# Advance Praise for *Cultural Comp Based Trauma with EMDR Therapy*

*After reading Nickerson's compelling and boldly comprehensive text, I have found myself sitting with clients in an entirely new way and so will you. With the multiple lenses offered in this book, you will start to think differently about the ways in which diverse cultural factors - social class, ethnicity, race, sexual orientation, religion, immigrant status, gender, discrimination, prejudice, and various disabilities interact to shape beliefs about oneself and one's experiences in the world. This book will heighten your awareness and cultural sensitivity, broaden your knowledge, and increase your repertoire of EMDR interventions. I suspect that you will be deeply moved by the book's many case presentations and ultimately left with a profound sense of hope and optimism about our capacity to help our clients heal.*

**—Deborah L. Korn, PsyD,**
Senior EMDR Institute Facilitator and Specialty Instructor,
Training Faculty, Trauma Center at JRI

*Finally there is a book that is thought provoking, insightful and rich in content, and which takes an in-depth look at the important role culture plays when treating trauma. With the strategies and protocols he provides in his book, Mark Nickerson has built a bridge for EMDR therapists to use our evidence based EMDR therapy to conduct more culturally effective trauma focused interventions. Mark's understanding of inclusiveness is reflected in his collaboration with other EMDR therapists. This book is a true guide in cultural humility.*

**—Diane DesPlantes, LCSW,**
Certified EMDR Therapist
Master trainer of Cultural Competency; New Jersey Department of Children and Families
Office of Training and Professional Development
EMDR International Association Board Director

*This is definitely a book whose time has come. From multiple contributions around the world, each chapter brings significant insights into how EMDR therapy can be culturally attuned and yet efficacious in preserving the individuality of each client. Highly recommended for those therapists who work in multi-cultural settings.*

**—Esly Regina Carvalho, PhD.**
Trainer of Trainers, EMDR Institute/EMDR Iberoamérica,
President, Trauma Clinic do Brasil/TraumaClinic Edições, Brasilia, Brazil

*This book may be one of the most important contributions to EMDR therapy literature so far in this century. Nickerson has astutely gathered together a collection of compelling articles that highlight the struggles of individuals and groups who have tragically and traumatically been affected by discrimination and discusses how EMDR therapy may be utilized to help them heal. Respectfully presented, this book offers information, strategies, and deviations from the EMDR standard protocol to deal with these diverse populations. Cultural Competence and Healing Culturally Based Trauma should be on the bookshelf of every EMDR therapy clinician.*

**—Barbara J. Hensley, EdD, LPCC,**
Author of *EMDR Therapy: From Practicum to Practice (2nd Ed.),*
EMDR International Association, Past President,
EMDR Research Foundation, Board Member,
Francine Shapiro Library, Creator and Curator

*This groundbreaking book edited by Mark Nickerson opens the field of psychotherapy to the importance of cultural competence. It gives the EMDR clinician the means of healing culturally based trauma by addressing a wide-range of important topics including social privilege and stigma, marginalized populations, LGBTQ concerns, and the special sensitivity needed when introducing EMDR Therapy to different cultures.*

**—Marilyn, Luber, PhD,**
Author of *EMDR SCRIPTED PROTOCOLS* series,
EMDR Global Alliance Co-Facilitator

*This book is a landmark contribution to EMDR therapy. In an increasingly culturally diverse society, clinicians need to understand the social forces and effects of culture, and how it shapes perceptions and consequently the memories that can become maladaptively stored. This will enable the clinician to develop a culturally informed treatment plan and provide more effective EMDR therapy treatment.*

**—Roger M. Solomon, PhD,**
Senior Faculty, EMDR Institute

*Having provided EMDR trainings in over a dozen countries and across three continents… I have learned that being blind to the culture you are teaching and practicing in can limit the effectiveness of what I believe is the psychotherapy of the 21st century. This volume gives the reader both the opportunity to see EMDR Therapy's cross cultural applicability, as well as develop the sensitivity and ability to adjust this great therapy to the specific culture of the client sitting in the room. Since different cultures exist in the present in our offices, not across the ocean, this book is a must read for today's EMDR therapists.*

**—Udi Oren, PhD,**
Past president, EMDR Europe Association

*This is a book of great scope and lucidity that examines the importance of culture and the impact of societal forces on individual and familial well-being, factors that have been frequently ignored by the field of psychotherapy. This scholarly offering is a clarion call highlighting the importance of cultural competence and will become an important contribution to the literature of our field.*

**—Uri Bergmann, PhD,**
Author of *Neurobiological Foundations for EMDR Practice,*
Past president, EMDR International Association

*This book delves deeply into the dimensions of EMDR therapy as it is applied to the hot spots of cultural challenges and cross-cultural differences. The EMDR community has made significant contributions to the latest critical and massive events occurring in Europe by working with victims of terroristic attacks and with the refugees and asylum seekers. Interventions have facilitated integration and adjustment into new cultures. A wide range of chapters in the book highlight innovative ways in which the EMDR approach and protocols can guide us amidst cultural differences, making adaptations when needed without losing efficacy.*

**—Isabel Fernandez,**
President EMDR Europe,
Past President EMDR Italy

# Cultural Competence and Healing Culturally Based Trauma with EMDR Therapy

**Mark Nickerson, LICSW,** is a psychotherapist with over 30 years of experience. He practices as a trauma treatment specialist in Amherst, MA. Mr. Nickerson is a graduate of Wesleyan University and the University of Michigan School of Social Work. He is on the faculty of the EMDR Institute and the EMDR Trauma Recovery Humanitarian Assistance Program, for whom he provides basic and advanced EMDR training sessions. He is a past president of the EMDR International Association, where he has served on the Board for the past 5 years. Mr. Nickerson conducts EMDR and other training sessions nationally and internationally on topics including treatment for problem behaviors and problematic anger; cultural competence and treating culturally based trauma and prejudice; conflict resolution; serving the needs of veterans and their families, and the effective use of EMDR protocols.

Trained as a social worker, Mr. Nickerson has a long-standing commitment to integrating the psycho and the social in his clinical work and teachings, as well as a passion for breaking down the barriers that divide people. Mr. Nickerson cofounded the Men's Resource Center of Western MA, a unique organization that developed violence intervention services and offered support and educational services for men. He is the Director of Parent Education for the Hampshire County Court's Bar Association, where he has developed two national award winning innovative programs designed to reduce and resolve interpersonal conflict. Mr. Nickerson is author of *The Wounds Within* (2015: Skyhorse, woundswithin.com), an exposé on the challenges for war veterans and their families. He also provides training sessions with the Veterans Education Project (markinickerson.com).

# Cultural Competence and Healing Culturally Based Trauma With EMDR Therapy

## *Innovative Strategies and Protocols*

*Mark Nickerson,* LICSW
Editor

Springer Publishing Company, LLC
11 West 42nd Street
New York, NY 10036
www.springerpub.com

*Acquisitions Editor*: Sheri W. Sussman
*Compositor*: diacriTech

*ISBN*: 978-0-8261-4286-3
*e-book ISBN*: 978-0-8261-4287-0

16 17 18 19 20 / 5 4 3 2 1



**Library of Congress Cataloging-in-Publication Data**

Names: Nickerson, Mark I., editor.
Title: Cultural competence and healing culturally based trauma with EMDR therapy : innovative strategies and protocols / Mark Nickerson, LICSW, editor.
Description: New York, NY : Springer Publishing Company, LLC, [2017] | Includes bibliographical references and index.
Identifiers: LCCN 2016020116 | ISBN 9780826142863 | ISBN 9780826142870 (ebook)
Subjects: LCSH: Eye movement desensitization and reprocessing. | Psychic trauma—Treatment. | Cross-cultural counseling.
Classification: LCC RC489.E98 N53 2017 | DDC 616.85/210651—dc23 LC record available at https://lccn.loc.gov/2016020116



Printed in the United States of America by McNaughton & Gunn.

*To the shared vision that human beings prefer to live in harmony,*

*To all those committed to making this possible,*

*And to the belief that*

*Our differences make life interesting, yet we are all one under the sun.*

# Contents

## SECTION III: INNOVATIVE PROTOCOLS 145



## SECTION IV: ADDRESSING SEXUAL/AFFECTIONAL ORIENTATION AND GENDER DIVERSITY 175



## SECTION V: SPECIFIC CULTURES AND SOCIAL STIGMA 229



## SECTION VI: GLOBAL FRONTIERS OF EMDR INTERVENTION 303

# Contributors

**Karen Alter-Reid, PhD** Clinical Practice, HAP Trainer, Co-Director, Integrative Trauma Program, National Institute for the Psychotherapies, New York, New York

**Cristina Angelini, MA** Clinical Practice, Gender-Based-Violence Expert, Child Specialist, Rome, Italy

**Sand C. Chang, PhD** Clinical Practice, Kaiser Permanente and Independent Practice, Oakland, California

**Paola Castelli Gattinara, MA** Cognitive Psychotherapy, Clinical Practice, MA EMDR Supervisor, Unit of Trauma Treatment of De Sanctis Clinical Centre, Rome, Italy

**Earl Grey, PhD** Clinical Practice, Consultant, Director of Field Experience, School of Counseling, Walden University, New York, New York

**John Hartung, PsyD** Clinical Practice, EMDR Trainer, Consultant, Director, Colorado Center for Alternative Psychology, Colorado Springs, Colorado

**Ruth Heber, PhD** Clinical Practice, Assistant Clinical Professor, Psychiatry, Mount Sinai School of Medicine, Supervisor, Integrative Trauma Program, National Institute for the Psychotherapies, New York, New York

**Josie Juhasz, MA, LPC** Clinical Practice, Institute and TR/HAP Facilitator, RTEP/G-TEP Trainer, Bend, Oregon

**Rajani Venkatraman Levis, MS, CTS, LMFT** Clinical Practice, San Francisco State University, San Francisco, California

**Barbara Lutz, PhD, MFT** Clinical Practice, Adjunct Faculty, The Chicago School of Professional Psychology, Chicago, Illinois; Adjunct Faculty, Hartnell College, Salinas, California

**Jamie Marich, PhD, LPCC-S, LICDC-CS** Clinical Practice, Director & Lead Trainer, The Institute for Creative Mindfulness, Warren, Ohio

**Rosemary Masters, JD, LCSW** Clinical Practice, Consultant, Founding Director, Trauma Studies Center of the Institute for Contemporary Psychotherapy, New York, New York

**André Maurício Monteiro, PhD, MSc** Clinical Practice, EMDR Trainer, Consultant, Brasília (DF), Brazil

**Elizabeth McConnell, MSW, LCSW** Clinical Practice, Pittsburgh, Pennsylvania

**Mark Nickerson, LICSW** Clinical Practice, EMDR Institute/HAP Basic Trainer, Advanced EMDR Trainer, Consultant, Amherst, Massachusetts

**John M. O'Brien, PhD** Clinical Practice, Consultant, Portland, Maine; Adjunct Faculty, University of Maine at Augusta, Augusta, Maine

**Antonio Onofri, MD** Psychiatrist, Emergency Psychiatric Care Unit, Santo Spirito Hospital, Cognitive Behavioral Psychotherapist, Unit for the Treatment of Trauma, Centro Clinico de Sanctis, Rome, Italy

**Natalie S. Robinson, LICSW** Clinical Practice, Consultant, Boston, Massachusetts

**Liz Royle, PhD, MA** Clinical Practice, Consultant, Bolton, United Kingdom

**Andrew J. Seubert, LMHC, NCC** Clinical Practice, Consultant, Seneca Lake, New York

**Robin Shapiro, LICSW** Clinical Practice, Trainer, Consultant, Author. Seattle, Washington.

**Laura Siniego, MA, MFT** Clinical Practice, Daly City, California

**Joseph C. Yaskin, MSS, LCSW** Clinical Practice, Bala Cynwyd, Pennsylvania

# Foreword

When Mark Nickerson told me he was planning a book about EMDR therapy and cultural competence, I was thrilled. These are both topics that are near and dear to my heart. EMDR therapy, of course, because we know it is an effective and efficient therapy that can be used to resolve trauma and disturbing life events. EMDR therapy has provided impactful interventions around the globe following natural and human created disasters. EMDR therapy is well grounded in neurophysiology, so it works with our human brains and our adaptive information processing system to facilitate healing, regardless of the language or local customs. With little modification, it is effective across cultures. At the same time, it can be used to address past events, current circumstances and inaccurate beliefs that create and maintain divisions between cultures and social groups.

Identification with a culture or a social group can bring many strengths and resources to individuals. It can make us feel connected to each other and to our communities. We also know that many of these cultural or group identities can be divisive and can be a painful source of trials and hardships. EMDR therapy provides a unique approach that is particularly well-suited to exploring the impact of culture and/or social groups on the individual. We, as EMDR therapy clinicians, can help to break down the barriers that divide people from one another, ranging from someone stuck in anger, to someone hurting from exclusion, or those social barriers impacted by prejudice.

And why is cultural competence important to me? I've learned that being or feeling different, no matter how seemingly small or insignificant can have a big impact on the individual. My father's family was tribal, both in heritage and lifestyle; my mother's family was northern European. As a child, I didn't understand the tension that existed because of these unaddressed differences, nor did I appreciate the impact that growing up in two worlds would have on me both personally and professionally. As an adult, I can appreciate the strengths that each perspective brings, as well as the challenges of trying to "fit in." As a psychologist, I've been drawn to teach cross-cultural communications at the college level, to work with students and clients from a variety of backgrounds and cultures, and to appreciate the richness that comes from exploring the beliefs, values and customs of others. Through volunteer work with EMDR humanitarian programs and associations around the world, I've been challenged to better understand the strengths and limitations that individuals embrace from their cultural and social upbringing. I've also learned to listen for the challenges that a decreased sense of safety and self-worth, marginalization, or discrimination can bring.

As therapists, cultural awareness and cultural competence are particularly important topics today. An appreciation for the impact of culture has been embraced by the fields of social psychology and social work, but has not been well developed in areas of psychology or individual therapy. I'm reminded of earlier times when individual therapy was offered without any awareness or attention to the family. Eventually, the field recognized the need to develop a family and systems perspective. From that vantage point, clinicians began to appreciate the impact of attachment experiences on individual development and relationship skills. Today, no competent therapist would consider providing comprehensive therapy without asking about attachment experiences or assessing attachment patterns and consequences. To extend that contextual and dynamic model, an attempt to understand the cultural framework and the impact of those experiences on individual and social identity is not only logical, but the essential next step. Whether our social experiences and identity are resources of strength and resilience, or sources of pain, marginalization, or discrimination in all its damaging forms, they impact our individual health and the health of our communities and the world in which we live. Mental health practitioners have an opportunity and an obligation to develop cultural competence in addressing these concerns, and in helping to break down the barriers that they create. Again, EMDR therapy is an ideal approach. From our various disciplines, we can create a dialogue around cultural competence that will help to integrate the fields of social psychology, social work and psychotherapy. We can help to unite an effort towards cultural competency that not only guides our EMDR treatment, but also creates a common goal among members of the mental health field.

Mark Nickerson brings awareness, expertise, passion, and his own cultural humility to this groundbreaking work. Not only does he challenge EMDR therapy clinicians with a clear imperative to develop cultural competence, he also provides a thoughtful model to guide us. *Cultural Competence and Healing Culturally Based Trauma with EMDR Therapy* brings together a cogent model of competence that is familiar to many EMDR therapy clinicians. Mark draws from concepts used to assess general clinical competency and applies the domains of attitude, skills, and knowledge as a method to define EMDR clinical skills in the social and cultural arena. The contributing authors bring their own cultural sensitivity and expertise as EMDR therapy clinicians working with individuals and communities that have faced many challenges. Their wisdom and insight in the use of EMDR therapy to address the impact of social identity is invaluable. The reader will find much to assist in the development of cultural awareness and competence in general, and the application of the adaptive information processing model and specific EMDR therapy protocols in particular. Whether working with distinctly different cultures, or exploring the nuances and implications of exclusion or marginalization from the dominant culture or social group, this book gives the EMDR therapy clinician a useful model and specific, practical suggestions for the use of EMDR therapy to heal cultural wounds.

I hope you read it, and I hope you enjoy it as much as I have.

*Rosalie Thomas, PhD, RN*
*Facilitator, EMDR Global Alliance*
*Board Member, EMDR Research Foundation*
*Past President, EMDRIA*

# Preface

The field of psychotherapy has frequently overlooked or minimized the importance of culture and the impact of societal forces on an individual's well-being. Culturally aware eye movement desensitization and reprocessing (EMDR) therapy provides a powerful alternative to this omission. From conceptual to practical, this book explores the interface of culture and EMDR therapy.

Cultural experiences and societal dynamics, for better and for worse, are fundamental dimensions of every human being's life and should be integrated into a general clinical approach. For many people, personal identity is intertwined with social identity and the welfare of one's cultural groups. Culturally linked experiences and values can be sources of great meaning and sustaining personal resources. At the same time, hostile social forces of discrimination, stigmatization, and oppression can define or confine an individual's sense of self and position in society. Whether explicit or more implicit, the many "isms" that persist in the world can limit human potential and threaten fundamental human dignity.

The movement for cultural competence is gaining greater recognition and momentum within the field of mental health. Service providers are increasingly aware of the need to keep step with an evolving multicultural world and to reverse the injustices that are perpetuated when cultural populations are marginalized and mistreated. As "culture-blind" psychotherapy models become obsolete, new approaches for culturally aware and effective intervention must be developed.

This book launches EMDR therapy both explicitly and dynamically into the broader movement for cultural competence. As EMDR therapy gains ever-broadening acceptance and stature throughout the world, it is only fitting that it aspires to excellence in this dimension. Indeed, EMDR therapy has the capacity to be a model of cultural competence for several reasons: EMDR interventions have already demonstrated effectiveness across a wide range of cultural contexts; EMDR humanitarian and membership organizations have reached out to serve culturally marginalized or underresourced populations throughout the world; the EMDR therapy model invites cultural awareness and attunement; and EMDR therapy's top-level evidence-based effectiveness in trauma treatment can be readily directed toward healing the impact of culturally based trauma including the effects of social discrimination and oppression.

And yet, each individual practitioner must make a deliberate and informed commitment to embrace cultural competence. This book offers EMDR clinicians information and guidance to move cultural competence from the abstract realm of an ideal to the applied methods of the real. Though the desire for cultural competence is an aspiration that is never fully achieved, its pursuit is inherently rewarding and the content of these pages illuminates the attitude, skills, and knowledge needed to move in this direction.

This book is written for EMDR therapists, EMDR leaders and supporting organizations, and others who want to understand and develop what EMDR therapy can offer as a culturally competent intervention. In a wide array of chapters, over 20 authors share their wisdom and bring their expertise to life with clinical examples. Suggestions are offered for weaving the cultural dimension into all phases of treatment, starting with a careful assessment. Information from allied fields of social psychology and social work are integrated into the adaptive information processing (AIP) model to provide a more nuanced understanding of innately human social tendencies toward inclusion and exclusion, including the neurology of social categorization. This knowledge helps EMDR clinicians transform maladaptive memories to more adaptive ones by informing protocols to undo internalized oppression and dismantle social prejudice. Readers will come away with new theoretical frameworks, useful language and terminology, in-depth knowledge about specific cultural populations, and practical intervention protocols and strategies.

In the end, clients will benefit the most from this book when the societal context of their lives, both external and internal, is more fully understood and welcomed in their psychotherapy work.

# Acknowledgments

I want to acknowledge the ongoing encouragement, support, and ideas that I have received from countless people along the path that has led to this book.

It is a privilege to showcase the work of each author in this collection. Their writings reveal a deep commitment to their work, the wisdom they have gained, and their innovative nature. When I first envisioned this book, I set out to try to cover this topic comprehensively by myself. What a breakthrough it was when I realized that a collection of voices could never be more fitting than for a book about culture and diversity, and what a relief when people stepped up to contribute. Their ideas helped me formulate my own.

I am grateful to Robin Shapiro, whose two *EMDR Solutions* books are models for the value of EMDR-themed books with multiple authored chapters. Hers and other such collections within the EMDR therapy literature offer a range of perspectives, are entry points for new ideas and emerging contributors, and build our EMDR community. I also appreciate Robin for being one of the first to write about treating culturally based trauma in EMDR therapy.

I thank Jane Porter, an EMDR clinician in my region, and others like her who heartily joined and contributed to my first EMDR study groups examining culture. Other close allies of mine who have advanced cultural consciousness within the EMDR community include fellow EMDRIA Board members Diane Desplantes, who has been a teacher to me as well, and Jim Cole, who had the nerve to train agencies in prejudice reduction. Also, I thank the many other kindred spirits in this work, including a dozen Jim Helling, Farns Lobenstine, David Eliscu, and Joany Spierings.

I am grateful to Francine Shapiro, not just for the obvious reason as the originator and developer of EMDR therapy, but for the 15-minute hotel lobby conversation 12 years ago, during which she encouraged me to integrate my cultural interests into the EMDR therapy model, and for her support since that time.

I want to thank Geneva Schmitt, who contributed both passion and objectivity to this project. She assisted me in providing editorial feedback to the authors, which they welcomed and appreciated. Ann della Bitta provided many valuable organizational suggestions. Finally, I thank Sheri W. Sussman from Springer Publishing Company, who sensed the time was right to make this book happen.

# Introduction

In 2007, I organized a study group designed to help EMDR clinicians explore the traumatizing effects of social discrimination and to integrate this awareness more fully into EMDR theory and practice. Several local clinicians joined in this multi-year experience. All of us had prior interests in this area, and we worked as allies to expand our thinking and "test drive" these ideas on ourselves and with our clients.

Prior to the group, my training as a professional social worker taught me the importance of social forces, both positive and negative. Yet, as I became a psychotherapist, I was disappointed to see how little attention was paid to the cultural component in advanced clinical trainings, writing, and discussion.

Many years ago, a wise mentor referenced the feminist movement and pointed out that as a clinician you have a choice. You can work with a woman who is in a confining sexist marriage and treat "her problems" of depression and "low self-esteem" to try to get her spirits up. Or, you can help her see herself in a social context with many other women who have been systematically "kept in their place" by cultural messages. Shifting the framework moves the problem from the person to the social context. It opens doors to a new range of problem solving.

As trauma-informed EMDR therapists, we have tools to liberate our clients from the restrictive effects of socially experienced dehumanization. As Robin Shapiro (2009) noted, EMDR therapy "can root out destructive cultural or generational introjects. . . . EMDR can target the cultural transmission of racism, sexism, class expectations, and the increasingly narrow parameters of acceptable appearance, interests and personality. It can also transform the effects of the generational transmission of destructive beliefs, identities and emotional states. . . . We can help people accept themselves even when they are bombarded with external messages that they are unacceptable."

The teachings of Francine Shapiro, originator and developer of EMDR therapy, convey great compassion for victims of trauma while bringing a theory and set of procedures that can be attuned to individual cultural context, help people recover from their adverse and traumatic experiences, and restore each person to their resilient potential.

In 2009 to 2010, I conducted a series of workshops titled *Undoing Stigma: EMDR Applications in the Dismantling of Socially Based Internalized Oppression and Prejudice.* Over 60 EMDR clinicians explored these issues in practicum sessions and agreed to keep detailed notes of their experiences. Frankly, the results of their reprocessing experiences were more impressive than I had anticipated and helped me further develop my thinking.

Along the way, I have learned how deeply committed many EMDR clinicians are to matters of social justice and diversity and how curious they are to explore ways EMDR therapy can help. The EMDR International Association (EMDRIA) special interest group on diversity and public practice has generated important contributions and created a bond among likeminded thinkers. David Eliscu (Eliscu et al., 2010, 2011) took initiative and organized two panel discussions of EMDR clinicians that offered valuable insight and guidance at EMDRIA conferences.

A major goal of this book is to explicitly move EMDR therapy into the discussion of cultural competence that is emerging within the field of mental health. In fact, I believe we can be a beacon of light within this realm. While there is ample evidence of cross-cultural effectiveness with EMDR treatment, relatively little has been written about the impact of culturally based trauma. I hope that this book helps build a body of knowledge that will more deeply embed cultural awareness into EMDR therapy and inspire more exploration, writing, and research.

Most immediately, the book will be a success if the many ideas offered throughout these chapters are put into use with your clients and create good results.

This book explores the interface of culture and EMDR therapy with a collection of chapters that cover a range of subjects and offer a variety of approaches. The book addresses the big conceptual issues as well as specific insights, strategies, and protocols that are brought to life with clinical examples. Please know that all clinical examples have been disguised to protect the identity of the client while maintaining the clinical truth of the points that are demonstrated.

This book is presented with the assumption that readers are EMDR trained and have a basic understanding of the core elements of EMDR therapy. So that attention could be focused on the integration of cultural issues, references are frequently made with limited explanation to the Adaptive Information Processing Model, the Eight-Phase approach of EMDR therapy, the Three Prong Protocol, Resourcing, and additional protocols and strategies that are frequently discussed in EMDR literature. Please make use of other EMDR texts as needed to further understand these fundamental EMDR concepts.

Finding common language about culture is both a challenge and a goal of this book. Efforts were made to use language that is current with updated perspectives, understandable, and acceptable to social groups being named. But getting it "just right" is impossible, so please be tolerant of some variations in language and terminology throughout the chapters. For example, becoming more familiar and fluid with pronouns that support gender diversity is a current linguistic challenge. In some cases, editorial decisions were made. For example, when discussing race and ethnicity, the term Black is used rather than African American, as it is more inclusive of people of African descent who do not identify as Americans.

In Section I of the book, I offer a collection of chapters with very different purposes. In Chapter 1, I define and explore the increasingly discussed concept of *cultural competence* and offer suggestions for how EMDR therapists and organizations can engage with and ultimately help lead this important trend. In Chapter 2, I integrate valuable terminology and knowledge from the fields of social psychology and social work to enrich the AIP model. I introduce information about how the brain processes social information and discuss the need for healing culturally based trauma and social prejudice. Chapter 3 focuses on clinical conceptualization and EMDR intervention strategies for treating culturally based trauma and exploring social identities. In Chapter 4, I present an EMDR protocol for treating social prejudice, discuss social privilege, and offer a protocol to target issues related to social advantages and disadvantages.

In Section II, Chapter 5, Rajani Venkatraman Levis and Laura Siniego write explicitly about integrating "the sociocultural, political, and legal realities that permeate" many clients' lives, and demonstrate uses of EMDR therapy as an "antioppression endeavor." In Chapter 6, Levis illuminates multiple categories of "cultural wealth" and guides clinicians to help clients develop these qualities to bring culture to "the heart" of EMDR work. Barbara Lutz writes in elegant detail about her culturally aware EMDR therapy with a recent immigrant in Chapter 7. Her writing reveals how she uses self-reflection about her own cultural background to strengthen the therapy. In a particularly current global issue, Paola Castelli Gattinara, Antonio Onofri, and Cristina Angelini offer a window into their work with refugees and asylum seekers in Chapter 8. Their adaptations of the EMDR approach to meet the most pressing needs of their clients are instructive.

Section III explores two specific innovative protocols. In Chapter 9, Natalie Robinson outlines several straightforward methods to integrate EMDR work into the context of a client's cultural ancestry, and conveys the potency of these methods. In Chapter 10, Andre Monteiro shares procedures for providing EMDR reprocessing experiences within the context of ongoing group-based therapy. He makes a compelling case for the added meaning that comes with reprocessing with group support.

Three chapters in Section IV explore different dimensions of identity as it relates to LGBTQQ (lesbian, gay, bisexual, transgender, queer, and questioning) issues. In combination, they dispel myths and misinformation, and help break down dichotomous either/or thinking. In Chapter 11, Sand Chang offers valuable information about affirmative care for transgender and gender nonconforming clients, and offers sage guidance for clinicians. John O'Brien talks about the realities, needs, and struggles for gay men and lesbians in Chapter 12. Earl Grey provides a fascinating protocol for helping a client assess his or her sex, gender, and affectional orientation along continua of characteristics in Chapter 13.

Section V includes several chapters that offer knowledge and insight into the experiences and needs associated with specific cultures, including the stigma they may battle, and provide specific recommendations for how the EMDR therapist can attune and help mold the EMDR approach to these groups. In Chapter 14, Ruth Heber and Karen Alter-Reid offer moving insight into the transgenerational impact of antisemitism and convey lessons that can be applied to treat the legacy of inherited trauma for other cultures, especially where oppression or genocide have been components. In Chapter 15, Joseph Yaskin and Andrew Seubert provide their longstanding expertise in working with intellectual disabilities, and speak of the power of EMDR therapy as an approach to overcoming socially dismissive attitudes.

In Chapter 16, Liz Royle presents her work with uniformed service workers in the United Kingdom, who must overcome mental health stigma to receive EMDR treatment. Addictions expert Jaime Marich portrays the profound value of the recovery community in Chapter 17, and offers ways that EMDR therapists can attune their treatment for clients in 12-step programs. In Chapter 18, Robin Shapiro offers clever strategies for helping clients undo the effects of culturally imposed social messages relative to physical appearance, aging, and social class.

Finally, Section VI includes accounts of efforts to bring EMDR to regions of the world with limited mental health services. In Chapter 19, Rosemary Masters, Elizabeth McConnell, and Josie Juhasz write about their important work in Uganda. With an attitude of cultural humility, they portray not only what they taught, but what they learned from those they met. In Chapter 20, John Hartung offers great wisdom from his extensive EMDR training around the globe. His deeply respectful approach explores the central questions of "When to Start , What to Do, and When to Leave," and provides fascinating and useful guidance for those fortunate enough to help bring EMDR to underdeveloped regions of the world, and for others who want to understand and support this pioneering activity.

## REFERENCES

Eliscu, D., Bergmann, U., Davis, K., Fitzgerald, J., Gomez, A., Janis, O., & Cloud, L. (2010). *Targeting oppression: Engendering empowerment*. EMDRIA Conference Panel Presentation.

Eliscu, D., Bergmann, U., Fitzgerald, J., Olivia, A., Oucault, A., DesPlantes, D., & Enjady, S. (2011). *Targeting oppression: Engendering empowerment*. EMDRIA Conference Panel Presentation.

Shapiro, R. (Ed.). (2009). EMDR *solutions II: For depression, eating disorders, performance, and more*. New York, NY: W. W. Norton & Company.

# SECTION I

# Components of an EMDR Therapy Approach to Cultural Competence

CHAPTER 1

# Cultural Competence and EMDR Therapy

Mark Nickerson

Developing *cultural competence* as a professional is a journey, not a destination. The quest for cultural competence is an ongoing pursuit and viewing it that way is the first step. Applying a culturally aware framework can reshape how clinicians understand and approach their interventions. This chapter explores the concept of cultural competence as it is being developed within the field of human services delivery, and integrates these ideas and best practices into eye movement desensitization and reprocessing (EMDR) therapy.

A purpose of this book is to advance the conversation about cultural competence among EMDR clinicians, to add new concepts and tools to the discussion, and to inspire continued attention and innovation. A second purpose is to advance EMDR therapy recognition for cultural competence in the broader field of mental health.

As EMDR therapy gains ever-broadening acceptance and stature throughout the world, I believe that it is important that those committed to its continued advancement explicitly engage in the movement to define and aspire to cultural competence, both for the benefit of EMDR therapy and for the contribution that it can make in this dimension to the field of mental health. EMDR therapy is well-positioned to become a model for culturally aware and effective trauma-informed intervention. Currently, I believe that there are three distinct ways in which EMDR intervention demonstrates cultural competence:

1. A guiding theory, fundamental mechanisms of action, and other procedures that have demonstrated effectiveness and adaptability across a wide range of cultural contexts
2. A clinical model that supports cultural attunement and a growing body of knowledge specific to different client cultural populations
3. The capacity to successfully treat the effects of culturally based trauma

EMDR therapy has been approved as a top-level, evidence-based treatment for trauma by many organizations and associations including the World Health Organization (2013) and the American Psychiatric Association (Ursano et. al., 2004). EMDR therapy has been implemented throughout the world as chronicled by increasing reports validating its effectiveness as a culturally adaptable treatment. Additionally, EMDR humanitarian and membership organizations are reaching out, sometimes through voluntary efforts, to serve culturally marginalized or underresourced populations throughout the world.

As individual EMDR therapists, striving for cultural effectiveness in our day-to-day clinical work is naturally aligned with our overall goals to best serve our clients. It behooves us to deliberately commit to an ongoing process of understanding and maintaining a culturally conscious approach. Indeed, as a collection of therapists, we have a solid base to build upon as individual EMDR clinicians are increasingly integrating their culturally aware insight and skills to improve their EMDR therapy work, as evidenced in the content of this book. The Francine Shapiro Library contains numerous citations to presentations and articles that reference a cultural component (emdria.omeka.net), although it is beyond the scope of this chapter to provide a literature review.

## THE NEED FOR A CULTURALLY-AWARE APPROACH

Cultural experiences, positive and negative, are fundamental dimensions of every human being's life. Well-being is intertwined with social relationships and the well-being of one's cultural groups. For many people, cultural values and affiliations are powerful and sustaining components of their lives. As EMDR therapists, these are resources we can help our clients develop. At the same time, as trauma therapists, we must be aware that many of our clients have grown up under oppressive conditions and have experienced significant social stigmatization and discrimination. Hostile social forces of disregard, intolerance, exclusion, and worse have been directed at many clients simply because of the way they look and talk, their social position, and the families they come from, or who they love.

To maximize our effectiveness as clinicians, we need to embrace our clients' full experiences including the role of cultural issues. While this seems like common sense, as psychotherapists we must understand that we operate in a broader "psychotherapist" culture that has been criticized for operating with a *culture-blind* approach that too often tries to separate "cultural" issues from "personal" issues.

Despite the fact that most psychotherapists have egalitarian values and are aware of the importance of cultural forces on a societal level, psychotherapy practice, including trauma-informed psychotherapy, has historically ignored or minimized the cultural context. Critics have described the Western psychotherapy model as being heavily influenced by a medical model that includes the preeminence of the *Diagnostic and Statistical Manual of Mental Disorders* (*DSM*; American Psychiatric Association, 2013) for diagnosis (which locates the problem within the individual and largely ignores etiology), the use of the *DSM* to determine "medical necessity" for insurance coverage, a focus on pharmacological interventions, the coopting of social workers toward an individual psychotherapy model rewarded with higher pay and higher status, and the established dominance of individually oriented treatment paradigms.

In a sobering caution about the risks of a "culture-blind" approach, Ridley (2005) cites over 80 studies showing that psychotherapists engage in discrimination during their clinical practice. In his review of research on this topic, he discovered that the following clinical decision points were influenced by prejudicial stereotypes: diagnoses, prognoses, referrals, treatment planning, selection of interventions, frequency of treatment, termination, medical therapy, reporting abuse or neglect, duty to warn, involuntary commitment, deciding the importance of case history data, and interpreting test data. Ridley suggested other clinical behaviors might also be impacted, such as seeking consultation, developing empathy, expressing support, advocating for the client, and identifying with a client's issues.

This culture-blind tendency to sidestep explicit attention to cultural issues may exist, in part, because therapists don't know how to productively integrate culture within the psychotherapy model. Overcoming this obstacle will be explored throughout this book. Despite the potential for inherent bias within clinical mental health practice, a more culturally competent one-on-one psychotherapy model can create conditions for recovery and growth for individual clients.

## DEFINING CULTURAL COMPETENCE

One of the most fundamental challenges to advancing the discussion about cultural competence in the field is simply defining the concept. The term *cultural competence* was established in the 1980s as part of a broad examination of the field of health and human services and their systems of care (Cross, Bazron, Dennis, & Isaacs, 1989). Since then, it has gained broader acceptance among individuals and organizations who seek to provide services that are culturally sensitive to a wide range of people.

In the original definition, *culture* is referred to as an "integrated pattern of human behavior that includes thoughts, communications, actions, customs, beliefs, values and institutions of a racial, ethnic, religious or social group" (Cross et al., 1989). This broader meaning of culture, which includes a range of socially salient groups in a person's life, is an important dimension. In fact, within the literature, the terms *cultural identity* and *social identity* are often used interchangeably to connote a person's identification with a larger group.

*Competence* is defined as "the capacity to function effectively" (Cross et al., 1989). A continuum of competence is depicted from one extreme to the other, which includes cultural destructiveness, cultural incapacity, cultural blindness, cultural precompetence, cultural competence, and cultural proficiency. Although others have added to the growing body of knowledge, definitions, and practice suggestions, the core definition has remained stable and will provide the foundation for the concepts covered in this book.

Since the concept was established, many organizations have aspired toward cultural competence (Denboba, MCHB, 1993; Lavizzo-Mourey & Mackenzie, 1996; National Alliance for Hispanic Health, 2001; U.S. Department of Health and Human Services, & Administration on Developmental Disabilities, 2000; U.S. Department of Health and Human Services, & Substance Abuse and Mental Health Services Administration, 2004). From an organizational perspective, Betancourt, Green, and Carrillo (2002) proposed that cultural competence within broader systems of care should have the capacity to (a) value diversity, (b) conduct self-assessment, (c) manage the dynamics of difference, (d) acquire and institutionalize cultural knowledge, and (e) adapt to diversity and the cultural contexts of communities they serve.

Pedersen (2002) identified three components of clinical competence: (a) awareness/attitude, (b) knowledge, and (c) skills. Awareness was characterized as both an awareness of other cultures and an active effort by practitioners to assess their own beliefs and values toward culture in general and different cultures in particular. This combination of external awareness and internal reflection has been echoed consistently by others as a core component of competence. Kaslow et al. (2004), for example, states that competence should include the capacity to evaluate and adjust one's decisions through reflective practice.

Related to this need for internal reflection, Tervalon and Murray-Garcia (1998) introduced the concept of *cultural humility* as an important mindset or stance from which to approach cultural issues. They proposed that three factors are fundamental for cultural humility: (a) a commitment to self-evaluation that includes qualities of humility, (b) a desire to fix unjust power imbalances, and (c) aspiring to develop partnerships with people and groups who advocate for others. They point out that the commitment to self-reflect should be lifelong and can build the capacity to respond flexibly with newly acquired knowledge. Yet, they warn that any insights are of limited value if not implemented in culturally informed clinical approaches that convey an understanding of a client's cultural experience, especially those who have endured social injustice. They emphasize that a commitment to diversity and undoing social injustices should be a collaborative effort with like-minded advocates for societal change.

Waters and Asbill (2013) have added that the term *cultural humility* is an attitude of openness from which one seeks to explore one's own cultural perspectives and biases. Cultural humility generates a natural curiosity that motivates one to learn and expand understanding. Cultural humility entails suspending one's own culture-centric views when entering the world of a client. Hook, Davis, Owen, Worthington, and Utsey (2013) describe cultural humility as the "ability to maintain an interpersonal stance that is other-oriented in relation to aspects of cultural identity that are most important to the [person]."

Other recommendations for cultural competence have been proposed. Goodman et al. (2004) suggested that counselors should act as "agents of change" and identified several competencies for a social justice approach to multicultural counseling, including (a) ongoing self-examination and self-awareness, (b) sharing power, (c) giving voice, (d) facilitating consciousness raising, (e) building on strengths, and (f) offering clients tools for creating social change. Gallardo, Yeh, Trimble, and Parham (2011) proposed six concrete stages of multicultural counseling: (a) connecting with clients, (b) conducting a culturally relevant assessment, (c) facilitating awareness, (d) setting goals, (e) taking action and instigating change, and (f) welcoming feedback and maintaining accountability.

Many of the professional organizations that represent the different mental health disciplines have made efforts to define and support cultural competence. Generally, these efforts fall into two categories: supporting diversity of membership and offering culturally attuned and effective services.

The National Association of Social Workers (NASW) highlights two major cultural forces requiring ongoing attention: the civil rights movement launched in the 1950s, including any disadvantaged and oppressed populations; and the increasing number of new immigrants to this country. An NASW statement acknowledges that "both helping professionals and society at large have a long way to go to gain cultural competence" while taking some pride in "social workers . . . longstanding history of understanding both people's differences and the impact of social injustices on their well-being" (NASW, 2011). NASW *Standards for Cultural*

*Competence and Social Diversity* emphasize three dimensions for social workers: understanding culture and recognizing cultural strengths; having knowledge of specific clients' cultures; and obtaining education to better understand social diversity and oppression.

The American Psychological Association Task Force on Inclusion and Diversity is developing a definition and standards for cultural competence and seeking to develop diversity among its membership. Their challenge has been described as "a complicated matter of defining diversity, attracting and engaging diverse members, sharing the power and accepting that the future will hold a very different climate of racial demographics" (American Psychological Association, 2011). The American Psychiatric Association has emphasized the need to assess and correct disparities in the delivery of mental health services related to cultural factors and to reduce stigma for those seeking care (psychiatry.org).

The International Society for Traumatic Stress Studies has established a diversity and cultural competence special interest group (SIG). The SIG has raised awareness of cultural factors and noted that "these factors mediate, moderate and in many cases, even determine traumatic exposure and post-traumatic response, such as through exposures to hate crimes, general community violence, forced internment, enslavement and other trauma or via contributing factors occurring within societies hostile to particular groups, such as social attitudes and actions contributing to a hostile environment" (International Society for Traumatic Stress Studies, 2016). The SIG also notes that "demographic characteristics may also be proxies for or directly countervail the effects of trauma through culturally-specific strengths and resilience factors" (International Society for Traumatic Stress Studies, Diversity and Cultural Competence SIG. Copyright ©2016 ISTSS. All rights reserved).

## EMDR AS A CULTURALLY COMPETENT THERAPY: EMBRACING THE CHALLENGE

### The Movement for Core Competencies

Having reviewed these and other efforts within the field of human services to define and implement cultural competence, my primary interest is in how these concepts can be effectively integrated into the application of EMDR therapy. Toward this goal, I believe it is wise to integrate another growing direction within the field of mental health, the establishment of general *core competencies* of clinical practice. This trend toward defining core competencies is a response to greater expectations for treatment outcome accountability. Generally speaking, these efforts tend to define competencies that are either evidence based as substantiated by research or are components that are generally considered to be essential for "best practices."

The EMDR International Association (EMDRIA) is currently in the process of defining and developing clarity about core competencies for EMDR therapy. The purpose of this initiative is to articulate the components of effective EMDR practice for the benefit of practitioners and to assist trainers and consultants in their roles. As part of this process, the EMDRIA Standards and Training Committee conducted a thorough survey of core competency models and selected a framework espoused by Len Sperry as the best tool available.

In *Core Competencies in Counseling and Psychotherapy* (2011), Sperry offers a comprehensive model for defining and developing core competencies. Sperry proposes six areas of clinical core competencies: (a) conceptual foundations, (b) therapeutic relationship, (c) intervention planning, (d) intervention implementation, (e) intervention evaluation and treatment, and (f) cultural and ethical sensitivity. Within each competency, the model calls for an articulation of the three dimensions necessary for effective clinical treatment: (a) knowledge, (b) skills, and (c) attitudes. These three dimensions echo the growing consensus of components for cultural competence within the field as previously cited.

As I seek to integrate the trend toward general clinical core competence with the specific momentum toward cultural competence, I believe that the Sperry model is a sensible choice through which to develop an articulation of cultural competence. The one twist I prefer is to list the three components in the order of (a) attitude, (b) skills, and (c) knowledge. This allows the use of the acronym *ASK*, which is not only easy to remember but also suggests an attitude of curiosity and humility that is a fundamental component to cultural effectiveness. As these components are interrelated and not linear, there is no reason the order cannot be changed.

## Applying the ASK Model to EMDR Therapy

The ASK model provides EMDR clinicians and organizations a tool through which to outline and develop a vision of core competence. The following is an example of the use of the ASK model for this purpose. In it, I have included some of the concepts that already exist in the core competency movement and integrated them with some of the core dimensions of EMDR therapy, with a few specific examples. This is *not* intended to be comprehensive. Hopefully, future collaborative work among EMDR practitioners will refine these concepts and delineate more details.

### Attitude

For the EMDR practitioner, a culturally competent clinical *attitude* is a state of mind that inherently understands and respects the role of culture in our society and in individual clients' lives. This attitude embraces a multicultural perspective that values diversity along many dimensions. An attitude of cultural awareness begins with a capacity to understand and appreciate one's own cultural background, which may necessitate creating opportunities for personal reflection to become aware of the strengths and difficulties that are associated with one's own cultural experiences. When therapists do their own "personal work" to explore culture, they are more able to appreciate this dimension in their clients. From a base of personal awareness of culture, cultural competence requires a capacity for humility whereby the clinician understands the limitations of understanding that come with one's own cultural perspective. Humility reduces assumptions about others and replaces it with an active curiosity to learn about cultural differences and show sensitivity to cultural needs.

An attitude of cultural curiosity seeks knowledge about a client's cultural values, experiences, needs, and general ways of being. This knowledge can be acquired from the client, although the therapist should actively seek out information from other sources as needed. A culturally competent attitude should go beyond merely understanding the client's experience and should be demonstrated by a commitment to active responsiveness to cultural needs.

## Skills

Culturally competent clinical *skills* are the clinical steps used by the clinician. They are developed with a culturally aware attitude and guided by learned cultural knowledge. EMDR clinicians begin with the impressive standard EMDR treatment skills that have demonstrated a high level of cross-cultural effectiveness. EMDR therapy encourages the customized adaptation of Phases 1 and 2 (Shapiro, 2001) to meet client needs, including the client's culturally related needs. Skills to attune other standard EMDR procedures for cultural effectiveness include building culturally sensitive therapeutic alliances as well as implementing culturally aware assessments, case formulations, and treatment plans. EMDR clinicians can employ culturally informed modifications to other aspects of the eight-phase approach as long as these modifications remain consistent with the adaptive information processing model (AIP) (Shapiro, 2001) and accomplish the primary goals of those phases.

There are many other additional specific skills that can be devised for cross-cultural effectiveness. For example, where language is a barrier, using fewer words and being sure to use culturally understandable metaphors is important. Other skills include conveying respect in culturally valued ways, sharing power by collaborating with the clients actively during the EMDR therapy process, being prepared to discuss cultural issues, allowing time for trust to develop, being able to self-disclose when appropriate, and conveying empathy for discrimination perpetrated upon the client's culture and allying with needs for change.

## Knowledge

Culturally competent *knowledge* refers to having an understanding of the importance of culture in general as well as an understanding about specific cultural realities of any particular client. A culturally curious attitude acquires knowledge as a natural and enjoyable part of attunement to the client's cultural world. Knowledge can be gained from many sources. Knowledge about specific cultures includes the norms, values, beliefs, and needs of the culture. Even with general knowledge about a specific culture, it is important to not make assumptions that any one client fits a "cultural profile." The clinician should assess the degree to which a client is attuned with these cultural ways, varies from them, or is in conflict with them.

Showing an awareness of cultural knowledge (a skill) can build trust. Some more specific examples of cultural knowledge include important aspects of communication such as forms of greeting and saying goodbye, the use and meaning of gestures, the meaning of eye contact, and norms for self-disclosure.

It is important to understand how the very process of engaging in EMDR therapy is viewed within a client's cultural identities. There may be support for it or stigma against it. Relatedly, the therapist should try to understand how the issues central to therapy would be viewed within the client's culture as well as within his or her family.

Again, this is only a partial formulation of content to demonstrate the use of the ASK model as a tool. It is my hope that as EMDR clinicians espouse and sustain a commitment to cultural awareness there will be increasing compilation and documentation of culturally effective clinical skills and valuable culturally specific knowledge. Chapters throughout this book provide just such information.

## More on EMDR Therapy and the Frontier of Cultural Competence

Though I am making the case for EMDR therapy to be more explicitly defined and allied within the movement in the field toward cultural competence, we have much to offer. As mentioned earlier, EMDR provides three key components that catapult it to the forefront of trauma-informed cultural effectiveness by offering (a) a guiding theory, fundamental mechanisms of action, and other procedures that have demonstrated effectiveness and adaptability across a wide range of cultural contexts; (b) a clinical model that supports cultural attunement and a growing body of knowledge specific to different client cultural populations; and (c) the capacity to successfully treat the effects of culturally based trauma.

EMDR originator Francine Shapiro's teachings have emphasized the importance of EMDR therapy as an integrative approach. Stewards of the development of EMDR therapy have skillfully balanced the need to maintain the core fidelity of the procedural components most essential to the transformative power of EMDR reprocessing with an openness and adaptability to the specifics of any one client's uniqueness. Shapiro (2002) has stated, for instance, that "all psychotherapies must be practiced in the context of interlocking systems" and must include an appreciation of cultural context.

EMDR has demonstrated tremendous range as a cross-culturally effective therapeutic intervention. EMDR therapists are active on all six major continents and there is ample evidence that the fundamental components of EMDR intervention can be used effectively across cultures with compelling results. EMDR interventions, particularly those associated with EMDR humanitarian assistance programs, have treated many people in underresourced parts of the globe, often in countries with limited and underdeveloped mental health services. Even when there have been significant cultural differences between therapist and client, including not speaking the same language, the effectiveness of the EMDR treatment has been validated.

Some core components of EMDR that appear to contribute to its effectiveness with a wide range of cultural populations include that EMDR:

- Is client-centered
- Places are limited demands on language
- Works effectively with translators
- Can use non-verbal modalities (drawing)
- Can be implemented with group treatment methods
- Allows clients to keep memories private
- Accesses multiple memory components (cognitions, emotions, and body states)
- Includes simple self-assessment tools (VOC, SUDs)

- Requires no homework
- Integrates universal brain biology into AIP model
- Respects inherent healing mechanisms
- Adapts bilateral stimulation methods
- Builds on existing cultural resources/beliefs
- Incorporates mindfulness skills valued in many cultures
- Encourages therapist attunement and non-intrusiveness
- Allows for the problem to be identified in client's terms
- Is effective for range of adverse experiences

Not only can EMDR standard treatment be adapted to different cultures, but it can be used to specifically treat the overall effects of culturally based trauma. This will be explored more in Chapter 3. The AIP model, the core theory behind EMDR methodology, offers a powerful framework through which to understand the constructive and destructive impact of cultural forces and other social dynamics. Generally speaking, the eight-phase approach, three-prong protocol, and many other EMDR protocols and strategies can be used successfully to treat culturally based trauma.

After reviewing the literature regarding cultural competence, clinical competencies, and assessing both the current effectiveness and potential of EMDR therapy, I generated a list of specific areas of focus for EMDR clinicians and EMDR organizations who are actively pursuing cultural competence. The chapters throughout this book provide extensive information and guidance to support clinicians along this path.

***Cultural competence focus areas for EMDR clinicians include:***

1. Understand the general importance of culture and the value of viewing individual client issues within a cultural context
2. Understand the important dimensions of culture to specific each client (including norms, values, beliefs, needs, etc.)
3. Maintain an attitude of curiosity and humility about other cultures while being aware of and seeking to overcome one's own cultural biases
4. Adapt EMDR therapy methods to a client's cultural context and needs
5. Provide psychosocial education to clients as appropriate
6. Empower clients in the face of culturally oppressive or stigmatizing conditions, including discrimination
7. Implement EMDR interventions that effectively treat the internalized effects of culturally based trauma
8. Implement EMDR interventions that effectively treat clients with culturally related prejudice and discriminatory behaviors, thus reducing the legacy of culturally based trauma
9. Support and ally with humanitarian efforts for social change including victim/survivor empowerment, social justice, and policy reform

10. Sustain EMDR therapist organizations which support the cultural competence of practitioners and which are culturally competent organizations
11. Seek ongoing education and training as needed to develop cultural competence

*Cultural competence focus area for EMDRIA as an organization include:*

1. Endorse, as an organization, the importance of cultural competence, diversity and inclusivity
2. Build and maintain cultural diversity of membership and leadership at all levels
3. Make EMDR treatment options available to and effective with people of all cultures
4. Define and develop standards of cultural competence within EMDR therapy and integrate them into overall core competency standards of EMDR therapy
5. Define and maintain cultural competence standards for EMDRIA approved educational programs, trainers, and EMDRIA approved consultants
6. Compile knowledge, and support education and training regarding culturally competent EMDR therapy
7. Support innovation and research related to culturally competent EMDR therapy
8. Promote to the public, mental health organizations and policy makers the ways in which EMDR interventions have demonstrated cultural competence and effectiveness
9. Collaborate regarding cultural competence with other EMDR and non-EMDR organizations

On the organizational level, the EMDR International Association (EMDRIA) has embraced the pursuit of cultural competence. The EDMRIA board of directors has established a Diversity and Cultural Competence Committee and an organizational policy is being drafted to make many of these specific focus areas a part of its organizational philosophy and goals. Some strategies that are underway include: recruiting, training, and retaining as EMDRIA members clinicians that meet diversity goals; establishing and maintaining standards for cultural competence in EMDR therapy practice; promoting trainings that are accessible and relevant to clinicians who serve diverse and underserved clinical populations and the practice settings; and supporting the development of effective treatment strategies to address the impact of social discrimination and culturally based adverse life experiences. The EMDRIA conference has sponsored two panel discussions on culture (Eliscu et al., 2010, 2011) as well as other culture related presentations. The commitment of EMDRIA and other EMDR organizations to ongoing attention and action will demonstrate leadership and can serve as a model within the field of mental health.

More globally, many EMDR clinicians and their supporting organizations are committed to bringing EMDR Interventions to underserved populations worldwide. Rolf Carriere, who has worked extensively with the UN, UNICEF, and World Bank, has estimated that over 500 million people globally suffer from unresolved trauma. EMDR humanitarian organizations have organized and sponsored EMDR trainings and interventions with a sense of mission that speaks volumes about the social awareness that exists within the EMDR professional culture.

An emerging frontier is the development of adapted EMDR treatment to fit the realities of the large numbers of people worldwide with little or scarce access to mental health services. EMDR innovations include implementing group treatment protocols and exploring the possible applications of EMDR interventions by paraprofessionals. Great care is being taken to balance innovative experimental approaches with the need to document procedures and evaluate results, so as to establish research-validated interventions. Early indications of these efforts are encouraging.

## SUMMARY

Within the field of mental health, there is a much needed conversation about cultural competence. EMDR clinicians and organizations can actively join this discussion for mutual benefit. EMDR therapy has the potential to be a leader in the field because of the cultural adaptability of our treatment model, and its capacity for alleviating the effects of trauma, including culturally based trauma.

At the same time, cultural competence is an ongoing challenge, and it is important that all clinicians take a clear look at how they can apply the ASK model to enhance a culturally aware attitude, stretch their skills, and deepen their knowledge. Culturally competent EMDR therapy welcomes cultural awareness, embraces social and cultural identity, integrates the EMDR approach within a cultural context, and implements EMDR therapy to dismantle culturally based trauma.

## REFERENCES

American Psychiatric Association. (2013). *Diagnostic and statistical manual of mental disorders* (5th ed.). Arlington, VA: American Psychiatric Publishing.

American Psychological Association. (2011). Diversity—what is it and what does it mean? Division Dialogue 11(1). Retrieved from www.apa.org/about/division/officers/dialogue/2011/03/diversity.aspx

Betancourt, J. R., Green, A. R., & Carrillo, J. E. (2002). *Cultural competence in health care: Emerging frameworks and practical approaches* (Fund Report 576). Washington, DC: Commonwealth Fund.

Cross, T., Bazron, B., Dennis, K., & Isaacs, M. (1989). *Towards a culturally competent system of care* (Vol. 1). Washington, DC: Georgetown University.

Denboba, D., & U.S. Department of Health and Human Services, Health Services and Resources Administration. (1993). *MCHB/DSCSHCN guidance for competitive applications, maternal and child health improvement projects for children with special health care needs.* Bethesda, MD: U.S. Department of Health and Human Services.

Eliscu, D., Bergmann, U., Davis, K., Fitzgerald, J., Gomez, A., Janis, O., & Cloud, L. (2010). *Targeting oppression: Engendering empowerment.* EMDRIA Conference Panel Presentation.

Eliscu, D., Bergmann, U., Fitzgerald, J., Olivia, A., Oucault, A., DesPlantes, D., & Enjady, S. (2011). *Targeting oppression: Engendering empowerment.* EMDRIA Conference Panel Presentation.

Gallardo, M., Yeh, C., Trimble, J., & Parham, T. (2011). *Culturally adaptive counseling skills: Demonstrations of best practices*. Thousand Oaks, CA: Sage.

Goodman, L. A., Liang, B., Helms, J. E., Lotta, R. E., Sparks, E., & Weintraub, S. R. (2004). Training counseling psychologists as social justice agents: Feminist and multicultural principles and actions. *Counseling Psychologist, 32*, 793–837.

Hook, J. N., Davis, D. E., Owen, J., Worthington E. L., Jr., & Utsey, S. O. (2013). Cultural humility: Measuring openness to culturally diverse clients. *Journal of Counseling Psychology, 60*, 353–366.

International Society for Traumatic Stress Studies. (2016). Diversity and cultural competence SIG. Retrieved from https://www.istss.org/about-istss/special-interest-groups/diversity-and-cultural-competence-sig.aspx

Kaslow, N. J., Borden, K. A., Collins, F. L., Jr., Forrest, L., Illfelder-Kaye, J., Nelson, P. D., . . . Willmuth, M. E. (2004). Competencies conference: Future directions in education and credentialing in professional psychology. *Journal of Clinical Psychology, 60*, 699–712.

Lavizzo-Mourey, R., & Mackenzie, E. (1996). Cultural competence: Essential measurement of quality for managed care organizations. *Annals of Internal Medicine, 124*, 919–926.

NASW. (2001). *Standards for cultural competence in social work practice*. Washington, DC: Author. Retrieved from http://www.socialworkers.org

National Alliance for Hispanic Health. (2001). *A primer for cultural proficiency: Towards quality health services for Hispanics*. Washington, DC: Estrella Press.

Pedersen, P. B. (2002). The making of a culturally competent counselor. In W. J. Lonner, D. L. Dinnel, S. A. Hayes, & D. N. Sattler (Eds.), *Online readings in psychology and culture* (Subunit 3, Article 4). Bellingham, Washington, DC: Center for Cross-Cultural Research, Western Washington University.

Ridley, C. R. (2005). *Overcoming unintentional racism in counseling and therapy: A practitioner's guide to intentional intervention*. Thousand Oaks, CA: Sage.

Shapiro, F. (2001). *Eye movement desensitization and reprocessing: Basic principles, protocols, and procedures*. New York, NY: Guilford.

Shapiro, F. (2002). *EMDR as an integrative psychotherapy approach*. Washington, DC: American Psychological Association.

Sperry, L. (2011). *Core competencies in counseling and psychotherapy: Becoming a highly competent and effective therapist*. New York, NY: Routledge.

Tervalon, M., & Murray-Garcia, J. (1998). Cultural humility versus cultural competence: A critical distinction in defining physician training outcomes in multicultural education. *Journal of Health Care for the Poor and Undeserved, 9*, 117–125.

Ursano, R. J., Bell, C., Eth, S., Friedman, M., Norwood, A., Pfefferbaum, B., . . . Yager, J. (2004). *Practice guidelines for the treatment of patients with acute stress disorder and posttraumatic stress disorder*. *American Journal of Psychiatry, 161*(11 Suppl.), 3–31.

U.S. Department of Health and Human Services, & Administration for Children and Families, Administration on Development Disabilities. (2000). Amendments to Pub. L. 106–402, 114 Stat. 1677 (2000). E:\Publaw 402.106

U.S. Department of Health and Human Services, Health Resources and Services, Administration, & Bureau of Health Professions Division of Medicine and Dentistry. (2004, September). Retrieved from www.hrsa.gov.

Waters, A., & Asbill, L. (2013, August). Reflections on cultural humility. *CYF News*. Washington, DC: American Psychological Association. Retrieved from http://www.apa.org/pi/families/resources/newsletter/2013/08/cultural-humility.aspx

World Health Organization. (2013). *Guidelines for the management of conditions that are specifically related to stress*. Geneva, Switzerland: Author.

CHAPTER 2

# Integrating Cultural Concepts and Terminology Into the AIP Model and EMDR Approach

Mark Nickerson

Human beings have an innate need to feel socially connected and included. The social richness that comes with a cultural connection can be a source of great satisfaction and meaning. On the other side of the coin, cultural experiences can be painful. Being excluded or devalued by people from another culture or within one's culture can be traumatizing. At the deepest level, it can tap into primitive fears of being "cut out of the herd."

As trauma-informed therapists, we need to include an understanding of culturally based trauma when assessing both our clients' strengths and vulnerabilities. Many clients have experienced harsh climates of social stigmatization and discrimination. Moreover, virtually all clients have experienced some social stigma and prejudice with lasting effects that are often more powerful than a client might understand.

Research confirms that stigmatized and oppressed people experience and report lower life satisfaction. Being a member of a low-status group can have many consequences including less access to resources such as employment, economic, political, medical, and educational opportunities. Discrimination has also been linked to greater health difficulties and a lower life expectancy (Stangor, 2009).

Cultural values of minority groups are often threatened by dominant cultures, leading to pressured acculturation or marginalization. Inaccurate perceptions and irrational fears of minority groups create intergroup competition rather than cooperation, which often increases the dynamics of oppression. Research patterns of racist police activity have led to the current rallying cry of "Black Lives Matter," reminding people of the ongoing realities of institutionalized racism.

A reasonable question is, how do social dynamics that are so meaningful and essential to human well-being go so bad? This chapter offers useful terminology as well as information and theory from the fields of social psychology and social work as they inform the adaptive information processing (AIP) model and the eye movement desensitization and reprocessing (EMDR) approach to culturally based trauma (Shapiro, 2001). Content will include a review of relevant social psychology theory including the innate mechanisms of group formation, social identity development, and learned prejudice patterns of social discrimination, depicting some of the experiences clients may need to address. The insights from this chapter guide clinical strategies that are detailed in Chapters 3 and 4.

## INCREASING INTERDISCIPLINARY COLLABORATION

In my search for insight and effective strategies to inform culturally competent mental health interventions, I have reviewed the work within three major realms of knowledge, each offering valuable information. Briefly and in very broad terms, the field of social psychology has focused extensive research and theorization on uncovering the dynamics and impact of social/cultural forces on individuals and groups. The field of social work has illuminated the impact of socially based discrimination, including systemic inequities, and has advocated for relief and fair treatment for those who have been mistreated and marginalized. The field of psychotherapy has developed procedures to help individual people and their families overcome and cope effectively with personal difficulties and achieve their personal goals, with inconsistent integration of cultural factors.

Each discipline has an abundance of information and expertise and yet I've been surprised by the limited interdisciplinary integration of this knowledge. Psychotherapists can benefit significantly from a solid understanding of social processes including a more nuanced awareness of the impact of socially based trauma resulting from stigma and of social behavior, both adaptive and maladaptive. At the same time, EMDR therapy offers a viable means to reduce or eliminate the internalized effects of stigma and oppression in a way that social psychologists and social workers continue to search for. For example, social psychologists have deep understandings of the mechanisms of social prejudice, yet methods used for creating change seem quite limited by EMDR standards. Clearly, better integration of these fields benefits all.

In my review of the literature, I found three collections of scholarly works from the field of social psychology particularly useful: *Stereotypes and Prejudice* (Stangor, 2000); *Handbook of Prejudice, Stereotyping, and Discrimination* (Nelson, 2009); and *The Oxford Handbook of Multicultural Identity* (Bebet-Martinez & Hong, 2014). Each of these collections offers comprehensive coverage and a window into current observations related to social behavior and cultural considerations.

As a starting point for the integration of concepts from social psychology and social work, I will introduce some useful terminology related to cultural issues. The following are my working definitions, which represent a synthesis of common understandings of these terms.

*Culture* is the composition of the multiple unique dimensions of a social group, typically including systems of belief, values, morality, interests, behavior, and customs.

A *social identity* or *cultural identity* is one's identity related to associations with social or cultural groups. These two terms are often interchangeable in the literature, which can be confusing. Although cultural identity is the more commonly familiar term, I generally prefer the term *social identity* because it is more broadly inclusive of social groups with less-developed cultures.

Categories that are most commonly associated with social identification include race/ethnicity, social class, nationality, religion/faith, age, sex, gender identity, sexual/affectional orientation, physical appearance, physical abilities/challenges, intellectual abilities, and mental health status. There are many other domains of socially meaningful identities not so commonly thought of such as health status, marital status, political views, educational differences, and a range of other interests and characteristics. In addition, most broad categories of identities can be expanded into subcategories. For example, within the category of physical abilities, there are innumerable other relevant categories including being a person who is blind, deaf, chronically ill, or lacking full mobility.

I view a social identity as composed of two important components. The first is the meaning a person gains through a chosen identification with a group. The second is the meaning that is ascribed by other people or groups of people to the person related to the identity, positive or negative. Social identities can have many other dimensions (Chapter 3) but these two are most fundamental.

The term *multiculturalism* is used to frame the social challenges and possibilities in a culturally diverse world. It has historically referred to ethnic diversity but it extends easily to include the diversity of other cultures. For organizations seeking diversity, identifying the types of diversity wanted can be challenging. The spirit of multiculturalism is one that promotes respect for the distinctiveness of multiple cultures while holding an expectation that coexisting harmoniously is possible and mutually beneficial.

*Entitativity* is a term introduced by Campbell (1958) that is rarely mentioned outside the field of social psychology but is a useful concept. Entitativity represents the degree to which members of a group are bonded together in a coherent social unit. Relevant factors that generally determine entitativity are group size, degree of spatial proximity, amount of interaction, importance of social identity, perceived common goals, outcomes of group, interdependence, interpersonal bonds, organization, and the behavior included among group members. The military, for example, seeks to strengthen entitativity to create group unity. Awareness of these factors can be used to both understand social difficulties and build social connection.

*In-group* and *out-group* distinctions depict the natural human tendency to evaluate whether someone is a member of one's own group or not based on a range of determinants associated with social groupings. The term *in-group* in social psychology language generally refers to one's own group, although the term is also commonly used to refer to the favored group, whether one belongs to it or not. This quick and often unconscious assessment of whether someone is "like me or not" can be highly influential.

*Stigma* is an ancient Greek term that originally referred to an indicator such as a mark burned into the body to designate the bearer as morally defective and to be shunned or disfavored. Stigma serves as a force of social control, often unjustly applied, and its impact can be profound and long lasting. It is safe to assume that all people have experienced stigma at one point or another in their life, thus making it a universal point of shared experience.

*Social oppression* signifies mistreatment of a person or a group of people in a way that reflects systemic inequalities. Oppressive injustices are typically embedded in social structures and reflected in laws, intolerant attitudes of a dominant culture, and lack of access to important social and economic opportunities and resources. Oppression is maintained through powerful social messages, and people in "positions" of social power may collude with cultural oppression through discrimination, the perpetuation of stereotypes, and other mistreatment.

*Bias* is a term that suggests an inclination for or against something that is not based on objective thinking. Social psychologists use the terms *prejudice, stereotype,* and *discrimination* to describe the components of social bias, which are learned responses to a person or group of people that reflect a misperception. These responses often result in misunderstanding, mistreatment, and other maladaptive responses to the person or group.

*Prejudice* refers to the *affective* or emotional response often elicited by the object of the prejudice. A *stereotype* is a *cognitive* perception. Stereotypes generally take the form of rigid and generalized beliefs about the traits of a person or characteristics of a group, often focusing on perceptions that differentiate groups or group members from other groups. *Discrimination* is the *behavioral* response or the actions a person takes, including avoidance of types of people that are often triggered by prejudice and justified by stereotypes.

Prejudices, stereotypes, and discrimination can be *explicit* (conscious, ego syntonic) for a person or more *implicit* (unconscious, ego dystonic) to a person. Explicit prejudice is more direct, close, and emotionally hot as compared with *implicit* prejudice, which has more subtle indications that are indirect, distant, and cool. Implicit prejudice is typically in conflict with a person's conscious belief system and is sometimes referred to as *aversive prejudice* because it is unwanted and disturbing to the bearer.

A *microaggression* is a term used to refer to an "unintended" act of discrimination that is often associated with implicit prejudice. The target of the microaggression may or may not be consciously aware of the act even though the target may feel it.

*Internalization* is the process whereby a person, as part of a coping response to mistreatment, adopts the negative messages conveyed to him or her. In the case of culturally based mistreatment such as discrimination, a person absorbs the messages of the adverse or traumatic experience, including the perpetrator's social judgment, value, belief, control, or prescription for conduct as his or her own and experiences it as a part of them. Clinical terms such as *internalized oppression, internalized stigma,* and *cultural trauma introject* can be used to depict a memory-related psychic structure that retains the characteristics of the cultural message. These *introjects* may have a constant chronic and defining impact on the person's life that become part of a personality trait or may be more contextually activated as an intermittent state. As with any trauma memory, culturally internalized introjects influence perception of both the self and others and can drive prejudices toward others.

*Acculturalization* is the process of adapting to the social norms of another culture. Berry (1984) depicted four types of intergroup relational possibilities related to acculturation. Successful *integration* within a multicultural model can be characterized by the metaphor of a salad bowl or tapestry. Different cultural identities mix together for the benefit of all while, at the same time, individual cultural differences are valued and supported. *Assimilation* fits the melting pot model in which a person surrenders his or her prior social identity in the process of taking on the cultural identity of the new group. One form this takes is when immigrants give up their prior language and take on the language of the new culture. Another adjustment, *segregation/separation* of different groups, keeps a separation of groups. *Marginalization* occurs when a group isolates to maintain its cultural ways and identity without trying to integrate, but remains in isolation from—and in a weaker position related to—the dominant culture.

Understanding these terms and their implications and offering them to clients can enrich the discussions of social and cultural experiences.

## UNDERSTANDING SOCIAL BEHAVIOR WITHIN THE AIP MODEL

As EMDR therapists operating with the AIP model, understanding how the brain processes socially related information is highly relevant. The AIP model views the human brain as a physical mechanism that translates perception into stored memories. These memories become the basis of knowledge that guides future activity. Memories are composed of complicated neuro networks that impact perception, response tendencies, attitudes, self-concept, and personality traits. We understand that the human brain functions on conscious and unconscious levels.

EMDR clinicians can appreciate that adverse and traumatic experiences of stigmatization and discrimination become physically stored memories that may remain "frozen" and isolated from other memory networks. When activated either consciously or unconsciously, these unresolved memories affect perception, feelings, and behavior.

### Innate Human Tendencies to Discriminate and Categorize

From the AIP perspective, we want to understand our client's adaptive tendencies. We may wonder, "What is adaptive and what is maladaptive in the realm of social behavior?" "How is the formation of culture adaptive or maladaptive?" and most importantly, "How can we assist our clients to adapt to challenges and opportunities?"

This section offers interesting insights from the field of social psychology regarding social behavior and group dynamics. The consensus within the field appears to be that many inclinations for social grouping, including social discrimination, are innately "hard wired" and instinctive (Bargh & Gollwitzer, 1994; Dasgupta, 2009; Devine, 1989; Devine & Sharp, 2009; Fiske et al., 2009; Gaertner & Dovidio, 2014; Hamilton, Sherman, Crump, & Spencer-Rodgers, 2009; Major & Sawyer, 2009; Nelson, 2009; Stangor, 2000).

Accepted thinking within the field is summarized in the following text. Starting from infancy, it is developmentally normal and important for all infants and children to have the ability to sort the many different objects, events, and people they encounter quickly and effectively into smaller numbers of meaningful categories. This capacity enables quick decision making, which supports efficient functioning because it spares the person having to reassess the details of every new situation that is encountered.

Social categorization occurs spontaneously on the basis of *entitativity* factors such as physical similarity, proximity, or shared fate. From the beginning, both attraction to and prejudice against are fundamentally related to social categorization and the perception of intergroup boundaries that define "we" from "they." Children show a natural interest in learning about social categories and seek to know how they fit in, especially between the ages of 7 and 11, although they are susceptible to believing stereotypes. Much of one's social values and judgments come from trusted caretakers initially, along with others of social importance to them and their social groups; in addition, the society at large has generated messages through the media.

Therefore, likes and dislikes are determined very quickly in life and related to fundamental needs for attachment. As clinicians, it is important to understand the importance of attachment at the social and societal level. The current surge of interest in attachment-focused psychotherapy tends to focus on early attachments with primary caretakers. Undeniably, unmet attachment needs during early formative years can have a profound impact. Yet Erikson (1968) makes it clear in his widely accepted model of developmental stages that one's psychological attachment needs extend beyond the initial primary caregivers. As life progresses, attachment needs widen to include the larger circle of the family, peers and friends, larger social groups, and ultimately society itself. Successes or failures of attachment at any level are significant. For instance, a girl can come from a very secure and loving family, only to head off to school and be shunned because she is ethnically different. Or an adolescent may have very solid friends until he comes out as gay and then feels suddenly unaccepted and withdraws into isolation.

## In-Groups and Out-Groups

Social psychologists have observed that people tend to quickly categorize others into *in-groups* and *out-groups* in relationship to their own group identity. Group membership is characterized by various criteria and boundaries. Given that groups shape a person's social identity, one's fate becomes intertwined with his or her groups. There are many proven benefits of in-group associations. People frequently derive material benefit, receive valuable information, and experience a sense of belonging and security from their in-groups. Research shows that even when the basis for group membership is randomly assigned, powerful instincts for ethnocentrism and group loyalty operate.

From childhood, people assign more positives and fewer negatives to members of their own groups. This is reinforced by exposure and information offered to them and is perpetuated as members of in-groups become more important and out-group members become less important in their lives. In times of threat or stress, these tendencies can become greater.

## Information Processing

As EMDR therapists are concerned with the information processing of our clients, it is important to appreciate that these in-group/out-group preferences are not just behavioral but are evidenced by differences at the information processing neurological level. The following findings provide revealing insight into the core workings of the socially adapted brain. While highly attuned to in-group information processing, the social brain can be very ineffective at accurately processing experiences with out-group members. These findings help us appreciate the mistreatment received by our clients when they are out-group members.

Research shows that people retain more information in a more detailed fashion about in-group members than about out-group members. People have better memory for information that confirms ways in-group members are similar and out-group members are dissimilar and they are more likely to forget positive information about out-group members. People think and act in ways that are more explicit and conscious about in-group experiences and more implicit and unconscious about out-group experiences.

Cognitively, people are more generous and forgiving in their interpretations of behaviors of in-group relative to out-group members. Neurologically, people encode observed behaviors of in-group and out-group members in memory at different levels of abstraction. For example, an undesirable action of an out-group member is encoded at a more abstract level that presumes intentionality and dispositional outcome (e.g., he's a drunken bum) when compared with the identical behaviors of in-group members (e.g., he drank too much last night). In contrast, desirable actions of out-group members are encoded at more concrete levels (e.g., she was nice to me that time) relative to the same behaviors of in-group members (e.g., she's a nice person). The impact of these human inclinations is profound and these cognitive biases help perpetuate social biases and stereotypes even in the face of countervailing evidence. Stereotypes are used to size up a person, to "make life easier"; eventually, they become quick and spontaneous, a matter of automatic categorization. As Allport (1954) observed, "the mind tends to categorize environmental events in the grossest manner compatible with action." Because positive behaviors of out-group members are encoded on the concrete level, they tend not to generalize to reduce stereotypes.

Furthermore, people don't remember that an out-group member was helpful, only that they did a helpful thing. Thus, out-group stereotypes containing information pertaining to traits, dispositions, or intentions are not likely to be influenced by observing counter stereotypic out-group behaviors. Pronouns like "we" and "they" are often paired with affective connotations. The pronouns alone can influence reactions to the associated matters.

Although social categorization generally increases pro–in-group orientation rather than anti–out-group orientation, pro–in-group bias can provide a foundation for generating hostility and injustice in relation to out-groups, especially when there is competition for economic resources and political power.

Though unsettling when we consider the negative consequences of these innate information processing tendencies to dismiss out-group members, the evolutionary benefit is apparent because it is generally adaptive to assume that a person or group that seems similar or has valuable attributes can be trusted and sought after while those seen as different or with undesirable qualities are to be avoided.

This information is useful as we seek to understand culturally based trauma. When people from one social group misjudge and mistreat a person simply because he or she is not an in-group member, it is understandable that the out-group member would be adversely affected.

## High Status/Low Status and Power Dynamics

Social psychologists have also observed that people quickly categorize according to another social dimension, *high status* and *low status*. People make surprisingly quick assessments of another person's social status relative to them and others. Of course, the currency of that social status varies with context. The boss at work may be the dullest person at a party.

Power is often associated with high-status groups. Yet, interestingly, research shows that when conflict arises, both high- and low-power groups may perceive that they are under threat. Although low-power groups are more likely to experience actual threats and these threats are more likely to be acted on with significant consequences, high-power group members, when they perceive threats, react more strongly to threat. High-power group members have more power to yield and, they perceive, to lose. The implications of these tendencies are significant and explain why challenges to authority are often avoided until they can't be contained. The fear of losing power explains sometimes aggressive defense of social advantages and privileges.

## The Neurology of Prejudice

Though an adaptive tool for some purposes, there are many downsides of the brain's tendency toward social categorization. While building in-group cohesiveness is generally beneficial, misperception of "out-group" members can be detrimental for all concerned. Just as social categorization establishes a template to allow for quick decisions based on limited information when needed, that template persists and biases perception. Once the template for judgment has been established, the bias resists any subsequent information that varies from the first impression.

Amodio and Lieberman (2009) studied the mechanisms of implicit prejudice using evidence from functional magnetic resonance imaging (fMRI) examination. They noted that the human subcortical response network, linked closely to the amygdala, provides information quickly when activated and interfaces strongly with autonomic and behavioral systems. Their study revealed that an amygdala reaction occurred within 100 milliseconds when stimulated by out-group faces rather than in-group. In a similar study by Cunningham (2004), White people were exposed to Black faces for 30 and 525 milliseconds. The study found that more amygdala activation occurred in the short exposure time. They also observed that activity in the prefrontal cortex (PFC), stimulated by the longer exposure time, correlated with lower amygdala activity. The prefrontal PFC was presumed to hold learned explicit information that countered the implicit prejudicial reaction in the amygdala region. They interpreted this to mean that the short exposure did not allow for the regulatory cortical activity to be activated. Their conclusions suggested that strengthening the PFC can reduce amygdala activity and serve to better regulate the autonomic bias system. They also noted that implicit prejudice toward a culture can be internalized by members of that culture as well.

Likewise, Hart et al. (2000) found that Whites demonstrated increased activity in their PFC when exposed to Black faces, suggesting the extra effort that was necessary to manage the amygdala response. This increased level of PFC activity has been correlated with others' scores on an implicit prejudice test (IAT) (Amodio & Devine, 2009).

## Implications for EMDR Therapy

This neurological insight into the mechanisms of prejudice is useful for EMDR clinicians. Amygdala activity is generally seen as a barometer of internal emotional disturbance often linked to traumatic memories. Like other emotional disturbances, a prejudicial reaction evoked in the brain stimulates midbrain activity and requires the resources of PFC regulation to manage the disturbance. As EMDR therapists, we often assist clients to strengthen the PFC system through resource development and installation (Korn & Leeds, 2002) and other strategies. However, we recognize that resourcing alone does not eradicate trauma-related responses altogether. EMDR reprocessing accesses disturbing memories in their "unmanaged" form (Pagani, Högberg, Fernandez, & Siracusano, 2013). When a memory has been fully reprocessed, it is no longer activating at the amygdala level. Therefore, we can predict that EMDR reprocessing can eradicate the prejudicial response. More on reprocessing prejudice will be covered in Chapter 4.

## THE IMPACT OF CULTURALLY BASED TRAUMA

Even with a better understanding of how human beings are susceptible to the negative side of social categorization, as clinicians we need to appreciate our clients' felt experience when they are victimized by social forces.

Prejudice and discrimination can take many forms including racism/ethnic discrimination, nationalism, classism, sexism, gay oppression, ageism, and religious/faith-based discrimination. Additionally, discrimination based on such parameters as physical appearance, physical ability, intellectual style or ability, and mental health issues are often reinforced by dominant cultural norms.

While most people can conjure up visible images of blatant examples of discrimination, less obvious patterns of discrimination can be *invisible* when they are pervasive in a culture. Subtle discrimination can be much like smog, invisible yet polluting.

### Microaggressions

Chester Pierce first introduced the term *microaggression* in 1970 to describe derogatory and dismissive actions he frequently observed non-Black Americans inflicting on Black Americans. The term has been increasingly used to describe casual denigrating and polarizing comments or gestures toward members of stigmatized or oppressed groups.

Some have suggested that microaggressions are the more visible face of discrimination in parts of society where explicit discrimination is less apparent. Sue, Bucceri, Lin, Nadal, & Torino (2007) divided microaggressions into three categories: microassaults, such as explicit racial slurs; microinsults that convey rudeness and insensitivity to a person's racial heritage or identity; and microinvalidations that exclude, negate, or nullify the thoughts, feelings, or experiential reality of a person belonging to a particular group.

Microaggressions, like overt acts of discriminations, can trigger and activate deeper cultural wounds. However "subtle" they may seem to some, microaggressions can sting and linger in a person's memories, often unconsciously, as reminders of social inequities and power imbalances.

Because of their less obvious nature, Sue et al. (2007) point out that microaggressions can put the target in a psychological bind. That is, the target may feel insulted but is not sure why. The perpetrator typically is unaware of the damage and so doesn't acknowledge the insensitivity, thus creating a rift between the two people. The target may not consciously identify the aggression but feels it. If the target does identify it, he or she often expects that bringing it up will only further the rift. If others are present and do not acknowledge the invalidation, the target may feel isolated and alienated from those others.

In the realm of gender and sexuality, Paludi (2010, 2012) discusses "microaggressable" themes including: sexual objectification, second-class citizenship, sexist language, assumptions of inferiority, denial of sexism, traditional gender role assumptions, social invisibility, denial of individual sexism, and sexist jokes. Members of sexual minorities commonly report experiencing microaggressions such as the sexual eroticization of lesbians by heterosexual men and prying questions about one's sexual activity. Transgendered people are commonly misgendered.

Microaggression experiences like these happen often in our clients' lives to varying effects. A client of mine reported that a male plumber she had contacted over the phone had called her "sweetie" and "hun" multiple times in a way that made her feel uncomfortable and demeaned. She asked politely for him not to use those terms. Two days later, she received a coldly worded letter in the mail saying that the man would not be willing to work with her based upon the phone interaction. While some people can shrug an experience like this off, for her, it was very disturbing. Women report this type of experience frequently as they try to deflect unwanted sexual attention or so-called "chivalrous" sexist gestures in the workplace.

Sue (2008) reported that young adult Black Americans in the New York metropolitan area indicated that microaggressive communications left them feeling like they didn't belong, were abnormal, or were untrustworthy. Some described the disturbing experience of being watched suspiciously in stores as they shopped.

Others have cited the pressure to represent one's group in a positive way. Meanwhile, Sue (2008) found that, in therapy, the more likely Black people are to perceive their therapist as using racial microaggressions, the weaker the therapeutic bond and the lower their reported satisfaction. It is no surprise that many studies indicate that microaggressions can lead people of color to fear, distrust, and avoid relationships with White people (Chambers, 2012).

A client of mine who came to the United States from a Caribbean country reported numerous microaggressions within academia as she pursued and earned her doctorate degree. These experiences often activated old experiences of exclusion or mistreatment. Like many minorities, she felt that she had to both positively "represent" her racial heritage and hide it. She stated repeatedly that were it not for the opportunities to process these experiences within EMDR therapy, she would have dropped out of the program and not completed the degree.

Social class is a remarkably unacknowledged dimension of social division. Many women have experienced "glass ceilings" in employment opportunities. Similarly, I have come to talk of *class ceilings* with clients as a reference to the common cap that people feel within a socioeconomically stratified society. While these limitations are generally real, the internalized effects can be addressed in therapy. Likewise, *class floors* is an equally useful term. Many people who have had money or a prominent socio/economic position and opportunities are very prone to shame and depression when life circumstances such as the loss of a job bring them to a different social position. Immigrants who were doctors in one country often have to start all over in another. People with PhDs sometimes end up driving cabs.

### Stigma and Mental Health Discrimination

In 2016, the World Bank Group and the World Health Organization sponsored "Out of the Shadows; Making Mental Health for Global Development Priority." I attended the multiday summit of policy makers and service providers. Overcoming stigma was seen as one of the three major hurdles to providing effective mental health services throughout the world. (The other two challenges were developing effective evidence-based interventions and accessing the resources to provide these interventions.)

Many of the clients we see in our offices have been discriminated against or felt judged about the very problems they seek help for in life and sometimes within the mental health system itself. A colleague of mine noted that in her work at a community mental health agency, three client descriptors are immediately treated with a "don't assign them to me" attitude and often get substandard treatment: bipolar disorder, borderline personality disorder, and cognitively limited.

Research findings indicate that people with "mental illness" report experiencing overt acts of discrimination rather than subtle ones, coming from family, friends, and authority figures. In a study involving college students and adults engaged in community care for mental health diagnoses, five common themes were identified related to mental health discrimination: (a) invalidation, (b) assumption of inferiority, (c) fear of mental illness, (d) shaming of mental illness, and (e) being treated as a second class citizen (Lundberg-Love, Nadal, & Paludi, 2011).

A client of mine was involved in a legal trial related to a personal injury claim. Under oath in a deposition, he was asked if he took medication. He felt a bolt of shame about his bipolar condition and reactively answered "No" for fear it would be used against him. After reprocessing that experience, along with other fear and shame-filled memories associated with his bipolar diagnosis, he was prepared to deftly correct the record without consequence.

Internalized stigma for "needing help" is a common struggle for many clinical populations including first responders and military veterans, clients with alcohol or drug problems, parents with acting out children, clients going through divorce, and a host of other circumstances related to families being different than the norm. I find that identifying and addressing the stigma is a crucial dimension of the therapy.

## SUMMARY

Information and terminology from the allied fields of social psychology and social work can help EMDR clinicians better understand and discuss the importance and impact of social and cultural forces, both positive and negative, in our clients' lives. Understanding how the brain processes socially related information enriches the AIP model and affirms the need for full reprocessing to create sustainable change.

As trauma-informed therapists, being fully aware of the destructive realities of stigmatization, oppression, and other discrimination is essential to understanding all dimensions of our clients' experiences. Like other traumatic memories, culturally based trauma may be minimized or walled from conscious recall. This chapter's insight can inform clinical strategies presented in other chapters of this book. As culturally aware therapists, we can support our clients to develop more constructive social realities.

## REFERENCES


Allport, G. (1954). *The nature of prejudice*. Reading, MA: Addison Wesley Publishing Company.

Amodio, D. M., & Lieberman, M. D. (2009). *Pictures in our heads: Contributions from the study of prejudice and stereotyping. Handbook of prejudice, stereotyping, and discrimination*. New York, NY: Psychology Press.

Bargh, J. A., & Gollwitzer, P. M. (1994). *Environmental control of goal-directed action: Automatic and strategic contingencies between situations. Nebraska symposium on motivation*. Lincoln, NE: University of Nebraska Press.

Bebet-Martinez, V., & Hong, Y. (Eds.). (2014). *The Oxford handbook of multicultural identity*. Oxford, UK: Oxford University Press.

Berry, J. W. (1984). Cultural relations in plural societies: Alternatives to segregation and their social psychological implications. In N. Miller & M. B. Brewer (Eds.), *Groups and contact: The psychology of desegregation* (pp. 11–27). New York, NY: Academic.

Campbell, D. T. (1958). Common fate, similarity, and other indices of the status of aggregates of person as social entities. *Behavioural Science, 3*, 14–25.

Chambers, C. R. (2012). *Black female undergraduates on campus: Successes and challenges* (pp. 83–87). Bradford, UK: Emerald Group Publishing (Diversity in Higher Education).

Cunningham, W. A., Johnson, M. K., Raye, C. L., Gatenby, J. C., Gore, J. C., & Banaji, M. R. (2004), Separable neural components in the processing of black and white faces. *American Psychological Society*. *15*(12).

Dasgupta, N. (2009). *Mechanisms underlying the malleability of implicit prejudice and stereotypes: The role of automaticity and cognitive control. Handbook of prejudice, stereotyping, and discrimination*. New York, NY: Psychology Press.

Devine, P. G. (1989). Stereotypes and prejudice: Their automatic and controlled components. *Journal of Personality and Social Psychology, 56*(1), 5–18.

Devine, P. G., Amodio, D. & Space M. (2006). Stereotyping and evaluation in implicit race bias: Evidence for independent constructs and unique effects on behavior. *Journal of Personality and Social Psychology, 19*(4), 652–661.

Devine, P. G., & Sharp, L. B. (2009). *Automaticity and control in stereotyping and prejudice. Handbook of prejudice, stereotyping, and discrimination*. New York, NY: Psychology Press.

Erikson, E. H. (1968). *Identity, youth, and crisis*. New York, NY: W. W. Norton.

Fiske, S. T., Harris, L. T., Lee, T. L., & Russell, A. (2009). *The future of research on prejudice, stereotyping, and discrimination. Handbook of prejudice, stereotyping, and discrimination*. New York, NY: Psychology Press.

Gaertner, S. L., & Dovidio, J. F. (2014). *Reducing intergroup bias: The common ingroup identity model*. Philadelphia, PA: Psychology Press.

Hamilton, D. L., Sherman, S. J., Crump, S. A., & Spencer-Rodgers, J. (2009). *The role of entitativity in stereotyping. Handbook of prejudice, stereotyping, and discrimination*. New York, NY: Psychology Press.

Hart, A. J., Whalen, P. J., Shin, L. M., Mcinerney, S. C., Fischer, H., & Rauch, S. L. (2000). Differential response in the human amygdala to racial outgroup vs. ingroup face stimuli. *Neuro Report, 11*, 2351–2355.

Korn, D. L., & Leeds, A. M. (2002). Preliminary evidence of efficacy for EMDR resource development and installation in the stabilization phase of treatment of complex posttraumatic stress disorder. *Journal of Clinical Psychology, 58*(12), 1465–1487.

Lundberg-Love, P., Nadal, K., & Paludi, M. (2011). *Women and mental disorders*. Santa Barbara, CA: Praeger.

Major, B., & Sawyer, P. J. (2009). *Attributions to discriminations: Antecedents and consequences. Handbook of prejudice, stereotyping, and discrimination*. New York, NY: Psychology Press.

Nelson, T. D. (Ed.). (2009). *Handbook of prejudice, stereotyping, and discrimination*. New York, NY: Psychology Press. (Collection of 26 topic-related chapters by experts in the field of social psychology.)

Pagani, M., Högberg, G., Fernandez, I., & Siracusano, A. (2013). Correlates of EMDR therapy in functional and structural neuroimaging: A critical summary of recent findings. *Journal of EMDR Practice and Research, 7*(1), 29–38.

Paludi, M. (2010). *Victims of sexual assault and abuse: Resources and responses for individuals and families (women's psychology)* (p. 22). Santa Barbara, CA: Praeger.

Paludi, M. A. (2012). *Managing diversity in today's workplace: Strategies for employees and employers*. Santa Barbara, CA: Praeger.

Shapiro, F. (2001). *Eye movement desensitization and reprocessing: Basic principles, protocols, and procedures*. New York, NY: Guilford.

Stangor, C. (Ed.). (2000). *Stereotypes and prejudice: Essential readings*. Philadelphia, PA: Psychology Press. (Collection of 24 topic-related chapters by experts in the field of social psychology.)

Stangor, C. (2009). *The study of stereotyping, prejudice, and discrimination within social psychology: A quick history of theory and research. Handbook of prejudice, stereotyping, and discrimination*, pp. 1–22. New York, NY: Psychology Press.

Sue, D., Bucceri, J., Lin. A., Nadal, K., & Torino, G. (2007). Racial microaggressions and the Asian American experience. *Cultural Diversity and Ethnic Minority Psychology, 13*(1), 72–81.

Sue, D. W. (2008). *Counseling the culturally diverse: Theory and practice* (5th ed.). Hoboken, NJ: John Wiley & Sons.

CHAPTER 3

# Healing Culturally Based Trauma and Exploring Social Identities With EMDR Therapy

Mark Nickerson

Understanding individual clinical issues within a societal context is fundamental to cultural competence. An approach to culturally competent eye movement desensitization and reprocessing (EMDR) therapy starts with an awareness of the client's cultural experiences and social identities. The importance of this understanding is explored in many ways throughout this book with emphasis on both general ways that culture is relevant and important dimensions of a client's particular cultural groups.

Assuming sufficient cultural attunement, as trauma-informed EMDR therapists, our job is to address our clients' treatment-related needs by offering them opportunities to recover from the effects of past adversity and trauma, to build resilience to cope with current challenges, and to enjoy greater overall well-being.

This chapter will review ways of assessing and treating the impact of culturally based adversity and traumatic experiences. It will also explore the importance of social identities both as they link to sources of positive meaning and resources within a client's life, as well as the ways in which social identities can be associated with cultural stigma and discrimination. Chapter 4 addresses dismantling socially related prejudice. The information presented in these two chapters builds on terminology, theory, and research presented in Chapter 2.

## APPLYING A CULTURAL LENS WITHIN THE EMDR APPROACH

As EMDR therapists, we have the basic tools to understand our clients' social and cultural realities and apply EMDR reprocessing and other strategies to heal and repair culturally based wounds. The adaptive information processing (AIP) model, along with the fundamental procedures of EMDR therapy, including the eight phase approach and three-prong protocol (Shapiro, 2001) for reprocessing culturally based trauma, are no different than for other types of trauma. All eight phases of treatment are important, and normal considerations for Phases 3 to 6 of the reprocessing steps remain the same. The challenge for cultural competence is weaving the cultural dimension into all phases of treatment, starting with a careful assessment.

The negative impact of culturally experienced stigma and discrimination has the characteristics of other traumatic assaults to the self. These experiences create state-based memories that impact an individual's sense of self, perceptions, and general well-being. The internalized impact of constant stigma and discrimination may take the form of chronic traits that go unnoticed. Or, the impact of cultural mistreatment may be more intermittent and periodically triggered. Ultimately, unresolved social trauma memories impact development, a sense of safety, and personal power, and influence how people view and treat others.

As trauma therapists, we know how to create conditions for clients to identify trauma in their lives. We take the first step and use direct but sensitive questions in this process. Yet, often standard assessments do not uncover culturally based trauma. Social issues sometime lies underneath a different rock, kept suppressed or unspoken and reinforced by patterns of cultural minimization and secrecy. As clinicians, we need to look under the right rocks.

## Clinical Example

The following is an example of a clinical case in which a cultural lens was essential to creating meaningful change.

Richard was a middle-aged man working in an architectural firm when he came to see me for anger management. Despite participating in an anger management group a few years earlier, he disclosed that he was often irritable, lost his temper occasionally, didn't know how to resolve conflict constructively, and typically avoided conflict altogether. He had a lot of resentments about his work where his career had plateaued. At group meetings, he felt his ideas were dismissed. He was very sensitive to criticism and had become increasingly reluctant to speak up in meetings.

As a practical type of person, he was eager to learn anger management strategies and conflict resolution skills. From the start, he used them in a disciplined way, although somewhat mechanically, with some success at home. But he still felt bad about himself, defensive about his shortcomings, and had grown hopeless that anybody could see his point of view. He agreed that a more full EMDR treatment might be valuable.

Richard was a multiethnic man and when we explored his history it was evident that his experiences growing up gave him plenty of reason to feel angry and excluded. His father, a White man stationed on business in Honduras, had married a local indigenous woman. Richard grew up in a primarily White neighborhood of U.S. citizens. Following hints he offered, I asked directly if he had experienced any racism. With that question, a flood of memories came forth. His memories contained his father's many racist remarks, including some toward Richard's mother. Another memory was of his father once saying to him angrily, "You're a banana eating (slur). You'll never be more than a shit house cleaner or a ditch digger." As we reprocessed that memory, Richard recalled parents of his friends refusing to include him in car rides. One day his best friend came to him and said, "I can't play with you, because my mother said that your mother is a (slur)."

As his painful memories were reprocessed, however, some silver linings appeared. He could recall many friends that did stick by him. He remembered one day speaking up to a parent who refused to offer him a ride. He recalled that a girl he liked very much seemed very sad when she said, "My mother said we can't be friends." Over the course of our sessions, Richard changed in many ways. His previously smoldering anger surfaced more vividly but then subsided as he realized the past was behind him. His previous Negative Cognitions of "I'm not good enough" and "I'm insignificant" shifted as he realized how strong he had been though it all, how loyal he was to his mother, and how ultimately in high school he had proved himself as a good student and athlete. In one moment of reevaluation, he said, "It makes no difference what race one is or where one comes from, we're basically the same and I am good enough. I can do what I set my mind to regardless of the opinions of others."

At work, he was rejuvenated. In one session, he reprocessed a subtle put down (microaggression) he received from his boss. The next day he confronted his boss with great skill and effectiveness. The boss apologized and went out of his way over the next few weeks to show how important Richard was to the team.

In reviewing our work together, it was clear to both Richard and I that had we not fully reprocessed the traumatic childhood memories of racism, he would have been unable to fully feel and maintain a dignified place in his current life, and that simply employing communication techniques would have been hollow and only partially effective.

### Phases 1 and 2: Engaging the Client's Cultural Experience

#### Psychosocial Education

Strategic *psychoeducation* is a common part of psychotherapy. Cultural effectiveness can be aided with an expanded *psychosocial education,* which can include information about the role of sociocultural forces in a person's life. As with all educational information we offer our clients, we look for the well-timed moments to provide needed perspective. Sometimes we remind clients of what they already know. Other times we introduce new bits of meaningful information. Psychosocial education may include concepts and perspectives described in Chapter 2 and throughout this book, including the importance and power of cultural identities, the cultural forces of stigma and oppression, and ways discriminatory experiences can alter perception and well-being.

Effective psychosocial education can increase the client's curiosity about social and cultural issues, create language for better understanding and discussion, reduce isolation or shame, and pave the way for productive therapy.

Also, as part of preparing a client for trauma reprocessing, EMDR therapy procedures and the AIP theory should be explained in a culturally comprehensible way by building on the client's existing knowledge and using accessible metaphors. Cultural attunement means adapting the methods of the treatment to the culturally informed needs of the client rather than the other way around.

## ASSESSMENT: HISTORY GATHERING AND ISSUE EXPLORATION

During Phase 1, initial or ongoing history taking and treatment planning, the task of cultural competence is to explore the client's social and cultural experiences, both positive and negative, and integrate them while formulating treatment strategies.

The more central culture is to the client's issues, the more attention should be put on it. Also, the more different the client's culture is from that of the therapist, the more careful the therapist should be to take the time necessary to attune to the client. Careful assessment not only brings important information to light for the client, but provides opportunities for the therapist to learn about the client. Sometimes these discussions are extended as the therapist seeks to learn about the client's culture. Sometimes the therapist should seek to learn more from other sources.

Expanding the therapeutic scope to more actively include culturally relevant issues can be a challenging shift for any therapist. Many clinicians have not been trained or exposed to effective ways to include culture. Standard clinical tools, including assessment techniques often include only a passing reference to culture, if anything.

How and when culturally focused questions are introduced depends on a variety of variables. How actively and explicitly the therapist engages in this topic depends upon the client's purpose and goals for therapy and the apparent relevance of cultural issues, combined with sensitivity to the barriers that might exist to exploring culturally. Naturally, when the focus of therapy is very narrow, such as in short-term work, history taking, case formulation, and treatment are tightly defined and cultural considerations, along with many other dimensions of a client's experience, are often omitted. Certainly, the degree of attention to social and cultural issues can be adjusted.

The important challenge for culturally competent therapists is to open up the cultural component rather than avoid it. It is important not to assume that culture plays no part in the issues the client has brought to therapy. Like many aspects of a client's life, such as his or her family relationships, if we don't ask we are missing important information. The therapist can inquire about cultural issues in a range of ways from the full culture-focused assessment included later in this chapter to well-timed questions that link directly to information the client is presenting.

Perhaps, the biggest fear that clinicians have about broaching the topic of culture is that it will backfire and actually derail the clinical focus or destabilize the clinical relationship. Of course this can happen, but it certainly doesn't need to. Although asking about culture is a new skill to develop, the therapist should be prepared to stretch beyond the client's comfort zone.

## Overcoming Therapist Barriers

The concept of "cultural humility" that is associated with cultural competence can be very freeing to the therapist. Permission to "not know" about a client's cultural experience allows the clinician to ask with a genuine curiosity and respect. Most clients are grateful that the therapist is interested.

Sometimes cultural issues are quite sensitive, although this may be all the more reason to find a way to talk about them. Some therapists may fear that if they introduce culture, especially if the client's cultural experiences have been different than the therapist's, it will lead to highlighting differences between client and therapist and create distance rather than connection. If the therapist has experienced advantages and privileges that the client has not, he or she may feel awkward, guilty, or helpless when relating to the client's experience. Without asking, the therapist may falsely assume that he or she understands the client's cultural experiences, perhaps because the therapist believes he or she can identify with them. The experience of being male or female, for instance, varies greatly between people.

In the end, many of these considerations can be approached with the same clinical skills that most clinicians have already developed. It's not a matter of whether a clinician should approach cultural issues, but how to do so in a constructive manner and with the right pacing and sensitivity so as to not overemphasize nor minimize culture. While there are potential risks in introducing culture, these can be managed. A therapist unskilled or avoidant in this area may be denying clients needed opportunities for understanding and healing. Certainly, social divisions have historically been a source of great pain and have separated people. By sensitively and constructively introducing culture, the therapeutic relationship can be a corrective experience.

## The Client's Perspective

Once the therapist feels comfortable enough in addressing cultural issues, it is easier to pay attention to the client's perspective when this subject is explored. From the start, it is important to understand the client's cultural norms about disclosure, especially if the client perceives a difference from the therapist. The therapist might start the conversation by asking, "Do you mind if I ask you some questions about your social and cultural experiences?"

It is important to remember that many clients don't know what to expect from the therapeutic process in general, especially if it is their first time in therapy. For those who do have prior therapy experiences, they may base their expectations on those past experiences which, quite possibly, did not actively address cultural issues. Either way, just as EMDR therapists typically find themselves explaining what the EMDR approach is at the beginning, they can simultaneously introduce a cultural lens.

Any discussion about culture experiences should balance identifying a client's positive experiences and cultural resources with a willingness to talk about the hard stuff. Regarding the many potentially sensitive topics, the client may be slow to warm to this discussion. Many members of marginalized cultures will not bring this dimension of their experience out unless they feel safe enough to do so. Like other painful past experiences, a trauma-informed therapist must make it explicitly possible to reveal. Sometimes culturally related trauma is walled off from other issues. If the therapist turns quickly away from a sensitive topic, it may reinforce a broader cultural pattern of avoidance or minimization. Trust issues are to be expected as a client is invited to share details of his or her cultural experiences or related trauma. When the therapist's culture or social identity appears different than the client's, the client may be more hesitant to risk sharing his or her realities.

Some clients may have coped with cultural trauma in the past by minimizing their own experience of discrimination or marginalization. For example, they may believe that their issues are small compared with what some others have gone through. Some clients may have hardened themselves to past discrimination or vowed to not use it as an "excuse" to get what they want in life. Some clients may think if they do admit to the impacts of these issues and face the memories associated with them, it will mean they have succumbed to them and become a victim. Or they may feel that if they admit to these injustices, they will feel compelled to do something about them which they aren't prepared for.

Some clients who object to the social injustice they have experienced may not want to "waste their time" exploring the internal effects of this injustice. They may believe that if they look at how they've been hurt by stigma/oppression, it will take their focus off advocating or changing the real problem. They may be focused on the externalization of responsibility for the problem to the point of denying the internalized impact. They may believe that if they reprocess the internal pain it won't change the world, so why should they bother?

In the end, a client's process of uncovering cultural issues should be understood through the AIP lens. Previously adaptive coping responses to cultural issues need to be respected and exploring cultural issues needs to be done with full client buy-in, in a culturally corrective manner. Ultimately, some clients may not feel ready to explore cultural considerations. While the therapist should be respectful of this, he or she should continue to internally ask the question, "What conditions might make it more possible to include cultural issues in the future?"

For therapists seeking to more actively include the cultural dimension, here is a brief exercise. Identify a few clients for whom cultural context or culturally based adversity seems particularly relevant. For each client, consider any reluctance that the client might have about opening up these issues in therapy. Next, as the therapist, identify any barriers or considerations you might have with how best to do this. Envision a plan for how to proceed. Consider strengthening your plan with the use of a future template.

This chapter contains three tools for exploring cultural issues: a general cultural assessment, questions to guide a cultural genogram, and the Social Identity Wheel (later in the chapter).

## General Cultural Assessment

The questions from the general cultural assessment (Figure 3.1) are designed to help elicit information about social and cultural identities and experiences, including past social/cultural trauma and adversity. It is important to get the client's explicit permission to discuss culturally related issues. Accessing relevant and useful information in a collaborative manner is the primary goal. Hence, these are guide questions *only* and should be offered in the most fitting wording for your client. Sometimes the clinician will find it more useful to select just a few of the questions and adjust or eliminate others depending upon the client's response. While it is ideal to gather this information early in treatment, the clinician should choose the best timing to explore these issues. These questions may introduce terminology such as a social identity, stigma, or oppression, and these terms should be explained. Given the newness of such direct questions about the social identity and culture for many clients, it is important to move slowly and to allow space for related discussions.

**Phase 1: Cultural Assessment: Exploring social identity, culturally based trauma, and prejudice.**

The following are questions to consider as part of an initial client history or when cultural issues emerge in other phases of the therapy. It is important to explore these questions in language that is attuned to the client. Offering examples of social identities can be helpful. Some psychosocial education may be needed to clarify the questions.

- Can I ask you some questions about your social and cultural experiences? If yes,

Social Identity:

- What social or cultural groups are most important to you?
- What are positive and negative qualities you associate with these groups?
- Are there any cultural or social groups that others identify you with and how has that been for you?
- Are there ways you can better understand yourself or the issues that brought you to therapy in a social/cultural context?
- What else would help me understand more about groups or cultures that are important to you?

Extended Exploration:

- What are sources of pride and shame for your social groups?
- Have you ever had to hide your social identity?
- (Consider introducing the cultural genogram)
- (Consider introducing the identity circle)

Social Trauma (discrimination, stigma/oppression)

- Have you ever felt seriously misunderstood or misjudged related to your social identity/culture?
- Are there ways in which you have been affected by discrimination, social stigma, or oppression during your life?
- Do you have early memories of being avoided, shunned, ostracized, or devalued related to social dynamics?
- Do you have any early memories of being included or excluded from a group based upon your race/ethnicity, social class, gender, physical ability/appearance, and so on?
- Do you currently experience social microaggressions (slurs, denigrating remarks, etc.)?
- Have you had difficulties related to assimilating into another culture?

Social Trauma (discrimination, stigma/oppression)

If issues have opened up at this point, continue with:

- How have these experiences impacted you?
- What beliefs did you form about yourself as you were growing up that might be linked to your social experiences and/or culturally based trauma?
- When did you first become aware of differences between types of people (wealthy people and poor people, different races)?
- Did these differences take on positive or negative meaning, or both?
- How did members of your family handle apparent differences between people?
- What were your earliest experiences related to observing social stigma, prejudice, or stereotyping? What was it like experiencing these dynamics?

**FIGURE 3.1** Conducting a general cultural assessment.

*(continued)*

**Phase 1: Cultural Assessment: Exploring social identity, culturally based trauma, and prejudice.**

- Do you avoid certain types of people? . . . Get upset by certain types of people? . . . . Feel powerless/unsafe or inferior/superior related to certain types of people? . . . . Have strong emotional or physiological reactions to certain types of people?

Strong Beliefs About Society

- Do you have any strong beliefs about culture or society that you think are extreme, inflexible, or problematic?

Prejudice

- Do you have any strong prejudices toward other people or types of people?
- How did you develop these beliefs?
- Do you see problems associated with having these prejudices?
- Do you want to better understand or change them?

Extended Exploration

- Explore the previous questions slanted toward illuminating exposure to prejudice.
- When have you objected to prejudice or stereotyping?

**FIGURE 3.1** Conducting a general cultural assessment. (*continued*)

## Cultural Genogram

Another means to help a client explore cultural dimensions is through a cultural genogram. Many clinicians are familiar with the use of a genogram as an assessment tool. Completing a genogram typically engages the client's curiosity at a deep level and generates discussion and insight. This process entails diagramming an ancestral family "tree" emphasizing a cultural component by identifying the major cultural groups from which a person descended. The next step is to use the guide questions that have been adapted from the work of Hardy and Laszloffy (1995; Figure 3.2) to elicit culturally linked information related to cultural norms, beliefs, and behaviors. Insights from the genogram also can be used in combination with Robinson's Legacy Attuned procedures (Chapter 9).

Each of these assessment methods can illuminate client strengths and resources as well as uncover potential areas of disturbance to be targeted for reprocessing. Some identified traumatic experiences will be obvious targets for reprocessing. However, adverse experiences (what are often called "small t" trauma) such as microaggressions are often linchpin memories that reinforce negative beliefs. Targeting these memories typically benefits clients as well.

# IDENTIFYING CULTURALLY INFLUENCED BELIEFS

EMDR therapy typically helps the client identify overarching metabeliefs, both negative and positive, as they relate to treatment issues that shape a client's perception. Negative self-referencing beliefs, generally referred to as Negative Cognitions, often

**Cultural Genogram Questions**

A culturally focused genogram can be a valuable tool to explore cultural identity. Diagramming your ancestral map can generate valuable insight into forces that may have shaped who you are today. These questions are designed to help you explore the perceptions, beliefs, and behaviors of members of your cultural groups. Please consider these questions for *each* group constituting your culture(s) of origin. Consider the implications of the answers in relation to your overall cultural identity.

1. What were the migration patterns of the group?
2. What significance does race, skin color, and hair play within the group?
3. What is/are the dominant religion(s) or beliefs of the group? What role does religion and spirituality play in the everyday lives of members of the group?
4. How are gender roles defined within the group? How is sexual orientation regarded?
5. What were/are the group's experiences with social stigma and oppression? What were/are the markers of stigma/oppression?
6. What issues divide members within the same group? Are there intragroup conflicts?
7. Describe the relationship between the group's identity and your national ancestry (if the group is defined in terms of nationality, please skip this question).
8. What prejudices or stereotypes does this group have about itself?
9. What prejudices and stereotypes do other groups have about this group?
10. What prejudices or stereotypes does this group have about other groups?
11. What occupational roles are valued and devalued by the group?
12. What is the relationship between age and the values of the group?
13. How is family defined in the group? What effect have they had on you?
14. How does this group view outsiders in general and mental health professionals specifically?
15. What are the ways in which pride/shame issues of each group are manifested in your family system?
16. If more than one group comprises your culture of origin, how were the differences negotiated in your family? What were the intergenerational consequences? How has this impacted you personally?

Modified questions for a cultural genogram (adapted from Hardy & Laszloffy, 1995)

**FIGURE 3.2** Developing a cultural genogram.

capture the essence of past adverse and traumatic experiences and are reflections of memory networks that shape a client's perception. As clients provide examples of their current difficulties, EMDR therapists often help them identify the internalized negative beliefs relative to those memories. Using the float back technique, the therapist often guides the client to identify earlier memories associated with those negative beliefs.

Clearly, cultural experiences impact a client's beliefs, both positive and negative. Culturally related positive beliefs provide important resources that can be accessed and enhanced. What follows are a series of unique and important considerations in pinpointing clinically useful, socially and culturally influenced beliefs.

Broadly speaking, negative beliefs can be formed by culturally based adversity and trauma and/or be reinforced by it. Likewise, social experiences of stigma and discrimination can often reactivate prior trauma by evoking painful emotions.

For example, when a child who has been shamed by a parent experiences further shaming in a cultural context, it reinforces his or her earlier trauma. Internalized stigma and oppression are represented by negative inaccurate self-referencing beliefs that reflect to discriminatory experiences and cultural messages. Whether it is a primary or secondary experience, the wounds of stigma and discrimination can both create and merge with other core Negative Cognitions.

## Socially Based Negative Cognitions

Within EMDR therapy, the commonly identified negative beliefs a client may have are often grouped within three categories (domains): responsibility, safety, and power/control. Each of these groups captures a fundamental human need that may have been violated by one or more traumatic experiences. Trauma in each of these domains is reflected by the client's distorted self-referencing beliefs linked to the effects of these unresolved memories. The need for self-worth is central to the realm of responsibility. Unresolved trauma in this realm is reflected by a tendency to hold oneself responsible for the trauma rather than being able to assign responsibility in a proper context. The need in the realm of safety is for the client to be safe and protect himself or herself. Unresolved trauma in this realm is often signified by the client's inability to feel safe in the present moment when thinking about the trauma. Within the realm of power/control, the client needs to feel his or her own self agency and be aware that he or she can make choices. Unresolved trauma in this realm is typified by the tendency to believe that the locus of control is outside of the client, and thus the client is powerless.

In my work exploring the social and cultural dimensions of the human experience, I have come to appreciate how fundamentally crucial it is to be connected to others and I think of this as its own realm of need. Human needs for connection include needs for acceptance, appreciation, belonging, closeness, community, friendship, inclusion, mutuality, partnership, shared realities, support, being "known" or "seen," and trust. Although the pursuit of these needs can become distorted by an individual or pathologized by others, they are fundamentally healthy.

Sadly, the normal fulfillment of these needs is often violated by social experiences including ostracism, exclusions, discrimination, stigmatization, and other microaggressions. Violations in this domain often lead to profound social insecurity and aloneness.

In the context of EMDR theory, I see these needs and related beliefs as being in an overarching realm of *connectedness and belonging*. Although this realm certainly overlaps with elements of self-worth and safety, I find that sensing connection is the fundamentally desired and needed state in and of itself.

Developmentally, this need for a group social connection emerges after early stages which focus on needs for secure primary attachment, and relate more to later developmental stages in youth as articulated by Erikson (1968) during which the individual seeks out positive experiences in broadening levels of connection from peer groups to the society as a whole.

Within some cultures, often called collectivist cultures, a person's identity is more connected to the cultural group than in societies considered to be more individualistic, such as the dominant U.S. culture. Likewise, some would say that conventional masculine development values independence as compared with feminine values of interconnectedness. In fact, feminist critiques have questioned the dismissive use of the term *codependent* when describing someone caring for a loved one with an addiction.

My clients have helped me appreciate the centrality of this need for connectedness and belonging. When I ask clients to identify negative and positive cognitions related to memories of adverse social experiences, the beliefs that resonate the deepest are frequently related to the need for connection and belonging.

Here are some examples of negative cognitions related to the need for connection and belonging:

- I don't belong
- I'm alone (and that is dangerous)
- I am disconnected from others
- I'm an oddball/weirdo/reject
- I'm out of it (I don't "get" what others "get")
- I'm not normal (from the dominant social norm)
- My "voice" doesn't matter/I'm invisible (in a social context)
- I'm different/don't fit in

In the aforementioned example, the Negative Cognition "I'm alone (and that is dangerous)" has dimensions of concern for safety; however, the desired solution is not to be physically safe in the moment, but rather for the client to know he or she is connected to others. The primary task of reprocessing is to resolve the dangers associated with the client's perception of being socially alone.

Overall, it is important to be aware that targeting socially based trauma is likely to uncover a particular type of Negative Cognitions. Being aware of this as a clinician makes it easier to help clients identify the beliefs that most accurately resonate with their experience.

## State-Based Social Identity Cognitions

A traumatic memory typically contains the perceptions and associations that were active for the person at the time of the experience. When a person has an experience that is closely associated with a social identity, elements associated with the identity are linked within the memory network. As people live their lives, there are times when different social identities are more present than others. For instance, over the course of a week, a person may have different experiences that seem more related to who that person is as a worker, a parent, a female, or a social activist. Each of these identities builds its own set of associations, positive and negative, based on the client's experiences. These experiences build in a "snowballing" manner, which further develops the importance of the social identity aspect of themselves. A person may feel great as a parent but badly as a worker. Disturbing experiences may occur while a person is within a certain social identity state. This understanding can be useful when helping our clients identifying meaningful Negative and Positive Cognitions.

Often in EMDR, we are trained to reduce Negative Cognitions down to the simplest statement that resonates as a belief that is negative, generalized, irrational, and about the self. A purpose for this is to access as much associated material as possible with any existing generalized negative belief. However, when the goal is to reprocess a disturbing memory associated with a specific social identity, it can be useful to include a reference to that social identity when establishing the Negative and Positive Cognitions. For instance, the Negative Cognition might be "I'm a bad *mother*," or "I'm a useless *old man*." This linkage seems to help keep the focus of reprocessing within the channels of memory most associated with the disturbance related to that social identity, and after reprocessing leads to installation of a social identity-related Positive Cognition. If the disturbance does not clear, the clinician can help the client access a more resourced aspect of the social identity to "come to the rescue"; thus, the healing is done within the identity. For example, a quality a client associates with his or her ethnicity, such as strength, might be accessed to help reprocess a trauma linked to his or her ethnicity. This technique is innately affirming and restorative of the social identity. It can lead to efficient reprocessing because the associations are more likely to be contained within the memory network associated with the particular social identity.

Examples of social identity linked cognitions include the following:

| Negative Cognition | Positive Cognition |
|---|---|
| I'm a weak cop. | I have feelings like any cop does. |
| As a gay man, I don't belong. | I'm a gay man, and I do belong. |
| I'm useless in a wheelchair. | I bring value and I use a wheelchair. |
| I'm just a dumb farmer. | I am proud of what I know as a farmer. |
| I'm a "SPED" kid. | I learn differently than others. |
| I'm a "second-class" person (immigrant). | I'm an immigrant and I matter as a person. |

## Exploratory Questions:

*When you think of yourself (as a specific social identity) in relationship to (a person of another social identity, group, or the larger society), what memories come to mind? (If negative, ask) What picture goes with that memory that represents the worst part? What words go with that picture that best describe your negative belief about yourself now?*

Float back to identify other memories. Target identified memories for reprocessing.

## Internalized Cultural Messages

Cultural messages can be imposing. Cultural expectations can be defining and confining. When a person is not aligned with these expectations, it can create great internal distress. For example, a woman who has decided she does not want to be a mother may feel bombarded by cultural expectations to have a child. When enough of these messages take root and colonize a client's beliefs, the client may need help separating cultural interjects from what he or she is inherently as a person.

Levis and Siniego introduce the term *Oppressive Cognition* in Chapter 5. When a client identifies an internalized negative belief that is linked to oppressive societal conditions, he or she has found it valuable to locate the origin of the negative beliefs in the culture that has historically perpetuated these beliefs through social oppression. Externally locating the source of the belief is another method that provides leverage for the client to separate from the belief. For example, a woman who thinks she "is stupid" because she thinks intuitively rather than linearly could see that belief as an Internalized Oppressive Cognition generated by sexism.

Examples of cultural messages include:

- Marines can't be weak.
- Transgendered people are weird.
- Sex is bad.
- If you aren't thin, you aren't attractive.
- People should stay in their place (social position).
- If you can't speak the language, be silent.
- One's value is based on how much one has/earns.

### Exploratory Questions:

*When you think of your current problem, what judgments or messages do you feel society making? or, What do you hear society saying? When in your life did you first hear that message?*

Target for reprocessing.

## Internalized Stereotypes

Stereotypes are another type of cultural message that can be internalized. Even when people know a social stereotype is unfair, the impact may remain internally embedded.

### Exploratory Questions:

*Is there a stereotype about some aspect of your social identity?*________________________

*When you think about that stereotype, what comes to mind (thoughts, feelings, or memories)? How disturbing does it feel to you now (Subjective Units of Disturbances [SUDs] [0–10])?*

*When in your life did you first hear that stereotype?*

Target that memory for reprocessing.

## TARGET IDENTIFICATION AND REPROCESSING

After all the work is done to uncover socially based adverse and traumatic experiences, the targeting procedures for reprocessing are largely similar to other types of trauma. Hence, although this is typically the most profound part of the treatment, this section will be relatively brief. However, the following are some examples of target issues related to social and cultural experiences that I have encountered in my work. Each target issue is listed alongside the related Core Negative Cognition. For most issues, the initial target image came from the first or worst related memory.

- A man who had lost his job (NC—I'm useless [without a job].)
- An alcoholic who only felt accepted in AA (NC—I'm bad, I can't fit in.)
- A Black teenager who dropped out of high school (NC—I'm done, there's no place for me.)
- A woman's lack of confidence in an all-male business meeting (NC—I'm not good enough for them.)
- An immigrant trying to get by (NC—I'm not wanted, I don't matter.)
- An overweight person being afraid to work out at a gym (NC—I'm gross, I'm unacceptable.)
- A person raised poor believing his or her opinion doesn't matter (NC—I'm not good enough.)
- A man with erectile dysfunction (NC—I'm not a man.)
- A young woman who believes she must wear makeup to be accepted (NC—I'm ugly.)
- An older person who feels disregarded (NC—I'm out to pasture.)
- A gay person afraid to come out (NC—It's not safe to be me.)
- A man who was physically impaired by a childhood stroke (NC—I'm an embarrassment.)
- A darker skin Black woman after a breakup (NC—I'm too Black.)
- A woman needing a wheelchair (NC—I'm a bother to others.)
- A blue-collar worker at a school meeting (NC—I don't belong.)

As mentioned, any of these Negative Cognitions might be more effectively accessed with the addition of wording that includes a social identity reference. For example, "As a woman, I'm not good enough," or "As a man, I'm weak."

Other targets associated with a particular culture or social identity might include:

- Secrecy connected with a social identity
- Traumatic experiences or challenges shared by a social/cultural group (AIDS crisis, anti-Semitism, being a political minority)
- Memories of being "taught" stigmatizing/oppressive beliefs (implicitly or explicitly)
- An unanticipated new and unwanted identity (cancer patient, unemployed person, divorced person, etc.)

## "What Does Stigma Look Like?"

An indirect way to uncover associations to stigma can be to simply ask the client, "What abstract image does stigma look like?" Once an image is identified, this can be followed by successive sets of bilateral stimulation. This can be used for exploratory reasons to generate understanding. It may also become a gateway into more specific memories to be targeted with the standard protocol. Abstract images related to prejudice or stereotypes can also be targeted.

One client of mine was charged with a DUI (driving under the influence) and his name was reported in the local newspaper. The shame was immobilizing until we directly named and targeted it. His abstract image was of a thousand eyes peering from all around him. This target image launched productive reprocessing. In the end, he was able to develop strategies for facing the consequences of his actions socially and was also better prepared to face matters internally.

## Interweaves

A culturally aware therapist might spot the intrusion of cultural messages that block processing and respond by offering a cognitive interweave. For example, a young male client of mine was grieving the loss of his two parents while reprocessing, with occasional constricted crying. "I shouldn't be this upset. I don't feel right about crying," he said. I asked, "When was the first time you remember getting the message not to cry?" He responded, "First grade, I felt different and no one expressed feelings so I thought it wasn't okay . . . in school, everyone is trying not to be different." We processed these memories and returned to more emotionally free processing of his grief.

## Clinical Examples of Reprocessing Culturally Based Trauma

Case 1—One client of mine, who is Black, had done years of effective EMDR therapy with me on a wide range of issues including childhood abuse. In one session, I deliberately opened the conversation about racial issues, including acknowledging my Whiteness, which he said he appreciated. Not too many sessions later, his reprocessing took a turn into a memory of direct and severe racism by a White adult that he experienced as a child. Later, we speculated that our explicit discussion of race likely made the memory more accessible for successful reprocessing. Increasingly, race-related issues became part of his reprocessing and our discussions.

Case 2—Carla, like many people, struggled with her weight. She felt overwhelmed by the countless invitations to consume food and drink, combined with an equal number of messages to look trim. She hated herself being what she considered overweight and her dieting seemed driven out of fear and self-loathing rather than a quest for greater health. When clients indicate that they want to lose weight in a serious way, I always suggest that we tackle their feelings about weight first. I don't want clients dieting in a spirit of self-hate or deprivation.

For Carla, this exploration led to reprocessing a series of incidents when she was 7 years old in which she was picked on by a group of girls. Her NC was "I'm not good enough to be treated the same as others." The memories cleared and Carla was able to carry a healthier attitude of, "I am who I am and I'll do what I can to manage my weight." A year later, she was eating healthier and had lost a few pounds. More importantly, she was not preoccupied in the struggle any longer.

Case 3—A female Japanese client reprocessed ambivalent feelings related to caring for her aging mother. Her mother had always been a "difficult person" in her life, yet she had always felt guilt ridden and helpless in the face of her mother's requests. As she reprocessed the issue, she suddenly linked into her cultural identity and realized that her culture put a high value on respecting the elderly. Simultaneously seeing the cultural expectation and the impossibility of meeting all of her mother's expectations, she felt a wave of self-acceptance. With the aid of a future template, she was able to envision how to set reasonable boundaries. Later, she commented that others had tried to tell her this; however, only with the reprocessing was she able to "find it on my own."

Case 4—Seth grew up in a Jewish family with a high-achieving father and brother. He chose a path to pursue countercultural values but struggled later in life to support himself, especially following a divorce and the loss of a job. He felt like a disappointment and did not seek the family help that was available to him. His reprocessing led him through both the pride in his Jewish heritage and the internalized judgments that came with these expectations. Following the reprocessing, he felt more self-acceptance for his path in life and was able to ask for some family financial assistance with less emotional activation, greater skill, and a positive outcome.

Case 5—One client feared that she would "outshine" her husband by making more money with a recent promotion at work, while her husband worked as a carpenter and had trouble finding enough work. As we targeted and processed her feelings, she realized that it was her issue related to feeling privileged growing up with a father who was a doctor. During the subsequent week, she discussed this for the first time with her husband, who was pleased for her career opportunities.

Case 6—Walter, a professor of Asian descent, taught about diversity as part of his course curriculum. Each semester, he dreaded the class on gay oppression and homophobia. He was afraid that just by talking about it, he would be perceived as gay. The reprocessing work linked to childhood memories of being sexually abused by a neighbor as a child and the shame, secrecy, and sexual confusion related to that. Over time, with the help of more reprocessing and future templates, he went from barely getting through the lectures and discouraging questions to being at ease in his presentations and looking forward to the class discussions. He dropped the tendency to "remind" people that he was heterosexual. In addition, he volunteered to lead a diversity initiative on campus, which included doing more public speaking.

## EXPLORING SOCIAL IDENTITIES

### Social Identity

Exploring social identities with a client can be a clinically relevant and rich experience. What follows are a variety of ways to assess and work with these dimensions of a client's reality.

A social identity has two components. The first is a person's sense of who he or she is based upon groups that he or she chooses to identify with. The second component is an identity assigned by others or the general culture based upon

## EXERCISE

Sometimes people new to this term of social identity need help grasping the concept. Here is a simple exercise for you or your clients to get in touch with the meaning of a social identity. It takes about 10 minutes.

Take a moment and notice what comes to mind when you think of yourself based upon your gender. Try to *feel* what this means to you for a minute or more. And as you get in touch with this aspect of who you are, write down five or more adjectives that come to mind. Now, think about yourself based upon your age. Again, write down several adjectives. And finally, think about some aspect of your ethnic or racial background, and again, write down some adjectives. Next, simply notice the array of adjectives. Notice that you may have a mixture of positive and negative associations. This is the beginning of understanding and exploring a social identity.

the person's association with a social group. This information may range from relatively accurate to highly inaccurate, but it can have a great impact on that person. For example, when most people learn about the sex of an unborn baby, they begin to have associations about who that person will be even with no real knowledge of that person.

Culturally influenced social identities are important dimensions of who people are and are highly related to self-identity and well-being. Sometimes people are aware of the importance of these identities, but often they are unexamined and need to be explored to be better understood. People can experience great meaning from the connection and intimacy related to their socially important groups. Positive social identities, sometimes taken for granted, can be accessed as positive resources to assist a client's approach to other difficulties. For the fortunate, individual social identities are accepted and affirmed by the broader culture. As trauma-informed therapists, it is important to realize, however, that social identities can be sensitive territory for many and can be painfully activated in particular social contexts.

## Social Identities as Parts of the Self

Many EMDR therapists are familiar with the exploration of *ego states* (Watkins & Watkins, 1997) as a way to illuminate the different aspects of a client's sense of self. These *parts of the self* often contain meaningful state-based memory associations linked to past experiences. Well-developed social identities are often laden with identifiable perceptions, beliefs, and affects that can be explored. Various therapeutic approaches to working with ego states can be used to enhance positive meaning, expunge negative associations, and aid in the integration of potentially conflicting identities.

In my opinion, considering how central social identification is to a person's sense of self, these dimensions of a person are underestimated in general and surprisingly underexplored in a typical psychotherapy. Sometimes social identities have been internalized at such a trait level that they are considered stable and permanent. Many of my clients have said that when social identity ego states are accessed and disturbing memories are reprocessed, the effects are more powerful than expected.

In my view, it is easy to overlook social identity issues or dismiss them as secondary to a primary problem, thereby underestimating their importance.

## Dimensions of Social Identities

Social identities can have many characteristics. The following is a list of important dimensions of these identities. Given the limits of space in this chapter, they will not be discussed in detail, though I am hopeful that the distinctions are evident and that this list will serve as an easy reference tool. Discussing these dimensions with the client can be helpful. Sometimes these differences can be more accurately viewed along a spectrum.

1. Visible to others *or* invisible to others (skin color/sexual orientation)
2. Conscious *or* unconscious (aware of the identity's meaning/unaware-meaning latent)
3. Ego syntonic *or* ego dystonic (aligned with identity/in conflict with it)
4. Chosen *or* not chosen (musician/physical appearance)
5. Shared with family *or* not shared with family (ethnicity/physical disability)
6. Valued by the person *or* not valued by the person
7. Valued by one's family *or* not valued by one's family
8. Valued by others beyond the family *or* not valued by others beyond the family
9. Constant *or* temporary (birth sex/mountain climber)
10. Accepted by self *or* rejected by self
11. Minority identity *or* majority identity (relative to social context)
12. Easily assimilated into broader culture *or* difficult to assimilate (English-speaking immigrant vs. non-English speaker)
13. In-group *or* out-group (relative to a particular social context)
14. High status *or* low status (relative to a particular social context)
15. Earned *or* unearned (college graduate/White person)

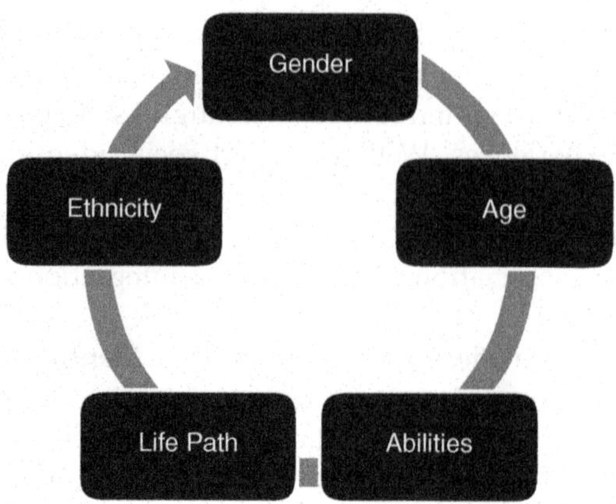


**FIGURE 3.3** Social identity wheel.

## Social Identity Wheel

The Social Identity Wheel exercise is a third tool for uncovering social and cultural issues (Figures 3.3 and 3.4). To get this started, as a therapist, you can ask a client to imagine a wagon wheel with his or her "whole self" at the hub of the wheel. Then surrounding the hub, ask the client to imagine spokes of the wheel extending to a series of circles that are located along the rim of the wheel. These circles can each contain a different social identity, as in Figure 3.3. A script for completing this exercise on paper is presented in Figures 3.4 and 3.5. The script guides the client to identify up to five different social identities that are important to him or her. A range of choices are listed including gender, age, race/ethnicity, social class background, and so forth. In the second portion of the exercise, clients are guided to identify a positive and a negative memory associated with each identity. The positive memories are enhanced as a resource, and used as a future template. The negative memories are available as possible targets for reprocessing.

**Social/Cultural Identity**

A social or cultural identity is a person's sense of who he or she is based upon groups the person identifies with or how he or she is viewed by others. Social identities can have both positive and negative feelings associated with them. Sometimes people are aware of the importance of these identities, whereas sometimes they need to be explored to be better understood.

Pick one or more of the following identities you would like to explore.

| | |
|---|---|
| Ethnicity/race | Political views |
| Age | Religion/faith |
| Sex/gender | Economic status |
| Family role (parent, child, sibling, spouse) | Intellectual style or ability |
| Work/career | Physical abilities/disabilities |
| Social class (past/present) | Physical appearance |
| Region (geographic)/citizenship | Health status |
| Sexual/affectional orientation | Mental health status |
| Social interests | Family/ancestral background |
| Life path | Other ________________ |

Continue on with the next step to explore identities.

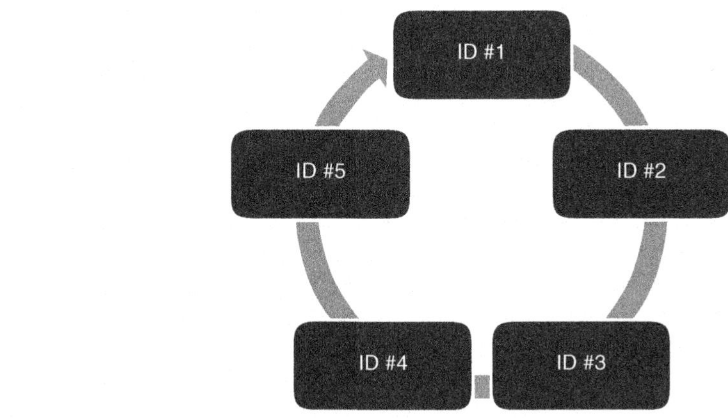


**FIGURE 3.4** Exploring social/cultural identity.

1. **Identify and list one to five personal social identities.**

**Social Identity 1**____________________________

**Good memory** ________________________________________

**Bad memory** ________________________________________

**Social Identity 2**____________________________

**Good memory** ________________________________________

**Bad memory** ________________________________________

**Social Identity 3**____________________________

**Good memory** ________________________________________

**Bad memory** ________________________________________

**Social Identity 4**____________________________

**Good memory** ________________________________________

**Bad memory** ________________________________________

**Social Identity 5**____________________________

**Good memory** ________________________________________

**Bad memory** ________________________________________

**Perform the following steps for each social identity.**

2. **Resource development and installation**—*As you get in touch with your positive memory, notice what positive qualities, feelings, or beliefs about yourself you associate with that memory.*
   - **Access positive associations and enhance with sets of bilateral stimulation (BLS).**
3. **Future template**—*Holding in mind those positive qualities/feelings/beliefs, imagine carrying those qualities into the future.* (Identify specific upcoming experiences if appropriate.)
   - **Enhance with sets of BLS.**
4. **Explore negative memories and identify targets for reprocessing**. *As you get in touch with your negative memory, how disturbing does it feel to you now on a scale of 0–10?*
5. **Consider targeting negative memories for reprocessing**.
6. **Repeat with other identities.**

**FIGURE 3.5** Exploring social/cultural identity worksheet.

## SOCIAL IDENTITY ENHANCEMENT STRATEGIES

### Identity Enhancement

Developing a stronger social identity can promote general well-being. Research affirms that developing a cohesive ethnic identity offers many potential gains including general psychological self-esteem, happiness, decreased self-destructive behaviors, and other markers of well-being (Greene, Way, & Pahl, 2006); and reduces the likelihood that discrimination will lead to depression (Torres & Ong, 2010). For adolescents in one study, greater family cohesion promoted feeling more connected to their ethnic group with related rewards (Kiang, Yip, Gonzales-Backen, Witkow, & Fuligni, 2006). As people age, identifying with groups based on achieved identity statuses reduced their risk for depression (Branch, 2001).

Given the pressure and rewards of assimilating into a dominant culture, some people drift from or abandon their original ethnic or other social identities. EMDR therapy can offer clients an opportunity to reverse that process and discover or recover a social identity. This process may be gradual, yet the rewards can be significant. Marcia (1991) describes a progression of identity stages for a person who seeks to reclaim a lost identity including: identity diffusion (no exploration or commitment), identity foreclosure (no exploration, yet committed), moratorium (exploration without having made a commitment), and identity achievement (exploration and commitment to the identity). We can collaborate with our clients by offering a pathway to this potentially rich growth process. Many strategies can be used to identify and strengthen cultural linkages to information such as the client's own positive identity-related memories, culturally related role models, learning about the culture, building relationships with others who share the culture, and envisioning and enacting culturally affirming activities.

### Supporting External and Internal Acculturation

Cultural minorities often face the challenge of fitting into a culture that is defined by majority norms. As introduced in Chapter 2, Berry (1984) depicted four types of acculturation. Successful *integration* within a society allows for both the maintenance of one's important social identities and an acceptance within the dominant culture. Unfortunately, oftentimes people adjust to the dominant culture through other types of acculturation that include *assimilation* by surrendering a prior social identity, *segregation* from the dominant society, or *marginalization* within it. As EMDR therapists, we can support our clients to acculturate in the external culture in various ways.

Within EMDR, resource development and installation are tool used to help clients build positive adaptive memory networks (Korn & Leeds, 2002). Resourcing is an important component of EMDR therapy as it builds positive memory networks of association that affirm the client's inherent nature and adaptive capacity. Resourcing can be used to enhance a client's culturally based strengths. It can also be crafted to help overcome negative cultural experiences and the internalized messages.

For clients who are seeking to assimilate across cultural or social boundaries that have divided them from others, or just want to fit into a new culture or group, resourcing can be designed to help bridge across cultural boundaries.

Resourcing can be a valuable strategy to build confidence in the possibilities. Research presented in Chapter 2 would predict that accessing and installing any of the following memories can assist a client in coping with cultural trauma:

- Positive experiences related to one's own social identity
- Positive associations of inclusion
- Resilience in the face of social justice
- Positive experiences of standing up against discrimination
- Positive associations of experiences with those from "other" groups
- Holding an affirming positive belief "I deserve the respect of all people."
- Empathy, respect, and so forth for other group members
- Identified similarities or common ground with other group members
- Shared values or other connections to group members
- Shared group identities with other group members
- Successful internal integration of different social identities

To create a future template, the therapist can guide the client to access the resourcing memory, enhance it with sets of bilateral stimulation, and then hold in mind as he or she imagines dealing effectively with an upcoming challenge. Resourcing with a future template generally builds the client's resilience and adaptability. As always, if it opens up distress that does not subside, the distress can be targeted for reprocessing.

In a parallel way, a client's internal constellation of social identities may not be well integrated. Sometimes these identities are in conflict with each other. For example, a client's learned notions of masculinity may dominate and invalidate other aspects of himself so that an older person who loses his sexual potency may not find compassion from his masculine identity. For most people, aging runs into conflict with other dimensions of who they are and what they want as it relates to their sex, their favorite activities, and their career identities.

EMDR therapy can support a process that allows for an articulation of different identities and create an atmosphere in which there can be internal integration and healthy coexistence. This can be dealt with clinically by identifying and exploring conflicting social identities. As an initial exploration, clients can be asked to hold both identities simultaneously. The EMDR clinician can then guide them through a series of sets of bilateral stimulation as the client "just notices." Typically, this will generate insights and varying degrees of progress. Aspiring for inner multicultural integration seems preferable to subjugating one social identity to the dominance of another. Once a therapist is comfortable in this territory, creative strategies begin to emerge.

## CULTURECTOMIES

Shapiro (2009, 2016) describes the use of the two-hand interweave as a strategy for expunging cultural messages, which she refers to as a *culturectomy*. As a general technique, the two-hand interweave can assist a client who is struggling with two conflicting forces. The client is asked to put one side of the dilemma in one hand and the other side in the other hand. The therapist then provides bilateral stimulation while the client "just notices" the experience. At the end of each set, the therapist asks the client what he or she is noticing. Typically clients who had felt paralyzed between two seemingly competing forces experience an adaptive shift.

As part of a culturectomy, the client separates the "true self" from the negative internalized cultural message by putting them in different hands. These negative messages can include stereotypes or oppressive cultural values. Additional steps can be taken to help the person identify, the source of the cultural message, and to clearly state his or her desire to disown it. Like Shapiro, I have noticed that clients struggling to conform to cultural messages can often release themselves from that expectation. For example, one woman feeling social pressure to have a child put that expectation in one hand, and her own right to choose in another. After several sets of bilateral stimulation, the pressure eased. Sometimes this creates only a momentary change of cognitive state or elicits disturbance. In those cases, disturbing memories may need to be fully targeted and reprocessed. But, overall, the exercise typically gives the client's adaptive self some separation and leverage over the cultural message.

I have also used this technique to explore and resolve inner conflict between two of a client's social identities. For instance, a client may feel a struggle between being a visible social activist and developing a career in which political visibility might pose difficulties.

## SUMMARY

Engaging clients in a culturally aware manner involves learning about and attuning to their cultural presentation, as appropriate. In addition to that, EMDR therapists can explore social and cultural experiences, positive and negative, as they impact our client's lives. EMDR offers a powerful opportunity to build upon a client's cultural resources and to reprocess culturally based adverse and traumatic experiences. In this chapter, several tools and strategies for history taking and issue exploration were offered for consideration. Cultural stigma, discrimination, and imposing expectations can be internalized and can colonize a client's belief system.

Several types of internalized beliefs were discussed to help clinicians identify and transform these negative beliefs into a more adaptive perspective. Examples of culturally based targets were offered along with clinical anecdotes. Finally, the uncovering and exploration of social identities can be integrated into other strategies for working with parts of the self. These often overlooked aspects of one's personality can carry great poignancy as an avenue to self-discovery. The cultural component is often overlooked and underappreciated as a force in client's lives. Once embraced, it can enrich the treatment experience and lead to more fulfilling client gains.

## REFERENCES

Berry, J. W. (1984). Cultural relations in plural societies: Alternatives to segregation and their social psychological implications. In N. Miller & M. B. Brewer (Eds.), *Groups and contact: The psychology of desegregation* (pp. 11–27). New York, NY: Academic.

Branch, C. W. (2001). The many faces of self: Ego and ethnic identities. *Journal of Genetic Psychology, 162*(4), 412–429.

Erikson, E. H. (1968). Identity, youth and crisis. New York, NY: W. W. Norton.

Greene, M., Way, N., & Pahl, K. (2006). Trajectories of perceived adult and peer discrimination among Black, Latino, and Asian American adolescents: Patterns and psychological correlates. *Developmental Psychology, 42*(2), 218–238.

Hardy, K. V., & Laszloffy, T. A. (1995). The cultural genogram: Key to training culturally competent family therapists. *Journal of Marital and Family Therapy, 21*(3), 227–237.

Kiang, L., Yip, T., Gonzales-Backen, M., Witkow, M., & Fuligni, A. J. (2006). Ethnic identity and the daily psychological well-being of adolescents from Mexican and Chinese backgrounds. *Child Development, 77*(5), 1338–1350.

Korn, D. L., & Leeds, A. M. (2002). Preliminary evidence of efficacy for EMDR resource development and installation in the stabilization phase of treatment of complex posttraumatic stress disorder. *Journal of Clinical Psychology, 58*(12), 1465–1487.

Marcia, J. E. (1991). Identity and self-development. In R. Lerner, A. Peterson, & J. Brooks-Gunn (Eds.), *Encyclopedia of adolescence* (Vol. 1). New York, NY: Garland.

Shapiro, F. (2001). *Eye movement desensitization and reprocessing: Basic principles, protocols, and procedures*. New York, NY: Guilford.

Shapiro, R. (Ed.). (2009). *EMDR solutions II: For depression, eating disorders, performance, and more*. New York, NY: W. W. Norton.

Shapiro, R. (2016). *Easy ego state interventions: Strategies for working with parts*. New York, NY: W. W. Norton.

Torres, L., & Ong, A. D. (2010). A daily diary investigation of Latino ethnic identity, discrimination, and depression. *Cultural Diversity and Ethnic Minority Psychology, 16*(4), 561–568.

Watkins, J. G., & Watkins, H. H. (1997). *Ego states: Theory and therapy*. New York, NY: W. W. Norton.

CHAPTER 4

# Dismantling Prejudice and Exploring Social Privilege With EMDR Therapy

Mark Nickerson

Can eye movement desensitization and reprocessing (EMDR) therapy be used to dismantle social prejudice? The answer is yes.

Viewed somewhat dispassionately through the adaptive information processing (AIP) model (Shapiro, 2001), social prejudice is an example of inaccurate perception based on misinformation, a lack of information, and information distorted by experience. Therefore, it is treatable through the EMDR approach. This is very good news for many obvious reasons because what might be considered a clinical "symptom" in a psychotherapy office has a particular social gravity that is different than many other "perceptual distortions" we see in our office.

On the macro-global level, social prejudice, especially when not contained, fuels ongoing stigmatization and other forms of discrimination in our world and perpetuates cultural intolerance. Institutionalized prejudice justifies and guides oppression. The vision of successful multicultural communities depends upon tolerance of cultural differences at the very least, and understanding and collaboration between cultures wherever possible. Many cultures, including nations and major religions, espouse morality, belief systems, values, ideology, and philosophies that are consistent with multiculturalism. And yet, individuals and groups struggle to live up to these ideals.

In our humble one-at-a-time clinical practices, putting a dent in the phenomenon of social prejudice may seem a small accomplishment. But just as we work to relieve the impact of each client's trauma, we can now be prepared to reduce or eliminate the prejudicial attitudes that can perpetuate it. Collectively, EMDR clinicians can learn to target and transform client prejudices and offer a unique treatment to this confounding human tendency. We just need to know how to identify prejudice as a relevance clinical issue and intervene.

This chapter presents an understanding of social prejudice that can be integrated into the AIP model and is supported by research-based knowledge from the field of social psychology. Strategies for targeting prejudice within the EMDR approach will be discussed and a protocol for reducing or eradicating prejudice is described. Finally, issues related to social privilege and social position are discussed in this chapter along with a protocol for targeting feelings related to social advantages and disadvantages. The potential of EMDR methods to support the exploration of other complicated social issues is discussed later in this chapter.

## UNDERSTANDING PREJUDICE THROUGH THE AIP MODEL

There is tremendous sensitivity surrounding the topic of social prejudice for many reasons. Just the mention of the word can be triggering. Most people's memory networks, clinicians included, are loaded with feelings about the very topic itself. While the sensitivity is understandable, it often leads to avoidance of the issue altogether, thus perpetuating the status quo.

Step one of getting beyond this hurdle is understanding that the internal mechanisms that are geared for social categorization and prejudicial response are innately human, common to all people, and, to some extent, adaptive. Although there is a significant range in the degree of prejudice among people, and a range of responsible and irresponsible ways people manage these feelings, all people have prejudices. Prejudice is viewed by social scientists as an emotional reaction, and like most feelings, the primary question of conscience is not if one has it but how one manages it. Now, with EMDR therapy we can offer our clients more than just emotional management skills. We can help clients who are willing to reprocess memories that have generated the reaction and transform our client's experience.

The word *prejudice* is a derivative of *prejudge*, which captures the core of the problem. Prejudice is part of the human tendency to assess a situation based on limited information. As discussed in greater detail in Chapter 2, prejudice is an essential adaptive tool that all human beings use to make quick assessments and quick decisions. Prejudice is based on past learning and the modeling of others. Evolutionarily, it has been an aid for survival when people don't know who to trust. From a young age, human beings determine who they can trust and who they cannot trust—based often on superficial, visual information.

However, often these judgments are shaped by misinformation and hardened by cultural messages and adverse life experiences that deepen prejudicial beliefs. Human beings also develop prejudicial response systems based on negative experiences related to intergroup relations that impair optimal functioning. Manifestations of these experiences include feelings, thoughts, and behaviors that devalue others and/or themselves on the basis of group identity.

## RESEARCH ON PREJUDICE

This section builds upon terminology and research presented in Chapter 2. Research in the field of social psychology documents how prejudice operates on the unconscious level, and that once a prejudice is learned it is not easily unlearned. Conscious antistereotyping values are not enough to prevent prejudiced responses. Once internalized, the prejudice response links to the amygdala and, when triggered, sparks automatic responses. Prejudice control mechanisms are in the prefrontal cortex and are important in managing these triggers. Prejudice reduction research shows that cognitive control can help but it's not enough to eradicate implicit prejudice; in fact, stereotype suppression as a technique led to a paradoxical rebound response in one study (Wegner, 1994). EMDR intervention offers the potential for not only strengthening control mechanisms but also for desensitizing automatic reactions.

## Implicit Prejudice

Much of the focus of this chapter is on working with people who have *implicit prejudice* (unconscious and ego dystonic) as compared with those with *explicit prejudice* who are likely more aligned and committed to their beliefs. Generally speaking, clients who have implicit prejudices are more likely to volunteer to target their prejudices for EMDR reprocessing, once they become aware of them.

Allport (1954) described a "state of conflict" for those who hold and identify with egalitarian beliefs yet have implicit (unconscious and ego dystonic) prejudice reactions that operate automatically in the subconscious associative mental processes. Though unconscious, these automatic biases can be observed internally as a gut-level emotional response, or thoughts that pop into the head. Externally, they may appear in subtle facial expressions and other involuntary movements.

Devine (1989) has explored unconscious indicators of implicit prejudice and her research showed that the automatic effects of stereotypes on behavior were not moderated by participants with low levels of explicit prejudice when they were unaware of racial primes (triggers). That is, when people were not conscious of wanting to be nonprejudiced, their nonprejudiced values had less effect. More recently, Gaertner and Dovidio (2014) have shown in several studies that many well-intentioned Whites who profess to egalitarian values act in unconsciously racist ways, particularly in ambiguous circumstances. Gaertner contends, "It's a monumental task to get White people to realize that they are delivering microaggressions, because it's scary to them. It assails their self-image of being good, moral, decent human beings to realize that maybe at an unconscious level they have biased thoughts, attitudes and feelings that harm people of color."

Dovidio and Gaertner (1986) reported that in experimental job interviews, Whites tended not to discriminate against Black candidates if qualification differences were clear. But when qualifications were close, Whites tended to favor White over Black candidates. They termed this tendency *aversive racism*, referring to the biased person's aversion to being seen as prejudiced.

Researchers report that most perpetrators of microaggressions typically consider themselves to be unprejudiced. One U.S. study found that even mental health professionals with extensive antiracist training engaged in microaggressions with Black clients (Gonzales, Davidoff, Nadal, & Yanos, 2015). They found that when challenged by the minority person or an observer, perpetrators often defended their microaggression as a misunderstanding, a joke, or something small that shouldn't be blown out of proportion.

EMDR practitioner Jim Cole has provided non-EMDR trainings and consulted with agencies and other organizations around reduction of prejudice in the workplace. He suggests different strategies for people who are open and willing to understand, explore, and change their prejudices compared with those who deny or justify their beliefs and attitudes (Cole, n.d.).

For those open to examining their *unintentional prejudice* (implicit), he suggests a more collaborative process. Participants can examine the habitual ways in which they viewed other people and reflected upon where these biases came from. More open-minded perspectives are developed and participants practice new responses.

Cole found that individuals with "intentional prejudice" needed a different level of intervention. He learned that it was important for these biases to be challenged directly. Cole found that a group member who expressed or demonstrated prejudice was enabled by a passive group and less changed by feedback from a targeted group member as compared with when the feedback was initiated or reinforced by a person who was identified as being within the same group as the person who had displayed the prejudice. These challenges were most effective when they came from authorities within the organization's power structure and in the same social group. Furthermore, he found that it was crucial not to "set up" any individuals who were targets of the prejudice by pressuring them to counter the beliefs of those with intentional prejudice.

## MAKING PREJUDICE A CLINICAL ISSUE

Engaging a client in a process of identifying and changing his or her social prejudices is an understandable challenge for any psychotherapist. Cole's work is instructive, though. His observation that an in-group authority is the best person to intervene in the face of prejudice is a reminder of why therapists are in an important position. Especially when a client is demonstrating a harmful explicit prejudice, we must be careful not to collude with the client's prejudices, even by ignoring them.

As with all clinical issues, before confronting a client's blind spots, the therapist must be prepared and skilled to do so in a constructive manner. It is a rare client who asks to examine his or her social prejudices or stereotypic views as part of therapy. However, any client can learn that prejudices are normal and that these sorts of generalized misperceptions about people can be therapeutic fodder. Also, many people who are well aware of the prejudices that have been directing them are prone to developing counter prejudices. Sometimes their path of healing moves from the victim's perspective to a desire to develop more unbiased views of others. Relatedly, some of my clients are committed to being more mindful of others and welcome the opportunities to get beyond their reactive judgments.

Yet, for most therapists, including prejudices as clinical issues is a new venture. Macleod (2013) has written about the ethical dilemmas and strategies that come with confronting more explicit (conscious and ego syntonic) prejudice in a clinical setting. He notes that therapists must balance a client-centered model that supports client empowerment with the reality that clients may use power in exploitive ways over others.

Various thoughts might go through a therapist's mind when trying to decide whether to make a client's prejudice a clinical issue, including:

1. Is it my place? Is it ethical?
2. Does this relate to therapy goals?
3. Is this prejudice affecting anyone else?
4. Will it do any good?
5. Is this the right time?
6. Can the therapeutic relationship handle it?
7. There is a lot of truth in that stereotype.
8. It offends me, but I'm supposed to put that aside.

In the end, the most solid justification for a therapist to confront a client's prejudice is being reasonably sure that you can do it in a way that will move the client forward. Secondarily, a therapist may choose to confront a prejudice on behalf of someone in the client's life who he or she believes is being victimized. Even in that case, the prejudice should be confronted with every intention to work with the client constructively. In some cases, therapists must manage their emotional reactions—such as hostility, fear, or disgust—to a client's prejudice.

In my own clinical experience working with people who have been abusive in relationships, part of my clinical responsibility has been to illuminate the beliefs that fueled or justified the client's behavior. Gender-based violence across cultures is a global concern. A fundamental component of standard interventions involves confronting the sexist attitudes and male privileges that justify the abuse. With both mandated and voluntary clients, I have learned to think and act outside the comfort zone of many clients to challenge them when necessary. However, my goal was always to convey respect and to help the client see that my intentions were constructive and for their benefit. A key to *compassionate confrontation* is separating the client as a person from the prejudice belief; he or she needs your help doing that.

An essential part of a constructive intervention is to offer a solution to a problem. EMDR therapists can offer clients a chance to target the prejudice for reprocessing. With an EMDR approach, the therapist is not telling the client how he or she "should" think, but simply offering the client a chance to reprocess feelings and discover on his or her own if there are new ways to think. Questions about the ethics of making prejudice a clinical issue evaporate when a therapist sees a pathway to getting his or her clients to a more adaptive perspective.

With all this said, spotting a client's prejudice and saying something about it doesn't have to be that hard. As a clinician becomes adept with it, the process becomes smoother and more routine. In the end, freeing a client from a prejudice he or she has been absorbed by can offer relief to that client and can deepen the therapeutic bond, rather than threaten it.

There are many ways to address a prejudice that emerges. Here is some possible language:

*I notice from what you said that you seem to think/feel*_______________ (reflect the client's words that suggest a prejudice or stereotype). *Can we explore that?* (If yes, then) *When did you develop that reaction* (or *those thoughts*)? (And when and if appropriate,) *Can we target that?*

(And, sometimes with humor with clients we know well,)

*Hey, did you just really say that? Do you really mean that? We should target that belief.*

## PREJUDICE REDUCTION

### Research-Supported Non-EMDR Intervention Strategies

Researchers within the field of social psychology have explored various ways of reducing the automatic biases associated with prejudicial responses (Bargh & Gollwitzer, 1994; Dasgupta, 2009; Devine, 1989; Devine & Sharp, 2009; Fiske,

Harris, Lee, & Russell, 2009; Gaertner & Dovidio, 2014; Hamilton, Sherman, Crump, & Spencer-Rodgers, 2009; Major & Sawyer, 2009; Nelson, 2009).

The findings from these studies suggest strategies for reducing prejudice that can be readily integrated into the EMDR approach. Core components of these successful strategies include:

- Activating mindful attention
- Increase motivation
- Decrease defensiveness
- Providing nonbiased information
- Strengthening prefrontal cortex awareness of nonbiased perceptions
- Desensitizing the amygdala reactivity to triggers of prejudice

Overall, these research findings indicate that prejudicial responses can be modified by various means with a multifaceted and tailored approach. The research found that reduction of prejudicial responses required adequate motivation to be nonbiased by the participants and a readiness to apply mindful, deliberate, and sustained attention to good information. Researchers found that participants could be motivated to change their attitudes toward out-groups on the basis of various factors including personal values, feelings of guilt, fear of punishment, or self-insight. Most techniques for reducing bias required that the target of the prejudice and/or the stereotype itself be activated by exposure to targets associated with prejudice. Some studies asked participants to actively employ the resources of direct attention and working memory to inhibit biased response tendencies with an intentional nonprejudiced response.

Not surprisingly, the research revealed that people with low to mild implicit prejudice were most able to modify their responses. They were more likely to learn from what they came to see as their mistakes. Researchers found that people with high self-esteem are more adaptable to view out-groups more positively.

Studies found that participants' defensiveness was decreased and motivation to change was increased when they were offered an explanation that social categorization is natural, that stereotypes may be based on some truth although they do not capture the whole truth, and by persuading people that their prejudice beliefs are dysfunctional.

## Research-Supported Resourcing Targets

Many clients' biases include misinformation and lack of information. Research experiments employed various strategies to provide information and create experiences that contradicted stereotypes and prejudices. The following strategies for prejudice reduction are all research-supported and can be creatively integrated into EMDR therapy resourcing strategies:

***Values driven*** reduction of bias:

- Enhance egalitarian values and motivation to be nonbiased
- Pair the goal of being egalitarian with the presence of the stereotyped person

- Reframe a proscribed stereotype (she's demanding) to a more socially permissible one (she's assertive)
- Understand and endorse multiculturalism over a color-blind philosophy
- Overtly reject stereotypic beliefs

***Wall crumbling*** strategies include ways to break down divisions between people:

- Engage in open discussion of intergroup prejudice versus color-blind approaches
- Notice variability among people of a targeted group
- Increase intergroup knowledge
- Decategorize salient group boundaries
- Regard other group members as distinct individuals
- Interact in an interpersonal rather than group-based manner
- Create positive intergroup contact

***Humanizing*** strategies:

- Activate the human caregiving system and related physiological responses
- Adopt the other's perspective
- Notice the other's personal attributes
- Create positive body/motor reinforcement (simple smiles toward the other groups)
- Notice counter-stereotypic role models

***Coming under one umbrella*** of common identity to build on a sense of in-groupness:

- Find overarching shared identity
- Identify other groups with shared identities

## EMDR Resourcing for Prejudice

As EMDR therapists, we can expect that using the earlier strategies (or derivatives of them) as target experiences for EMDR resourcing will help reduce a client's prejudicial barriers. Generally speaking, the goal of resourcing is to increase the adaptive and positive neural network linkages by providing valuable new information. Procedurally, the client is asked to imagine a positive experience related to one of the categories that have been identified as reducing prejudice, to access it as fully as possible, and then to notice the adaptive information, feelings, or perspectives. The positive awareness is enhanced over a series of sets aided by bilateral stimulation. Once it has reached its peak potency, asking the client to imagine handling a future challenge with this resource awareness can create a future template. Again, sets of bilateral stimulation (BLS) can be used to increase the vividness of the future template.

For example, a client reported feeling distracted by various thoughts about the one woman who showed up for weekly pick-up basketball. During resourcing, he focused on his common ground with that person as someone who enjoyed basketball, played hard, and was a good passer. As a future template, he envisioned keeping this in mind the next time they played. He later reported that the distraction went away and he enjoyed having her on his team.

Sometimes a client cannot sustain a positive focus during resourcing. When this is true, the therapist can help the client identify the disturbance what interferes with the resourcing. Often that links to an adverse memory which becomes a target for future reprocessing.

### Reprocessing Considerations

Despite the valuable insights from these studies regarding ways to reduce the power of bias by increasing prefrontal cortex (PFC) awareness of anti-bias knowledge, the studies are equally valuable in revealing the limits to their effectiveness. The research reveals that strengthening PFC helps people better manage bias, yet it does not eliminate it at the amygdala reaction level. This is where the deep reprocessing power of EMDR therapy can make a major contribution. Having reviewed the many non-EMDR approaches to prejudice reduction, and based upon my own clinical experiences, it is clear to me that by offering full Phase 3 to Phase 6 reprocessing, more significant gains can be made. Hopefully, research can be carried out to evaluate this reasonable prediction.

## AN EMDR PROTOCOL FOR TARGETING PREJUDICE AND NEGATIVE EXTERNALIZED BELIEFS

In 1954, psychologist Gordon Allport established some foundational theory about prejudice. He defined *prejudice* as having the following four characteristics: (a) negativity, (b) overgeneralization, (c) inaccuracy, and (d) it is directed at others. This may sound very familiar to EMDR therapists who view Negative Cognitions in a parallel way as being negative, generalized, inaccurate, but directed at the self.

EMDR therapists typically guide clients to identify their negative self-referential beliefs related to traumatic memories as part of the process of creating inner oriented change. However, I have found that many clients hold significant negative beliefs about others. These externalized negative beliefs, often in the form of prejudicial opinions about others, reflect perceptions that inform actions. The actions generate consequences, sometimes significant. Although these consequences are often negative, the beliefs that guide them are often resistant to change. Bad experiences do not lead to change but rather to deepening the dysfunctional belief.

I have come to view these negative beliefs about others as not just symptoms of the client's difficulties, but as part of the client's core problem. These beliefs perpetuate the client's difficulties, often hurting others along the way, and therefore need to be explicitly uncovered and addressed. The *Protocol for Targeting Prejudice and Negative Externalized Beliefs* is designed to target and transform externalized negative beliefs such as hostile attitudes, negative stereotypes, and prejudice.

## EMDR PROTOCOL FOR TARGETING PREJUDICE AND NEGATIVE EXTERNALIZED BELIEFS

Phase 2: Preparation (if needed)

- Normal preparation as needed.
- Consider reprocessing prior memories of being the target of discrimination. This builds adaptive empathy and realizations that can assist the prejudice reprocessing.
- *What is a personal quality of yours that will help you address this prejudice (e.g., open-mindedness, sense of fairness, curiosity)? Can you think of a time in your life where you had this quality?* Access memory and enhance with BLS.

Target selection: Identify prejudice. *What is the prejudice (stereotype, hostile belief) you would like to reprocess today?*

Phase 3: Assessment

*Picture/image: What memory/thought related to the subject of the prejudice evokes the strongest reaction? What specific picture comes to mind?*

*Externalized Negative Cognition (ENC): What words go with that picture that best describe your negative belief about the subject of the prejudice now?*

*Negative Cognition (about self): What words go with that picture and that belief (repeat ENC) about the subject of the prejudice that best describes your negative belief about yourself now?*

*Positive Cognition: When you bring up that picture, what would you prefer to believe about yourself instead?*

Validity of Cognition (VoC): *When you think of that picture, how true do those words _______________ (previously identified PC about the other) feel to you now on a scale from 1 to 7 where 1 feels totally false and 7 feels totally true?*

*Emotions: When you bring up that picture and those words (Repeat the NC), what emotion(s) do you feel now?*

*SUDs: On a scale of 0 to 10, where 0 is no disturbance or neutral and 10 is the highest disturbance you can imagine, how disturbing does the incident feel to you now?*

Body: *Where do you feel it in your body?*

Phase 4: Desensitization and Reprocessing

Proceed to reprocess with normal procedures. If a recent memory, consider a float back to earlier memories.

Phase 5: Installation

Positive Cognition: *When you bring up the original subject of the prejudice, do the words "repeat the original PC" still fit, or is there another positive statement you feel would be more suitable?*

Assess VoC (1–7): *Hold the PC and the subject together. Use sets of BLS to strengthen.*

*Externalized Positive Cognition (EPC): When you bring up the original subject of the prejudice, what positive or neutral words describe a revised belief that you now hold about the subject of the original prejudice?*

## EMDR PROTOCOL FOR TARGETING PREJUDICE AND NEGATIVE EXTERNALIZED BELIEFS (*continued*)

Assess VoC (1–7): *Hold the EPC and the subject together. Use sets of BLS to strengthen.* If the client is unable to identify an EPC with a VoC of 5+, return to reprocessing.

Phase 7: Closure

If desensitization is incomplete, identify a temporary self-related PC and externally related EPC. A temporary Positive Cognition is the most positively adaptive attitude toward the self and subject of the prejudice as possible in order to hold a VOC level of five or above (e.g., "I'm learning that there is a lot more to that person than I have realized").

I first became aware of this externalizing dynamic in my specialty work with people with problematic anger. I repeatedly observed that when clients identified the worst part of a disturbing memory about which they were still angry, they were often highly externally focused. During the Phase 3 assessment, I would ask a client for the worst image from the target's memory and follow it with the standard question, *What words go with that picture that best describe your negative belief about yourself now?* This was often followed by a puzzled, somewhat annoyed look. Just the wording of the question itself, "negative belief about yourself," seemed off-putting and sometimes created defensiveness, as if I was "turning the table" of the disturbing incident on him. Because most clients don't respond that way, I became curious about this pattern. I noticed it was common to clients who tended to externalize the *locus of control* of their problems onto others when they were upset, which was often associated with anger and hostility.

One particular clinical experience sticks in my mind, as it was the day I fully grasped this phenomenon and adapted my approach. A regular client of mine, who had previously successfully reprocessed many EMDR targets, shared a recent incident about which he was very upset. He had a verbal "blow-out" with his 14-year-old son over the weekend. His son wanted to visit a friend and the father said "No." They had a brief, heated exchange and the son huffed away, muttering, "You're a dick." My client was triggered by the comment, which ignited a stormy argument.

The worst part of the memory for my client was his son's words. When I asked my client to think about those words and identify a negative belief about himself, he looked at me defensively as if I was implying there was something wrong with him. I noticed this uncharacteristic response, paused, and said, "Okay then, what words describe a negative belief about your son?" To this question, I got an instant response, "He's obnoxious and self-centered!" I paused again, and then said, "Okay, and when you remember those words, 'You're a dick,' and believe that your son is obnoxious and self-centered, what words describe a negative belief about yourself now?" He looked at me with less defensiveness and a wry, knowing look and said, "*I'm* obnoxious and self-centered!" In that moment, with his externalized belief about his son already spoken, he could see that *he* was a part of the problem and that he had probably projected an undue amount of the blame onto his son. From there we processed the incident to a Subjective Units of Disturbances (SUDs) score of zero. We installed a Positive Cognition about my client, "I'm a good parent doing my best." At that point, I had the presence of mind to ask him for a Positive Cognition about his son, and he delivered. "He's a good kid, doing what 14-year olds do." Both cognitions were of high validity and we installed them both. As I reflected upon the session, I realized that it was important for him to identify and strengthen a positive, more adaptive view of his son, just as it was about himself.

Since that time, I have come to sense when a client might benefit from those extra steps and I have formalized it into a protocol that can be used whenever an externalized negative core belief is a part of the client's difficulties. Prejudicial beliefs can be effectively reprocessed through this protocol.

I have found that many times clients have little awareness of the self-related negative beliefs that are linked to their hostile perceptions and attitudes toward others. The protocol helps illuminate and transform both the external *and* the internal previously frozen beliefs.

As part of the protocol, I developed the term *Externalized Negative Cognition* (ENC) to designate the negative belief about the "other." Getting familiar with this term and the concept behind it is useful for an EMDR clinician learning to spot the externalization process. Clients familiar with identifying NCs about the self often grasp the concept of ENCs and can quickly learn that developing ENCs is a normal part of how some people cope with past adverse or traumatic experiences. Because these beliefs often lie unexamined, I believe that the ENCs need to be explicitly articulated as part of this process and then linked to internal experiences.

Sometimes, as in the case of more explicit prejudice, these prejudicial ENCs are quite vivid and come to light in such forms as "justified" emotional rage, "reasonably" drawn negative judgments, and echoing "commonly accepted" stereotypes. They may not be seen as a problem by the client and can go unchallenged by others in the client's life. On the other hand, more implicit biases may emerge as more modest negative judgments of others. Either way, they can be targeted for reprocessing.

Even after establishing the ENC, it may take some clinical effort to help direct the client's focus inward. When a client feels justified in his or her extreme judgment, he or she may not be ready to share responsibility for a disturbing experience. However, the client may be able to access a Negative Cognition such as "I'm powerless" or "I'm unsafe."

Sometimes an ENC may be identified as a treatment issue to be addressed during Phases 1 and 2, as in the case of choosing to work on prejudice or hostility. Other times, a strong ENC may become evident during the Phase 3 assessment questions. Also, an ENC may emerge during Phase 4 reprocessing and can be seen as a form of blocking beliefs that might block reprocessing until it is recognized and addressed.

As part of Phase 5 installation, the protocol calls for the identification of an *Externalized Positive Cognition* (EPC). This is important to correct the original ENC. That's why EMDR treatment includes an installation and body scan. My original protocol offered an option of asking the client for a more adaptive EPC during the assessment phase in a manner parallel to how a client is standardly asked for a PC about the self. This may be useful to keep in mind for some clients. However, I found that most clients were not ready to generate an adaptive EPC before the reprocessing and asking them to do so seemed to induce guilt or an attempt to give the right answer. After the reprocessing, most clients readily generate a meaningful and adaptive EPC that then can be installed.

It is important to note that with any client who is preparing to target a prejudice, I try to be aware of what experiences he or she may have had being discriminated against. Often, I suggest that we reprocess those experiences prior to targeting a prejudice. Reprocessing a client's own victimization helps prepare that client for adaptive empathy toward the subjects of his or her own prejudice. Another type of preparation is for the client to identify a personal quality that may help him or her address the prejudice, such as empathy or open-mindedness. This serves as a resource that can be enhanced with bilateral stimulation. Many times, however, with clients who are proficient at reprocessing, these strategies are not necessary.

## Client Examples

Case 1—Jack, a client of mine, was discussing his initial reaction to someone he met through online dating. He admitted to having mixed feelings when he realized she was "heavier" than she looked in her online picture. He liked her but was somewhat "turned off" by her size and felt a little tricked by her misleading photo. At the same time, he was uncomfortable that he felt that way, especially as he was heavy himself. I mentioned that attraction is a very personal inclination, but that it is influenced by many factors including learned prejudices about appearance that can limit a person's options. Jack had experienced many breakthrough realizations in our prior EMDR reprocessing; therefore, when I said that there was a protocol for prejudice, he was all for it. As I often do, I suggested that we first do a session on any ways he had experienced prejudice. We targeted and successfully reprocessed childhood memories of being bullied related to his weight. In the next session, we used the prejudice protocol. The reprocessing was effective and his feelings shifted not only about her size but also because he realized why, with all the cultural messages, she would try to conceal her size on a dating site. He then chose without ambivalence to move forward in the relationship.

Case 2—Ron was a recently retired policeman who realized that he viewed "dark skinned" people differently than Whites. As part of the prejudice protocol, he accessed a prior disturbing memory in which a Black fellow officer was befriending two suspicious Black men while they were on duty together. He realized it made him feel afraid. His ENC toward the other officer was, "He's one of them, he's dangerous." His internal NC was, "I'm out of place, I'm different and not safe." His processing over multiple sessions took him through many memories connected with race and ethnicity, both within his police experiences and outside them. It also linked in with memories of his father's own intolerance toward "people who were different." Ron not only cleared the disturbance but also realized that he learned a lot from that officer about the relational side of police work. He also became openly interested in culture and began to date a Latina woman.

Case 3—Marge, a 65-year-old woman, had a prejudice toward Spanish-speaking people. She believed, quite vehemently, that they should learn English if they wanted to live in this country. Marge was the receptionist at a large community service agency. She began to rant at a session about how much it bothered her when somebody called in asking to speak to someone who speaks Spanish. She was highly emotional, mocking their "broken English" and saying that she had insisted that several of them try to speak with her. While I was trying to stay empathic to her experience, I also put myself in the position of the people calling for help. Marge and I had a good rapport and we had made good use of EMDR reprocessing before, so I felt I could interrupt her and said, "That's a strong reaction, can we target it?" She agreed. What followed were several sessions of powerful work. We started with her own experiences of discrimination. Marge grew up in a second generation Polish-American Catholic family that worked hard to assimilate to this country. She had also struggled throughout her life with cerebral palsy and was currently in a wheelchair. We first targeted her own mistreatment as an adolescent related to her physical disability, including derision from a Catholic school nun. At one point she said, "All my life I've struggled to be accepted, wanted, and loved. I resent those who don't have a clue what it's like."

When it came to targeting her reaction to people wanting to speak with a Spanish speaker, her ENC was, "They're lazy and don't care about this country. They just want handouts." Her NC about herself was, "I'm a bad person," and she felt an immediate wave of shame and guilt. "I'm supposed to be a Christian," she said. The reprocessing went back into more of her own mistreatment growing up, and it continued for several sessions. Along the way, she remembered how a Latina personal care attendant had meant so much to her. As we wound up the work, and without any interweaves, she had come to many adaptive insights, including appreciating how difficult it must be to learn a new language and that no one was excluding her "personally." She shared that a group of Cambodians who ate lunch together at her agency had always "annoyed her" for speaking in Cambodian, so she couldn't participate. "Now," she said, "I don't know how they can even wait until lunch to talk in their own language."

## Evidence Supporting the Protocols for Culturally Based Trauma and Prejudice

In 2010, I conducted four one-day trainings throughout New England, USA, for EMDR-trained clinicians on the topic of *Undoing Stigma: EMDR Applications in the Dismantling of Socially Based Internalized Oppression and Prejudice.*

The training included a morning and afternoon didactic presentation, each followed by a practicum experience. The information presented covered topic-related theory and clinical strategies that explored cultural identities, culturally based trauma, and interventions to reduce prejudice. The didactic information presented was consistent with content from Chapters 2 through 4 in this book. The practicum experiences were strategically organized as a progression through three types of practicum exercises. Participants were asked to: (a) identify and enhance positive associations with a social identity (to access and enhance internal resources); (b) identify and reprocess a disturbing memory associated with an adverse/traumatic social/cultural experience; and (c) identify and reprocess a self-identified prejudice toward others.

In the morning practicum, participants completed exercises one and two. In the afternoon practicum, participants completed exercise three. For practicum exercises two and three, 50 minutes were allotted for each participant to be in the role of both client and therapist. In the client role, participants selected personally meaningful issues. The participant acting as therapist kept process notes during the sessions and both client and therapist answered questions to evaluate their experience after each session. Notes were submitted on a voluntary basis and 60 submissions were fully completed. These 60 were reviewed and tabulated as part of an overall evaluation of the practicum experiences. Due to space considerations, this is a brief report; however, it is included to provide readers with a better "feel" for these protocols in action.

Overall, participants' reports strongly validated the effectiveness of the standard protocol for reprocessing a memory associated with an adverse/traumatic social/cultural experience. Likewise, most participants were able to successfully reprocess a prejudice using the protocol for prejudice.

*Target issues for reprocessing adverse/traumatic social/cultural experience:* The most common target issues were related to socioeconomic status (social class), racial discrimination, gender (sexism and male conditioning), sexual orientation, gender identity, age, and experiences of exclusions.

*Pre- and postsession SUDs:* Seventy-five percent of participants identified an initial SUDs of five or above. At the end of the session, 85% of participants reported a final SUDs under two. Sixty-seven percent reported that they completely cleared the disturbance associated with the target memory.

Session transcripts and comments indicated a typical progression of memory associations as part of the reprocessing, including fading of the original target image, decreased emotionality, and reevaluation of the targeted experience. Most participants remarked about the power of the reprocessing session. None reported an unproductive experience.

*In their postpracticum observations, participants noted:*

- How quickly accessible stigma feelings were
- How I moved through my resistance to unpacking these memories
- It was not easy to speak about an issue I had buried
- How the final PC linked up with strengths of Latina identity
- How many social issues were uncovered
- How closely social and personal issues are related
- Impact of social consciousness tied to my personal psychology
- Social messages made my childhood confusing
- How social class colored my lenses, and to be more aware
- I was able to say how much words stung from a powerful White woman

*Target issues for the prejudice protocol:* These are the are the most commonly targeted issues related to age, wealthy people, nationalism, race/ethnicity, appearance, political views, and other ways people seem "different."

*Presession and postsession SUDs*: Eighty percent of participants identified an initial SUDs of five or above. At the end of the session, 85% of participants reported a final SUDs under three. Sixty-seven percent reported that they completely cleared the disturbance associated with the target memory altogether.

After the session, participants responded to the same questions as in the first practicum. All comments indicated a positive experience.

Clients shared insights about the nature of prejudice both general and specific:

- Prejudice in one's life goes back to themes early in life
- So many connections between a prejudice and current behavior
- A connection to being bullied and carrying racial prejudice
- My prejudice linked to my own fear and shame
- Profound shift. I targeted prejudice of severely handicapped people—instant float back to an age 7 memory
- Helped me to get at underlying feelings

Clients reported shifts in their attitudes and perceptions toward others including:

- I may be able to think more about individual wealthy people and their behavior rather than making a blanket judgment.
- I'm feeling more curious about members of the group I have been avoiding.
- I gained clarity about seeing the essence of a person beneath physical attributes.
- Yes, acceptance of other cultures and myself.
- Shift from focus on the actions of the other to what I can do to change the situations.
- Reinforced awareness that so much of my fear is my mom's core belief.
- Everyone's different.
- I can comfortably explore this topic.
- I didn't realize how much I had aligned with the oppressor.
- I had a rewarding shift in understanding, less blaming of myself.

The protocol calls for identifying an initial ENC about the subject of the prejudice. Following the desensitization phase, the client is asked to identify a more positive and adaptive EPC. Some examples of the transformation of these cognitions after the reprocessing are:

| ENC (before reprocessing) | EPC (after reprocessing) |
|---|---|
| She misuses her power. | She is a reasonable person doing the best she can. |
| They're idiots. | They are different than I am and that's okay. |
| They are gross, indulgent. | Being fat is only one aspect of that person. |
| They are trying to take over the world. | We are all part of the same human family. |
| That person is worthless. | That person is doing his or her best, better than I realized. |

*Clients and therapists were asked: Did the extra steps in the protocol for prejudice seem useful in facilitating a more meaningful session?* Most participants responded to this question, all positively. Some comments included:

- Yes, a , the "double layering" of ENCs and EPCs helped
- Saying out loud what one believes about "the other" was great
- What the NC is of self and of the ENC of the other is helpful
- Yes, a greater focus on the issue got to the core
- Yes, it focused on specifics of the target, fast processing
- Yes, the extra steps helped me as a therapist, and the revised EPC about prejudice was important
- Helped clarify the prejudice

Overall, the detailed session data and written comments from the 60 participants showed that both practicum experiences had a remarkable impact. Consistent comments from these EMDR therapists who, of course, are all familiar with trauma reprocessing found that the intentional focus on social/cultural trauma including prejudice opened up a surprisingly meaningful new dimension.

The most interesting comments came from a participant who said, "I have worked with a fair number of people of color and never sought to address stigma so directly. I'm eager to do so." The comment confirmed my observation that many EMDR clinicians may not think to target adverse cultural experiences, but gave me hope that more will do so.

## MORE ON FINDING TARGETS FOR REPROCESSING

### Targeting Stereotypes

Stereotypes are typically rigid beliefs that are culturally reinforced and are generalized when applied to an object of the stereotype or the situation. Within EMDR language, stereotypes can be seen as blocking beliefs because they interfere rigidly with a true understanding and are thus maladaptive.

Examples of client stereotypes that were transformed by reprocessing include the following:

- Old people make things difficult.
- White people are all the same.
- Men don't understand their feelings.
- Gay people just want attention.
- Overweight people are undisciplined.
- Teenagers are selfish.
- "Borderline" people won't change.
- Muslims don't care about human life.
- Children don't know what's good for them.

- Cognitively different people can't contribute.

As with other blocking beliefs, the therapist might ask:

> *Do you have any stereotypes you'd like to work on?*
> *Where did you first learn that belief?* (Sometimes it is useful to ask)
> *Is there some part of you that believes something else? Just notice that?*

This information can lead to full reprocessing with the protocol for prejudice.

Other possible target memories associated with prejudice include:

- Witnessing prejudice
- Colluding with prejudice when it felt wrong
- A current situation in which the client was aware of his or her prejudice
- Stereotypic beliefs and when they were learned
- Being criticized for being prejudiced
- Current triggers
- Future fears related to exposure of prejudice

## Running Into One's Own Prejudice

Sometimes a person's life changes create circumstances whereby the person moves into a social category that he or she had an established prejudice against. For instance, this occurs for many people as they realize that they are getting older. When the client is grappling with aging issues, I often ask, "What stereotypes did you have about older people when you were younger?" Of course, these stereotypes may still be alive even though the shoe is on the other foot.

One 64-year-old client of mine was terrified of getting old. When we processed it, he discovered that his judgments about what it was like were formed when he was 19 years old and worked for a year in a nursing home. After reprocessing, he was much more adaptively equipped to negotiate his aging process.

For this issue, a client could be asked:

> *Do any disturbing feelings come up when you think of being around an older person?* or
>
> *What stereotypes did you have about older people when you were younger?*

Information from these questions can be used to select a target for reprocessing.

Other examples in which the client may run up against his or her own prior prejudices include becoming ill or handicapped, having a child with a drug problem, or needing therapy.

Sometimes social identity ego states have their own prejudices that need to be identified and targeted. Roberta grew up in a poor family that distrusted others with money. As she sought to become a middle-class professional, she felt a judgment of herself for "getting too big for her britches" and turning her back on her family's roots.

### Countertransference

Therapists are trained to identify countertransference with their clients. Countertransference may well be influenced by prejudices or stereotypes. Indeed, as mentioned in Chapter 1, studies have shown that therapists are more biased than they think. Ridley's (2005) report of over 80 studies showing evidence of psychotherapist discrimination during their clinical practice is a chilling reminder that a culturally competent therapist needs to spot and perhaps reprocess countertransference to determine if there is a culturally based bias operating. In my workshop practicums, several therapists have worked on countertransference issues with their clients and all reported valuable shifts in perception and empathy for the client.

## EXPLORING SOCIAL PRIVILEGE AND SOCIAL POSITION

Social stratification is a reality in almost every culture and social group, from families to nations. Hierarchies of power are determined in many ways, ranging from the meritocracy of an athletic team to the genetic privilege of a royal family. Oftentimes in most societies, these hierarchies are linked to social inequities. However, social hierarchies are often intertwined with the established ways that societies function, and trying to bring about systematic change to correct inequities is a complex and long-term undertaking way beyond the scope of this section.

*Social privilege* is generally defined as an advantage or right available only to a particular person or group of people. Social privilege is a hot topic of focus currently, in particular on college campuses and other communities that are pushing the edges of social consciousness. Discussion about social inequalities and discrimination quite appropriately includes attention to those that are advantaged by social position as determined by race, socioeconomic class, gender, or other variables. For those in advantageous social positions, there are many secondary gains to maintaining this position. When directly challenged about having advantages, those in power sometimes assert that they have, at least in part, earned their positions, adding further complications to determining what is just.

As EMDR psychotherapists, our opportunities to create change are on the individual level. If we think it is hard enough to find appropriate moments to confront client prejudices, we may find it more unlikely to imagine how targeting social privilege can be a clinically appropriate issue. And yet, I have found that some clients, often in a more integrative personal growth phase of their therapy, are quite open to facing the prejudices, biases, and social advantages that are aversive to them and in conflict with their core values.

Within the scope of this chapter, my goal is to make a case for EMDR reprocessing as a useful means by which a person can explore dimensions of his or her social position. Indeed, powerful feelings and complicated thoughts are often associated with perception of oneself as having either social advantages *or* disadvantages. It is human nature to take advantage of opportunities in life, to take pride in what one earns, and to protect what one has. At the same time, those with social advantages have greater opportunities and resources to accomplish their goals. Many people have been in positions of advantage or disadvantage at one time or another in different social groups and sometimes acknowledging this shared experience can reduce defensiveness and increase curiosity.

However, when it comes to the dynamics reinforced by social oppression and the "isms," the advantageous opportunities that come with privilege can be significant. A very active discussion is going on in the United States about the importance of examining White privilege. Helms (as cited in Sue et al., 1998) created a White racial identity development model that has been frequently referenced. She suggests a phased psychological process for examining social privilege and transforming prejudice. She notes that a person embarking on this path typically starts with the belief that he or she is not racist but rather "color blind." The challenging process of self-discovery typically leads to realizing his or her own unconscious discrimination and the inconsistencies between his or her chosen beliefs (humanism/egalitarianism) and the discovery of latent biases. Ultimately, the process can lead to a more conscious integration of one's Whiteness into other parts of his or her identity. It can lead to choosing to surrender privileged forms of power while discovering fulfillment in newfound power including appreciating differences.

Amid the sometimes strong feelings associated with social justice analysis, EMDR therapy can offer a process to sort out feelings of social privilege that are inherently nonthreatening. EMDR therapists create a means by which the client's brain discovers the most adaptive way to sort through his or her feelings and thoughts. Nevertheless, in my experience, for the client opening up feelings related to social privilege, it can feel like new territory and surprisingly threatening. Sometimes an immediate wave of guilt or shame can overwhelm and shut down the process. Clients reprocessing privilege need to be kept within the "optimal window" of effective processing. They may need to be reassured, for example, that if they uncover and face their feelings related to being wealthier than most people in the world, they do not need to immediately arrange to donate all of their money to those that are less fortunate. In my experience, adaptive resolutions for people examining their social advantages are often nuanced and may take time to become clear.

Here are some questions to explore feelings related to social advantages or disadvantages:

*Have you ever felt any unfair advantage or disadvantage because of your cultural or social identity?*

*Do you have strong feelings about this that you'd like to work on?*

Or, *Are there ways you take advantage of others because of your social position?*

This second question is especially sensitive and needs to be delivered skillfully. Yet it is important as many exploit their social position in a variety of ways such as controlling group decisions and excluding or devaluing others. A responsible person seeking to examine his or her use of social power can address this through EMDR reprocessing.

## PROTOCOL FOR TARGETING SOCIAL ADVANTAGES AND PRIVILEGES

*Would you like to explore issues related to any advantages or privileges that you have in life related to any dimension of your social identity such as race/ethnicity, nationality, social class, sex, appearance, age, education, and so forth?* (If yes, then)

*When you think of one or more of these advantages, what comes to mind? Take a moment to notice some of these advantages with an attitude of appreciation and gratitude.* (Enhance positive associations with sets of BLS. Instruct the client to put any disturbing feelings into a "container.")

*What is a personal quality of yours that will help you consider the experience of those who do not have these advantages (e.g., honesty, courage, curiosity)? Can you think of a time in your life where you had this quality? Access memory and enhance with BLS.*

*When you think of another person or group of people who have been disadvantaged, what comes to mind? What specific image most clearly captures these disadvantages?*

(Proceed with the standard protocol.)

### Targeting Social Disadvantages

*Would you like to explore issues related to any disadvantages that you have in life related to any dimension of your social identity such as race/ethnicity, nationality, social class, sex, appearance, age, education, and so forth?* (If yes, then)

*When you think of one or more of these advantages that you do have in life, what comes to mind? Take a moment to notice some of these advantages with an attitude of appreciation and gratitude.* (Enhance positive associations with sets of BLS. Instruct the client to put any disturbing feelings into a "container.")

*What is a personal quality of yours that will help you consider the reality that others have advantages that you don't (e.g., strength, courage, resilience)? Can you think of a time in your life where you had this quality? Access memory and enhance with BLS.*

*When you think of another person or group of people who have advantages that you don't, what comes to mind? What specific image most clearly captures these advantages?*

(Proceed with the standard protocol.)

I have crafted a Protocol for Targeting Social Advantages and Privileges that includes a modification for targeting social disadvantages. The steps outlined in the protocol are relatively simple and are strategically designed for optimal processing effectiveness.

In my experience, following either of these protocols is a serious undertaking. It can open up very deep feelings. Most people have developed internal boundaries to protect themselves from feelings about social inequities, and yet awareness of these inequities can accumulate and gnaw at a person. For many clients, clear and strong associated memories will come quickly to mind, and because few people have had opportunities to process this material, emotions can be strong and wide ranging.

Regarding targeting social advantages and privileges, the protocol is likely to take a client into the experience, as he or she imagines it, of another person who has experienced cultural disadvantages. This is a potentially deep well to enter. Accessed emotions may include grief, guilt, fear, confusion, anger, and despair. At the same time, as with processing other disturbing memories, it will predictably yield to adaptive resolution. Signs of successful resolution that I have observed include a lessening of the extreme painful emotion, a reduction in immobilizing guilt, an increase in curiosity about the experience of the target, and stimulation of actions the person can take to assist in some way to rebalance particular injustices, especially that they feel directly connected to. Especially because this is uncharted territory for many, special care should be taken to close sessions thoughtfully with follow-up evaluation.

## Client Examples

Case 1—One woman, who is a second generation White immigrant, realized that her pathway to higher education and a professional job was undoubtedly easier because she was White. When asked (as part of this protocol) to consider an experience of someone who had been disadvantaged, she remembered driving through Georgia as a child. Her father pointed out shacks inhabited by Black families. There was a sobering moment of empathy that was still vivid in her mind. Her Negative Cognition as she thought of that image was, "I'm selfish." Her Positive Cognition was, "I can share." As she processed, her feelings went from sharp sadness to curiosity. At the end of the session she said she had often thought about contributing to Black children's education. She felt this more strongly than ever.

Case 2—A man using this protocol conjured up an image of a young Syrian girl as an example of someone disadvantaged. The Negative Cognition was, "I'm helpless." The reprocessing brought guilt and then fantasies of rescuing this girl. Those fantasies yielded to the understanding that he could not do that himself. His perspective shifted to seeing the world as he imagined it through her eyes, which brought feelings of fear and deep sadness. The session was wrenching in many ways for him but he felt deeper for having faced a reality of the world. He left the session speculating about what he could do to contribute to social change on a global level.

So far, my experience with targeting issues of social privilege are too anecdotal to present broader patterns of response to this protocol, but I believe it is reasonable to predict that EMDR reprocessing will lead to more adaptive insights, beliefs, and choices. And, I think this tool can support individual processes of those with humanitarian values who seek social change.

To further speculate, as EMDR clinicians we might wonder, "What is adaptive resolution when one examines social privilege in an unjust world?" Kohlberg and Lickona's theory of development (1976) suggests that people have the capacity to evolve from lower to higher levels of morality of "obedience and punishment orientation" to the highest level of principled conscience. It seems reasonable to think that EMDR reprocessing of feelings can allow a person to better face and come to terms with social realities, and in that process be able to draw from greater and greater depth of perspective and conscience. Indeed, it is predictable that EMDR reprocessing strategies could provide opportunities to support people examining other complicated social issues. Hopefully these possibilities will be better studied in the future.

Case 3—Another clinical example related to social position is a client who targeted her shame about having inherited money and not having to support herself. She did work for pay, but was also ashamed about earning money given her inheritance. Her negative belief was, "I don't deserve it." Her touchstone early memory was at age 5 when she suddenly felt that a hardworking janitor who she liked very much might have been overly nice to her because her father owned the building. She felt confused about what was real. During reprocessing, her thoughts took a path that included: "I'm not better than he . . . . I'm less worthy because I have more . . . . I am allowed to take advantage of my opportunities . . . . It doesn't make me less than to be in a position of having more . . . . I'm not less worthy to have more . . . . There is no right way . . . . I can do the best I can . . . . What I do is fine . . . . My intentions are good . . . . I might be able to do more . . . ."

At the end of the session, her shame had eased. She said, "This session was more relevant than I expected . . . powerful!" (It should be noted that this client lived modestly and volunteered extensively.)

Some people consciously choose to give up social privileges either because they realize they are confined by them or because they feel their privileges are oppressive to others. I know one man who donated most of his family fortune because of his deep moral objection to how the fortune was gathered, and so that he would not have that advantage. This is not easy and the feelings related to these "sacrifices" can be targeted for reprocessing. EMDR reprocessing can also allow a person to face fears of anticipating surrendering privilege so he or she can make a clear decision for them.

Case 4—Brad, a White Anglo-Saxon Protestant (WASP) in his 60s, was born into an upper middle class family, and was educated at an elite private high school and college. He was handsome, an athlete, a good student, likeable, and received praise and awards for his achievements. With each recognition, however, he felt increased pressure to live up to the expectations of others. He had other interests that were outside the socially valued mold. As a male he felt constricted by norms of masculinity and lived in two realities, his high achieving public face and his hidden, softer "more authentic self." After college, many high-paying career opportunities were available to him, but he pulled away completely to pursue a countercultural life. Although he eventually prospered in his alternative pursuits, he never truly felt that it was okay to be who he really was and he felt he had abandoned the good parts of his school experiences. The multisession EMDR therapy created a process of internal integration. Brad was able to reclaim and appreciate the many positive aspects of his youth, while feeling less rebellious and more proud of the brave choices he made to live a more authentic life. During the sessions, he articulated greater awareness of his hard-earned power to love, affirm, and support others, and to be a socially conscientious person.

## SUMMARY

This chapter has offered an AIP understanding of the mechanisms of social prejudice along with EMDR strategies for reducing or eliminating prejudice. On one level, distorted perception of other people is a normal fact of life; indeed, all people have prejudices. At the same time, prejudices that fuel the mistreatment of others through stigmatization, discrimination, and exploiting social power are poisons to a civil society. Non-EMDR research has shown that social prejudice can be managed by motivated people with egalitarian values. However, even then, people with more subtle illicit prejudice tend to manage prejudice by avoiding certain "others."

EMDR reprocessing offers the potential to more radically reduce or eliminate prejudice. The chapter described a protocol for prejudice that explicitly uncovers the negative beliefs associated with a prejudice or stereotype. Early results from this protocol show promise. In addition, a protocol to examine thoughts and feelings related to social privilege was described along with some case examples of its use. It is interesting to speculate about the potential societal benefits that can come if EMDR treatment further develops its capacity to effectively dismantle prejudice. Likewise, by providing a means to examine socially related realities such as those connected to social privilege, EMDR methods hold promise for a socially responsible exploration of the many complicated issues in society, and to otherwise support successful multiculturalism.

## REFERENCES


Allport, G. (1954). *The nature of prejudice*. Cambridge, MA: Addison Wesley.

Bargh, J. A., & Gollwitzer, P. M. (1994). Environmental control of goal-directed action: Automatic and strategic contingencies between situations. *Nebraska symposium on motivation*. Lincoln, NE: University of Nebraska Press.

Cole, J. (n.d.). *Beyond prejudice* [website]. Available at beyondprejudice.com

Dasgupta, N. (2009). Mechanisms underlying the malleability of implicit prejudice and stereotypes: The role of automaticity and cognitive control. In T. D. Nelson (Ed.), *Handbook of prejudice, stereotyping, and discrimination* (pp. 267–284). New York, NY: Psychology Press.

Devine, P. G. (1989). Stereotypes and prejudice: Their automatic and controlled components. *Journal of Personality and Social Psychology, 56*(1), 5–18.

Devine, P. G., & Sharp, L. B. (2009). Automaticity and control in stereotyping and prejudice. *Handbook of prejudice, stereotyping, and discrimination*. New York, NY: Psychology Press.

Dovidio, J. F., & Gaertner, S. L. (Eds.). (1986). The aversive form of racism. *Prejudice, discrimination and racism* (pp. 61–89). San Diego, CA: Academic Press.

Fiske, S. T., Harris, L. T., Lee, T. L., & Russell, A. (2009). The future of research on prejudice, stereotyping, and discrimination. *Handbook of prejudice, stereotyping, and discrimination*. New York, NY: Psychology Press.

Gaertner, S. L., & Dovidio, J. F. (2014). A common in-group identity: A categorization-based approach for reducing intergroup bias.

Gonzales, L., Davidoff, K. C., Nadal, K. L., & Yanos, P. T. (2015). Micro aggressions experienced by persons with mental illness: An exploratory study. *Psychiatric Rehabilitation Journal, 38*, 234–241.

Hamilton, D. L., Sherman, S. J., Crump, S. A., & Spencer- Rodgers, J. (2009). The role of entitativity in stereotyping. *Handbook of prejudice, stereotyping, and discrimination*. New York, NY: Psychology Press.

Kohlberg, L., & Lickona, T. (Eds.). (1976). Moral stages and moralization: The cognitive-developmental approach. In *Moral development and behavior: Theory, research and social issues*. New York, NY: Holt, Rinehart and Winston.

MacLeod, B. P. (2013). Social justice at the micro level: Working with clients' prejudices. *Journal of Multicultural Counseling and Development, 41*(3), 169–184. doi:10.1002/j.2161 1912.2013.00035.x

Major, B., & Sawyer, P. J. (2009). Attributions to discriminations: Antecedents and consequences. *Handbook of prejudice, stereotyping, and discrimination*. New York, NY: Psychology Press.

Nelson, T. D. (Ed.). (2009). *Handbook of prejudice, stereotyping, and discrimination*. New York, NY: Psychology Press (Collection of 26 topic-related chapters by experts in the field of social psychology.)

Ridley, C. R. (2005). *Overcoming unintentional racism in counseling and therapy: A practitioner's guide to intentional intervention*. Thousand Oaks, CA: Sage.

Shapiro, F. (2001). *Eye movement desensitization and reprocessing: Basic principles, protocols, and procedures*. New York, NY: Guilford.

Sue, D. W., Carter, R. T., Casas, J. M., Fouad, N. A., Ivey A. E., Jensen, M., . . . Vazquez-Nutall, E. (1998). *Multicultural counseling competencies: Individual and organizational development* (pp. 47–58). Thousand Oaks, CA: Sage.

Wegner, D. M. (1994). Ironic processes of mental control. *Psychological Review, 101*, 34–52.

# SECTION II

# Strategies for Marginalized Cultures

CHAPTER 5

# An Integrative Approach to EMDR Therapy as an Antioppression Endeavor

Rajani Venkatraman Levis and Laura Siniego

## A NOTE OF GRATITUDE

Chicano and Latino scholars have long acknowledged that their personal and academic experiences are inseparable. As therapists who identify as immigrant Women of Color,[1] we are pleased to present this chapter on culturally attuned eye movement desensitization and reprocessing (EMDR) therapy that furthers this academic tradition.

Laura Siniego was born in Argentina and raised in Mexico, while Rajani Venkatraman Levis was born and raised in India. Each of us migrated to the United States in the 1990s and has made it our home since. Primed by our own experiences as immigrant Women of Color, our clinical work has focused on immigrant communities both documented and undocumented. Our practice of EMDR therapy has also been strongly influenced by our intimate familiarity with the intersection of race, gender, class, immigration status, and dominant perceptions. As living mirrors for our clients' experiences of immigration, bilingualism, discrimination, marginalization, microaggressions, racism, and sexism, this chapter is part of our ongoing exploration of the issues that impact us both personally and professionally. While this chapter focuses on the experience of undocumented Latinos in the United States, it is intended to offer support to professionals who are immigrants, as well as those who serve immigrant communities around the world.

We would like to thank our undocumented clients for their patience, trust, and courage. We are made alive by their stories, their resilience, and especially their resistance, which we feel honored to set forth in this chapter. Without a doubt, our work with these clients has been strongly informed by our lived experience, and in turn, has helped us to make meaning of our personal and professional

[1] "Women of Color": The intentional capitalization, which rejects the grammatical norm, represents a grammatical move toward social and racial justice through empowering this group and their resources. This rule also applies to "People of Color," "Community Cultural Wealth Resources," and "Clients of Color" throughout this chapter.

experiences as immigrant Women of Color in the United States of America. We are immeasurably transformed and offer this chapter as proof of the abundance of our most marginalized clients.

## INTRODUCTION

### The Background Through Numbers

The world's largest corridor of international migration is between the United States and Mexico (United Nations Department of Economic and Social Affairs, 2014). In 2012, Latinos, a heterogeneous group that includes persons of varying racial and socioeconomic backgrounds from more than 20 countries of origin (Harwood, Leyendecker, Carlson, Asencio, & Miller, 2002), accounted for about 78% of undocumented immigrants (see Passel & Cohn, 2014). It is estimated that over 60% of the Latino undocumented immigrants were of Mexican origin (see Passel & Cohn, 2014). These numbers serve to explain our emphasis on a sociopolitical and cultural understanding of Latino families, their reasons for immigration, and their contemporary experiences in the United States.

### EMDR Therapy as an Antioppression Endeavor

Therapy needs to integrate the sociocultural, political, and legal realities that permeate our clients' existence in order to be an effective instrument of healing (Arredondo, 1999). The importance of such an integrative framework is to reach beyond the client's presenting problem in order to understand how philosophical, contextual, experiential, and pragmatic considerations affect the client (James & Prilleltensky, 2002). The following are a few complementary considerations specific to undocumented immigrants in the contemporary United States.

In a country that prides itself on being a nation of immigrants, there is a significant anti-immigrant trend that has a major impact on the well-being of both documented and undocumented immigrants in the United States (Arbona et al., 2010; Furman, Ackerman, Loya, Jones, & Negi, 2012). The contemporary framing of the immigration debate in the U.S. media falsely simplifies it as a problem created by immigrants and the failure of governmental control (Lakoff & Ferguson, 2006; Romero, 2008). In the North American media, the blame has been squarely placed on the backs of the immigrants who crossed the border "illegally." This generally accepted notion fails to acknowledge the devastating impact of U.S. foreign policies like NAFTA (North American Free Trade Agreement; see González & Fernandez, 2002) upon Mexico, the country from which we see the greatest number of unauthorized immigrants.

A more balanced contextual consideration from a socioeconomic justice perspective recognizes the reality of difficult living conditions south of the border, including gang violence, financial hardship, and the lack of opportunity that resulted from U.S. foreign policy and influenced the migratory trend (Cervantes, Mejía, & Guerrero Mena, 2010; Perreira, Chapman, & Stein, 2006). This basic understanding of the sociopolitical realities introduces us to a person far removed from the stereotype of the "illegal alien" popularized by the media. In place of the dishonest law-breaker who deserves to be deported, we might encounter a man who willingly sacrifices his own safety and dignity in the hope of securing a better economic future for his *familia* (including those on either side of the border). We might discover a woman who strives to honor the Latino values of *respeto* (respect, or appropriate courtesy and decorum in varied social contexts) and *familismo* (loyalty, reciprocity, and feelings of community toward members of extended family—including close friends—that incorporates the notion of the family as an extension of self [Buriel, 1993; Falicov, 1998; Harwood et al., 2002; Perreira et al., 2006]) by reuniting with family members who are already in the United States. Often, this "illegal alien" is a parent removing his or her children from violent and impoverished living conditions and acting on the promise of better educational opportunities in a safe environment.

An integrative framework of this nature allows therapy to reach beyond the client's presenting problem and acknowledge the impact of intersecting domains. Thus, the reason the client originally enters into therapy may only be a minor portion of the trauma narrative, and, like an iceberg, much of it may be hidden from view. It is the culturally attuned therapist's responsibility to integrate the sociopolitical and cultural environment within which trauma occurs and to help the client better integrate his own healing resources through rewriting the narrative and claiming his own identity (Malott & Schaefle, 2015). Through integrating a range of complementary considerations and the negative beliefs that the client internalizes due to social oppression, we conceptualize this form of EMDR therapy as an antioppression endeavor.

## A Note About Our Use of the Term *Undocumented*

While the official or technical label for foreign-born noncitizens residing in the United States without legal status is "illegal aliens" (IRS, 2014; U.S. Citizenship and Immigration Services, 2015; U.S. Customs and Border Protection, 2014), academic researchers such as those from the Pew Hispanic Center use the term *unauthorized immigrants*. Romero (2008) and Gomberg-Muñoz (2012) denounced the punitive immigration-enforcement strategies that have resulted in the social construction of Mexicans and Latinos as criminal and foreign. Gomberg-Muñoz (2012) also supported the argument that the concepts of illegality and criminality act to veil racism while creating what appear to be legitimate bases for exclusion and oppression.

Following this train of thought, allowing a client to be framed as alien, illegal, or criminal within the therapeutic context is to bear witness to racism, criminalization, and dehumanization through nomenclature. As therapists who work in immigrant communities, in our sessions we have witnessed directly the suffering of our clients due to this unfair framing (see Thompson & Neville, 1999, on the impact of ideological and structural racism on mental health), which unfairly targets a specific population. Therefore, we have deliberately chosen to use the term *undocumented immigrants*, because it takes into account the challenges experienced by individuals who lack documented status without imposing a criminalized identity upon them.

## EMDR THERAPY WITH UNDOCUMENTED CLIENTS

### Building a Strong Therapeutic Alliance

Most therapists will easily agree that the more adept a clinician is at identifying the client's internal and external resources, the more likely it is that she[2] will build a strong therapeutic alliance with the undocumented client. Identifying, acknowledging, and installing resources is one key to creating strong clinical engagement with a client who experiences himself as disenfranchised, marginalized, and discriminated against in society. As a result of being seen as strong, capable, and resilient in the therapeutic context, the client is restored to a more empowered version of himself. This, then, strengthens the client's trust in the therapeutic alliance, and creates the foundation for more positive treatment outcomes.

As a result of our clinical experiences, we believe that the preparation phase is a powerful means of building the therapeutic alliance with this population. It can also provide an inroad into the history taking process by beginning from a strengths-based orientation. In addition, many of the common questions in the history taking process can be threatening and/or disempowering for a client who is entering into a new relationship with an unfamiliar provider. The authority role and status of the EMDR provider in society places the undocumented client at a disadvantage. In order to honor the client's need to protect his or her undocumented status and various other details surrounding this information, we encourage clinicians to build a strong therapeutic alliance and install *Community Cultural Wealth Resources* (CCWR) (See Chapter 6, Phase 2) before attempting to gather sensitive history from the client. Thus, Phase 1 (history taking) and Phase 2 (preparation) run parallel to, and intertwine with, each other, with Phase 2 often taking the lead. However, for the sake of simplicity, we have chosen to present them in the order of the standard eight-phase protocol (Shapiro, 2001).

### Phase 1: History Taking

We assume the greatest confidence in our colleagues' ability to gather a general client history under typical circumstances. Here, we outline some nuances of this phase that are specific to working with undocumented clients.

In our experience, addressing the client's entry into the host country must be handled very delicately. Given the prevalent social climate of hostility toward undocumented immigrants, it is of particular importance that a therapist approach questions about the immigration narrative and border crossings with utmost compassion and respect. Maintaining a nuanced understanding of the relevant socio-political factors will allow us, as clinicians, to honor the clients' protective instincts,

---

[2] He and She: To reduce the awkward construction that results from using he/she, and because both authors are female, we have chosen to use the female pronoun in regard to clinicians, as needed. With respect to clients, we have chosen to use the masculine pronoun to distinguish client from therapist in narrative that does not contain a vignette.

as well as any hesitation, prevarication, and resistance to the inquiry. We have also noticed that asking a less direct question acts as a collaborative step toward increasing client safety and comfort in therapy.

Due to these special circumstances, we offer a few sample questions that we have successfully used with undocumented Latino clients. As always, we trust our therapist colleagues to use their clinical judgment regarding the timing and appropriateness of the questions for each individual case.

1. *If your high school teacher, Mrs. Roberts, who is White, asked about the border crossing, what might you say? And if your cousin, Julia, in Michoacan asked about the border crossing, how might you explain it? What is different about what you would say to each of them?*

   Although this is a long-winded way of asking the question, the intent is to acknowledge the reality that the client needs to present different versions of his or her story based on who asks the question. Therefore, instead of asking the client directly to speak about his or her experience of crossing the border, this format honors the ways in which the client has learned to read the environment. By incorporating the element of race as well as the more implicit element of social status within the question, the therapist acknowledges the intersection of race, class, and immigration and its importance in the client's experience. In addition, the therapist allows the client some freedom in how to answer the question, and respects that the client's resistance to answering the question may well serve a necessary protective function.

2. *If your cousin Tenoch said he was going to move to the United States, and your cousin Maria said so too, what fears or concerns would you have for each of them, especially based on their gender?*

   Incorporating gender as an important element acknowledges yet another facet of the client's reality. Furthermore, many female clients report both witnessing and experiencing sexual assault during their journey across borders. The relational framing of the question allows the clinician to acknowledge this specific vulnerability of female clients while allowing the client to choose how much or how little to reveal at this time in therapy.

3. *What is your first memory of being in this new country?*

   This relatively simple question often allows the therapist to gather the context around a client's entry into the host country. There are many possibilities for follow up based on the client's response, such as:

   *Tell me some other memories from that period in your life.*

   *What were some of the first clues that this was a different country/society?*

   *How do you feel when you hear the stories of other people's first memory of being in this country?*

4. *If you could have had the most ideal farewell party before you left, who would be there? What would they say to you and what would you say to them?*

   This question may aid in the identification of other targets for reprocessing, and it may also elicit familial capital or social capital resources (see Chapter 6, Phase 2) that can be installed during the preparation phase, or may be useful as a cognitive interweave during desensitization.

5. *If your best friend from back home asked you what you liked most and least about living in your new country, what would you say? Has this answer changed over the time that you have been here? How do you think this answer might change in 3 to 5 years?*

   Incorporating a friend into this scenario reduces the intrusiveness of the question. In addition, it invites a greater level of honesty than the client may feel comfortable in directly sharing with the clinician, especially if the client feels particularly disadvantaged by the racial–socioeconomic–educational gap between therapist and client. By allowing the client to reflect on how the answer may already have changed, or may change in the coming years, the practitioner acknowledges the client's ability to adapt, adjust, grow, and heal. Such questions can unearth valuable resources to develop and install during the Preparation phase.

6. *What kinds of sacrifices does a person need to be willing to make in order to leave his or her home country and make a new life in this country?*

   Asking the question in a very generic manner allows clients to choose how much of their own experience they wish to share. If a client is particularly hesitant to answer the question, it may be helpful for the therapist to offer examples of sacrifices that other clients may have made, such as loss of status, loss of home, experiencing racial discrimination, being separated from family, and others.

7. *If your young cousin asked you what skills he or she should develop in order to be successful in your new country, what would you say in reply?*

   Usually, clients answer this question in general, but this typically generates a dialog within which the therapist can reinforce the client for the skills that he or she has developed. Through this, the clinician can also uncover CCWR that the client may not have seen as valuable, but can be installed to empower the client. In addition, this question helps to reveal the client's aspirations as well as fears and concerns.

## Phase 2: Installation of CCWR in the Preparation Phase

Refugees and undocumented immigrants are typically seen as lacking in resources because they may be poor, illiterate or uneducated, lack English or other dominant language skills, and work in low-paid, undesirable occupations. Although many common forms of preparation can be used with these clients, including imaginary container, safe place exercise, light stream, and guided visualization, we have found the installation of CCWR to be an indispensable resource for this population. CCWR encompasses an impressive array of hidden knowledge, contacts, abilities, and tools that can be vital sources of empowerment for communities of color, immigrants, refugees, and other minority groups. We invite our colleagues to elicit and install multiple CCWR, such as aspirational, familial, social, cultural, navigational, and spiritual capital, using the resources in Chapter 6, Phase 2.

## Phase 3: Uncovering Oppressive Cognitions

During the Assessment phase with undocumented clients, we began to notice a subcategory of Negative Cognitions (NC) that were linked with social oppression.

Although NCs in this subcategory follow the typical criterion of being self-referential, they are applicable not just to the individual, but also to a specific minority group. While they focus on the presenting issue and are generalizable to other related events, these NCs are typically sociopolitically influenced and culturally reinforced in an ongoing and insidious manner by the dominant majority as well as the media. Thus, the desensitization and reprocessing of this type of NC requires a broadening of the therapeutic focus, and their successful resolution depends on an acknowledgment of the impacts that historic and ongoing social oppression have upon the presenting problem. We label such an NC as an *Oppressive Cognition (OC)*.

While NCs indicate pathology (Shapiro, 2001) and locate the problem within the client, OCs locate the problem within the client while colocating the problems in the context that have resulted in the creation and/or maintenance of the client's issues. While NCs represent inappropriate and objectively untrue negative beliefs (Shapiro, 2001), we hold that OCs represent inappropriate negative beliefs that are based in repeated social evaluations that lend the semblance of objectivity. While NCs are self-denigrating or self-limiting (Hensley, 2016), OCs take into account the role played by external circumstances in creating limitations for the individual and his cultural group. Thus, OCs can represent personal, irrational cognitions, while also highlighting external and internalized oppression. It is our belief that without eliciting, naming, addressing, and challenging the sociopolitical realities that present as OCs, a client's narrative is not contextualized. Further, we posit that with targets related to social oppression, the distinctive labeling of an OC builds the therapeutic alliance and expands the therapeutic scope of intervention, leading to trait change.

For example, an intelligent undocumented Latina student whose lack of English language skills leads her to believe "I am stupid" cannot easily shake off this irrational belief because it is being reinforced by a dominant value system that privileges English language skills above her linguistic and navigational capital. Viewed through an integrative framework, we delineate "I am stupid" as a sociopolitically influenced cognition in this scenario, where the primacy of English has rendered the client's capabilities invisible. When all information in her environment is provided in English, when she is repeatedly shamed in society for lacking English skills, and when she is verbally denigrated and told "All Mexicans are ignorant and should just go back to where they came from," these repeated and ongoing events serve to reinforce her negative beliefs. When the media, which purports to be objective, paints a biased picture of her and her heritage as "less than," it reinforces her belief that not only is she stupid, but that all people of her heritage are stupid and, therefore, most suited to low-paid undesirable jobs. Her self-limiting beliefs are further strengthened by the prevailing social culture of the dominant group which verbally denies, but continues to practice, institutional forms of racism through educational curricula, employment practices, incarceration, and economic discrimination (Perrin, 2013). Thus, it is not completely irrational for someone in her shoes to begin to question his or her own intelligence, even though this is a dysfunctional belief. Therefore, we label this NC as an OC.

When the client's voice is drowned out by the environment in which he lives, the attuned therapist must become an explorer, a discoverer, a tracker, and an ally in empowering the client to reclaim his voice. Thus, successful trauma treatment relies on the clinician's ability to address the social construction of reality as an element of the client's trauma. Even when the NC is due to internalized oppression, we name it as an OC in order to clearly delineate the sociopolitical realities within which that cognition originated and therefore to locate the problem in the context as well as the client.

We offer the following case study to further illustrate the concept of OCs, as well as our integrative approach to EMDR therapy as an antioppression endeavor.

## Case Study: Gabriela

Gabriela was referred by her school counselor for individual therapy. Her uncle Juan, with whom she was living, agreed to pay out of pocket for her to receive EMDR therapy and signed a release for the therapist to speak with the school counselor.

The school counselor described a depressed 14-year old whose attendance hovered at just under 50%, with a history of poor grades and social isolation at her school. Her uncle shook his head in despair, visibly emotional as he talked about his worry that Gabriela would not complete high school due to her depression. When asked about her family, he mentioned that her parents and older siblings worked as migrant farm workers, and had sent Gabriela to live with him so that she could have a stable education.

Although Gabriela was slow to warm up, she was quite vocal in many of her opinions. When asked what she would like to accomplish in therapy, she rolled her eyes and said:

> Cuál es el punto? Todo esto no tiene sentido. Mi tío sólo está desperdiciando su dinero. [What's the point? What is the point of anything? My uncle is wasting his money on this.]

Some of her statements in that first session were both critical and revealing, such as:

> I'm stupid, I hate history, English sucks and homework is a waste of time, so why keep going to school?
>
> I ain't like the others in my class. I don't belong.

Using James and Prilleltensky's integrative framework (2002), some helpful complementary considerations in this case study are highlighted as follows.

### Philosophical Considerations

Given the Latino value of familismo, Gabriela's distress may be related to her separation from her family, wherein she is being offered an easier situation than the back-breaking manual labor and harsh living conditions that her siblings and parents are subjected to. Gabriela may be having a hard time seeing herself as a good person, because she does not feel like a part of her familia and is not sharing their burden. It is likely that her depression, as well as her school avoidance, are related to her struggle to be a good person. The challenge truly lies in the fact that Gabriela is living between two cultures and each of them defines the values of a good person quite differently.

### Contextual Considerations

A culturally attuned review of standard educational curricula reveals that schools often socially reproduce forms of cultural oppression (see Freire, 2000). The prevailing educational curriculum that privileges White, middle-class values and ideas as the good, universal, or ideal not only disadvantages Gabriela, but also intensifies her distress at being wrong, immoral, illegal, and bad. Discrimination, marginalization, microaggressions, and othering, as well as pressures to acculturate to an often rejecting culture (Flores, 2013), are likely structural threats that are impacting Gabriela's well-being.

### Experiential Considerations

Experiential considerations usually relate to what might be missing or desirable in a living environment. This can often involve an exploration of the social context that identifies what is needed to improve the individual and community mental health. A major challenge within the educational and societal context is that English language learners are seen as lacking in "the basics." Thus, Gabriela might be missing an environment within which she can be seen as strong, resourceful, capable, and competent. Instead of being seen as deficient in English language skills, reinforcement for her bilingual, bicultural abilities (see linguistic capital and navigational capital in Chapter 6, Phase 2) would dramatically alter her experience of herself.

### Pragmatic Considerations

Pragmatic considerations in this case include a plan for Gabriela's future that goes beyond therapy. Through collaborative acknowledgment of this integrated perspective of her situation, Gabriela may feel empowered to join a group of activists campaigning for the rights of the undocumented. Another desirable outcome of the pragmatic considerations relates to therapists as agents of social change. Seeing the human face of undocumented immigrants might motivate therapists to act in ways that increase the social awareness of challenges faced by this community. This may also facilitate greater community engagement in finding more equitable solutions.

Due to space limitations, certain facets of the standard protocol have been emphasized in order to exemplify this integrative approach, as well as the uniqueness of this population. However, each client must be treated as an individual, and each treatment plan needs to be evaluated within its relevant biopsychosocial ecology.

### Phase 1: History Taking

With Gabriela, the therapist explored her familial context, immigration history, and other background information throughout the course of their work together.

The therapist was deliberate in emphasizing the strengths and resilience, which were evident in Gabriela as an individual, in her family, and in her culture.

### Phase 2: Preparation

Beginning with the very first session, the therapist's goal was to empower Gabriela through identifying and installing CCWR, beginning with her aspirational capital.

*Identifying Aspirational Capital*

The therapist asked Gabriela about her dreams for herself, and her family's dreams for her. When she spoke about her mother wanting to see her graduate from college, Gabriela's eyes misted over. Making note of this, the therapist asked Gabriela whether this was one of her goals as well.

**Gabriela:** "I'm undocumented. I won't be going to college, because I don't have papers. So what's the point of even going to high school right now?"

**Therapist:** *What emotions do you feel when you imagine your mother witnessing you in your graduation gown and cap?*

**Gabriela:** "I feel so proud that I have made my mother's dream come true. I feel my mother's pride in my accomplishment, and I feel my pride in mother and father for working so hard and never giving up."

**Therapist:** *Would you like to hold onto that feeling of pride in your parents for working so hard and never giving up?*

Gabriela's face lit up as she smiled while nodding her head vigorously.

**Therapist:** *While this graduation is not happening in this moment, and we don't know if and when it will happen, the pride that you feel in your parents for working so hard is very real, and certainly worth holding onto.*

The therapist then assisted her in vivifying this picture, as well as the accompanying emotions and sensations, so that it could be installed as a positive resource.

Gabriela was able to use this as a resource in session, and to test it with a mild disturbance, such as her uncle calling her lazy when she didn't get up on time. In addition, this resource was matched with a cuing word, "Orgullo" (pride).

### Target Selection

Next, the therapist decided to focus on Gabriela's belief about the reason she was in therapy. She willingly acknowledged that her refusal to attend school and low attendance was related to several factors, stated in the following list in her words:

1. I have poor grades.
2. My English teacher hates me.

3. My history teacher is an idiot.
4. I don't belong in this school.
5. What's the point of going to school?
6. I have no future.

Some of the early work with Gabriela involved addressing the personal NCs that had led to the depression, while also tracking the OCs that often coexist.

## Initial Target: Why Go to School When I'm Stupid?

Gabriela acknowledged that she felt unmotivated to attend school because of her failing grades in English and history. While assessing this target, the therapist concluded that her negative belief of "I am stupid" was actually an OC because of its context. The public school educational curriculum in the United States was designed with White students in mind, and disadvantages many students of color (Delgado Bernal, 1998). The historic devaluation of non-English-speaking immigrants as having lower IQs and the social constructs that perpetuate low self-esteem for Latino students are additional factors influencing Gabriela's self-limiting belief. Gabriela clearly did not believe herself to be stupid, but felt this way because of the grades she was receiving, the school environment, and ongoing negative evaluations of the Latino community in the media. By acknowledging the context, the therapist recognizes that the problem is co-located outside of the client and labels this as an OC.

OC: I am stupid.

Through reprocessing, Gabriela arrived at the statement:

> I am intelligent, even if I am not good at English and history.

While some EMDR therapists might see this as a Positive Cognition (PC), the culturally attuned therapist saw this as incomplete processing. The fact that Gabriela was still linking her intelligence to the educational curriculum reflected the ways in which the dominant culture of education and society was preventing her from being able to see herself as intelligent, smart, or intellectually capable.

The goal in therapy was to acknowledge and challenge the dominant cultural context and values that were rendering Gabriela's own innate cultural capital and cultural knowledge both invisible and worthless. The therapist recognized that the educational tasks on which Gabriela was not performing well were not created with communities of color in mind. The therapist hoped that Gabriela too would ultimately come to this understanding.

**Therapist:** *Gabriela, how many languages do you speak and how many languages do your classmates and teachers speak?*

**Gabriela:** "They speak only English, but their English is good, and mine is broken."

**Therapist:** *Is your English good enough to attend school? How would your teacher or your classmates cope if they had to move to Mexico?*

This simple interweave elucidated the dominant ideology inherent in Gabriela's negative self-evaluation. Gabriela spoke two languages, as opposed to the English-only environment prevalent at her school. Instead of being lauded for her bilingual abilities, she found herself in an environment that solely valued the language in which she was weaker and completely devalued her primary language.

Having this reality named and acknowledged in the therapeutic context allowed Gabriela to access a range of experiences in which she saw herself as valuable because she spoke two languages, and had successfully navigated two cultures.

Despite good progress, the work of challenging the dominant ideology through raising Gabriela's critical consciousness (Freire, 2000) was not yet done. Next, the therapist decided to address the OC of "I am stupid" and its link to the history class.

The therapist proceeded by asking Gabriela about the topics covered in the history class this semester. The goal was to highlight the cognitive dissonance experienced by People of Color when history is presented solely from the perspective of the victor or the colonialists. Gabriela was able to highlight the cognitive dissonance she experienced when she heard statements from her teacher, such as:

> The Aztecs were uncivilized people who murdered babies in the name of human sacrifice to their gods.

and

> The colonialists brought culture and civilization to the natives.

Gabriela's eyes widened as she said: "I stopped going to history class because I always felt angry afterwards, so I figured it was stupid to sit there and get angry. Now, I realize that any Latina would be angry about how history is presented in the classroom."

As they continued reprocessing, she began to integrate this information, and arrived at:

> I get poor grades in history, because I don't attend class. I don't attend class because it makes me angry. Latinos are characterized as weak, inferior, and less-than in the history books, and it makes me feel weak, inferior, and less-than.

She was able to access a new PC.

PC: I am more than my history grades.

At this point, Gabriela's depression began to lift, but she still did not want to attend school.

## Target: My English Teacher Hates Me

Initial NC: I am worthless.

During the floatback, Gabriela landed on some incidents from early childhood when she was rejected by her cousins. She was able to reprocess those incidents, and see herself as worthy in those situations.

Asked to identify targets related to her English teacher, Gabriela pointed to two instances in which she felt shamed and confused by her teacher.

Incident A: "When the teacher said to the class, 'In my class, we only speak English. We are not in your village.'

Incident B: Another time when the teacher said: "For the potluck, please bring American food. Please do not bring something that I cannot pronounce."

These incidents were linked to several other distressing memories of times when she had experienced microaggressions in the United States. Many of the microaggressions experienced by clients usually generated the NC: I don't belong. Based on the social climate and structural racism, we do not see this as an irrational cognition for People of Color in the United States. Thus, we label this as an OC.

OC: I don't belong.

During the early phase in therapy, it is helpful for a culturally attuned therapist to introduce the topic of race as well as any relevant immigration history, thus placing race and immigration squarely in the therapeutic arena. Through similar discussions, Gabriela was able to see her own experience through a broader lens. She began to understand that her sense of not belonging at the school was part of a larger narrative: the Latino experience in the United States. Through an exploration of her minority experience within a largely White student body, with no visible presence of Latino/as, except for janitorial staff, she could see how her sense of not belonging was a systemic issue, and not a personal one. This led to the emergence of a PC.

PC: I am carving a unique place for myself in a society that is still learning to value people like me.

## Target: School Refusal and Anger

At this point in therapy, Gabriela became very engaged and spent a lot of time at the library reading, but would become angry if her uncle even mentioned school. Her attendance was now at a historic low. In accordance with an understanding of CCWR, the therapist saw this as indicative of Gabriela exploring her own agency through resistance. So during sessions, the therapist added a theoretical frame within which self-defeating resistance could be distinguished from transformative resistance (Solorzano & Bernal, 2001). The therapist explained to Gabriela that the act of not attending school or not performing her student role could be either form of resistance, depending on how she engaged with it. Gabriela proceeded to research the topic of resistance and started viewing her own process from a standpoint of curiosity, rather than shame and judgment.

Gabriela spent the next session fantasizing about picking fights with her classmates, mocking her teachers, and even throwing a hand grenade through the window of the principal's office. She identified the following NC.

NC: I am bad.

What emerged through this piece of work was the root of her sadness, depression, anger, and frustration. Gabriela was struggling against the marginalization of her family and her culture. She felt like a bad person for having an easier life than others in her family and for being in school, while her parents and siblings continued to struggle as migrant farm workers. At the same time, she saw that she didn't have it easy at school and was constantly feeling "othered."

As the therapist desensitized her anger in session, Gabriela saw her refusal to attend school in a different light:

> I'd rather be out there making money than sitting in some stupid classroom trying to become White.

As the weeks went by, Gabriela began to attend school and when asked about this change reported:

> If I don't show up, how can I speak up when they get it wrong? And it makes me happy to point out when my history teacher is getting it wrong.

Gabriela benefited from the acknowledgment of her various complementary considerations, including the difference in values between school and home, language-bias in the system, historic devaluation of Latinos, and Latino history, as well as the challenges of being othered at school. She was able to transform her self-defeating resistance of school refusal into a motivation to speak up in class, thereby challenging the structural norms that privilege White values.

She came to her last session smiling:

> **Gabriela:** "I used to avoid school because I felt stuck. But really, it was the school that was stuck in a White groove that made it so hard for me to just be me. In my sadness, anger, confusion, and frustration, my behavior was feeding the negative stereotype that immigrants are ungrateful and don't work hard to take advantage of the opportunities offered to them. But now that I know that the problem isn't me, I know that I will never stop speaking up for the rights of people like me. This is why I'm going to school, and I will find a way to keep getting an education, so that I can be the voice for my family and others like me."

PC: I am proud to be a Latina and I have the power to speak out against injustice.

Due to space limitations, only the critical parts of this case which exemplify OCs have been highlighted.

## Targets That Generate Oppressive Cognition

Although this list is far from comprehensive, we believe it is important to highlight a few targets that relate to the social challenges faced by undocumented immigrants. These are usually not the presenting problems that bring clients into treatment. However, we believe that treatment is often unsuccessful or incomplete, when it fails to unearth and address some of these targets that relate to social oppression. It is important to be mindful of the OCs that lie hidden in these and other targets.

1. Microaggressions
2. Housing or employment discrimination
3. Colorblindness and meritocracy, wherein discrimination or structural racism might be veiled by a statement such as "There is equal opportunity for anyone who works hard."
4. Supremacy of English
5. Accent-based discrimination
6. Issues related to skin color
7. Feeling torn between two cultures
8. Issues around those who have been left behind, both geographically and metaphorically
9. Immigration narrative and immigration trauma
10. Conflicting loyalties in mixed status families where only some members are documented.

## SUMMARY

This chapter focuses on the use of an integrative approach to working with undocumented Latino clients in the United States. However, we see this framework as having benefits for immigrant communities and many other marginalized populations around the world. We believe that the naming and acknowledgment of systemic oppression allows EMDR therapy to become a powerful instrument of both individual and community healing. It is also our belief that each individual enacts transformative resistance in the manner that is unique to and appropriate for his or her situation. Therefore, therapy fails to meet its full potential when it does not sufficiently empower the client to challenge injustice and sociopolitical inequalities. It is the therapist's understanding of the sociopolitical and cultural realities within which therapy exists that allows EMDR therapy to become an agent of social change. By addressing oppression that is external to the client, practitioners can continue to effect change in ever widening circles around us. We thank you for joining us on this journey to make EMDR therapy an antioppression endeavor.

We end this chapter by emphasizing, once again, the greatest rewards of our work with undocumented clients: the gift of vicarious resilience. Vicarious resilience (Hernandez, Gangsei, & Engstrom, 2007) reveals the mutuality in the therapeutic relationship by focusing on the positive transformation in the therapist's inner experience through empathic engagement with the client's traumatic material. We have found ourselves buoyed by the hope, determination, courage, and tenacity of our undocumented clients. Through our shared histories of being "othered," we have arrived at a new sense of belonging. And from bearing witness to their healing from oppression, we have made meaning of our own experiences as immigrant Women of Color in the United States of America.

## REFERENCES


Arbona, C., Olvera, N., Rodriguez, N., Hagan, J., Linares, A., & Wiesner, M. (2010). Acculturative stress among documented and undocumented Latino immigrants in the United States. *Hispanic Journal of Behavioral Sciences, 32*(3), 362–384.

Arredondo, P. (1999). Multicultural counseling competencies as tools to address oppression and racism. *Journal of Counseling and Development, 77*(1), 102.

Buriel, R. (1993). Childrearing orientations in Mexican American families: The influence of generation and sociocultural factors. *Journal of Marriage and Family, 55*(4), 987–1000.

Cervantes, J. M., Mejía, O. L., & Guerrero Mena, A. (2010). Serial migration and the assessment of extreme and unusual psychological hardship with undocumented Latina/o families. *Hispanic Journal of Behavioral Sciences, 32*(2), 275–291.

Delgado Bernal, D. (1998). Using a Chicana feminist epistemology in educational research. *Harvard Educational Review [H.W. Wilson—EDUC], 68*(4), 555.

Falicov, C. J. (1998). *Latino families in therapy: A guide to multicultural practice*. New York, NY: Guilford Press.

Flores, Y. G. (2013). *Chicana and Chicano mental health: Alma, Mente, Y Corazón*. Tucson, AZ: University of Arizona Press.

Freire, P. (2000). *Pedagogy of the oppressed*. New York, NY: Continuum.

Furman, R., Ackerman, A. R., Loya, M., Jones, S., & Negi, N. (2012). The criminalization of immigration: Value conflicts for the social work profession. *Journal of Sociology and Social Welfare, 39*(1), 169–185.

Gomberg-Munoz, R. (2012). Inequality in a "Postracial" era: Race, immigration, and criminalization of low wage labor. *Du Bois Review, 9*(2), 339–353.

González, G. G., & Fernandez, R. (2002). Empire and the origins of twentieth-century migration from Mexico to the United States. *Pacific Historical Review, 71*(1), 19–57.

Harwood, R., Leyendecker, B., Carlson, V., Asencio, M., & Miller, A. (2002). Parenting among Latino families. In M. H. Bornstein (Ed.), *Handbook of parenting: Social conditions and applied parenting* (Vol. 4, pp. 21–46). Mahwah, NJ: Lawrence Erlbaum Associates.

Hensley, B. (2016). *An EMDR therapy primer from practicum to practice* (2nd ed.). New York, NY: Springer Publishing Company.

Hernandez, P., Gangsei, D., & Engstrom, D. (2007). Vicarious resilience: A new concept in work with those who survive trauma. *Family Process, 46*(2), 229–241.

IRS. (2014). Immigration terms and definitions involving aliens. Retrieved from https://www.irs.gov/individuals/international-taxpayers/immigration-terms-and-definitions-involving-aliens

James, S., & Prilleltensky, I. (2002). Cultural diversity and mental health. *Clinical Psychology Review, 22*(8), 1133–1154.

Lakoff, G., & Ferguson, S. (2006). The framing of immigrants. Retrieved from http://www.cognitivepolicyworks.com/resource-center/rethinking-immigration/the-framing-of-immigration

Malott, K. M., & Schaefle, S. (2015). Addressing clients' experiences of racism: A model for clinical practice. *Journal of Counseling & Development, 93*(3), 361–369.

Passel, J. S., & Cohn, D. (2014). Unauthorized immigrant totals rise in 7 states, fall in 14. Retrieved from http://www.pewhispanic.org/2014/11/18/unauthorized-immigrant-totals-rise-in-7-states-fall-in-14

Perreira, K. M., Chapman, M. V., & Stein G. L. (2006). Becoming an American parent: Overcoming challenges and finding strength in a new immigrant Latino community. *Journal of Family Issues [H.W. Wilson—SSA], 27*(10), 1383.

Perrin, P. (2013). Humanistic psychology's social justice philosophy: Systemically treating the psychosocial and health effects of racism. *Journal of Humanistic Psychology, 53*(1), 52–69.

Romero, M. (2008). Crossing the immigration and race border: A critical race theory approach to immigration studies. *Contemporary Justice Review, 11*(1), 23–37.

Shapiro, F. (2001). *Eye movement desensitization and reprocessing: Basic principles, protocols, and procedures* (2nd ed.). New York, NY: Guilford Press.

Solorzano, D. G., & Bernal, D. D. (2001). Examining transformational resistance through a critical race and latcrit theory framework: Chicana and Chicano students in an urban context. *Urban Education, 36*(3), 308–342.

Thompson, C. E., & Neville, H. A. (1999). Racism, mental health, and mental health practice. *The Counseling Psychologist, 27*(2), 155–223.

United Nations Department of Economic and Social Affairs. Population Division. (2014). International migration 2013: Migrants by origin and destination (No. 2013/3 Rev.1). Retrieved from http://esa.un.org/unmigration/documents/PF_South-South_migration_2013.pdf

U.S. Citizenship and Immigration Services. (2015). Glossary. USCIS. Retrieved from http://www.uscis.gov/tools/glossary

U.S. Customs and Border Protection. (2014). Reporting illegal activity. Retrieved from https://help.cbp.gov/app/answers/detail/a_id/735/~/reporting-illegal-activity

CHAPTER 6

# Placing Culture at the Heart of EMDR Therapy

Rajani Venkatraman Levis

## PLACING CULTURE AT THE HEART OF EMDR THERAPY

*If we are to achieve a richer culture, rich in contrasting values, we must recognize the whole gamut of human potentialities, and so weave a less arbitrary social fabric, one in which each diverse human gift will find a fitting place.*

—Margaret Mead, anthropologist

The emergence of eye movement desensitization and reprocessing (EMDR) therapy as the premier treatment for posttraumatic stress disorder (PTSD) has been accompanied by a recognition of the healing role played by the relationship between EMDR therapist and client (Dworkin, 2005; Marich, 2009; Shapiro, 2001). In her 2012 client-centered exploration of what makes a good EMDR therapist, Marich highlighted the importance of empowering clients while Silver and Rogers (2002) recognized the need for therapist self-awareness. This chapter offers a culturally attuned approach to the therapeutic alliance and therapist self-awareness by placing culture at the heart of EMDR therapy. Such a practice facilitates healing through the integration of the five intermingling cultures identified by Vontress (1988)—universal culture, ecological culture, national culture, regional culture, and racioethnic culture. It further acknowledges that all aspects of counseling, including the relationship, diagnosis, treatment plan, and the intervention strategy, are influenced by the culture of both the therapist and client (Vontress, 2012, p. 9). In addition, it mitigates the risk of epistemic violence, or the therapist's insistence on imposing a different worldview on the client, by acknowledging the impact of the therapist's own socialization and values.

This culturally attuned practice of EMDR therapy embraces the historical and current realities of clients from culturally diverse backgrounds. It takes into account the trauma experienced by minority groups, defined by Corey, Corey, Callanan, & Corey (1988) as people who have been discriminated against or subject to unequal treatment. It does so by embracing the distinct cultural, subcultural, racioethnic, sociopolitical, and economic environments within which each client has been socialized. While revealing hidden targets related to social oppression and historical trauma, it simultaneously uncovers invisible and undervalued forms of cultural wealth. Thus, it offers an expansive scope of healing by exposing deeper layers of trauma as well as the culturally congruent means of healing such wounds. Such a culturally attuned practice of EMDR therapy broadens the therapeutic lens as well as the possibilities for healing by using an integrative framework to place culture at the heart of therapy.

## PRESENTING AN INTEGRATIVE FRAMEWORK

James and Prilleltensky's (2002) framework provides a valuable integrative approach to mental health by honoring the culture and dignity of clients from diverse cultural backgrounds. This framework extends beyond the individual to include a cultural awareness of needs, norms, context, values, and social change. Comprised of four complementary considerations—*philosophical, contextual, experiential,* and *pragmatic*—it merges considerations like politics, philosophy, religion, and anthropology with social, moral, and cultural domains (James & Prilleltensky, 2002). Thus, it supports the practitioner in providing culturally attuned and effective services with increased awareness of her[1] own cultural values and biases, as well as the client's worldview (Malott & Schaefle, 2015). The application of these four vital considerations can provide a more holistic understanding of the role of culture within the therapeutic arena.

### Philosophical Considerations

James and Prilleltensky (2002) noted that each culture has a different set of social values, which shape the vision of the good person, the good life, and the good society. Philosophical considerations reveal that liberal societies emphasize autonomy and the rights of the individual, whereas collectivist societies emphasize the benefit of the greater good. Therefore, approaching clients from a collectivist culture in terms of self-interest, self-advocacy, or a purely internal locus of control may fit with a Western psychotherapy model, but lacks the necessary consideration of moral obligations and commitments linked with culturally congruent values. For example, many individuals in the West consider honesty to be a universal value. However, their understanding of honesty may be limited to the notion of truthfulness and, therefore, a refusal to lie, steal, or deceive in any way. In collectivist cultures, however, honesty may be better understood in terms of integrity or the adherence to a code of moral values that requires attending to fairness and honor first. In the latter culture, a man who does not have the means to pay for the drug that will save his mother's life might make a conscious decision to steal it, while being in full integrity with his code of moral values, wherein family must be valued above all else. As a philosophical consideration, the therapist's ability to identify her own values as only a possible set of values, but not as universal, is an important precursor to culturally attuned EMDR therapy.

[1] Her: To reduce the awkward construction that results from using he or she, and because the author is female, the feminine pronoun has been used in referring to clinicians. For clarity, in narrative that does not contain a vignette, the masculine pronoun has been used with respect to clients.

## Contextual Considerations

James and Prilleltensky (2002) identified contextual considerations as the actual state of affairs in which people live. A contextual assessment identifies the social norms and cultural influences on people's choices and behaviors, as well as how this might affect their mental well-being. Cultural influences include the effects of historical trauma such as genocide, forced relocation, and internment camps. Duran (2006) emphasized that a culturally congruent therapist must be aware of oppression that has its roots in the colonization process, whereas Helms, Nicolas, and Green (2012) identified racism and ethnoviolence as forms of trauma. Ivey (2006) identified migration and immigration as trauma and Vontress (2012, p. 67) categorized the types of problems faced by immigrants into three groups: preimmigration problems, cultural anxiety, and postadjustment problems.

Other contextual considerations include the issue of universalism, or the presumption that psychotherapy theories are equally applicable to other cultures. Given that symptom expression is socially and culturally influenced, diagnostic categories are also socially constructed and may not apply outside of the practitioner's culture (Watters, 2010). Thus, James and Prilleltensky (2002) encouraged practitioners to identify historic and prevailing sociopolitical conditions, as well as the applicable cultural, religious, and moral norms.

By establishing the intersectionality and positionality of therapist and client, the complex interplay of race, ethnicity, culture, gender, sexualities, immigration, age, and other factors becomes centrally located in EMDR therapy. Thus, both parties are able to explore how this interplay contributes to the construction of mental health as well as disease and distress.

## Experiential Considerations

The experiential component of the integrative approach focuses on identifying wants, needs, and aspirations based on lived experience (James & Prilleltensky, 2002). This allows therapists to work toward the changes in each social context that would improve the mental health of the communities in which they work. This component may include actual, ideal, and desirable states of affairs as well as ways to affirm the dignity of each client.

A review of the literature reveals a wealth of hidden resources possessed by immigrant clients, including the aspirations that guide them (Delgado Bernal, 1998; Huber, 2009; Yosso, 2005). These valuable but often invisible resources, such as spiritual capital and navigational capital (see Phase 2: Preparation Phase), highlight the experiential dimensions of many minority groups. Other repeated themes echoed by clients from minority groups reveal the presence of widespread structural racism, heterosexism, discrimination, and microaggressions that have a negative impact on their physical, emotional, and mental health. An understanding of such experiential considerations allows psychotherapy to support healing in multiple domains by broadening the focus beyond the therapy room and from the individual to the community.

## Pragmatic Considerations

A thoughtful consideration of pragmatics seeks to bridge the gap between the actual state of affairs on the one hand, and desirable, ideal visions on the other hand. This allows both therapist and client to focus on therapeutic and social goals that can be realistically accomplished (James & Prilleltensky, 2002). Improvement of community mental health through social action and social intervention is a desired outcome of pragmatic thinking (Prilleltensky & Nelson, 1997).

One simple pragmatic goal for practitioners is to acknowledge the degree to which Western psychotherapeutic modalities are culture bound. By recognizing and addressing this, practitioners give appropriate consideration to how power is embedded in and conveyed through the therapeutic relationship. Thus, they become more transparent about the authority role of the EMDR therapist, as well as how the therapist is influenced by her own sociopolitical cultural system with its own set of values.

Viewed through this integrative framework, therapy may be yet another arena in which social hierarchy is reinforced. The average EMDR therapist in the Western World is White, educated, able-bodied, and upwardly mobile. This places clients from many minority groups in a challenging situation where the verbal adherence to neutrality begins to render the therapist's racial, social, class, gender, and other privileges invisible, thereby reinforcing White, middle-class cultural and social norms. Even Therapists of Color[2] have found this to be true, as their assimilation into Western cultural norms and the Western practice of psychotherapy places them in a privileged position, thus reproducing social inequalities. In spite of these challenges, the therapist's own awareness of her position, culture, and values will allow her to be more effective in building a strong therapeutic alliance with a client from the minority group.

Acknowledging the stigma experienced by individuals with limited English proficiency is another example of a pragmatic consideration for English-speaking therapists in the United States. In this situation, naming the historical devaluation of Spanish and other heritage languages, as well as the challenges posed to nonnative English speakers, is a step in the direction of equal access for all. Addressing the English-only bias in the U.S. educational curriculum is an example of a social action that would serve to improve the collective morale and mental health of both Native and immigrant communities.

Pertaining to the EMDR community, training more Spanish speakers to provide EMDR therapy in the United States is one pragmatic goal. Motivating more EMDR therapists to become competent clinicians cross culturally is another goal that will have far-reaching benefits for community mental health. The use of cross-cultural team approaches with an emphasis on community-based interventions allows practitioners to mold their interventions in a more culturally sensitive manner.

---

[2] Color: The intentional capitalization, which rejects the grammatical norm, represents a grammatical move toward social and racial justice through empowering this group and their resources. This rule also applies to "Communities of Color," "CCWR," and "Students of Color" throughout this chapter.

## Phase 2: Installation of Community Cultural Wealth Resources in the Preparation Phase

This section identifies a culturally sensitive framework for increasing client resilience as well as strengthening the therapeutic alliance by building upon Yosso's (2005) concept of community cultural wealth. Yosso (2005) defined *cultural wealth* as "an array of knowledge, skills, abilities and contacts possessed and utilized by Communities of Color to survive and resist macro- and micro-forms of oppressions" (p. 77). She described six forms of capital originating within Communities of Color—*aspirational, linguistic, familial, social, navigational,* and *resistant capital*—that comprise community cultural wealth and may often go unacknowledged or unrecognized. Huber (2009) added *spiritual capital* as an additional form of capital that emerged from her research. Earlier on, Delgado Bernal (1998) introduced the concept of *cultural intuition*, which highlighted that members of marginalized groups may have a unique sensitivity, perspective, and ability to interpret information based on their experiences. This is yet another hidden resource that needs to be named, acknowledged, and developed during the Preparation phase. Yosso (2005) wrote that these forms of resources are not mutually exclusive or static, but that they often build upon each other in dynamic processes. Since these assets may be entirely invisible from the perspective of the dominant majority, they may also have lost their importance and/or availability for an oppressed client.

While the original concept of community cultural wealth referenced Students of Color in institutions of higher education, this chapter expands on those terms. It proposes the umbrella term of *Community Cultural Wealth Resources (CCWR)* as an important resource for minority groups. CCWR have the potential to transform the process of EMDR therapy for the clients whose voices are in the margins. The acknowledgment and installation of the client's invisible and undervalued resources restores the client to a more empowered version of himself. This, in turn strengthens the therapeutic alliance, creating a healthy foundation for the desensitization and reprocessing of trauma.

By placing culture at the heart of EMDR therapy, clients feel empowered to teach us what we need to know in order to be the best therapists for them. In alignment with the proposed integrative framework, a clinician can empower clients by owning her own expertise in EMDR therapy, but consistently highlighting that the client's CCWR hold unique and important therapeutic insights as shown in the following text.

### Community Cultural Wealth Resources

#### *Aspirational Capital*

Yosso (2005) defined *aspirational capital* as the resiliency that allows clients to maintain hopes and dreams for themselves and their children, even when faced with both real and perceived barriers. This is evidenced by many immigrant communities, including Chicanos in the United States, who demonstrate the ability to maintain consistently high aspirations for the future, even in the absence of objective means to achieve those goals. In addition, a family's migration experiences are a form of cultural knowledge that helps many clients to feel connected to the aspirational capital of the family. The following example demonstrates the use of aspirational capital in EMDR therapy.

> *Maria, 49, a recent immigrant, was referred to therapy as a victim of gang violence. During the Preparation phase, the therapist elicited Maria's aspirational capital—the hopes and dreams that led her to the United States—by asking questions such as:*
> *What made you decide to come to the United States?*
> *and*
> *What did you hope that your children might be able to accomplish by coming here?*
> *Thus, the therapist highlighted Maria's dreams for her childrens' future that allowed her to face so many challenges thus far. Her resilience, as well as the belief that each of her children could have a better life, was then installed as a positive resource. This also strengthened the therapeutic alliance by reinforcing Maria's experience of her therapist's attunement and hope.*

Some questions that may be helpful in revealing aspirational capital, depending on the cultural specifics of the client, include:

- During the hardest times before this, how did you keep going? What made you so determined to survive such difficult circumstances?
- Who, other than you, benefits from your being in this country/being out/being courageous/being alive?
- Who relies on your presence or your income for support?
- Are there other people whose dreams depend on your continuing to walk this path or for whom you are a role model?

Expanding the concept of aspirational capital as a valuable resource for other marginalized communities, we can modify these questions for individuals with disabilities and older adults, among others. For LGBTQQ[3] clients, a culturally attuned intake practice may include asking for both legal name as well as preferred name. The clinician's acknowledgment of his or her chosen name places the client's cultural context at the heart of therapy, as do the aspirations that led to the choosing of this preferred name. In the case of immigrants, the honoring of the client's name in his or her own language, as well as the client's adopted Western name (when there is one), is an opportunity to identify hidden targets related to colonization and oppression, while also highlighting the aspirational capital related to given and chosen names.

### *Linguistic Capital*

Yosso (2005) identified linguistic capital as the intellectual and social skills attained through communication experiences in more than one language, style, or context. It can also describe a variety of skills related to language and communication that go beyond speech and the written word. The ability to communicate through

---

[3] LGBTQQ: This umbrella term includes lesbian, gay, bisexual, transgender, queer, and questioning individuals, although some may prefer other terms or no labels at all.

sign language, dramatic pauses, oral storytelling traditions, visual art, music, and poetry are other aspects of linguistic capital that may not be readily apparent to monolingual English speakers. The skills of culture-specific communication, including unique phonemes, tonal languages, gestures, gendered speech, and honorific speech, are other examples of linguistic capital. The use of memorization, math skills, and street smarts are important forms of linguistic capital that may even be demonstrated by clients who are functionally illiterate or underperform in the academic setting. Clients need to be acknowledged and validated for their ability to use such varied resources in order to navigate complex social and cultural situations.

> *Binh is a 10-year-old boy who often misses school. His school counselor is worried that he will not graduate from elementary school because he has missed too many days. When asked about his frequent absences, Binh mentions that he is the only one in his family who can speak English and is therefore needed as a translator. He has a younger brother with a neurological disorder and Binh has often missed school, in order to accompany his brother to the pediatrician, specialist doctors, and occupational therapist. Since none of these specialists speak Vietnamese, Binh is the only one who can help his family to access these services.*

A therapist who highlights Binh's poor attendance but fails to acknowledge his linguistic capital unwittingly emphasizes the dominant narrative that Binh is not benefiting from the education offered by the school. In a more culturally aware environment, instead of assuming that the current form of school-based learning is superior to all other forms of educational and cultural capital, equal emphasis would be placed on acknowledging and rewarding the ways in which Binh navigates an adult system, while acting as a translator of both culture and language. Reinforcing a client's cross-cultural awareness, metalinguistic awareness, "real-world" literacy skills or street-smarts, and social maturity are ways in which a therapist can acknowledge and reinforce the linguistic capital that a client may not have recognized as a key survival strength. For example:

> *Jimena, who was a teacher in her village but now has to work as a housekeeper in her new country, has learned how to modulate her facial affect, vocal tone, and volume. She knows that speaking in the same authoritative tone of a teacher will not please her domestic employers and she has made the requisite adaptation, almost seamlessly. During the course of therapy Jimena begins to see this adaptation as her linguistic capital, rather than as a complete devaluation of her self-worth. By internalizing it as a strength, she finds a way to move past the shame about her loss in status from teacher to domestic help.*

LGBTQQ clients often reveal a specialized understanding of the gendered nature of speech, language, and communication patterns. These can be installed as forms of linguistic capital, navigational capital, and resistant capital.

### *Familial Capital*

Yosso (2005) stated that family capital refers to cultural knowledge nurtured among extended family networks and "engages a commitment to community well-being and expands the concept of family to include a more broad understanding of kinship."

A therapist may conceptualize that a client who is geographically separated from his family, sometimes with scant hope of reunification, is an isolated individual. Despite the distance, many clients benefit from the therapist's acknowledgment of extended family networks that include immediate and extended family as well as friends, some of whom may have long passed on, as a vital and ever-present internal and external resource for some clients. For example, in the Latino culture, *madrinas* (godmother to the child) and *comadres* (the bond between biological mother and godmother) are often an important part of *la familia*, but because they are not blood relatives and seldom appear on a genogram, the practitioner might miss the opportunity to develop and install these valued resources during the Preparation phase.

> *Luna, a victim of domestic violence, was seen at the local domestic violence shelter for individual and group therapy. She reported a decrease in her feeling of isolation once she began to communicate with her familia through video chat technology. During the Preparation phase, the therapist created a family tableau, where she could visualize a scene with her whole family, relatives, alive and dead, all standing in a green meadow under a blue sky and smiling at her. This resource emphasized her aspiration and familial capital, and was often accessed by her as an anchor during reprocessing.*

Here are a few possible questions that might elicit a more inclusive picture of the client's *familia*.

- Whom are you supporting through being here in the United States?
- Who cares about you and misses you?
- When your *familia* would gather for happy occasions, who are some of the people you always looked forward to spending time with?
- We learn different things from different people. From whom did you learn lessons about love and friendship? Travel and adventure? Family values? Education? Faith and religion?
- Who in your *familia* would be proud that you are making a life for yourself in this country?
- Who in your *familia* inspired you to come to this country?
- If you could magically bring one person from your *familia* to be here with you right now, who would that be?

Despite the significance of family in many cases, it is always of relevance to note the exceptions. Some clients may not be able to count on their familial capital and may be estranged from their families, or may need support in creating strong boundaries from their family. Alternatively, some individuals receive support from their family-of-choice, which can also be installed as a valuable resource that represents both familial capital as well as social capital.

### *Social Capital*

Yosso's (2005) concept of social capital includes the networks of social contacts and community resources that provide instrumental and emotional support.

It references an individual's ability to resolve crucial personal issues by tapping into social networks. Social capital can serve a bonding function, which "helps people get by," or a bridging function, which "helps people get ahead" (Putnam, 2000). Thus, bonding capital supports individuals and helps them to cope, while bridging capital acts as leverage and helps people solve problems in order to get ahead (Briggs, 1998; Irwin, LaGory, Ritchey, & Fitzpatrick, 2008).

Churches, synagogues, mosques, gurdwaras, and places of worship provide spiritual as well as social support for many immigrant families, regardless of documented status. Religious traditions such as *bar* or *bat mitzvah* (Jewish coming of age tradition) or *Khatam Al Quran* (a Malaysian Muslim tradition for 11-year-old girls) augment bonding social capital, as well as familial capital and spiritual capital. Family gatherings and celebrations such as *quinceañeras* (the celebration of a girl's 15th birthday, which marks the transition from childhood to womanhood in Latino culture) or *Seijin-no-hi* (Japanese coming of age tradition celebrated each January to honor 20-year-olds as they come into their maturity) offer culture-specific means for reinforcing social capital. The celebration of cultural festivals, traditions, and holidays, such as *Diwali* (the Hindu festival of lights), Chinese New Year, and the Gay Pride parade all represent valuable forms of bonding social capital and can be installed as resources during the Preparation phase.

Some older clients have a connection with their peers through community centers or senior centers. In a study that measured the five indices of social capital, that is, norms, trust, partnership in community, information sharing, and political participation, Kim, Auh, Lee, and Ahn (2013) found that partnership in community was significantly associated with lower levels of depression for older Chinese and Korean immigrants.

It is important to note that language usually plays a very important role in bonding and bridging, so therapists must endeavor to connect clients to social resources that honor the client's language, culture, and context.

While bonding capital reinforces homogeneity, bridging capital links people to those of another social strata and is used as a strategy to secure economic stability, as well as upward mobility. Many immigrant, asylee, and refugee communities lack critical economic resources. However, social networks and community resources can offer a wealth of material and emotional support, as well as the means to economic sustainability and can be installed as useful resources. For Latino communities, *rifas* (raffles) and *tandas* (a form of rotating no-interest savings pool) are other ways of creating social, capital, and economic support, especially when denied formal means of savings and economic support due to lack of documentation.

### *Navigational Capital*

Yosso (2005) defined *navigational capital* as the skills of maneuvering through social institutions that were not created with Communities of Color in mind. Expanding on that definition, this form of capital draws on the critical navigational skills found in marginalized communities as well as the strategies of resiliency that allow individuals to transcend the hurdles that they consistently encounter. Thus, navigational capital includes inner resources, social competencies, and cultural strategies that draw upon a lifetime of personal and community experiences of living as a marginalized individual.

The culturally attuned therapist plays a significant role in giving importance to the client's experiential knowledge, as well as eliciting the alternative understandings conveyed by clients who do not belong to the dominant culture. Naming this capital acknowledges the resourcefulness and tenacity of culturally diverse clients, who manifest a high level of strategic intelligence in navigating their way to safety, better living conditions, and an improved quality of life for themselves and their kinship network.

For LGBTQQ clients, there are specific forms of navigational capital that the client may be able to identify when the culturally attuned clinician acknowledges that our society primarily operates under heterosexual and cisgender cultural norms. Sometimes, therapy might include the installation of navigational capital in the form of the client's historic or ongoing ability to pass or not draw attention to his or her gender identification or sexual orientation. Other times, navigational capital may present as the finely tuned skill of the client to read the social environment and dress, act, or speak in certain ways that match, defy, or modify dominant expectations.

For clients who are living in poverty, their basic survival is a testament to their navigational capital. In spite of tremendous odds, these are individuals who have not given up and who have often acquired street smarts and specialized skills in order to survive. Acknowledging their navigational capital may also allow us to uncover the aspirational capital that sustains them. In the face of harsh realities, their ability to find enough food to live and finding shelter, even if only temporary, is a vital resource.

The following areas also offer opportunities to discover and install navigational capital as a resource.

- Honoring the mastery of living and surviving in two worlds, two countries, and two paradigms
- Acknowledging the distance traveled from place of birth and the resilience that allowed the client to navigate this dangerous journey
- How clients negotiate for their basic needs in an unfriendly environment, including a place to live, employment, food, education, medical aid, and more
- Reinforcing the aspirational and linguistic capital, which allow clients to navigate to and negotiate for resources when lacking dominant cultural capital
- The ability to function in an environment designed by and for able-bodied, heterosexual, cisgendered individuals

### *Resistant Capital*

Resistant capital refers to the knowledge and skills that are generated or fostered through thought or acts that challenge inequality. Huber (2009) defined *resistant capital* as the "knowledge and skills developed in opposition to oppression, grounded in a legacy of resistance to subordination." Resistance theories emphasize human agency by demonstrating how individuals negotiate with oppressive structures in order to create meaning of their own from these interactions (Solorzano & Delgado Bernal, 2001). Oppositional behavior that challenges inequality or combats assimilation serves the purpose of increasing self-esteem and preserving native culture. Solorzano and Delgado Bernal (2001) identified transformational resistance as a tool for naming, acknowledging, and addressing resistance as a resource, and a tool for empowerment and agency. Transformative resistant capital includes cultural knowledge of racism, sexism, and discrimination, as well as the motivation to confront and transform such oppressive structures (Yosso, 2005).

The Dreamers movement in the United States is an excellent example of transformative resistant capital. These students and young people who are children of parents who migrated without documents began pushing for legal alternatives by drawing attention to their plight as citizens without a nation. They mobilized the media into pointing out that there was no legal avenue for them to become lawful citizens of the United States and this movement spurred President Obama's "deferred action" order effectively protecting their status.

The various social movements within the LGBTQQ communities that advocate for recognition of alternative social and sexual values are examples of transformative resistant capital. With a focus on equal rights for all, these movements have incorporated political activism and cultural activity, including lobbying, street marches, social groups, media, art, and research. Currans (2012) described how the marchers at NY Dyke March (and other similar events) attempted to take the power away from value judgments privileging monogamous heterosexual experiences by claiming and celebrating deviant identities. These are powerful acts of transformative resistant capital.

### *Spiritual Capital*

From an existential perspective, it is the ability to make meaning of our difficulties, pain, suffering, and trauma, which allows us to transform it into healing (Duran, 2006, p. 74). Thus, spirituality and a connection to a reality greater than oneself serve as valuable resources for many culturally diverse individuals.

Religious and indigenous traditions, as well as ancestral beliefs and practices that are learned from one's family, community, and inner self, act as a reservoir of hope and faith (Huber, 2009). Wearing a crucifix, lighting a candle, displaying a picture of *La Virgen de Guadalupe*, praying to saints, communicating with relatives who have passed on, a belief in the afterlife, and committing acts that might ensure a better afterlife are all ways in which Latino clients might practice varying forms of spirituality. Group prayer as a communal activity allows clients to connect to others, thus reducing their social isolation and reinforcing their social capital. In addition, the religious and cultural rituals that accompany birth, coming-of-age, weddings, and funerals allow many clients to overcome feelings of hopelessness and helplessness, and increase their feelings of well-being.

In the prevailing social climate of hostility toward Muslims in large parts of the Western hemisphere, a culturally congruent approach includes an understanding of the everyday challenges a Muslim client faces in staying connected to his or her faith-based practices. These may include the need to hide his or her religious beliefs, the lack of a prayer space at work, the banning of the client's traditional clothing, or the pressure to consume alcohol or intoxicants at social gatherings. A culturally attuned therapist can play an important role in validating a client's spiritual practice by installing it as a resource during the Preparation phase. This may provide the needed safety for the client to reveal important targets related to repeated instances of harassment, name-calling, racist, or discriminatory attacks on the client and others close to him or her.

### *Cultural Intuition*

Most therapists are familiar with the notion of clinical intuition despite its rather elusive nature (Jeffrey & Stone Fish, 2011). Delgado Bernal (1998) articulated cultural intuition as a unique way of "knowing" that relates to both personal experience as well as collective experience, which includes community memory. The ability to accurately perceive a situation or assess others has greater importance for members of socially stigmatized or marginalized groups because of their status as a numerical minority who often experience prejudice and discrimination. Cultural intuition often involves deliberately utilizing the substance and expressions of one's minority cultural experience in order to thrive and evolve. It is, therefore, a valuable, yet undervalued and invisible resource that can greatly empower clients in and out of therapy.

In her 2009 article, Huber highlighted how undocumented students develop intuition about the appropriateness of whom, when, and where to share information about their status. She suggested that this might be a navigational strategy "amassed from a lifetime of personal and familial experiences living as an undocumented Latina/o immigrant in the United States."

Sociopolitical and cultural conditions also necessitate the evolution of social skills, such as *gaydar*. Gaydar, a popular culture term that refers to the ability of one individual to correctly identify the sexual orientation of another (Woolery, 2007), is another form of cultural intuition. Ambady, Hallahan, and Conner (1999) theorize that due to their numerical minority, the ability to identify potential romantic partners is of great consequence to gay men and women. They further state that due to antigay prejudice, "inaccuracy may have greater costs for gay men and lesbians, such as the risk of homophobic hostility and violence." Thus, gaydar as cultural intuition offers protective functions, as well as social ones.

Delgado Bernal (1998) described four sources of cultural intuition as they relate to Chicana researchers: personal experience, existing literature, professional experiences, and analytical research processes. Often, therapists who identify with a minority group report that the four sources of cultural intuition, especially their own personal and collective experiences of immigration, migration, bilingualism, discrimination, marginalization, microaggressions, racism, sexism, and ableism, play an important role in therapy. Inviting clients to bring their cultural intuition into the therapeutic realm allows a more client-focused, strengths-based approach to EMDR therapy.

A culturally attuned therapist's work offers many examples of cultural intuition interwoven with other forms of capital, especially aspirational, navigational, and spiritual capital. It may be beneficial to develop and install these resources during the preparation Phase and to use them as cognitive interweaves when processing might be blocked. For colleagues who come from the dominant culture, ongoing consultation with culturally diverse practitioners can offer relevant context and an expanded therapeutic perspective.

## UNCOVERING TARGETS THROUGH THE INSTALLATION OF CCWR

Oftentimes in therapy, when a client has lied and/or chosen not to disclose certain information, it can be beneficial to set aside the Western notions of resistance and to explore how the client's resistant capital, cultural intuition, and navigational capital may be guiding him to be protective of information. Thus, the therapist can help the client to use his CCWR to feel empowered rather than ashamed, which usually leads to a deepening of the therapeutic process. This acknowledgment of CCWR may serve to uncover targets that were invisible to either the clinician or the client, or both. While these targets may not be the reasons that the client entered into treatment, they may be linked to the client's self-evaluations and Negative Cognitions, as well as historic or ongoing social oppression. Although the following list of targets is far from comprehensive, it offers a starting point from which therapists can pursue their own process of discovery.

1. **How I look:** Physical appearance, including skin color, hair, size, gender, ability, and other physical characteristics associated with stigma or discrimination
2. **How I speak:** Issues related to language, accent, cultural mannerisms, disfluencies, and speech impediments
3. **Whom I love:** Racioethnic and cultural identity, gender identity and sexual orientation, issues of loss, and conflicting loyalties
4. **How I see myself:** Historical trauma, immigration narratives, personal identity versus social identity, media portrayals, intersectionality
5. **How my family sees me:** Issues related to assimilation, acculturation, gender identity, sexual minority status, and conflicting loyalties
6. **How others see me:** Microaggressions, sexism, racism, ableism, discrimination, and issues of social identity, including issues related to colonization and social oppression, such as media portrayal
7. **Cognitive dissonance:** Related to any of the earlier aspects or related to personal, cultural, social, racial, and family identity

## SUMMARY

Duran (2006) wrote that by understanding the sociocultural, historic, and political origin of their problems, individuals "can assume responsibility for their lives and gain an objectivity that has not been available to them until this moment of awareness." An integrative framework, such as the one presented in this chapter, opens up the possibility of empowering clients through unearthing and healing such trauma. Furthermore, CCWR help therapists to privilege the client's invisible resources through increased awareness of self and the intermingling of cultural influences. This type of cultural understanding has implications for therapist and client that will ripple outward in ever widening circles through the community, expanding the potential for individual and community healing through EMDR therapy.

## REFERENCES

Ambady, N., Hallahan, M., & Conner, B. (1999). Accuracy of judgments of sexual orientation from thin slices of behavior. *Journal of Personality and Social Psychology, 77*(3), 538–547.

Briggs, X. de Souza. (1998). Doing democracy up close: Culture, power, and communication in community building. *Journal of Planning Education and Research, 18*, 1–13.

Corey, G., Corey, M., Callanan, P., & Corey, G. (1988). *Issues and ethics in the helping professions.* Pacific Grove, CA: Brooks/Cole.

Currans, E. (2012). Claiming deviance and honoring community: Creating resistant spaces in U.S. dyke marches. *Feminist Formations, 24*(1), 73–101.

Delgado Bernal, D. (1998). Using a Chicana feminist epistemology in educational research. *Harvard Educational Review, 68*(4), 555.

Duran, E. (2006). *Healing the soul wound: Counseling with American Indians and other native peoples*. New York, NY: Teachers College Press.

Dworkin, M. (2005). *EMDR and the relational imperative: The therapeutic relationship in EMDR treatment*. New York, NY: Routledge.

Helms, J., Nicolas, G., & Green, C. (2012). Racism and ethnoviolence as trauma: Enhancing professional and research training. *Traumatology, 18*(1), 65–74.

Huber, L. (2009). Challenging racist nativist framing: Acknowledging the community cultural wealth of undocumented Chicana college students to reframe the immigration debate. *Harvard Educational Review, 79*(4), 704–729.

Irwin, J., LaGory, M., Ritchey, F., & Fitzpatrick, K. (2008). Social assets and mental distress among the homeless: Exploring the roles of social support and other forms of social capital on depression. *Social Science & Medicine, 67*(12), 1935–1943.

Ivey, A. E. (2006). Foreword. In E. Duran (Ed.), *Healing the soul wound: Counseling with American Indians and other native peoples*. New York, NY: Teachers College Press.

James, S., & Prilleltensky, I. (2002). Cultural diversity and mental health. Towards integrative practice. *Clinical Psychology Review, 22*(8), 1133–1154.

Jeffrey, A., & Stone Fish, L. (2011). Clinical intuition: A qualitative study of its use and experience among marriage and family therapists. *Contemporary Family Therapy, 33*(4), 348–363.

Kim, B., Auh, E., Lee, Y., & Ahn, J. (2013). The impact of social capital on depression among older Chinese and Korean immigrants: Similarities and differences. *Aging & Mental Health, 17*(7), 844–852.

Malott, K., & Schaefle, S. (2015). Addressing clients' experiences of racism: A model for clinical practice. *Journal of Counseling & Development, 93*(3), 361–369.

Marich, J. (2009). EMDR in the addiction continuing care process: Case study of a cross-addicted female's treatment and recovery. *Journal of EMDR Practice and Research, 3*(2), 98–106.

Marich, J. (2012). What makes a good EMDR therapist? Exploratory findings from client-centered inquiry. *Journal of Humanistic Psychology, 52*(4), 401–422.

Prilleltensky, I., & Nelson, G. (1997). Community psychology: Reclaiming social justice. In D. Fox & I. Prilleltensky (Eds.), *Critical psychology: An introduction* (pp. 167–184). Thousand Oaks, CA: Sage.

Putnam, R. D. (2000). *Bowling alone: The collapse and revival of American community*. New York, NY: Simon & Schuster.

Shapiro, F. (2001). *Eye movement desensitization and reprocessing (EMDR): Basic principles, protocols, and procedures* (2nd ed.). New York, NY: Guilford Press.

Silver, S., & Rogers, S. (2002). *Light in the heart of darkness: EMDR and the treatment of war and terrorism survivors*. New York, NY: W. W. Norton.

Solorzano, D., & Delgado Bernal, D. (2001). Examining transformational resistance through a critical race and latcrit theory framework: Chicana and Chicano students in an urban context. *Urban Education, 36*(3), 308–342.

Vontress, C. E. (1988). An existential approach to cross-cultural counseling. *Journal of Multicultural Counseling and Development, 16*(2), 73–83.

Vontress, C. E. (2012). The awakening of a cross-cultural counselor: A personal retrospective. In R. Moodley, L. Epp, & H. Yusuf (Eds.), *Counseling across the cultural divide* (pp. 7–11). Ross-on-Wye: PCCS Books.

Watters, E. (2010). *Crazy like us: The globalization of the American psyche*. New York, NY: Free Press.

Woolery, L. (2007). Gaydar: A social-cognitive analysis. *Journal of Homosexuality, 53*(3), 9–17.

Yosso, T. J. (2005). Whose culture has capital? A critical race theory discussion of community cultural wealth. *Race Ethnicity and Education, 8*(1), 69–91.

CHAPTER 7

# Culturally Attuned EMDR Therapy With an Immigrant Woman Suffering From Social Anxiety

Barbara Lutz

The prevalence of cultural elements in trauma-based disorders has been widely neglected in evidence-based treatment of immigrant populations. This case report explores how culturally based trauma in immigrant populations may be addressed in eye movement desensitization and reprocessing (EMDR) therapy. The approach is illustrated with the case of a young Hispanic woman suffering from the effects of multiple distressing cultural transitions and their significant impact on her well-being.

Alma's (pseudonym) case is significant, because upon adjusting to her California cultural context, she spent her adolescence back in Mexico where she had difficulty adjusting again. Her return to California created yet another complicated cultural adjustment phase for Alma. As a result, she developed extreme social anxiety to the point of developing panic attacks that ultimately had her avoid social situations at her university and later at work.

Alma's situation was evaluated with a holistic lens, attending to social, cultural, and societal contexts along with EMDR-specific assessment categories. In the course of EMDR therapy, Alma became increasingly able to integrate memories about her painful transition within various cultural contexts and to reevaluate the Negative Cognitions associated with them.

Alma's case demonstrates how effective steps for developing a culturally attuned EMDR therapy process allow for integration of complex trauma work. It ultimately positions EMDR therapy as a primary treatment modality for complex trauma in the face of increasing global migration.

## THE CULTURAL DIMENSION IN FIRST ENCOUNTERS

As I opened the door to my therapy office in our rural town in Northern California, several different worlds intersected: using the English language with my still recognizable German accent, I greeted Alma and noticed the pale, younger woman standing there, avoiding eye contact. Her name led me to believe that she was of Mexican American descent, but I was not sure whether she had been born in the

United States or in a Latin American country, nor whether English or Spanish was her first language. She sat down on the couch, kneading her fingers. I introduced myself using a friendly tone of voice, explaining that I had a heavy German accent in both English and Spanish, that I knew both languages reasonably well, but that I wanted her to let me know if my pronunciation made comprehension hard. She looked up at me for the first time, and quickly stated in perfect English that she understood me very well.

The implications of first intercultural encounters are many. According to Perry (2009), "The human experience is characterized by clan-on-clan, human-on-human competition for limited resources" (p. 247). The intercultural encounters in our past "were as likely to result in harm as in harmony" (p. 247). Thus, when people interact with an individual from a different culture than their own and grew up biased against a race, ethnicity, or religion, their stress and fear responses can become extremely aroused. Consequently, Matsumoto, Hee Yoo, and LeRoux (2007, p. 77) proposed that the capability to regulate one's affective response to a culturally foreign situation "is a gatekeeper ability that allows people to engage in successful conflict resolution that leads to effective, long-term intercultural communication" (p. 77).

Community psychologists Nelson and Prilleltensky (2010) offered a related set of skills for approaching work with different populations. "It is important for researchers and writers to own their location and position in their field and the larger social order" (p. 18). The authors encouraged an honest look at personal subjectivity and emphasized a passionate approach to the work practitioners did. Thus, I will address the cultural identity of the therapist as well as placing emphasis on the cultural and historic context of both therapist and client, since understanding it can counteract assimilationist implications in the therapy room.

## WHITE CULTURAL IDENTITY DEVELOPMENT

Sue and Sue (2013, p. 313) introduced a model for "White identity development," referring to the therapist's cultural awareness about his or her own immersion in the dominant culture. In order to prevent letting our own cultural background interfere with the work with our clients from a different culture, the authors suggested that we examine our cultural identity considering seven phases: (a) the "naiveté phase," (b) the "conformity phase," (c) the "dissonance phase," (d) the "resistance and immersion phase," (e) the "introspective phase," (f) the "integrative awareness phase," and (g) the "commitment to antiracist action phase" (pp. 331–335).

During the first stage or "naiveté phase" (p. 331), the "White child begins to associate positive ethnocentric meanings to his or her own group and negative ones to others." Upon reflection, I can remember a walk with my mother in Germany by the river at age 3, with my baby brother in a stroller. Small children crowded around the stroller and wanted to look at the baby. One of them, a boy with brown complexion, smiled at the baby and let my brother close his little fist around his finger. My mom interfered and shoed the boy away. Her explanation to me was "He is a gypsy, they are dirty" when I asked. This is an example of how a negative, ethnocentric association was presented quite early on in my own childhood.

The following "conformity phase" centers on experiencing life as a White person as "morally neutral, normative, average and also ideal, so that when we work to benefit others, this is seen as work which will allow 'them' to be more like 'us'" (McIntosh, in Sue & Sue 2013, p. 324). The Germany of my childhood in the 1960s was predominantly White.

However, as soon as the Second World War was discussed in school during my early adolescence, I was forced to confront the racism, anti-Semitism, and the horror of the Nazi reign, ushering in the phase that Sue and Sue referred to as "dissonance" (p. 333). After seeing film footage about the death transports and camps in school, I asked my parents if they had known what had happened. They told me stories of their own early childhood and hardships during the war, but avoided the Holocaust whenever possible. I became more and more curious, and at the same time disgusted with my cultural history of efficient, exact, and calculated genocide based on the idea of creating a superior race. The feelings of guilt, shame, anger, and depression, typical for this phase, followed me through adolescence into adulthood. Traveling a lot, I enjoyed learning about different cultures. However, most of the people I encountered around the world had one common association with Germany: Hitler and the Nazi rule. Sue and Sue state that in the dissonance phase "guilt and shame are most likely related to the recognition of the White person's role in perpetuating racism in the past" (p. 333). Rather than taking refuge in the fact that my parents had been children during the war and that I personally had not directly experienced fascism, I became more aware of the powerful international and intergenerational effects of this period. I felt shame and anger about what my grandparents' generation had done.

The "resistance and immersion phase" (p. 334) is characterized by challenging and questioning one's own racism. During my own process, I took responsibility for having benefitted from the legacy of German fascism, travelled to Israel, and apologized in the name of my people for the atrocities committed by the Nazis, being still mainly motivated by guilt. As a German, I became aware of culture's intrinsic potential to become destructive and violent. The former United Nations official and senior advisor to the Nonviolent Peaceforce, Rolf Carriere, defines this as "cultural violence" (2014).

I became aware how racism can operate hidden by normalcy and everyday language. For example, to this day some Germans use the expression "bis zur Vergasung" (until death by gas poisoning), when describing routines they are fed up with. The term was used first by soldiers during World War I, when they stayed in the field until poisonous gas killed them, but was later associated with the Holocaust (Bibliographisches Institut GmbH, 2013).

Sue and Sue named the following phases "introspection," "integrative awareness," and "commitment to antiracist action" (pp. 334–335). These encompassed "a searching, observing, and questioning attitude," as well as valuing—and feeling comfortable with—multiculturalism (p. 335). This process has become a continuing significant part of my personal and professional development.

## Alma's Biography

Alma's story began in rural Mexico in the early 1970s. She was the middle child of five siblings, with an older and a younger brother and sister pair. When Alma was 5 years old, the family emigrated to the United States to escape poverty. During this period, the Mexican peso was devaluated, causing a financial crisis across the country that left many families struggling for survival (Ratnikas, 2015). In the United States, Alma's family moved to a farm labor camp outside of a rural Californian town. The children played together while the parents worked long hours harvesting vegetables, berries, and strawberries. "I do not remember much about our move to the States" Alma stated, "but in the camp I was happy and had lots of friends." Isolated from the dominant Anglo culture, she was still unaware of the effects of structural injustice that many immigrant families face to this day. However, she knew that "we were poor and could not just buy things."

During our first session, Alma soon shared her presenting problem. "There must be something wrong with me. I don't want to have children." Her speech was pressured, her gaze downcast, and she was wringing her hands while relating this to me. I thought of the importance of gender roles in the traditional Mexican culture, and how specifically the role of the mother generally entails self-sacrifice and self-denial (Sue & Sue, 2013). The knowledge of cultural generalities, however, does not suffice in establishing a culturally attuned therapy. While it is important to recognize culture-specific tendencies, it is essential to be open and curious about the specific cultural client–therapist constellation and context.

## TRANSFERENCE AND COUNTERTRANSFERENCE DIMENSIONS

As Alma's therapist, I needed to be aware of how my own cultural beliefs, values, and experiences created countertransference. Alma's presenting problem of feeling "wrong" for wanting to remain childless created in me an immediate sense of "sisterhood." I also knew from my own experience that the initial decision not to enter the mother role could later shift. Another part of Alma's story touched me deeply; at two major intersections in her life, first when attending an English-speaking school, and later after her reimmersion into the Mexican culture, she had learned to see herself as an outsider and value herself less than her peers. I could relate, since I had felt like a misfit in the small Catholic German town that was my home. Becoming an immigrant in the United States, I experienced being an outsider to the mainstream culture in my chosen new country. Cultural pressure to adjust can be stressful in itself, even if it does not directly threaten an individual or a group with violence. When the individual characteristics of a person and the norms of a specific culture do not match, the person will be exposed to the relentlessly felt demand to adjust to the dominant culture.

I experienced little of such cultural stress in California as a White European immigrant, but Alma had to face the effects of cultural violence in the form of a segregated upbringing, racism, and power structures going back all the way to colonialization. While I could impress people with my language skills and foreign ways, Alma's cultural heritage and bilingualism were not met with admiration by the Californian mainstream. I remember mispronouncing the word *psychology* with emphasis on the "p," as it is pronounced in German. People considered this "cute," or a sign of how "smart" I was for speaking more than one language. Alma, in contrast, noted that her classmates whispered behind her back and laughed about her accent in her California grammar school.

Even though I felt, and continue to feel, strongly about emancipation and social injustice, I had to respect that while these themes were related to Alma's social context, her lens could be very different. Alma preferred privacy and financial fairness to building relationships in her work and private life. Whereas I appreciated the closeness and supportiveness of the Mexican family and community, Alma sought refuge in the Anglo American emphasis on individualism from what she called the "drama" of Mexican family relations. In her marriage Alma did not choose the traditional Mexican woman's role as mother and cook, but she still adhered to the cultural norms of what was proper behavior for a woman in public. She did not deem it appropriate to speak to a male to whom she was not related or married, which also contributed to her problems at work.

## PRACTICE IN THE PRESENCE OF COLONIAL HISTORY AND ETHNIC/ SOCIOECONOMIC DIVIDES

In order to practice within the historical context, culturally attuned EMDR therapists need to consider the complex international, national, and local context since, generally speaking, the discipline of psychology has surfaced and developed within an exclusively Western colonial paradigm. Sue and Sue (2013) maintain that as a result of the "predominantly Euro-American perspective, mental health practitioners . . . have done great harm to culturally diverse groups by invalidating their life experiences, by denying them culturally appropriate care, and by imposing the values of a dominant culture upon them" (p. 38). As I have previously discussed, for example, the functioning of the parental unit is often seen through the lens of family systems therapy, where "the quality of the marital relationship is the key to overall family functioning" (Rothbaum, Rosen, Ujiie, & Uchida, 2002, p. 330). Attachment theory and family systems theory assign "pejorative labels [such as] 'overinvolved', 'enmeshed', 'undifferentiated', 'overly dependent', and 'symbiotic'" (Lutz, 2012; Rothbaum et al., 2002, p. 330). EMDR therapy also retains a firmly Western character as an evidence-based treatment approach defined by the American Psychological Association (APA Presidential Task Force on Evidence-Based Practice, 2006). In their chapter on multicultural evidence-based practice, Sue and Sue (2013) therefore pointed out that "contextual, cultural, and other environmental influences are [often] not adequately considered" and that "the importance of the therapist-client relationship is [often] not adequately acknowledged in such therapies" (pp. 240–241). The inclusion of the historical and sociopolitical background in the case conceptionalization is therefore a necessary step for deconstructing bias.

As I have previously stated, U.S. rule has led to "cycles of exploitation/expulsion of major sources of labor roughly in the order of their arrival" (Friedman et al., 1996, p. 11) from the 1600s to present times. This is evident in the California history of immigration:

- Native Americans (genocide, slavery, expulsion)
- Enslaved people of African descent (slavery, involuntary servitude, slavery outlawed in all states in 1856, continued structural racism, emancipation, civil rights movement, continued legacy of slavery, continued racism)

- Chinese (Post-Civil War: contract labor, residential/educational/occupational segregation, denial of legal rights and citizenship, eventual immigration ban, resettlement, and expulsion)
- Japanese (Late 19th century: contract labor, residential/educational/occupational segregation, denial of legal rights and citizenship, eventual immigration ban, internment during World War II)
- Filipinos (1920: contract labor, residential/educational/occupational segregation, denial of legal rights and citizenship, immigration ban)
- Mexicans (various periods, especially after 1910: contract labor, residential/educational/occupational segregation, denial of legal rights, immigration bans, expulsions) (Friedman et al., 1996, pp. 11–12, in Lutz, 2012, p. 39)

The effects of historic colonization and discrimination are present in our current sociopolitical environment and have consequences for the mental health of immigrant populations. As I have previously discussed, roughly half of the local Latino population's income in 2007 still fell below the area's self-sufficiency standard, which indicates the actual cost of living on a county-by-county basis (Lutz, 2012). In order to culturally attune EMDR therapy, we cannot afford to ignore the historical macro perspective that includes both ourselves and our clients.

## RELATIONSHIP BUILDING WITH CULTURE-SPECIFIC ELEMENTS

When I asked her to let me know if she had difficulties understanding me due to my heavy German accent, Alma lifted her gaze up from the floor to me for the first time. I noticed a slight opening up in Alma due to our shared multicultural histories, even before I realized that cultural shifts and language issues comprised a large part of her distressing and traumatic experiences. I continued by disclosing when I had come to the United States, and that try what I might, my accent remained even after now having lived 27 years in an English-speaking country. This part of introducing myself often creates a more equal relationship between me and my immigrant clients, relates to my understanding of language barriers, and helps build a solid emotional and interpersonal bond for the therapeutic relationship.

Sue and Sue (2013) confirmed that "the importance of feeling accepted by a therapist on an emotional and cognitive level seemed to be a universal prerequisite for an effective therapeutic alliance" (p. 245). Pocock (2010) hypothesized that "there is no difference between the idea of culture and that of relationship" because "both culture and relationship are about managing otherness; we are always in danger of not belonging," and "every encounter with another is to some degree cross-cultural" (p. 366). Regulation of the emotions that interpersonal encounters brought forth depended on the quality of the "relational system," consisting of "interactive regulation and self-regulation" (p. 369).

While an exclusively factual history would have focused on Alma as the patient, it was important to include our cultures, commonalities, and differences as we shaped our therapeutic relationship. Paying particular attention to the Hispanic culture, "personalismo" (the value of personal relationships) had to be factored in, and time had to be allowed for "presentaciones" (introductions) with exchange of personal information and exchange about acculturation difficulties (Sue & Sue, 2013, p. 241). I find it important at this early point in getting to know each other that we not only focus on communalities between us, but also acknowledge our differences, in order to create space for exploring their cultural historical and sociopolitical reasons: Whereas I openly admitted my German accent, Alma paid close attention to the proper English pronunciation. Her professional dress and subdued color scheme were also in contrast to my more colorful, relaxed wardrobe. These differences alerted me to Alma's possible wish to blend in in order to feel safe and comfortable, while I deemed it safe to express my idiosyncrasies.

Our "presentaciones" also covered other themes: for instance, Alma grew up in the United States in a rural Mexican labor camp, with Spanish as her only language until she entered the U.S. school system. English and Spanish had been part of my curriculum in Germany. When I expressed my curiosity about how the transition from Spanish to English had gone for her, mentioning my formal language training, she commented, "I wish I had had that." Alma continued: "Well, we don't speak real Spanish here, you know?" I commented that I had noticed variations in the vocabulary used by people living in the United States versus different parts of Mexico and Spain, carefully avoiding judgmental terms in order to model for Alma a neutral and curious stance toward language differences.

This allowed Alma to open up about a language barrier she had encountered: Once her parents could afford to send her and her sister from the U.S. labor camp to a private school back in Mexico, she noticed that her Spanish was being ridiculed by her peers. Alma had not only faced a language gap between the "Spanglish" common among farmworkers in the United States and the language spoken in Mexico, but also a large class difference. Children who can attend a private school in Mexico mostly belong to the upper middle class, while in the United States migrant workers often struggle with poverty and illiteracy. I related that I had taken a professional training in Mexico with EMDR trainer Lucina Artigas, where I found myself at times grappling with the differences in register between the colloquial Spanish I used with my clients in California and the more sophisticated language used by psychotherapists in Mexico. Alma then pointed out to me that in the Mexican culture, not wanting children was "not acceptable." I acknowledged that while this was similar in most of the traditional cultures around the world, the Mexican culture put a high emphasis on the role of motherhood in a woman's life. When she asked, I told Alma that I had no children. My self-disclosure was intended to further establish a therapeutic bond. However, it was also meant to interfere with harsh criticism of disobeying cultural norms when they hinder personal development. Exposing my resolution to remain childless allowed Alma to notice, criticize, or accept my decision, thus externalizing part of her process.

Blending "personalismo" with the History-Taking phase of Alma's EMDR therapy, I began to identify, in a holistic fashion, indicators of stability, integrative capacity, affect tolerance, attachment history, and readiness for change, as well as current psychological factors and the level of complexity and resource availability. However, my initial findings were hypotheses that still needed confirmation through the process of learning from and with Alma about her life and circumstances.

## ADAPTIVE INFORMATION PROCESSING

Alma experienced a lot of distress. While talking about her issues, she cried and wrung her hands in obvious pain. She needed tools to enable her to be in the presence of overwhelming feelings and negative beliefs about herself, and to trust that she could shift out of such old and ongoing negative states. What she had done in the past to manage was very similar to what Ana Gomez (2010) described as a common strategy in Latino populations for treating trauma and distressing memories: "If you don't think about it and don't talk about it, it will go away" (p. 3). I carefully explained the adaptive information processing model and how negative past experiences are connected to present issues, as well as the healing effect of reprocessing maladaptively stored materials. Alma consented to the treatment approach.

I then introduced her to a HeartMath tool and breathing technique in order to provide her with a sense of manageability and immediate relief. Alma learned to shift out of tension and anxiety quickly, and enjoyed how this and other grounding exercises provided her some relief from her painful emotions. Breathing deeply and regularly, she was able to imagine petting her cat, sitting in her bedroom, or looking into the eyes of her husband. She was able to shift into a more coherent calm state. Later she referred to grounding herself in a tender self-appreciative tone as "I am doing my breathing."

## ESTABLISHMENT OF NEGATIVE COGNITIONS

During her early childhood in the labor camp, Alma had no contact with more affluent children. She nevertheless understood when entering the local school system that her family was considered "poor." Alma recounted how hard the transition had been for her when she had to learn English, as instruction was held exclusively in that language. One of the events she chose to work on in EMDR therapy was a time at age 8 when she was writing an essay. Her teacher criticized her for using the brand name "Colgate" instead of the term *toothpaste*. Alma reported: "I felt mortified, ashamed and worthless. I knew that I needed English to get ahead, but at home we were not allowed to speak English." Another time, she remembered being alone in the cafeteria of her middle school, feeling betrayed by a friend who came from the same camp but paired up with the popular English-speaking girls, leaving her on her own. Her negative self-judgments from this time that surfaced in therapy centered on "not being likeable," "not being good enough," and "not being important." Alma's negative beliefs about herself further developed during the next cultural transition in her life.

Considering the local social context, it is easy to understand why Alma's parents decided to send her back to Mexico once they were able to afford it. As I have previously discussed, in Alma's home town the incarceration rate of Latino children was skyrocketing during the 1990s, and the youths "experienced a rate of gang involvement and heroin use higher than that of children in other California communities of similar size" (Lutz, 2012, p. 41).

Thus, when Alma was 13 years old, her parents dropped her off with an aunt in Mexico near a prestigious private school. With tears in her eyes, Alma remembered "a shameful silence" when she first spoke up in her new class. Her classmates' Spanish was more sophisticated and she was sure that they thought of hers as "vulgar" and "low-class." In addition, the other children were driven to school while she had to take the bus. Her classmates lived in "fancy houses" and she in a rural outskirt of town with her aunt. She did not know how to answer questions about what her father did for a living. "My classmates' parents were doctors, dentists, or in business. My father was a farmworker. I constantly tried to hide that we were poor," Alma remembered. "I never talked more than absolutely necessary and never socialized." The other teenagers engaged in activities after school, but she went home and helped her aunt with household chores. Alma finished school in Mexico at age 18. Her negative beliefs about herself stemming from the time in Mexico were: "I don't fit in anywhere," "I am defective," and "I am incompetent."

On her subsequent return to the United States as a young adult, Alma reconnected with a childhood friend, her future husband. She left her California home town for college, a stressful time filled with anxiety about her competency and social skills. In her early twenties and after finishing her degree, Alma married her boyfriend and started working in the financial department of a large U.S. company. Her husband was employed by the same company, but worked for a different division. Alma now organized her whole day and work schedule around limiting social encounters to only those absolutely necessary for getting her work done. She arrived at work before her coworkers, went home by herself for lunch, and stayed late, avoiding social break times. The most difficult situations for her were company events such as Christmas parties and birthday celebrations, where she said she froze, turned bright red, and could not communicate. She enviously observed colleagues who "talked so easy" and criticized herself mercilessly for any of her own comments or her silence for days and nights after the events. In regular business meetings, she stayed silent even if she knew that she had important information to share, and when having to discuss work with her superiors she felt as if she was "wasting their time." She passed up promotions for the sole reason of avoiding increased social interactions. Her Negative Cognition, "I am incompetent," which had begun when entering school in California and later solidified during her time in Mexico, became even more prevalent.

While I learned about Alma's increasing social anxiety, I continued "personalismo" and connected with her by sharing how much the Californian work culture differed from the European one. By relating from my outsider view the estrangement with Christmas games such as "White Elephant," or small talk and frequent self-praise, I normalized some of the social discomfort that someone like Alma could experience on the outside of a dominant culture, and brought the culturally different social customs into focus. Alma noted with relief: "That is how I thought about it! So it's not all me being crazy!" While I was at first unsure of Alma's expectations of therapy, I was aware that Hispanic immigrants were "more likely to fear embarrassment or social discrimination from family, friends, and employers if they acknowledge psychological distress" (Sue & Sue, 2013, p. 417). Thus, continued relationship building, strengthening of the therapeutic bond, and highlighting the commonality of stressful intercultural estrangement help the cultural attunement of the therapy process.

Alma's relationship to her parents further illuminated how existing family issues can become increasingly complicated by cultural elements. Alma's father had started drinking during his early years in the fields, but later became a pillar in the local Spanish-speaking Alcohólicos Anónimos group. Alma felt closer to him than to her mother. The mother complained about many health issues that required constant consideration, and created a closed home environment where not many outside influences were invited and the children knew their place without much communication. Alma stated that her mother never asked about school, friends, or interests, and that at age 12, when Alma was a tomboy, she received a doll as a Christmas gift. She hated the doll, but never voiced her opinion. "How should I have criticized a gift?" she wondered with tears in her eyes. Later, during her time in the Mexican private school when she found herself in need of a bag for her books, Alma's mother sent her a "huge bright red satchel that was definitely not in fashion." When her classmates teased her, Alma felt mortified, but she had to accept the gift without communicating what she would have liked instead. She experienced her own preferences as unattainable, since gift giving in her culture symbolized the bond between her and her parents (Erickson, 2001).

Neither of Alma's parents ever spoke or understood English, nor did they have high school educations in Mexico. They could not help her when she felt lost at school. However, the parents took pride in displaying to their countrymen that their hard work away from their native land had paid off, allowing them to send their child back to a private school in Mexico. What the parents took as a status symbol representing that they had overcome poverty (Jimenez, 2010) left Alma struggling with experiencing her lower social standing.

Alma never told her parents about the difficult times she had in Mexico. She had learned that her individual needs were not important, and that asking for help would overwhelm her mother and "make her sick," which has been identified as a typical way to express discomfort in the Mexican culture (Tofoli, Andrade, & Fortes, 2011). While Alma's mother's capacity to emotionally nurture seemed limited, much of her relationship with her children was based on cultural traditions. Thus, Alma felt she had no right to express her needs, which deepened her overwhelming sense of helplessness.

Caught between the demand to comply with her family's culture on the one hand, and the need to find her way in California and Mexico on the other, Alma felt strong pressure to fit in. She believed that she had "to be perfect," that she didn't belong, and that she couldn't rely on anyone. When she was not thriving, she was not only disappointing her family, but also unable to meet the general cultural expectations in California and in Mexico.

In her professional interactions at her work in California, Alma became highly socially anxious and avoidant. When dealing with family affairs, such as planning the parents' retirement and supporting her sister and nieces after a divorce, Alma took on a rigid traditional role as the oldest daughter and selfless caretaker. She gave sound advice, took into her home whoever in the family was stranded even if it made her feel intruded upon, and presented herself as "the flawless matron." She mentioned that she took off her jewelry before meeting her sister in a coffee shop in order to model modesty. While Alma secretly lived the life of a modern Western woman in her marriage, she retreated to the traditional female role in front of her family. Noticing this, she expressed feeling "like a fake" in both the dominant and her family cultures.

## RESOURCES AND PRESENTING ISSUE

Despite the tension in her familial and peer relationships, Alma was happy and felt like an equal partner throughout her 15 years of marriage. Here, she had freed herself from the traditions she found limiting and that did not support her. For example, she lived a modern lifestyle, with both spouses pursuing a professional career, became a vegetarian, and refused to cook regular meals, but went dining out with her husband instead. She also decided not to attend church anymore soon after their wedding. However, when her parents came to visit, she felt like she was losing her balance in the one area where she felt in control, her home. She resented her mother's sporadic visits and made a point of not letting her help out in her household in any way. When the mother cooked, Alma did not eat the food. When the mother wanted to shop or clean the house, Alma went out of her way to do it herself. Now that Alma was nearing menopause and facing the finality of her decision to stay childless, she sought professional help.

In our conversation about her history and current life issues, it became evident that Alma had not been prepared to perform well as a professional woman in the Anglo culture, or having to perform with assertiveness in a less authoritarian social structure than that of Mexico: She had been brought up as the traditional Mexican girl that followed her parents' rules without discussion of her own opinions or wishes, as the immigrant child who had to adjust to the dominant culture, and as the girl groomed to become a traditional woman by practicing self-denial and not leaving the family home but for education and, later, marriage. According to Sue and Sue (2013, p. 413), women of Mexican heritage in the United States often struggle with role expectations and develop "anxiety or depression over not being able to live up to these standards."

In her marriage with a former playmate from the immigrant camp, however, Alma was largely able to create an integrated feminine role for herself. She felt free to be an equal partner, to focus on what she liked, and to eliminate what she did not want. Nevertheless, while she openly expressed to her husband that she preferred "having a puppy to having a baby," she doubted herself enough on this departure from her traditional values to call herself "crazy" and to seek professional help. Moreover, Alma kept the fact that she was consulting a therapist a secret from her husband and other family members.

## THE THERAPEUTIC PROCESS

In the initial phases of EMDR treatment, Alma expressed that she felt a lot of pressure to make a final decision about becoming a mother or staying childless since she was approaching menopause. She agreed to imagine the two scenarios in the future, one with a baby, and one without, while staying grounded and working with slow bilateral stimulation. With relief she realized that "there is no wrong decision, just a decision." When we continued to look at the future with a baby in the following sessions, Alma's anxiety noticeably increased, especially when she thought of child-related social events such as children's birthdays. During this phase, she made statements like "I would have a lot of work and would worry all the time," and "I like my life quiet, calm, and safe as it is." When we discussed the baby scenario again at the next session, Alma calmly stated that she needed to work on her "non-existent social skills." She did not, after all, want to stay childless out of fear.

We looked at early distressing and traumatic social events and clarified that the first strong thoughts of herself as "misfit" and "not loveable" manifested when she entered the California school system. Alma later identified experiences at the private high school in Mexico as the most painful memories, when she started thinking that in order to be accepted she would have to "speak perfect, dress perfect, and be perfect." This fragmentation in her personality likely accounted for the intense affective charge that came up when she talked about her mother's lack of support as she learned how to face the world. She started "connecting the dots" between overwhelming challenges for a girl her age, and the lack of outside support. Imagining a girl that age in the Mexican school, and knowing herself as a wiser older adult, Alma realized that it was hard for her to like the little scared girl she had been. However, she responded well to reprocessing the events in EMDR therapy and challenged herself with practicing "being more social at work" in the time between sessions.

Three weeks into treatment, Alma surprised me. She was 5 minutes late to a session to which she had typically arrived before our arranged time, stating "I am practicing not having to be perfect." When I laughed with her, she had more good news: "I have accepted an invitation for lunch with one of my coworkers!" she reported with a smile, intently watching my response. I clapped my hands and exclaimed excitedly what a huge step that was. I noticed that I was feeling like a proud mother. Alma added: "I have never been asked before." At another occasion, she planned on joining a group of coworkers going to a baseball game and felt very distraught and fearful. She defined what she wanted from our session in the following manner: "I have to find out if I just don't want to connect, or if it is fear." While working on her fear of not being likeable, she announced: "I actually like to connect sometimes." I asked her to listen to herself while she said it again, and she became teary with joy. She had moved into a more regulated emotional state and accessed an inner truth that was a discovery for both of us.

Over time, Alma befriended the little scared girl she once had been, and explained to this part of herself that it did not matter what others thought about her, offered to help her, gave her advice on how to make friends, and hugged her, telling her she loved her. She noticed: "The little girl was so scared, she did not see or hear anyone." Alma's merciless inner critic slowly yielded to a gentler voice. Her anger against her mother slowly gave way to detecting that the mother herself did not know much about how to behave in different social situations. While Alma actively practiced allowing more social contact in her life, she also relaxed about criticizing herself when just wanting time alone. She was proud when she reported that she had developed a real friendship with a Japanese-American woman at her work: "I have not had a friend, except my husband, since I started elementary school." The isolating social restrictions predominant in her family culture started to cede and allow her to experiment with a more integrative social stance.

After an intensive EMDR therapy session where Alma focused on the negative impact of forcing herself to be more outgoing in order to be perfect and likeable, she accessed the following wisdom from within herself: "I don't need to get on with everyone. There are people I like and ones I don't like." Her progress in accessing adaptive strategies eventually led to a reevaluation of her relationship with her parents.

When Alma's parents came to visit from their retirement home in Mexico, Alma and her husband took them in, because out of all the siblings they were the only ones who owned a large home. Alma was pleased that her self-reliance and prudence had afforded her a nice house, but dreaded having her parents in her private sanctuary. She expressed fear that they might want to move in permanently. She did not want her mother to talk with her or about her, or be involved with her in any other way but providing her mother and father shelter. She saw no way to explain her discomfort and felt guilty, knowing that their cultural norm that "family comes first" was not negotiable. She reported: "I forgot my breathing and am sliding back into the miserable feelings of childhood." I told her about Bowen, the famous family therapist, who examined the great challenge of going back to one's family of origin, trying to hang on to being an adult (Brown, 1999). I had normalized for her the difficulties she experienced to a degree that allowed her to look deeper into the issue. As a result, we reprocessed a childhood event where Alma's mother overreacted when she wanted to know the end of a story and inquired about it by saying, "So?" as in "What happened then?" The mother misinterpreted this as being disrespectful in terms of "So what?" and punished her. Alma's Negative Cognition about herself from that time was "I am weak and cannot say what I mean." Within the hour of EMDR therapy she affirmed as a personally felt truth the positive statement: "I am strong enough now to express my thoughts." In the following session, Alma reported how her husband had agreed to buy an apartment for her parents, should they want to permanently live back in California, since this was also a good investment. She had been able to creatively think of a solution to protect her sanctuary, instead of staying overwhelmed by her emotions.

In one of our last sessions, Alma mentioned hearing her mother talk about Alma's wedding to an aunt. She described how Alma had gotten married to her childhood playmate from the labor camp after coming back from college. Alma brought this event to therapy in tears: "My husband and I have had to lie for over 15 years now about the fact that we both went to the same college. We always had to calculate the years and make up stories. I have to make sure they don't know that I chose the college only because he went there." I asked her to clarify: "In my culture," she explained, "you cannot just go away living with your boyfriend. You have to choose your college thinking of what makes sense and what best fits your career." Sobbing heavily, she judged herself as a "bad person," "a liar," and "a fraud." I asked how she thought people from the dominant Anglo culture decided on which college to attend. "The one you want!" was her immediate response. We agreed to focus on the day she made the decision to study at the same college as her future husband, sitting in the college counseling office with her acceptance letter for the college, feeling dread, fear, and shame instead of joy. Although her negative beliefs about being a deceptive, bad person were clear, she struggled to find what she would rather think about herself until she came up with "I am independent and strong." Following her associations during reprocessing, Alma got stuck judging herself for how wrong she had been: "I should have been stronger, I should have gone to college for learning!" I interjected that I was confused. "How long have you now been happily married?" "Fifteen years," she smiled under tears. Coming to the end of the process, Alma surprised me by calmly stating: "If I had to do it over again, I would!" and "Everyone needs something different. Some people need to focus on their career first. I needed Carlos (pseudonym) then!" She saw herself as strong and independent, and said: "The real me is so much happier than my family's image of me!" Alma had accessed her authentic self and separated it from what she had thought of as a fixed cultural norm which did not fit for her anymore. When I checked in with Alma the next session about this revelation, she said: "It's strange. I feel really relaxed, but also a little sad. I know now that I made a good decision going to college together with Carlos, but it is as if I lost something—as if I lost another tiny piece of my culture." I continued to review the treatment process with Alma. When I asked her how she felt now about her initial question of whether to have children, she replied: "I actually think now that I could have become a good mom!" She quickly added: "but I am glad Carlos is supporting me not to go that way." Alma had chosen to create her feminine identity by becoming a wife and a professional woman, separate from the traditional Mexican mother role. She also had repaired her relationship to the lost little girl she once was.

In a final session, Alma resolved that after having applied her strong Mexican work ethic to her social issues with good success in treatment, she was ready to reveal to her husband that she had undergone therapy. When asked about how she would explain it to him, she used a striking metaphor, saying she had developed "a new muscle," meaning an approach that was not merciless criticism but a new strength based on kindness and acceptance. Alma now saw herself as "an autonomous individual who is unique (individual level of identity), a member of her own racial–cultural group (group level of identity), a member of a larger society, and a member of the human race" (Sue & Sue, 2013, p. 304). She had successfully worked though her treatment plan and had gained a perspective of integrative cultural awareness.

## SUMMARY

The combination of EMDR therapy and cultural attunement, as illustrated with the case history of Alma, shows promise in the treatment of clients undergoing traumatic cultural transitions. As part of a process involving the therapists' willingness to explore their own cultural identity, their knowledge of cultural themes, application of a holistic lens, as well as a practice in the presence of colonial history and ethnic/socioeconomic divides, culturally attuned EMDR therap may prove to be an essential ingredient in reaching underserved populations worldwide, providing relief, evoking hope, and cocreating sustainable better futures.

## REFERENCES

APA Presidential Task Force on Evidence-Based Practice. (2006). Evidence-based practice in psychology. *American Psychologist, 61*, 271–285.

Bibliographisches Institut GmbH. (Ed.). (2013). *Duden*. Retrieved from http://www.duden.de/rechtschreibung/Vergasung#Bedeutung2

Brown, J. (1999). Bowen family systems theory and practice: Illustration and critique. *Australian & New Zealand Journal of Family Therapy, 20*(2), 94–97.

Carriere, R. (2014). Scaling up what works: Using EMDR to help confront the world's burden of traumatic stress. *Journal of EMDR Practice and Research, 8*(4), 187–195.

Erickson, H. (2001). *Before you go: A short-term mission manual*. Cherokee Village, AR: Deeper Roots Publications & Media.

Friedman, R. M., Hernandez, M., Zirps, F. A., Greenbaum, P., Sengova, J., Uzzell, D., . . . Larsen, C. (1996, March 3). *Watsonville: A clinical ethnography*. (Report submitted to the Center for Mental Health Services by the Comprehensive Community Mental Health Services for Children and Their Families Evaluation Team). Tampa, FL: Department of Child & Family Studies, Louis de la Parte Florida Mental Health Institute, University of South Florida.

Gomez, A. (2010, October 3). In EMDRIA (Ed.), *EMDR and diversity: A panel presentation discussion* [Panel transcript]. Retrieved from www.emdria.org

Jimenez, T. R. (2010). *Replenished ethnicity: Mexican Americans, immigration and identity*. Berkeley, CA: University of California Press.

Lutz, B. (2012). *Rey: An intensive single case study of a probation youth with immigrant background participating in Wraparound Santa Cruz* (Doctoral dissertation). Retrieved from ProQuest Dissertations and Theses (Accession Order No. UMI 3556382).

Matsumoto, D., Hee Yoo, S., & LeRoux., J. A. (2007). Emotion and intercultural communication. In H. Kotthoff & H. Spencer-Oatey (Eds.), *Handbook of intercultural communication*. Berlin, Germany: Mouton de Gruyter Publishers.

Nelson, G., & Prilleltensky, I. (2010). *Community psychology: In pursuit of liberation and well-being*. New York, NY: Palgrave-MacMillan.

Perry, B. (2009). Examining child maltreatment through a neurodevelopmental lens: Clinical applications of the neurosequential model of therapeutics. *Journal of Loss and Trauma, 14*(14), 240–255.

Pocock, D. (2010). Emotions as eco systemic adaptations. *Journal of Family Therapy, 32*(4), 362–378.

Ratnikas, A. (2015, March 25). *Timelines Mexico*. Retrieved from http://timelines.ws/countries/MEXICO_B.HTML

Rothbaum, F., Rosen, K., Ujiie, T., & Uchida, N. (2002). Family systems theory, attachment theory, and culture. *Family Process, 41*(3), 328–350.

Sue, D. W., & Sue, D. (2013). *Counseling the culturally diverse: Theory and practice* (6th ed.). Hoboken, NJ: John Wiley & Sons.

Tofoli, L. F., Andrade, L. H., & Fortes, S. (2011). Somatization in Latin America: A review on the classification of somatoform disorders, functional syndromes, and medically unexplained symptoms. *Revista Brasileira De Psiquiatria, 33*, 70.

# CHAPTER 8

# The EMDR Approach Used as a Tool to Provide Psychological Help to Refugees and Asylum Seekers

Paola Castelli Gattinara, Antonio Onofri, and Cristina Angelini

*It's not because I cannot explain that you will not understand, it is because you do not understand that I cannot explain.*
—Wiesel (1996)

The aim of our work is to describe the psychotherapeutic intervention for a particular clinical population: refugees and asylum seekers. These individuals live in a state of great vulnerability. For them, migrating was not a choice, but a decision forced by the particular conditions in their country of origin (wars, religious or political persecution, etc.). They have often been tortured, suffered material deprivation, witnessed violence, and lost dear ones. They are affected by cultural isolation, the inability to return to their country, and concerns over the fate of family members back home (Aragona, Pucci, Mazzetti, & Geraci, 2012; Miller & Rasmussen, 2010). Silove, Sinnerbrink, Field, Manicavasagar, and Steel (1997), in a survey of asylum-seekers living in a community resource center, showed that as many as 79% of them had experienced traumatic events such as witnessing killings, being attacked, or suffering torture or imprisonment.

In addition, the living conditions that this population found in the receiving country played a role comparable to that of the trauma suffered in their homeland. This is why various authors (Aragona et al., 2012; Mazzetti, 2008; Silove et al., 1997) speak of *postmigration trauma*. Inadequate reception conditions seem to amplify the traumatic experience they have already been through.

This chapter focuses on our work in Italy, where the long procedures related to the recognition of asylum, the fear of being repatriated, and the kind of life offered by the detention centers puts an additional strain on the mental health of this population, which is already at high risk. In these centers, migrants spend their days waiting with nothing to do. They have to share their personal space with strangers who speak other languages and belong to different religions, making it difficult to build meaningful relationships. They are subjected to many restrictions and feel like unwanted citizens with little access to employment and education. Often, these centers are far from cities, exacerbating the feelings of isolation and discrimination.

In addition, there are specific risk conditions that affect the asylum seekers' ability to adapt, such as deculturalizing social contexts and social loneliness as well as exposure to triggering stimuli such as repeated interrogations by police (Mazzetti, 2008).

## COMPLEX PTSD AND SOMATIZATION DISORDERS AMONG IMMIGRANTS, REFUGEES, AND ASYLUM SEEKERS

The immigrant population is very heterogeneous due to different factors: their migration history and the reasons at the root of their migration (economic, political, religious, familial, etc.); their social, cultural, and economic conditions; their status (some have a legal residence permit, some have had their refugee status recognized, others are asylum seekers or still illegal immigrants); and their ability to access national health care.

One aspect that unites this population, however, is that they are particularly at risk for complex posttraumatic stress disorder (PTSD; Sabin, Sabin, Kim, Vergara, & Varese, 2006). Since the 1980s, a growing number of studies have shown how the phenomenology of individuals who have suffered an individual trauma is very different from that of persons exposed to repeated and chronic trauma, especially of an interpersonal nature (Herman, 1992, 1997; van der Kolk, 2005).

Several studies have shown the presence of this complex symptomatology in the migrant population, which has been subjected mainly to interpersonal violence, both by witnessing it or by having directly suffered it (Heptinstall, Sethna, & Taylor, 2004; Rasmussen, Rosenfeld, Reeves, & Keller, 2007; Spitzer, Barnow, Wingenfeld, Rose, Lowe, & Grabe, 2009; van der Kolk et al., 1996). Furthermore, high rates of somatization were found among this population, so much so that the somatic symptomatology is considered in this particular clinical population a "primary" therapeutic target (Aragona et al., 2010).

The importance of considering somatization disorders as a possible sign of PTSD symptomatology is particularly evident if we consider that in developing countries, emotional distress is often expressed through the body (Saxena, Nepal, & Mohan, 1988). In addition, recent research studies on the migrant population have highlighted how severe premigration traumas increase the sensitivity to postmigration difficulties and how the consequent discomfort created by them amplifies the tendency to develop somatic symptoms (Aragona et al., 2012; Aragona, Pucci, Mazzetti, Maisano, & Geraci, 2013).

## PSYCHOTHERAPEUTIC TREATMENT FOR COMPLEX PTSD

Before processing traumatic experiences directly, patients must acquire some ability to regulate their emotions sufficiently, control their impulses, commit to the therapeutic relationship with enough confidence, and develop at least some positive sense of their self and their lives.

These considerations benefit from an articulated therapeutic strategy divided into phases (Courtois & Ford, 2009; Miti & Onofri, 2011). Pierre Janet, one of the most influential psychiatrists of the past two centuries, had, since 1889, developed the idea of a treatment in consecutive stages (van der Hart, Nijenhuis, & Solomon, 2010). According to Janet, the first phase of treatment should be dedicated to the construction of the therapeutic alliance and to the stabilization and reduction of symptoms. It is not realistic to start clinical work while there is still a serious uncertainty about the current living conditions, as often happens in the case of torture victims applying for asylum or international protection and refugees coming from war zones or extreme poverty, and so forth. The intermediate stage is focused instead on processing memories related to the traumas. The third and last phase aims at the integration of the personality and on relational rehabilitation, in particular on the progressive integration of the dissociated mental functions and on the development of social skills, self-care, and personal growth. This sequence is not strictly linear: although the orientation of the treatment is in "phases," it follows a rather spiral course, with the themes of the three phases alternating.

## PSYCHOTHERAPY WITH REFUGEES AND ASYLUM SEEKERS

Victims of multiple traumas, both prolonged and interpersonal, such as those who have suffered torture, are annihilated to the point that personal, social, and cultural differences no longer seem to exist (Caizzi & Ciambellini, 2008). The main therapeutic goal then is to allow them to rediscover themselves as "people who have the right to live" through initial work on self-narration that integrates the traumatic experiences into their personal history without forgetting them, but by making them part of their individual life experience. In this sense, it is very important to make the client feel that they are in a "safe enough relationship" that will enable them to tell the therapist their own story with confidence, without feeling forced to do so and with the certainty of remaining anchored to the present. The active work on trauma within a therapeutic relationship, in fact, can only be successful when the patient no longer feels alone in front of the horror (Dworkin, 2005).

Another key element of the treatment, especially in this type of population, and in general in those suffering from complex PTSD, is attention to the body. The changes occurring at the somatic level represent a critical link to the whole process of change. The impact of major trauma may include a continued perception of absolute impotence, which is experienced in the body; overcoming it means finding a way to help the person remember and feel that he or she has in effect survived it. Eye movement desensitization and reprocessing (EMDR) targets memories felt in the body, promoting full access, reprocessing, and integration of the traumatic experiences.

In particular, the articulation and extension of the EMDR protocol proposed by Gonzalez and Mosquera (2012) provide flexible answers in all stages of the phase-oriented therapy and is an effective clinical intervention in dealing with severe and prolonged traumatic experiences. This is a progressive approach, which works on the "peripheral" behavioral and mental processes before facing the traumatic memories. The bilateral stimulations are used and dosed in accordance with the development of the clinical process, working on small fragments and encouraging the stabilization and strengthening of resources. The patient is thus assisted in developing those psychological conditions that allow him or her to overcome avoidance and dissociation tendencies.

## THE PROCESSING OF TRAUMAS: THE PATIENT'S NEED OR A NEED OF THE THERAPIST?

After reflecting on our clinical experiences, we realized that the processing of past traumas in this particular clinical population was a mode of intervention that was reassuring for the psychotherapist but rather unsuitable and detached from the patient's needs. The users of the service appeared in fact quite reluctant or resistant to going over a painful past at a time when their current day-to-day lives still appeared to be unstable, uncertain, and sometimes even threatening. The first patients that were recruited by this program usually had other priorities, such as:

- Improvement of their symptoms
- Control and regulation of the frequent dissociative episodes and states of anxiety—related to the possibility of being relocated again to another country
- Preparation for the hearing regarding their request for asylum
- Dealing with the difficulties associated with their current lives (relationships with other guests of the reception centers and their operators)
- Keeping up their hope for the future

For this reason, we encourage therapists to remain acutely attuned to their client's present needs and not force reprocessing of past traumas if it is not considered useful by the client. It was in fact observed that changes in the clinical status of the patients were directly correlated to acceptance or rejection of their asylum application.

## EMDR AND RECENT TRAUMATIC EPISODE PROTOCOL

EMDR offers clinicians a particularly flexible way of working with patients, providing a range of interventions for all three stages of the treatment of complex trauma cases (Gonzalez & Mosquera, 2012; van der Hart, Brown, & van der Kolk, 1989).

In the case of refugees, especially during the process of applying for asylum (but not only then, given the difficulties related to integration and postmigration stress), the trauma cannot be fully processed and cannot be considered as "passed" or even "recent," but must still be considered "in progress." There are so many traumatic events, scattered throughout an entire existence, that they can actually be looked at as one large, single, and still "ongoing" trauma.

Psychotherapists looked for those EMDR and sensorimotor interventions that were best able to stabilize the patient, such as those used in ongoing emergency situations like the "EMDR recent traumatic episode protocol (R-TEP)" proposed by Shapiro and Brurit (2012). This form of intervention offers some advantages when compared with more popular alternatives used on survivors of organized violence, such as the Narrative Exposure Therapy (NET; Schauer, Neuner, & Elbrert, 2011). In both procedures, the main objective is to build an explicit and semantic narrative of the events experienced, integrating the sensory, emotional, and cognitive aspects within a space–time continuum and one of autobiographical memory. While in the NET, this process follows the chronological order of traumatic life events and is fully guided by the therapist; the EMDR R-TEP lets the patient drive the narrative by gradually identifying the episodes to be processed, counteracting by doing so the feeling of powerlessness and loss of control so easily activated in victims of torture and intentional violence.

In the current guidelines for the treatment of multiple and repeated traumas, the care process is divided into three phases in which a special emphasis is put on the interpersonal and intersubjective dimension. In working with asylum seekers, a first and fundamental objective is to allow these patients to experience emotional help—sometimes for the first time in their lives—that will enable them to finally feel like people worthy of attention.

Therefore, we offered "modular packages" of five to seven sessions, each with progressive and spaced targets. The starting point was work on current problems, followed by the construction of an idea of the future, and only then (and when possible and required) to work on past traumas. All of the aforementioned are still using the EMDR R-TEP.

## The First Session Package

The "package" of sessions is centered on stabilization and involves:

- History taking (not too detailed) and symptoms evaluation
- Psychoeducation on trauma
- Techniques to deal with hyperarousal or/and hypoarousal symptoms, like grounding techniques and four elements exercise
- Imaginary work on the "creation of a safe place"
- Strengthening positive resources
- A series of somatosensory and mindfulness exercises to increase personal awareness and coping strategies to manage emotions

This package's goal is to teach the client techniques, including bilateral stimulation (butterfly hug and tapping), for stress management that can be used by the patients themselves when in difficult situations (Shapiro, 2012). This first package corresponds with EMDR protocol Phases 1 and 2.

## The Second Session Package

The second "package" of sessions mainly concerns preparation for the hearing; application of the techniques learned; and building a narrative that gradually becomes more coherent through the use of bilateral stimulation—as provided by the EMDR R-TEP.

- The first session is dedicated to the life timeline, like in the NET therapy, to recollect the main events of the life of the client.
- In the second session, the therapist asks for the narrative of the period starting from the arrival in Italy until the present.
- In the following reprocessing sessions, the therapist follows the R-TEP protocol, focusing on desensitization of the most disturbing events.

Providing this type of aid, designed to master the difficult emotional obstacle of hearing more effectively, the therapist becomes a new and present time relational resource, allowing the patient therefore to have a corrective emotional experience to which he or she can recall in times of need. Developing a narrative integrates positive experiences of the self and facilitates the construction of a "*postmigration plan*" that works. The intervention can go beyond "saving one's life" to further generate meaning to one's existence through the visualization of the future (Mazzetti, 2008).

This second package uses the EMDR R-TEP to focus mainly on the present and the future rather than the past.

## The Third Session Package

Only the third "package" follows the plan of complete treatment provided by the EMDR standard protocol. This phase can be deferred to a time when living conditions have become more stable and the motivation for undertaking it have become stronger. It can include the entire history of the patient, and is aimed at the reprocessing of the most difficult and still active aspects of past trauma.

The following clinical cases were chosen to best illustrate the type of work that has been done, the difficulties encountered, and the objectives that can be achieved using this method of clinical intervention.

## Fatima's Case

Fatima is a 28-year-old Somali girl belonging to an ethnic minority. Recently, she has been denied refugee status. The commission did not believe her story, so she is waiting for a new hearing. She was sent to the outpatient clinic of the "Santo Spirito Hospital in Rome" suffering from insomnia, nightmares, flashbacks, irritability, and intense pain in her hands, legs, and head. She also suffers from a strong sense of desperation and worthlessness that are leading her to suicidal ideation. Her symptoms have increased significantly since she was denied refugee status and since two of her friends left the center, having been given the right to stay and having finally managed to find a job.

### History

Fatima was one of the first patients of this clinical facility addressing migrants. She was offered 15 meetings focused on processing the traumatic events she had experienced. This included those related to the forced migration and the terrible journey to Italy, but also her previous experiences. She lost her parents when she was 7 years old during the war, the only memory of which is "people running and fire everywhere." She was taken in by an aunt, where she was abused and forced to be a servant while her cousins went to school. She got married at a very early age to a husband belonging to another religion for which he was persecuted and ended up fleeing to the mountains. Fatima was also threatened with death and forced to flee her country, leaving two small children behind. During the journey through different African countries, she was repeatedly tortured, raped, and jailed. She had not heard from her husband or her two children—who she had abandoned, but still believed to have left in good hands—for more than 2 years. She missed her children very much and felt guilty, convinced that she would never see them again.

## The Treatment

The first phase of the therapeutic process involved building a therapeutic alliance with the patient, which had to start with the patient recognizing her trauma and the fact that she was a victim. It is no surprise that Fatima's symptoms were exacerbated after the commission rejected her asylum request.

The therapist's initial task, therefore, was to investigate Fatima's cultural identity in order to understand how the mental distress and adversities she had met over time had impacted her. Establishing a therapeutic relationship requires meeting the other's cultural universe in order to find a common ground that will constitute the interaction container (Moro, Neuman, & Real, 2008). The function of a cultural linguistic mediator as a witness and a bridge between the two cultures, the patient's and the therapist's, can be of great help to achieve this goal.

Fatima came to the psychological support meeting with a guarded demeanor. It was apparent that she was scared and unsure about what she was supposed to be doing. During the first session, she shared her current struggles: nightmares that kept her from sleeping and physical pain. She was very suspicious and spoke only with the mediator, never looking into the therapist's eyes.

Spontaneously, she told of a dream, which appeared to be very significant for her. However, she did not accept the interpretation offered by the therapist, but only the one offered by a friend who belonged to her same ethnic group, who told her that it was an auspicious dream. In this way, she was immediately letting the therapist know that she must take her culture into account.

According to protocol, the first two objectives of Fatima's treatment were the construction of a therapeutic alliance and the stabilization of her symptoms.

The work on stabilization of the symptoms took place through:

- The therapist's attention to the somatic pain
- The psychoeducation on the reactions to traumatic events that provides legitimization and understanding of her symptoms
- Recommendations about medication to help her sleep at night
- Teaching of relaxation techniques

The construction of the therapeutic alliance was achieved through:

- Attentive listening to how the patient's symptoms were explained in the country of origin
- A clear definition of the achievable goals within the available time
- The reassurance that the intervention was not going to affect her legal position in Italy

The presence of the cultural linguistic mediator, whom she had met before, allowed Fatima to accept the proposed aid without feeling completely disoriented. The psychoeducation about her symptoms and the respect shown to her and her culture formed the background to the clinical work, making it possible to diminish her mistrust. After the first meetings, Fatima, who used to turn almost exclusively to the mediator, started to look the therapist in the eye more while waiting to understand what was being translated. Moreover, she was explicit in linking the increase in her symptoms, especially the sense of despair and futility, with the disappointment regarding her reception in Italy, indicating a decrease in her fear of being rejected because of her criticism toward the country that was hosting her. She had dreamt of Italy as "the land of salvation."

A relationship built on trust, which led to a real commitment in the therapy, was reached after two events took place, both of which occurred during the fourth session: the first was related to the therapist's proposal to build a common vocabulary by asking Fatima to teach her two new words, which were particularly significant in that session, in her language at every meeting, a proposal that Fatima welcomed with great enthusiasm; the second event was related to Fatima's late arrival at the session, to which the therapist responded by rising to greet her without reproach.

Both experiences were emotionally charged for both patient and therapist, which allowed a qualitative leap in the rapport to take place. In the first event, the wish expressed by the therapist to learn Fatima's language helped the patient perceive the two cultural horizons as less distant, making the therapy more acceptable and in harmony with the beliefs of her country of origin. In the second event, recognition of the patient's dignity as a human being was a central element of the healing process, especially in those who have seen this right eroded. It was Fatima herself who stressed this point by explaining that not being reproached for arriving late and the respect shown by the therapist in getting up to greet her represented a "corrective emotional experience," in which she felt acknowledged for her value as a subject and not as an object. During the following sessions, Fatima attempted to speak in Italian using the few words that she had learned. Her desire to establish a direct relationship with the therapist became clear, and the mediator promoted this shift of relational focus. Fatima decided to start a course to learn the new language and became very cooperative when the proposal of working on the traumas with the EMDR protocol was offered to her.

The first step with Fatima was to work on the present, as it was not possible to effectively work on the past because it was too painful and a source of anxiety. Nor was it wise to work on the future, as it could not be represented after the recent asylum application rejection. Therefore, the work focused on her somatic pain and, through the creation of a safe place and installation of her present resources, on preparation for the second commission hearing.

The possibility of locating a safe place proved to be very difficult for a person so strongly traumatized from childhood, but in the end it was found in the place where the therapy was being conducted, which also included the social worker who had been following Fatima since her arrival in Rome. Opening the setting to the people who belong to the patient's social network is sometimes a crucial element in the start of a clinical path for torture victims, who have always found themselves at the mercy of a hostile environment (Caizzi & Ciambellini, 2008).

The use of the protocol on somatic pain was accompanied by the search for a suitable form of bilateral stimulation, which in Fatima's case were circular eye movements. The NC that emerged immediately as she focused on the somatic pain was that typical of torture victims: "I am nothing," and initially it was impossible to identify the PC. Asked to describe the pain through a drawing, Fatima illustrated the impossibility of distinguishing between physical and mental pain, representing the fragmentation of her inner world with the faces of loved ones floating around (Figure 8.1).

Through mindfulness exercises accompanied by bilateral stimulation, Fatima was helped in strengthening her capacity for nonjudgmental attention and recognizing her current physical security.

The decrease, but not disappearance, of the somatic pain, together with greater ability to regulate anxiety and physiological hyperreactivity, made it possible to start work on her traumatic history.

Using the EMDR R-TEP, Fatima identified two targets to work on her hasty escape from home and the subsequent abandonment of her children and the torture and rapes suffered. We decided together to start from her escape from home, a less frightening memory than the torture.

The first target was processed rather rapidly. The prevailing emotions were sadness and guilt toward her children, which she connected to the loss of her parents. This demarcated the beginning of her suffering. She repeatedly stated: "If they were alive all this would not have happened to me!" Through desensitization and reprocessing of the most painful images, Fatima showed an important change in her perspective: escaping was no longer seen as abandonment and an act of cowardice against her family. Escape was a way of saving her life that would allow her to reconnect with her children in the future, children who, unlike her, have not lost their own mother. This change in perspective allowed Fatima to imagine a future again.

It was not possible, however, to fully reprocess the second target. After three difficult sessions, in which the intensity of emotion fell to then rise again in the following ones, we decided to set those memories aside. Despite feeling slightly relieved about having been able to share, for the first time, the horrors suffered, Fatima still needed to work on stabilization and focus on the imminent hearing.

**FIGURE 8.1** First drawing, Fatima's inner world

**FIGURE 8.2** Fatima's drawing at the end of therapy

At the 3-month follow-up, Fatima was smiling and cheerful. She emphasized the usefulness of the therapeutic work, although not with respect to the most painful memories. She was speaking better Italian and obtained refugee status, having been able to offer a more coherent and credible account of her story. She had decided to start looking for news of her children, something she had avoided doing before.

The elaboration of some traumatic experiences, especially those of escape, had allowed Fatima to build a migration plan, which gave her a sense of continuity of the self, as is evident from the drawing that she wanted to give the therapist (Figure 8.2). She represented herself as a full-length figure next to a chicken eating and a monkey, a typical landscape of her country. At the bottom of the picture, there is a colored snake, representing her positive thoughts.

With the thought of a possible family reunification, the process of integration into the culture of the host country in which she is learning the language has started.

## Sultan's Case

Sultan is a 20-year-old Afghan young man who has been in Italy since 2010. He arrived in the country as a minor and then had his refugee status recognized. His goal is to go to university and become an engineer like his father. He is fluent in Italian and writes poetry in both Italian and his own language.

He has several friends, but feels very lonely. Since the move to the new center, he is suffering from gastritis and vitiligo, which doctors attribute to emotional stress. Sultan has many flashbacks involving his father being riddled with bullets, and episodes of captivity suffered in the different countries he went through, accompanied by constant fear of being raped. Nightmares, depression, and negative thoughts about himself and his future, as well as nostalgia for his mother and brother, often turn into moments of acute desperation leading to suicidal thoughts.

## History

Sultan fled Afghanistan in 2009 with his mother and brother, following his father's assassination by the Taliban. From there, he reached Iran and then Turkey. Here, he lost sight of his family, who were stopped and sent back to Iran, while he continued his journey across Europe. He did not report traumatic episodes before fleeing his country. He described the relationship with his father, an atheist and communist, as very important in his life. His father taught him ideas and values and always encouraged him to be curious and open toward what is new. He was a reference point for Sultan and losing him left Sultan with a terrible void. The relationship with his mother, a Muslim, had always been rather conflicting as he did not share her religious values, but she nevertheless gave him a strong sense of family that he now missed.

## The Treatment

Sultan arrives at the psychological support facility under the recommendation of a psychiatrist. During the first interview, he appears very discouraged about the usefulness of these meetings, despite the fact that he requested treatment. He had seen a psychologist in another hospital the previous year. He shows a state of continuous stress characterized by negative thoughts and a constant reactivation of the image of his dead father. He feels that he is surviving rather than living and believes to be hopelessly damaged by all that has happened to him, especially when he was still very young. He constantly repeats that he was only 14 when he had to flee his country and alternates moments of despair with moments of anger.

It is clear that the forced migration and the cultural identity crisis, linked to the loss of his father, represents the main risk factors for his mental health. However, Sultan's ability to integrate quickly into the new reality the social support he received upon his arrival in Italy and his attitude toward planning constitute major resilience factors. This was also determined by a childhood development characterized by a relationship of positive attachment with his parents and by the absence of early interpersonal traumas.

The therapist decides to try to reach an agreement on a therapeutic plan with Sultan from the first session. The plan will initially be focused on the stabilization of the symptoms through psychoeducation on trauma, and on relaxation techniques and exercises of mindfulness to manage negative thoughts. The therapist also points out that the treatment will initially consist of only five sessions to clarify expectations.

Sultan very quickly becomes so familiar with the relaxation techniques that he starts using them to his advantage to handle disturbing emotions. He also finds the work done with EMDR on resources extremely useful. Positive memories about his father and moments spent in Italy start emerging, giving him hope in his ability to build his future. His sleep has improved and negative thoughts about himself and his future have decreased; however, the intrusive images about his father's death remain.

By mutual agreement, the decision to extend the therapy by adding five more sessions is made. This will allow work on Sultan's traumatic experiences, through the reelaboration of the most disturbing aspects, to take place. Sultan appears to be more collaborative and willing to trust the therapist, but he still manifests fear of being abandoned: "I feel safe here and I am able to tell my story, but what will happen when it will end?"

The R-TEP makes it possible to identify the more traumatic memories: the threats received by Sultan's father, Sultan's father's death, the imprisonment in Greece where Sultan feared being raped, and the separation from his mother and brother.

The first image on which the therapeutic work centers is that of Sultan's father's body riddled with bullets. The NC is: "I am damaged." The PC is: "I can plan my future, I can continue my father's work." The prevailing emotions are: anger and sadness, with a Subjective Units of Disturbance score of 10.

After the EMDR standard protocol has taken place, the picture is much less vivid, although a fair degree of disturbance remains. The boy is feeling better and stops having flashbacks, and asks to devote the last meeting to the reconstruction of the episode of forced separation from his mother and brother. However, he does not accept the proposal to address this theme in greater depth. His need to avoid the full activation of these painful memories is clear. Before saying goodbye he gives the therapist a piece of paper with a sentence his father would often repeat: "Accept your past, live stably your present, and be ready for your future."

At follow-up, Sultan has retained his ability to regulate his emotions. He continues with his studies with great results and is much more confident about his future and the chances of reuniting his family. He speaks a lot about his relationship with the psychiatrist whom he sees as a father figure and an important reference point, despite the few and hurried contacts they have had. Once again, as at the beginning of our work, he makes the therapist feel his need to keep his distance from a female figure who, perhaps, is still too much a reminder of his mother's absence.

Upon the psychiatrist's suggestion, it is Sultan who picks up contact with the center 18 months after the last meeting. He feels again distressed, even though he has implemented his plan to join the Faculty of Engineering in Rome and has received a scholarship. He is finding it difficult to study and is terrified of losing his scholarship and relapsing into the condition of a refugee having to depend on others for help. Behind this demand, however, his affective needs soon emerge: he has met a girl that he likes and would like to start a relationship with, a girl he feels he does not deserve because he is without a family and roots. At the same time, he is finding it extremely difficult to decode the nonverbal messages coming from girls who belong to a different culture from his own. The themes of inadequacy and shame, accompanied by the feeling of not having the basics for living, seem to be reemerging.

In order for the therapist to fully understand his emotional distress, she must consider three aspects:

1. The cultural dimension of his country, which emphasizes the importance of an identity primarily linked to the family rather than the individual. Therefore, not having a family could involve a rejection and isolation from the social context (Dwairy, 2006).
2. The lack of guidance throughout the delicate stage of his adolescence, which makes him feel lost and confused during his first affective approaches.

3. The difficulty in processing the emotional trauma of the separation from his mother; since both his parents had always stressed the importance, for a son, of being strong and not showing emotions.

In the light of these factors, EMDR therapy included a series of integrative interventions aimed at guiding him through the aspects typical of his developmental stage. A brief description of the typical nonverbal cues of flirting in Western society, and a comparison with those of his own Muslim culture, were enough to make him feel closer to the girls. However, it is only by recognizing and processing the pain caused by the dispersion of his family and the separation from his mother that Sultan will be able to get involved in an emotional relationship—an elaboration, which is now possible, thanks to the materialization of his migratory plan, which is proving to be realistic and feasible.

In both clinical cases described, we believe that the EMDR approach has facilitated the construction of a migratory plan, which is realistic and flexible, that helps the patient build a narrative that can integrate different experiences of the self.

Sultan had a plan from the very beginning: to follow in his father's footsteps and study engineering, which he started to implement by learning Italian at evening class. However, what he is lacking is the presence of parental figures who will enable him to carry it forward and overcome the sense of injustice and damage suffered. In his case, EMDR is done through the articulation of various integrative cognitive interventions that will help Sultan face the issues linked to his stage of development.

With Fatima, however, it was necessary to help her develop a more benevolent attitude toward her sense of self, which had been severely damaged by torture. This work will stop her from getting stuck in the role of victim, and enable her to imagine a future.

While retaining a clarity of rules and objectives, both therapists who have been collaborating in following these patients have chosen interventions that go beyond a strictly clinical setting in order to enhance the more supportive and self-care aspect of the therapeutic process and at the same time allow them to build a bridge between the various ways of giving meaning to mental suffering.

## SUMMARY

Based on our experience with refugees and asylum seekers, we can say that an effective clinical intervention is characterized by a number of factors:

- The importance of not working immediately on traumatic experiences
- The use of a phased approach that pays particular attention to the stabilization of the patient and the avoidance defensive mechanism
- The proposal of brief interventions, built around the patient's present context, with a continuous balance between stabilization and processing of traumatic experience
- The use of the EMDR R-TEP

- Attention to the way in which the patient's problem is considered within the culture of origin, to the way it would have been addressed in the country of origin and by which supportive figures. In this work, the role of the mediator is extremely important
- Special attention to the therapeutic relationship as an opportunity for a corrective emotional experience (Alexander & Thomas, 1946) through a rapport based on cooperation and equal partnership

The work with refugees and asylum seekers involves a therapeutic approach that cannot be linear and rigid. It must operate on different levels (psychological, social, cultural), with attention to what is being done during the session, rather than to what is being said (Telfner, 2010). In this perspective, EMDR becomes a tool that can facilitate connection with "the other," provided that the therapist is able to reflect on this otherness by bringing to the table an attitude of openness and mutual exchange. The emphasis that this method places on the natural tendency of the individual to find an adaptive solution to adverse events allows the therapist to convey care rather than determining the healing process. The purpose of this type of intervention is to stimulate the resilience of this suffering population, helping them recognize the resources they already have, and increasing their "emotional capital" (Papadopoulos, 2002), which is their ability to relate to other human beings and to integrate in the new way of life. For this to be possible, it is not enough to simply administer clinical procedures that have been developed to overcome traumatic experiences. It is also necessary to build a relationship that allows them to perceive the two cultural horizons, that of the country of origin and that of the host country, as less distant.

The recognition of their dignity as human beings, for those who have felt this right crumbling, must be a top priority of the entire health care community. This core respect integrated with thoughtful interventions facilitates a recovery and healing process.

## REFERENCES

Alexander, F., & Thomas, M. F. (1946). *Psychoanalytic therapy: Principles and application.* New York, NY: Ronald Press.

Aragona, M., Catina, E., Pucci, D., Carrer, S., Colosimo, F., Lafuente, M., . . . Geraci, S. (2010). The relationship between somatization and posttraumatic symptoms among immigrants receiving primary care services. *Journal of Traumatic Stress, 23*(5), 615–622.

Aragona, M., Pucci, D., Mazzetti, M., & Geraci, S. (2012). Post-migration living difficulties as a significant risk factor for PTSD in immigrants: A primary care study. *Italian Journal of Public Health, 9*(3). Retrieved from ijphjournal.it/article/download/7525/6784

Aragona, M., Pucci, D., Mazzetti, M., Maisano, B., & Geraci, S. (2013). Traumatic events, post-migration living difficulties and post-traumatic symptoms in first generation immigrants: A primary care study. *Annali Istituto Superiore di Sanità, 49*(2), 169–175.

Caizzi, C., & Ciambellini, S. (2008). An ethnopsychiatric approach to healing trauma in involuntary immigrants and torture victims: A clinical case. *Transactional Analysis Journal, 38*(4), 273–284.

Courtois, C. A., & Ford, J. D. (2009). *Treating complex traumatic stress disorders*. New York, NY: Guilford Press.

Dwairy, M. (2006). *Counseling and psychotherapy with Arabs and Muslims. A culturally sensitive approach*. New York, NY: Teachers College Press, Columbia University.

Dworkin, M. (2005). *EMDR and the relational imperative: The therapeutic relationship in EMDR treatment*. New York, NY: Routledge.

Gonzalez, A., & Mosquera, D. (2012). *EMDR and dissociation: The progressive approach*. Charleston, SC: On Demand Publishing.

Heptinstall, E., Sethna, V., & Taylor, E. (2004). PTSD and depression in refugee children: Association with pre-migration trauma and post-migration stress. *Child and Adolescent Psychiatry, 13*, 373–380.

Herman, J. L. (1992). Complex PTSD: A syndrome in survivors of prolonged and repeated trauma. *Journal of Traumatic Stress, 5*, 377–391.

Herman, J. L. (1997). *Trauma and recovery. The aftermath of violence from domestic abuse to political terror*. London, UK: Basic Books.

Mazzetti, M. (2008). Trauma and migration. A transactional analytic approach towards refugees and torture victims. *Transactional Analysis Journal, 38*(4), 285–302.

Miller, K. E., & Rasmussen, A. (2010). War exposure, daily stressors, and mental health in conflict and post-conflict settings: Bridging the divide between trauma-focused and psychosocial frameworks. *Social Science & Medicine, 70*, 7–16.

Miti, G., & Onofri, A. (2011). La psicoterapia dei disturbi dissociativi: Dalle tecniche cognitivo-comportamentali all'approccio EMDR. *Cognitivismo Clinico, 8*(1), 73–91.

Moro, M. R., Neuman, D., & Real, I. (2008). *Maternités en exil. Mettre des bébés au monde et les faire grandir en situation transculturelle*. France: La pensée sauvage.

Papadopoulos, R. K. (2002). *Therapeutic care for refugees. No place like home*. London, UK: Karnac Books.

Rasmussen, A., Rosenfeld, B., Reeves, K., & Keller, A. S. (2007). The subjective experience of trauma and subsequent PTSD in a sample of undocumented immigrants. *Journal of Nervous and Mental Disease, 195*, 137–143.

Sabin, M., Sabin, K., Kim, H. J., Vergara, M., & Varese, L. (2006). The mental health status of Mayan refugees after repatriation to Guatemala. *Revista Panamericana de Salud Publica, 19*, 163–171.

Saxena, S., Nepal, M. K., & Mohan, D. (1988). DSM III: Axis I diagnosis of Indian psychiatric patients presenting somatic symptoms. *American Journal of Psychiatry, 145*, 1023–1024.

Schauer, M., Neuner, F., & Elbrert, T. (2011). *Narrative exposure therapy (NET). A short-term treatment for traumatic stress disorders*. Goettingen, Germany: Hogrefe Publishing.

Shapiro, F. (2012). *Getting past your past: Take control of your life with self-help techniques from EMDR therapy*. New York, NY: Rodale.

Shapiro, E., & Brurit, L. (2012). The recent traumatic episode protocol (R-TEP) for early EMDR intervention (EEI) revised. *Journal of EMDR Practice and Research, 2*, 113–115.

Silove, D., Sinnerbrink, I., Field, A., Manicavasagar, V., & Steel, Z. (1997). Anxiety, depression and PTSD in asylum-seekers: Associations with pre-migration trauma and post-migration stressors. *British Journal of Psychiatry, 170*, 351–357.

Spitzer, C., Barnow, S., Wingenfeld, K., Rose, M., Lowe, B., & Grabe, H. J. (2009). Complex post-traumatic stress disorder in patients with somatization disorder. *The Australian and New Zealand Journal of Psychiatry, 43*, 80–86.

Telfner, U. (2010). Il lavoro con i migranti in Italia: Per una pratica etica basata sul rispetto. *Terapia Familiare, 92*, 57–79.

van der Hart, O., Brown, P., & van der Kolk, B. A. (1989). Pierre Janet on post-traumatic stress. *Journal of Traumatic Stress, 2*(4), 365–378.

van der Hart, O., Nijenhuis E. R., & Solomon, R. (2010). Dissociation of the personality in complex trauma-related disorders and EMDR: Theoretical considerations. *Journal of EMDR Practice and Research, 4*(2), 76–92.

van der Kolk, B. A. (2005). Developmental trauma disorder: Toward a rational diagnosis for children with complex trauma histories. *Psychiatric Annals, 35*, 401–408.

van der Kolk, B. A., Pelcovitz, D., Roth, D., Mandel, F. S., Mcfarlane, A., & Herman, J. L. (1996). Dissociation, somatization and affect dysregulation: The complexity of adaptation to trauma. *American Journal of Psychiatry, 153*, 83–93.

Wiesel, E. (1996). Interview. Washington DC: Academy of Achievement, Museum of Living History. Retrieved from http://www.achievemt.org

# SECTION III

# Innovative Protocols

# CHAPTER 9

# Legacy Attuned EMDR Therapy: Toward a Coherent Narrative

Natalie S. Robinson

There is ample evidence that eye movement desensitization and reprocessing (EMDR) therapy is recognized as a powerful method of psychotherapy by domestic and worldwide organizations (American Psychiatric Association, 2004; Department of Veterans Affairs and Department of Defense, 2004, 2010; World Health Organization, 2013). EMDR therapy alleviates suffering and promotes positive self-worth (Shapiro, 2001). The standard three-pronged EMDR therapy protocol addresses past disturbances, present triggers, and future actions, but it does not specifically address the internalized ancestral, familial, cultural or archetypal influences from the distant past. Legacy attuned EMDR therapy contains narrative, transgenerational, and integrative components. It allows clinicians to access and reprocess transgenerational associations, and memories that negatively impact current lives.

Legacy attuned EMDR therapy promotes the reprocessing of distilled associations that may have originated from family or cultural narratives, media or photographic images, or from imaginal perceptions of the distant past. The adaptive processing model (AIP) of EMDR therapy (Shapiro, 2001) asserts that associations from the past can be dysfunctionally stored and manifest in present time as disturbing images, negative beliefs about self or others, affect dysregulation, and/or distressing bodily sensations. The impact of dysfunctionally stored memories, stories, and beliefs can be transmitted to descendants from dominant and from minority cultures as well as to people raised by birth or adopted families.

Legacy reprocessing can benefit any individual but may be especially therapeutic for people who have experienced transgenerationally based familial, cultural, or institutional abuse. Legacy attuned EMDR therapy resonates for people exposed to terrorism, war, and genocide, as well as for those stricken by devastating natural disasters. It stimulates hindsight and compassion for ancestors forced to migrate from homelands in order to survive or to serve the greed of others. It is germane for people persecuted by racial, religious, and gender discrimination, including gay, transgendered, and minority individuals who have felt betrayed and invalidated by the culture at large or by their cultural heritage. Legacy processing also allows descendants to notice and honor positive traditions and beliefs of forebears.

Legacy attuned EMDR therapy includes target selection, knowledge interweaves, and dysfunctionally stored experiences and is consistent with the AIP model. It draws upon resources that may have been dormant and helps discard deficits such as negative self-beliefs that have accumulated over longer periods of time, even generations. Legacy components are introduced as part of a broad-brush exploration that does not focus on accumulating factual ancestral or historical details. Nor does it entail past life regression or access to deceased ancestors. The intent is to reprocess select transgenerational memories of experiences or narratives. It brings an edge of awareness to relevant resources or disturbances from the *collective memory*, which is passed down from one generation to another. The goal is not to reprocess all or even many specific memories, just enough to help clients perceive sufficient associations to formulate a coherent life narrative and develop a legacy-based Core Positive Cognition (CPC). Legacy attuned EMDR therapy fosters a deeply rooted sense of wholeness and therapeutic completeness. It is predicated on the wisdom and concepts of the AIP model and a range of EMDR therapy procedures as well as other multidisciplinary clinical, scientific, and philosophical predecessors.

## VOICES OF PREDECESSORS

The narrative, transgenerational, and integrative components of legacy attuned EMDR therapy are informed by multifaceted psychological theories and practices that recognize the significant impact of the past on current dynamics and symptomatology. Freud (1954) developed and popularized the concept of the unconscious, Jung (1916) that of the collective unconscious, and Klein (1955/1975) explored projective identification. Attachment researchers (Ainsworth, Blehar, Waters, & Wall, 1978; Main & Solomon, 1986) recognized a transgenerational and a narrative perspective when they discovered that the best predictor of secure attachment of a newborn infant is the ability of the primary caretaker parent to tell a coherent life story. Narrative therapy, popularized in the 1990s (White & Epston, 1990), has traditionally emphasized the healing power of storytelling. White's Dulwich Centre in Australia currently utilizes story telling as a healing modality with indigenous peoples. McAdams defined the *life story* as, ". . . an internalized and evolving narrative of the self that incorporates the reconstructed past, perceived present, and anticipated future in order to provide a life with a sense of unity and purpose" (McAdams, 2009, p. 10). This definition resonates with the past, present, and future prongs of EMDR therapy.

Family therapists and researchers have understood and attempted to treat the negative transgenerational residue of familial and societal dynamics such as loyalties (Boszormenyi-Nagy & Spark, 1984; Hoffman, 1990), secrets (Imber-Black, 1993), and trauma (Kellermann, 2013). Family systems group therapist Satir (1983) identified and worked with negative family scripts. More recently, family constellation therapy (Wolynn, 2015) utilized a unique form of psychodrama to encourage group participants to resolve previously unrecognized family dynamics that span multiple generations.

The impact of the distant past on the present day has also been explored by mythologist Joseph Campbell (1991) as well as psychoanalyst and author of archetypal stories Clarissa Pinkola Estés (1995). Claire Frederick (2009), a psychiatrist and specialist in dissociative disorders, integrates personal mythology and narratives through hypnotic processing. Current epigenetics research (Jablonka & Raz, 2009; Kellermann, 2013) has introduced yet another piece of intriguing data about the transgenerational transmission of trauma. There are indications that life experiences may be encoded in genetic material and transmitted to descendants. Thus, people might show symptoms of trauma without having suffered through those experiences themselves. Siegel (1999), a noted psychiatrist and interdisciplinary author of *The Developing Mind* (1999), gives voice to the vital importance of integrative elements for good mental health and general well-being. Dr. Siegel (2010) defines nine domains of integration that promote a sense of wholeness and well-being. The EMDR protocol incorporates several of Siegel's domains of integration, including bilateral, consciousness, vertical integration, and memory. Legacy attuned EMDR deepens the integrative component of EMDR therapy through two additional domains: temporal and narrative.

Legacy attuned EMDR therapy acknowledges and incorporates ideas and implementations from diverse schools of psychological thought and innovative EMDR practitioners (Kitchur, 2005; Korn & Leeds, 2002; Lendl & Foster, 1997; Lovett, 1999; Nickerson, 2011; Shapiro, 2001; Shapiro, 2005; Yoeli & Prattos, 2009). These practitioners inform the temporal and narrative foundation as well as the time-free implementation of legacy attuned EMDR. Francine Shapiro, the originator and developer of EMDR therapy (Shapiro, 1989, 2001, 2013), stresses the influence of the past on the present. Shapiro also identified the time-free nature of the AIP as healing "because rapid treatment effects can be observed when EMDR is applied, regardless of the number of disturbing events and no matter how long ago they occurred" (Shapiro, 2001, p. 48). Joan Lovett (1999) successfully utilized story telling with EMDR therapy, which she does with young children. The model for the development of legacy-based resources comes from resource development and installation (RDI) (Korn & Leeds, 2002). Maureen Kitchur (2005) introduced the developmental timeline. Robin Shapiro (2005) noted the importance of generational introjects and Mark Nickerson (2011) presented the strategies for undoing stigma with EMDR therapy. Yoeli and Prattos (2009) detailed a use of the genogram (McGoldrick & Gerson, 1985) with EMDR therapy. Legacy attuned EMDR emanates from the aforementioned innovators and the AIP model of processing.

## WHAT LEGACY ATTUNED EMDR DOES FOR CLIENTS

EMDR therapy accesses and reprocesses disturbing fragments of memories, emotions, thoughts, and bodily sensations that interfere with current well-being. These fragments may emanate from earlier life experiences, current triggers, or future anxieties. Legacy attuned EMDR extends the reach of EMDR reprocessing into transgenerationally linked associations and can facilitate the ability to:

- Access legacy-based strengths
- Desensitize maladaptively encoded trauma and beliefs generated by negative familial, cultural, societal, or ancestral patterns and institutions
- Embrace a CPC that resonates with the distant past
- Develop a legacy-inclusive coherent life narrative that reconsolidates fragmented threads from the distant past, the remembered past, current being, and future vision

*For example, 24-year-old Bobby had come into therapy depressed and continually getting into scrapes with the law. Bobby had been adopted from another country and had felt unwanted all of his life. During his course of EMDR therapy, he had successfully targeted incidents of feeling ostracized by family and schoolmates, a recent failed romantic relationship, and an inability to envision a positive future. He had become able to hold a job, maintain a positive intimate relationship, and was no longer getting into trouble. As he and I began to discuss termination, he felt that something was still missing and he agreed to do the legacy reprocessing. Although he had few facts on which to base his assumptions about his birth family and country of origin, he utilized the legacy attuned EMDR therapy protocol to access and reprocess images, events, and people as he imagined them to have been. He articulated a succinct narrative at the end of a series of reprocessing sets as well as a CPC that was installed.*

*When he completed the legacy reprocessing, he began to understand why his birth parents may have put him up for adoption. He reasoned that they were hardly surviving back there; there had been a struggle to survive for generations. They couldn't feed another child and wanted something better for him. They had brought him to a safe place with a blanket and that meant that they cared about him. He had hated feeling so different growing up. He had been bullied and felt he didn't belong anywhere. But now he concluded that his parents did love him, those who raised him and those who birthed him. His coherent life narrative at the conclusion of his therapy was "I do belong. I belong to the world. I'm beginning to feel like a grown up. I can make my way and be the man I want to be."*

The legacy processing enabled this young man to move beyond his belief that he was given away for adoption because there was something wrong with him. He developed a coherent life narrative that included his envisioned distant past, his known past, his present sense of being, and his future vision. Adoptees can utilize legacy attuned EMDR as readily as other clients. They process whatever comes up during the sets. Clients who have been adopted may reprocess thoughts, affects, bodily sensations, or images related to either birth families or adopted families, or both, as in the case of Bobby.

## WHEN TO USE LEGACY ATTUNED EMDR

There are several times in the course of EMDR therapy that legacy attunement is productive. It can be utilized to procure a comprehensive client history and plan treatment, develop resources for strategic use, identify and reprocess legacy-rooted triggers and residue that exacerbates current suffering, and promote the clinical integration of a course of EMDR therapy.

### Client History and Treatment Planning

Client history for legacy attuned EMDR therapy is expanded with the use of a multigenerational family genogram (McGoldrick & Gerson, 1985; Yoeli & Prattos, 2009). An initial genogram exploration opens an awareness of legacy-based associations. The observation of forebears, patterns, and influences serves as precursors for legacy-based resources and for the development of a legacy-informed coherent narrative. The genogram is a brief sketch that can include names, nodal events and dates, birth order, and countries of origin on both the paternal and maternal sides.

I typically express interest and curiosity about how the gathered information or family patterns might be relevant to the client's presenting problem.

*For example, Mary, a 43-year-old married woman of Irish descent, came into therapy feeling overwhelmed, angry, and depressed. During the first session Mary asked, "Why am I stuck having to be the one to take care of my mother?" I told Mary that she asked a good question and that a genogram might provide some clues. Perhaps others in her family felt burdened. Although Mary said she was interested in the family history, she added that her family didn't speak about the past. I reassured her that they would just note the information that was known and put in question marks if there was doubt. As they drew out the family positions, I noticed some patterns and expressed curiosity about what it might have been like for Mary's great aunt to be the first born girl in her family. Mary responded that it must have been hard. After three generations of Mary's family were sketched out, Mary commented that she had come from a family of hard workers. On her mother's side, the men drank and provided for their families and the women worked hard and did what they were supposed to do. On her father's side, both the men and women raged at one another and the women let everyone know that they felt used and abused. Mary said that "the women were plenty strong on both sides." In this case, the genogram's transgenerational lens brought into focus ancestral resources (plenty strong) and patterns that related to the client's presenting problem (angry, hardworking, and resentful).*

As part of treatment planning with a legacy perspective, a desired CPC is identified as part of the goal. Clients are asked what they would like to believe about themselves by the time the therapy is completed. The statement from Mary, in the aforementioned case, that "the women were plenty strong on both sides of my family," gave me a natural opening to ask her about her desired CPC. Mary answered that she'd like to believe that she was strong but she really wasn't. I asked her how much she believed the words "I am strong" on a scale of 1 to 7, where 7 is completely true and 1 is completely false. Mary said it was a 1. I replied that it was understandable that she would feel that way for now and that it was possible that she would change her mind about herself as they proceeded. EMDR therapy fosters an opportunity for clients to embrace a positive self-belief that fits for them. Final development of the CPC is done toward the end of the legacy attuned EMDR therapy.

## Legacy Attuned Resources

Resources such as the container, lightstream, and safe place (Miller, 1994; Shapiro, 2001; Twombly, 2001) are often established as part of the preparation for EMDR reprocessing. Additional resources are sometimes advised for vulnerable clients for stabilization and affect regulation, closure, looping, or to mitigate overwhelming anxiety related to processing specific triggers or events. The RDI protocol (Korn & Leeds, 2002) can be applied to elicit ancestral resources. Clients are asked what quality or strength they need in their life now. The therapist helps the client identify an ancestor or a personage from the collective memory, perhaps an historical figure who resonates with a client, whether or not this figure has a personal cultural or a family-linked connection. Renowned figures such as Martin Luther King, Jr., Mahatma Gandhi, or Helen Keller are among those often chosen by clients because they have a desired quality or have overcome a challenge similar to one that the client is currently facing (incredible loss/hardship, unjust or unrelenting opposition, disheartening set-backs, incessant depression, or anxiety). In one case, a legacy resource was developed and installed for a client anxiously facing major surgery. The client identified the source and the quality that she felt she needed right now, the patience of Gandhi in her heart. Slow, short, bilateral stimulation sets (BLS) were used until the client felt her patience grow as strong as possible with a deep sense of calmness in her chest. I helped her identify and install a gesture to anchor and to self-cue the calm feeling. She placed her hand over her heart to reexperience that sense of calmness.

Clients also use legacy attuned resources to expand their window of tolerance when the EMDR reprocessing is looping rather than moving ahead.

*Sally, a 51-year-old survivor of chronic and severe sexual abuse and neglect, wanted someone or something strongly protective to be there for her as she reprocessed a terrifying early abuse memory. She loved the mental images evoked for her by the book,* Women Who Run With the Wolves *(Estés, 1995). Sally kept images from that book in mind while doing a floatback to search for a resource. A mental picture of herself as an ancient woman warrior emerged without any assumption being made that this image was a part of her ancestral lineage. She then imagined herself in the center of a circle surrounded by women warriors facing outward. Each woman was a fierce replica of herself and each had a quiver of poisonous arrows in readiness. Her imagined sense of being transformed into multiple powerful ancient warriors was installed with BLS. She reactivated the warrior image for psychological armor, a source of personal strength and protection she needed for processing memory and current life experiences.* This state change led to Sally's ability to process trauma and achieve trait changes.

Clients who are able to locate resources that arise from legacy-based sources report that they are incredibly empowering both in and out of sessions. Deeply scarred clients who are able to develop personally relevant legacy-based resources can utilize them to expand their window of tolerance in order to reprocess traumatic memories whether or not those forebears are familial relations. Jung (1916) or Estés (1995) might have considered an associative link to be part of the collective memory.

Once a legacy attuned resource has been identified, developed, and installed, it can be used in several ways during the course of the therapy.

*Mary, the client cited earlier, was agitated at the end of an incomplete session. She needed additional stabilization and self-soothing for closure and between sessions. She was not able to utilize the safe/calm place imagery or lightstream that day. I asked what or who she needed for a good closure and for the upcoming week. Mary thought of having her great grandmother sitting by her side singing soothing lullabies to her. This image of her and her great grandmother and her PC "I am lovable" was installed with BLS. Mary also used this resource to soothe herself in between sessions when she was awakened by nightmares.*

Legacy attuned EMDR resources can be developed (Korn & Leeds, 2002) to be used for anticipated anxiety and affect management as part of a float forward (Browning, 1999).

*George, age 45, had already used EMDR to reprocess childhood sexual abuse by a sadistic uncle. But he was deeply anxious about an upcoming family event being attended by that uncle. He wanted to confront the uncle, but felt he was too weak to do so. I asked if he could think of someone who might have the quality that he needed now. His answer was General George Patton, not a blood ancestor, but a cultural icon for him. George developed an image of standing like Patton with his feet firmly planted on the floor and a bodily sensation of feeling the courage of Patton in his gut. He then imagined himself at the family function and anticipated himself standing and confronting his uncle. The Negative Cognition (NC) was "I am weak," the Positive Cognition (PC) "I am courageous." His anxiety was at Subjective Units of Disturbance (SUDs) level of 8, where 10 was the highest imaginable. Set after set of BLS was done until his anxiety went down to a zero. The PC "I am courageous" was strengthened and installed with slow sets of BLS. George reported that he had stepped into his Patton shoes as needed during the processing of the anticipated event. When he returned from the event itself, he spoke of being proud of himself for speaking up to his uncle and proud that he did so in his own shoes. Legacy-based resources need not be blood related nor heritage linked to be powerful for clients.*

## Target Legacy-Based Trauma

Refugees, victims of racial, religious, or identity persecution, and those suffering from natural disasters often enter therapy with both historical and more recent trauma. Media accounts or memories of family or cultural stories may retrigger the terror or exacerbate posttraumatic symptomology of recent events. These painful reactions are particularly likely to manifest in people who have felt invalidated or endangered by the dominant culture or those who were raised in families with those central concerns. A floatback can identify an earlier target, perhaps a story heard as a child or a photograph seen. The standard EMDR protocol can then be used to desensitize legacy-based fears that intensify current triggers.

## Develop a Coherent Life Narrative and a CPC

Developing a coherent life narrative and legacy-informed CPC are important components of legacy attuned EMDR. EMDR therapy typically includes a three-pronged approach of targeting and reprocessing disturbing past memories, current triggers, and anticipated challenges. As part of the wrap up and integration of the overall work completed through EMDR therapy, developing and installing a legacy-oriented CPC can enhance the integrative process. Clients are invited to briefly explore, desensitize, and discard the negative residue of self-selected ancestral images and beliefs and to incorporate residual positive qualities from the distant past. The adaptive information that emerges promotes the development of a coherent life narrative and legacy attuned CPC.

Legacy attuned EMDR enriches the termination process and deepens the integration of the EMDR therapy. Client and therapist circle back to the beginning of the therapy by refocusing on the genogram. Permission is secured from clients to process self-selected associations to their distant past. Clients are set-up for that processing with an appropriate journey metaphor. Disturbances are managed. A brief timeline review of the therapy is done with BLS sets advancing from the associations to the distant past, to the remembered past, on to the client's current state of being and ending with a future vision. Clients are encouraged to verbalize a brief coherent life narrative encompassing the essence of what they have learned about themselves through this EMDR process. The CPC that emerges is installed.

The therapist activates legacy attunement by redirecting a client's attention to the beginning of the therapy. *As we think about ending our work together, let us revisit the beginning and thread together what we have done here.* Details and examples of the steps for implementing legacy attuned EMDR therapy follow.

## HOW TO INTEGRATE LEGACY ATTUNEMENT INTO THERAPY

The specific steps of legacy attuned EMDR therapy are: (1) refocus on the genogram, (2) set-up for legacy reprocessing, (3) reprocess the distant past, (4) manage disturbances, (5) review life with timeline reprocessing, (6) codevelop a coherent life narrative, and (7) elicit and install a legacy informed CPC.

1. *Refocus on the genogram*—Therapist and client direct their attention to a client's transgenerational history. The genogram serves as a template for clients to elicit initial transgenerational images and perceptions. Clients with a foundation steeped in oral traditions may prefer to relate ancestral stories, myths, or inspirational legends rather than to use a genogram to begin to access associations. Suggestions are made for clients to imagine how ethnic ancestors may have lived and prospered, struggled, or suffered through generations. They may notice socioeconomic shifts, migrations, or conflicts. Questions can include *What beliefs or values may these ancestors have held? What qualities and coping skills were transmitted to descendants? What qualities do clients need for life now and in the future?*
2. *Set-up for legacy reprocessing*—The therapist will explain how noticing associations to the distant past is similar to the other EMDR associations that they have been doing. Legacy reprocessing may make them aware of specific or imagined ancestral places, events, and people. Clients are to just notice what comes up, gather whatever is useful to them now, and discard what is not. There are no right or wrong ways to do this and it is not about facts or accuracy. If a client expresses serious disturbance about the distant past, the disturbance itself might be targeted with the standard protocol.

   Appropriate journey metaphors for distant past travel are suggested. They may choose to travel by canoe, be transported along a moving waterway or walkway, float via a hot air balloon, or ride aback a bird. It is essential to encourage clients to personalize this process as much as possible. In one session, a client said, "The canoe or water does nothing for me. I'm a mountain person." The therapist encouraged the client to choose his own way. He took the imaginal journey on foot.

   Specific questions are asked to encourage initial distant past images such as whether ancestors might have lived in a city or countryside or how a client thinks that they may have made a living. The therapist may suggest that the client choose to start the processing on one side of the family or the other. Although it is helpful for clients to choose an initial image for the processing, it is not unusual for images, emotions, and thoughts to veer into unforeseen directions with legacy processing as is true for other EMDR processing. The process goes where it goes.

   *For example, Rebecca, a high-functioning teacher who had endured early life losses, expressed interest in starting on her maternal side as the legacy processing was to begin. But to her own surprise, she found herself following her paternal grandmother down dark streets of a rough city. The grandmother was followed in the shadows by a suspicious husband. This non-English-speaking immigrant mother and grandmother challenged the streets and her husband to attend a Parent Teachers Association (PTA) meeting to learn what her children were being taught. She had been a school teacher in her native Russia. Rebecca later remembered hearing this story from a cousin. She was astonished that she had never given any thought to the determination and strength of her father's side of the family. They became part of her newly developing life narrative. For her, it was no longer about how young she was when she had lost all of her family, but of the resilience that they had passed down to enable her to go on without them.*

3. *Reprocess the distant past with BLS*—Clients are not expected to identify or reprocess all nodal events but just to notice enough associations to help them make a connection to their distant past and to desensitize deeply disturbing associations. *Jonathan, a writer, was intensely interested in the narrative component of the legacy therapy. He had entered therapy with issues of poor self-worth and lifelong bouts of serious depression. Jonathan had a sense of being unlovable in spite of evidence to the contrary, including a loving spouse. The ancestral image that emerged for him with the legacy focus was dreamlike but historically relevant. He envisioned a scene with men in hats and long black coats dancing joyfully in a circle and bouncing something up and down in the center. When he looked closer, he realized that they were laughing and bouncing a baby boy. "That's me. I am their future and I made it even if they were lost in the Holocaust."* In the case of Jonathan, I had incorrectly assumed that the client would use the legacy processing to reprocess Holocaust remnants that filtered through his family history. But the legacy reprocessing is associative and can be unpredictable for client and therapist alike. It often reveals powerful protective or soothing themes as happened with Sally and her self-warriors and with Jonathan and his vison of loving ancestors.
4. *Manage disturbances*—At times during reprocessing, highly disturbing images or emotions emerge and clients ask to pause the processing. They are offered the option of targeting and desensitizing the disturbance, halting the legacy processing entirely, or refocusing in another area. *In one case, Ellen suddenly realized that some of her ancestors were slave owners. At first she wanted to stop and focus elsewhere but she quickly reconsidered and decided to target the disturbing self-beliefs that this realization elicited within her. Her worst image came from a drawing she had seen in a book that prompted her to imagine seeing an ancestor buying slaves. The NC attached to that image was "I am shameful." She wanted to believe, "I am innocent." But when she looked at that image of an ancestor buying slaves, Ellen did not feel innocent and was filled with a high level of self-disgust and nauseated in the pit of her stomach. The target was processed with EMDR but a remnant of disgust and shame remained. Ellen knew that these negative feelings were not at a zero level for her. She searched to find a suitable PC. "I am innocent" did not fit. She came up with a complex self-belief, "I am a good person. I can fight grave injustice in our society. Maybe that is why I've felt so badly about myself." Her later articulated PC was "I'm doing what I can do now and will continue to work on this."* Clients are often surprised to find that residual shame or other negative emotions have affected their sense of self-worth in spite of a lack of conscious awareness. Some, Ellen included, feel the need to do some genealogical research to learn whether

perceived associations may be valid. Ellen also decided that she needed to do more work on herself because of the unresolved feelings of shame.

5. *Review life with timeline processing*—After the distant past associations are completed, a timeline review of the therapy is undertaken. This comprehensive overview serves as a framework for the development of the coherent narrative and the integration of the therapeutic process as a whole. Timeline processing with EMDR has been used for strategic development (Kitchur, 2005), as part of the recent events protocol (R-TEP; Shapiro & Laub, 2015), and to promote life enhancement (Robinson, 2001).

Life review sets for legacy attuned EMDR therapy are generally done with BLS in chronological order to give a sense of historical continuity. Portions of a client's life periods may have already been processed as targets earlier in the therapy. They are now connected as part of the whole therapy experience. Clients refocus on images from life periods and are asked to just notice what comes up for them. Sets may go from prebirth to school age, from elementary school to adolescence, from adolescence to adulthood, from young adult to mid-life to old age, as is appropriate for each client. If unprocessed or new disturbances emerge, the client is given the opportunity to target the disturbance or to move ahead.

For example, a man came into therapy due to relationship problems. Therapy was drawing to a close and he was reprocessing with a focus on his own prebirth period of life and his parents' relationship. Between two of the sets he exclaimed, "I'm a mistake. I wasn't supposed to be born." The therapist asked him if he wanted to target that. He responded, "Hell no, that explains a lot. That's their problem, not mine. I'm fine now. I'm moving on." Life review processing often assuages the self-doubt about salient missing or incomplete fragments as therapy is drawing to a close.

6. *Codevelop a coherent life narrative*—The timeline processing encourages coherence. It includes distant past associations and serves as a baseline from which clients can help to develop personally meaningful life narratives. When processing is completed, clients are helped to integrate the experience by developing a brief coherent life narrative that contains threads from ancestors, lifetime, and a glimpse of the future. There is compelling affirmation that narratives are a vital part of the life experience (Estés, 1995; Siegel, 2010; White & Epston, 1990) and psychological research (Main & Solomon, 1986) that affirms the importance of coherent narratives (Siegel, 2010). The legacy-informed narrative brings a sense of continuity and wholeness to both the EMDR therapy and to the lives of clients. The narrative is not intended to be a comprehensive life story. Clients are asked to briefly summarize their experience with a few sentences about what their story says about them. Many clients begin their narrative some time before they were born and extend them to a positive sense of themselves in the future. Others start the narrative with their presenting problem. The narrative is generally personally affirming, integrative, and an indicator of resilience. These narrative summaries are often remarkably short in length but touchingly expressed.

Mary's narrative was: "I came in here bitter, ready to give up and hating my sister for not helping me. I thought I had had a miserable life. But my people went through life-threatening times including a famine. My great grandmother buried many children and sent one over here alone to this country with a hope of survival. I am from strong stock. I can manage what I have to do now and whatever will come up in the future."

Jonathan realized that he had not wanted to think about why he and his folks were so depressed. His narrative addressed it. "My ancestors were victimized for centuries. And what did my father see in that war? I thought he just hated me. I came close to destroying myself with addictions. But I got myself out of that with a lot of help. I've worked hard. I'm whole. I'm proud of how far I have come. I am lovable." The final step of the legacy attuned EMDR is to elicit and install a CPC.

7. *Elicit and install a legacy informed CPC*—A PC relates to a desired self-referencing belief that a client wants to hold when thinking of a specific event or image. A CPC represents a client's deeply held self-belief without reference to a specific event or image. A legacy informed CPC is a positive self-belief that is enriched with a transgenerational foundation. It is predicated on my own belief that culture and history impact one's core beliefs. The legacy based CPC often emerges directly from the coherent life narrative. A CPC is installed using BLS. If the CPC does not materialize spontaneously, the therapist may say, "As we finish our therapy together, what positive self-belief do you want to hold for yourself now and take away with you for the future?" Jonathan completed therapy feeling and believing, "I am lovable." Examples of other CPCs that have emerged are, "I am strong like my forebears," and "I am able to survive and thrive like my great grandmother." Legacy attuned EMDR therapy, with its transgenerational and narrative lenses, promotes both an integrated and a deeply rooted core positive cognition.

## SUMMARY

Legacy attuned EMDR therapy was developed within the context of my clinical EMDR practice and is designed to be practice oriented. Case examples in this chapter had the client's permission or are composites of my clinical cases. Legacy attuned reprocessing provides resources and brings an edge of awareness of the impact that historical associations may have on current disturbances. These associations may emanate from a client's cultural, familial or archetypal history. The reprocessing encourages the reconsolidation of threads from the distant past and remembered past with current being and future vision, and it encourages the formation of a coherent narrative. It lays the foundation for a legacy-based sense of wholeness for the EMDR therapy. Research is necessary to ascertain the effectiveness of legacy attuned EMDR therapy. However, there is no doubt about the unremitting level of worldwide human suffering and trauma as the result of familial, societal, and institutional malevolence perpetrated by abuse, war, oppression, migration, prejudice, and slavery as well as hardships from accidental or natural disasters. The effects of these traumas can be passed on for generations. EMDR therapists are already working to mitigate worldwide distress. Legacy attuned EMDR therapy can enrich the therapeutic process and stimulate the deeply rooted resilience that humankind needs for well-being and to pass down to descendants.

## REFERENCES

Ainsworth, M. D. S., Blehar, M. C., Waters, E., & Wall, S. N. (1978). *Patterns of attachment: A psychological study of the strange situation.* Hillside, NJ: Erlbaum.

American Psychiatric Association. (2004). *Practice guideline for the treatment of patients with acute stress disorder and post-traumatic stress disorder.* Arlington, VA: American Psychiatric Association Practice Guidelines.

Boszormenyi-Nagy, I., & Spark, G. M. (1984). *Invisible loyalties.* New York, NY: Brunner/Mazel.

Browning, C. (1999). Floatback and float forward: Techniques for linking past, present and future. *EMDRIA Newsletter, 4*(3), 12.

Campbell, J. (1991). *The power of myth.* New York, NY: Knopf Doubleday.

Department of Veterans Affairs and Department of Defense. (2004, 2010). *VA/DoD clinical practice guideline for the management of post-traumatic stress.* Washington, DC: Author.

Estés, C. P. (1995). *Women who run with the wolves: Myths and stories of the wild woman archetype.* New York, NY: Ballantine.

Frederick, C. (2009, May). *Bridging two worlds: The integration of personal mythology.* Lexington, MA: NESTTD Workshop.

Freud, S. (1954). *The origins of psychoanalysis: Letters to Wilhelm Fliess, drafts and notes: 1887–1902.* New York, NY: Basic Books.

Hoffman, L. (1990). *Foundations of family therapy: A conceptual framework for systems change.* New York, NY: Basic Books.

Imber-Black, E. (1993). *Secrets in families and family therapy.* New York, NY: W. W. Norton.

Jablonka, E., & Raz, G. (2009). Transgenerational epigenetic inheritance: Prevalence, mechanisms, and implications for the study of heredity and evolution. *The Quarterly Review of Biology, 84*(2), 131–176.

Jung, C. G. (1916). *Analytic psychology.* New York, NY: Moffat.

Kellermann, N. (2013). Epigenetic transmission of holocaust trauma: Can nightmares be inherited? *The Israel Journal of Psychiatry and Related Sciences, 50*(1), 33–39.

Kitchur, M. (2005). The strategic developmental model for EMDR dysfunctional behaviors. In R. Shapiro (Ed.), *EMDR solutions: Pathways to healing* (pp. 8–56). New York, NY: W. W. Norton.

Klein, M. (1975). On identification. In *The writings of Melanie Kein* (Vol. 3, pp. 141–175). London, UK: Hogarth. (Original work published 1955)

Korn, D. L., & Leeds, A. M. (2002). Preliminary evidence of efficacy for EMDR resource development and installation in the stabilization phase of treatment of complex posttraumatic stress disorder. *Journal of Clinical Psychology, 58*(12), 1465–1487.

Lendl, J., & Foster, S. (1997). *EMDR performance enhancement in the workplace: A practitioner's manual.* San Jose, CA: Performance Enhancement Unlimited.

Lovett, J. (1999). *Small wonders: Healing childhood trauma with EMDR.* New York, NY: Free Press.

Main, M., & Solomon, J. (1986). Discovery of an insecure-disorganized/disoriented attachment pattern. In T. B. Brazelton & M. W. Yogman (Eds.), *Affective development in infancy* (pp. 95–124). Norwood, NJ: Ablex.

McAdams, D. (2009). *The person* (5th ed.). Hoboken, NJ: Wiley.

McGoldrick, M., & Gerson, R. (1985). *Genograms in family assessment*. New York, NY: W. W. Norton.

Miller, E. (1994). *Letting go of stress*. Menlo Park, CA: Source Cassette Tapes.

Nickerson, M. (2011, June 25). *Undoing stigma: EMDR applications in the dismantling of socially based internalized oppression and prejudice theory, examples and practicum*. Waltham, MA: Workshop.

Robinson, N. (2001, September). Time-line EMDR for life enhancement. *EMDRIA Newsletter, 6*(3), 11–12.

Satir, V. (1983). *Conjoint family therapy*. Palo Alto, CA: Science and Behavior Books. (Original work published 1967)

Shapiro, E., & Laub, B. (2015). Early EMDR intervention following a community critical incident: A randomized clinical trial. *Journal of EMDR Practice and Research, 8*(1), 17–27.

Shapiro, F. (1989). Eye movement desensitization: A new treatment for post-traumatic stress disorder. *Journal of Behavior Therapy and Experiential Psychiatry, 20*, 211–217.

Shapiro, F. (2001). *Eye movement desensitization and reprocessing: Basic principles, protocols and procedures* (2nd ed.). New York, NY: Guilford.

Shapiro, F. (2013). *Getting past your past: Take control of your life with self-help techniques from EMDR therapy*. Emmaus, PA: Rodale Books.

Shapiro, F., Kaslow, F. W., & Maxfield, L. (Eds.). (2007). *Handbook of EMDR and family therapy processes*. Hoboken, NJ: Wiley.

Shapiro, R. (2005). EMDR with cultural and generational introjects. In R. Shapiro (Ed.), *EMDR solutions: Pathways to healing* (pp. 228–240). New York, NY: W. W. Norton.

Siegel, D. J. (1999). *The developing mind: Toward a neurobiology of interpersonal experience*. New York, NY: Guilford Press.

Siegel, D. J. (2010). *Mindsight: The new science of personal transformation*. New York, NY: Bantam.

Twombly, J. H. (2001, December). Safe place imagery: Handling intrusive thoughts and feelings. *EMDRIA Newsletter*, Special Edition, 35–38.

White, M., & Epston, D. (1990). *Narrative means to therapeutic ends*. New York, NY: W. W Norton.

Wolynn, M. (2015, March 6–8). *Creating great relationships through family constellations*. Kripalu. Retrieved from www.hellingerpa.com

World Health Organization. (2013). *Guidelines for the management of conditions specifically related to stress*. Geneva, Switzerland: Author.

Yoeli, F. R., & Prattos, T. (2009). The EMDR-accelerated information resourcing (EMDR-air) protocol. In M. Luber (Ed.), *EMDR scripted protocols: Basics and special situations* (pp. 31–45). New York, NY: Springer Publishing Company.

# CHAPTER 10

# EMDR in a Group Setting (GEMDR)

André Maurício Monteiro

There are voices and laughter at the reception of the clinic. They signal uncommon social interaction before a session. We go into the consulting room and everyone quiets down a bit, concentrating on how they feel and what is about to come. The session with a group has begun. They come from different walks of life, but their purpose is the same: to overcome haunting ghosts from the past and to enjoy what life has to offer. Could this happen with the aid of eye movement desensitization and reprocessing (EMDR)?

To date, there have been several successful efforts to adapt the standard EMDR protocol to a group setting. In the aftermath of natural disasters and collective trauma, reports were documented with the aid of the "EMDR Integrative Group Treatment Protocol (IGTP)," developed by Lucina Artigas, Ignacio Jarero, Nicté Alcalá, and Teresa López Cano; "the Imma EMDR Group Protocol," by Brurit Laub and Esti Bar-Sade; and "A Written Workbook for Individual or Group EMDR," by Aiton Birnbaum; all of which were published in Luber's (2009) book on EMDR scripted protocols. These protocols refer mainly to short-term focused intervention. These examples provide useful guidelines that help clinicians to work especially with individuals and groups in postcatastrophes as part of posttraumatic stress disorder (PTSD) prevention interventions (Jarero, Artigas, Uribe, & Miranda, 2014; Monteiro, 2014).

However, EMDR in a group setting may become a suitable venue for some clients who wish to face the consequences of early childhood traumatic experiences, as well as for those who do not really feel they fit into the mainstream culture. This has been my experience in Brazil, where I work. These clients may regard themselves as belonging to a minority and feel discriminated against because of their cultural and ethnic backgrounds, their gender or sexual orientation, or simply wander through life with the Negative Cognition "I don't belong," which often reflects the generalization of childhood rejections.

This text provides general guidelines for conducting a more long-term psychotherapeutic process in a group setting, where these issues may be systematically addressed and reprocessed with the aid of EMDR. Before delving into practical steps and clinical examples, let us begin with some theoretical considerations concerning the pros and cons of an EMDR intervention at individual or collective settings.

EMDR has been primarily regarded as an individual-centered approach to psychotherapy. With the aid of specific procedural steps, outlined in Phase 3 of the standard EMDR protocol, clients activate traumatic memories that are dysfunctionally stored in the brain. They are then reprocessed and integrated in the person's autobiography. Reactions to these traumatic experiences impact the individual at both emotional and neurophysiological levels. When triggered, these emotional reactions tend to be avoidant and dissociative in nature, making it harder for clients to face the reality of what happened to them during the traumatic event that took place in the past. Meanwhile, neurophysiology is altered by what appears to be either excessive sympathetic symptoms, such as anxiety, intrusions, hyperalert states, and startle responses; or excessive parasympathetic activation of the brain, with clients presenting complaints of depression, lack of motivation, or little engagement in life, plus feelings of shame, guilt, and indecisiveness. Both emotional and physical dysregulations compromise the clients' ability to grow and to adapt to environmental changes.

Integrated with these neurobiological underpinnings, the theoretical model emphasizes the importance of the therapeutic relationship in the process of emotional healing, as expressed by Dworkin (2005) in his work on the relational aspects of EMDR therapy. The adaptive information processing (AIP) model addresses hypotheses based on the dovetailing of an interactional preparation of the client and consequent neurobiochemical changes that occur in the brain during and after information reprocessing procedures. A therapeutic challenge is how to find the right balance between these two poles: a technical, almost surgical intervention and the more predominantly interpersonal exchange between therapist and the client. In short, the therapist interacts more with the client during the initial rapport stages of preparation for reprocessing, and tries to stay out of the way during the reprocessing phases of the protocol so the brain can do its job as unimpeded as possible. This may be viewed as a kind of a game, where the therapist gets closer and collaborates like a team player at times, or withdraws to the audience and supports the client from afar.

Many authors suggest that at a dyadic level, the client's emerging dynamics, history, and emotional interaction are not only reported, but also cocreated with the therapist, the team player. The resulting relationship cannot be evaluated in isolation (Aron, 1996; Bohleber, 2013; Ginot, 2015; Mitchell, 2000). It can be understood as an intersubjective third witness. The focus of a more interactive approach can be experienced with a relational third element, the surrounding others in the group, which at the same time encompasses and exceeds the clinical system formed between client and therapist. But there is more to that interaction than simply emotional support.

According to Cozolino (2014), relationships are our natural habitat, and the brain is to be considered not only as an isolated organ, but as a social one. Considering the plasticity of the brain, especially the neuronal changes that take place due to the interaction of the individual with his or her environment, one should recognize the importance of human relationships, and how one may benefit from the emotional exchanges in the social milieu, which suggests the relevance of social interaction for emotional health.

Additional attention should be given to the importance of a more interactive ambience for the development of the person as a whole. Both Siegel (2012) and Cozolino (2014) resort not only to the emotional but also to the biological regulation that stems out of early interactions between mother and child, in particular, its relevance for the maturation of the child's right hemisphere of the brain, including the formation of an implicit self (Schore, 2012). This specific form of cerebral hardwiring would be the result of the natural maturation of the brain, or an expression of the environment that allows for its gradual genetic expression, not to mention the active communication between the right hemisphere of the primary caretaker and that of the baby. Setting up this attachment system successfully is vital to exercise the homeostatic maintenance of affect regulation and social skills of the adult in the future. Cozolino affirms how human babies strive, thanks to the developed skills of caretakers who identify the needs and intentions of those around them. Some aspects of this argument still correspond to a maturational perspective, though the implications are socially significant in terms of emotional regulation and the manifestation of mental health.

## GEMDR

I theorized that if the power of EMDR therapy includes the more intersubjective exchange between therapist and client, then it seemed possible that this human interaction could extend to a group setting, with EMDR therapy being carried out within the power of a group. I think of this form of intervention as Group EMDR, or more simply GEMDR. Expanding EMDR therapy to a group version as a treatment option on a regular basis can offer new venues for clients with particular needs and cultural profiles.

EMDR may be regarded not only as a psychotherapeutic tool to heal the past, but as a potential strategy to help outcasts address and redefine their social and political statuses. A collective awareness and support can improve the chances of political position in the quest for a more equitable society.

I found that there are also clients who are so satisfied with the results obtained through their first encounters with EMDR therapy being applied to specific purposes that they sometimes want to remain in therapy, to go a step further in their quest for self-knowledge, and explore deeper layers of their identities and relationships with others, but not necessarily with the intensive care of individual sessions. A woman in her mid-40s, for instance, joined our group because she wanted to explore the issue of having witnessed her mother's sudden death more thoroughly. In individual EMDR therapy, she had overcome initial complaints of anxiety outbursts; eventually, she realized how her expressions of panic were linked to having seen her mother die of a stroke when she was still very young. There was intense relief after reprocessing this touchstone event and bidding mom farewell. The presence of others offered her the comfort of a family she no longer had.

She had not realized at first how the childhood event would forever interfere with her affective relationships in her adult life. She suffered from chronic feelings of not belonging to any group, or to anyone. The triggering event to come to individual EMDR therapy was a tearful breakup, with her boyfriend leaving her for being too clingy and demanding. After the breakup, the loneliness returned and she felt abandoned, just like it had been for many years before the boyfriend. Right after joining the group, the issue of emotional connections came up. In the beginning of a session she started sobbing as another group member described her anger and confusion during a recent divorce. The client shared that she identified with the story of divorce, but did not know exactly why. She felt confused, which was an indicator of old material blending with current issues. Then a scene from her childhood popped up in her head. Her stepmother had forgotten to pick her up after school.

When the reprocessing was over, and with her consent, the group peers encircled her silently and gave her a collective hug. She admitted to feeling a sense of warmth and belonging for the first time ever. The emptiness was no longer inside of her. A few sessions later she hooked up with a recent acquaintance. This time the boyfriend was not seen as a lifeboat anymore.

Like this woman, these clients may not be afflicted by open crises, such as having been struck by a recent catastrophe. Still, they want to benefit more from their personal resources, to observe and to learn from what other humans do to face inevitable challenges in life, as well as to improve their emotional and social skills. Their focus goes beyond a specific problem-solving situation. They want to thrive and to find out what else there is to learn about themselves.

Some other clients may feel victimized by cultural and social profiles that make them stand out in the crowd and increase the risk of prejudice, bullying, or mobbing. What they suffer from is not the ghosts of the past, but current discriminatory issues that make them feel isolated and deprived of communal bonding. Since many of these complaints are of a collective nature, it makes sense to consider some pros and cons when thinking about this project of regular collective intervention.

A man in his late-30s had problems related to being gay at a homophobic workplace. He felt constantly observed and refrained from making comments or gestures that might give him away. He was successful at his job, but suffered from bouts of depression and excessive drinking. After having come out in the group, and with nothing disastrous happening, we reprocessed a scene from the past when he was 6 years old: He fell from his new bicycle, grazed his knees and hands, and cried. His father shouted at him that he would rather have a dead son than a gay son. With the reprocessing, he gradually accepted the positive thoughts: "This is who I am," "I exist," and "I deserve to live." Shortly after this session he started a relationship with a younger man at his work. This experience and others showed that it was clear that he was able to reprocess in front of others effectively, and that rather than the group inhibiting his processing, the presence of others seemed to help. Experiences like these also made me realize the importance of evaluating how GEMDR benefits are similar or different than individual EMDR.

## Dyadic Interaction

I consider GEMDR to be a viable alternative to individual EMDR therapy for some clients. In GEMDR, we want to assess the importance of the group in the emotional healing process. The therapist provides his or her technical EMDR skills to aide the client's process. The therapist also offers other needed emotional support and containment and helps maintain appropriate emotional regulation during sessions. This may be needed in particular with those clients who lack these self-care skills, resulting from previous emotional deficiency or overall lack of parental engagement and general childhood deprivation. GEMDR can enhance the therapeutic effect by numerically multiplying the support component while at the same time diluting this expectation of the therapist. It is not solely up to the therapist to provide answers or to regulate emotions. Group peers who have undergone challenging experiences also relieve the burden by holding the emotional load of a group member with the therapist. The therapist may talk the talk, but the experiences in the group setting are strengthened by the support from other survivors who have walked the walk. In other words, therapists can be seen as engaging the humanity of the group, while group peers can be viewed as part of a therapeutic team, regardless of a common background of difficulties they share with the client.

I have observed that at certain times group members have been exposed to the same traumatic experience of a certain client. This is common in situations related to a postdisaster intervention, and when everyone comes from a homogeneous background. However, even when that is the case, if everyone in the group has an alleged common link to an unexpected disaster that struck group members at the same time, the way the experience is stored in the brain of each individual varies from person to person. They also differ according to their personal autobiographical idiosyncrasies. Despite a common link set up by the unforeseen fate, individuals react according to their habitual strategies, not as a cohesive cohort.

Therefore, the idea of a common historical profile is not a requisite for GEMDR to function nor is having endured the same trauma a barrier. On the contrary, I have found that a heterogeneous emotional diversity supplies the ingredients for the richness in a group. The emotional and cultural diversity establish a set of mirrors, just like a mirror room that reflects back multiple versions of how different people see the client differently, as well as a pallet of adaptive behaviors presented from peers, such as stories of endurance, coping, and success a given client may benefit from. Indeed, the therapists can take advantage of the presence of other group members to provide extra emotional and cognitive support.

## Screening

In addition to the usual screening prior to EMDR reprocessing, including dissociative features, certain physical disorders, suicidality, self-mutilation, and so forth, prospective group clients should comply with certain criteria before being accepted for GEMDR. They should, for instance, be able to preserve dual attention, and be able to tolerate some level of exposure to traumatic content without fully decompensating. This resiliency should be coupled with the capacity to relate to others, without the need for too much intensive individual attention.

The screening process should be carried out individually, and its purpose is to evaluate both inclusion and exclusion criteria. The latter may refer to acutely dysregulated clients, such as those in crisis, or those going through an acute psychiatric decompensation, such as a psychotic episode. Another counterindication would be those who fit into cluster A of personality disorders (paranoid, schizoid, and schizotypal), which portray unavailable or suspicious clients who will not tolerate group interaction. Apart from dual attention challenged clients, antisocial and narcissistic personality disorders are likely to be very disruptive for the co-construction of an atmosphere of trust and compassion that is needed in the group.

Clients with histrionic or compensated borderline disorders, however, may benefit from the interaction with others, as well as clients who fit into the category of cluster C personality disorders (avoidant, dependent, and obsessive-compulsive).

These seem to tolerate better the presence of other group members and profit from the collective context.

Eligible clients should have the adequate capacity to self-stabilize. They should also have adequate emotional literacy and be able to access and use resources to reestablish balances caused by temporary loss of dual attention. They should also be able to postpone gratification and wait for their turn to speak. The desire to help and to be accepted is fairly common in traumatized clients, notably those who had to take care of others in their childhood. GEMDR may offer these clients an opportunity to use their empathic skills in a constructive manner.

Once this initial evaluation is over, the therapist may proceed with psychoeducation for higher functioning clients, so they can practice resource development and installation (RDI; Korn & Leeds, 2002) and establish clearer communication channels with the therapist. This preparation phase helps clients develop a more adaptive interaction in the GEMDR. The diagnostic process does not end with the initial evaluation. Individual and collective assessment of group components are a continuous process. Should a group member relapse into an acute phase, he or she would be encouraged to take temporary leave from the group, or continue in the group, while pursuing parallel individual sessions.

## Phases of a GEMDR Session

Group sessions are relatively unpredictable. One cannot abide by strict rules, but a phased intervention helps clients to open and especially to close each session adequately grounded in the present, which is an important principle in EMDR therapy. Despite previous planning, therapists cannot know beforehand what is going to happen in an upcoming session, even after it has begun, even if a group may have gathered for an intervention with a specific theme.

One or more group members may be in crisis or may be more defensive and withdrawn, for instance. Overall, therapists have less control over the content. They are also unable to predict the different levels of emotional impact provoked by the disclosure of one person's trauma upon other group members. The coordination of such a diversified environment requires additional care on the part of therapists, patience, and spontaneity, in order to understand and follow how the multiple threads of activated stories interplay. According to the *Diagnostic and Statistical Manual of Mental Disorders* (5th ed.; *DSM-5*; American Psychiatric Association, 2013), one may develop PTSD simply by watching or by learning that someone has gone through a traumatic experience. At the same time, it appears that witnessing group members reprocess some of their issues in a group helps other clients vicariously. The group may provide such a therapeutic frame of reference.

The structured eight-phase approach and three-pronged protocol provides parameters for therapists to organize treatment strategies. Once the group targets are set, and clients recognize possibilities of improvement, participation in the group can be a powerful tool of change. On the whole, the sessions can be divided in a beginning, a middle, and a closure phase, which include the warm-up, the intervention, and the sharing phases. This arbitrary division reflects in one session an equivalence to the EMDR three-pronged protocol, where past, present, and future follow a coherent sequence. The following description will further clarify some of the basic steps for the GEMDR. Some components are adaptations from the phases of a psychodrama session (Kellerman & Hudgins, 1988), which also deals with the treatment of trauma through group intervention.

## Introduction or Warm-Up Phase

After initial greetings, there is a first round of follow-ups so clients can report what has happened since the previous session. This first round helps the therapist and group members evaluate how mobilized and cohesive the group is at the beginning of the session. In order to preserve a space for each participant to speak and be heard, it is prudent to set up limited time for each to share important updates during this introductory phase, so as to avoid one client monopolizing the whole session. If the group lasts for about 2 hours, about half the time should be devoted to this warming up process. Time restriction is a rather loose item of the group contract, but it may be called upon in case someone monopolizes the time. Other contract items may include commitment to attendance, confidentiality, duration of the group, criteria for the inclusion of new members, and other issues deemed necessary by group members.

Depending on what theme comes up, the therapist and the group may decide to prolong this initial conversation and let the emotions cool down a little. Often the group can assist with emotional regulation of an animated member and provide a sense of holding within the group context. In the long run, clients learn that extreme emotional outbursts are not generally useful for integrating emotion and cognition, and they learn how to keep themselves within an emotional window of tolerance and build skills for emotional titration. They benefit from this contained approach to therapy to deal with traumatic memories, whereby emotions and cognition seem to more easily integrate into a coherent understanding of the event. On the other hand, sometimes the group will become intensely focused on a specific story, and feel the relevance of immediate reprocessing. The unfolding of a personal story brings the storyteller to the foreground and the other group members typically empathize with that person. For example, in one group, a client reported an experience when she felt morally harassed at work and another client shared that he was bullied as a kid and finds it hard to relax in a group with strangers. The theme of being uncomfortable and threatened in the presence of others began to "resonate" in the group as each person recalled fearing potential aggressions and criticism from others and feeling somewhat impotent to defend themselves. The client whose report has mobilized the emotions of the group members emerged as the natural candidate for EMDR reprocessing during the session.

Cozolino (2014) describes this resonance as an attribution of importance to the social brain by suggesting that "mirror systems and resonance behaviors evolved into our ability to attune to the emotional states of others. They provide us with a visceral-emotional experience of what the other is experiencing, allowing us to know others from the inside out" (p. 51). Therefore, a psychotherapeutic framework that fosters corrective interaction through group members, and offers mutual observation, should serve as a social paragon; a reference for reciprocal learning and emotional regulation. Through observation of other group members, mirror neurons may provide individuals with a corrective opportunity for reprocessing and rewiring, especially for those who did not benefit enough from the interactional patterns with their primary caregiver or an individual therapist.

*Decision Taking*

After this first round of individual disclosure, the group decides together who is to be chosen for EMDR reprocessing in the session. Therapists explain that the votes are not supposed to be assigned to a certain group member, based on the display of emotion, but rather on how the specific stories have moved each client's associative network. It is not, therefore, a tear contest, but a matter of whose reprocessing would be most advantageous for the group to witness and to learn from. A client may vote on himself or herself, depending on what issues arise during this initial warm-up phase.

*Intervention*

Once a client's story is voted on, that client sits with the therapist in the middle, while the others form a circle around them. Should someone not feel like taking part in the circle, they are free to sit elsewhere. Each one is responsible for evaluating the emotional/concrete distance they want to preserve between themselves and the heart of the action.

At times, another group member may feel so connected to the story being reprocessed that he or she may volunteer to help with tactile tapping on the client's shoulders during reprocessing. The chosen storyteller may also willingly request this form of assistance from a group member with whom there is perceived attunement. In the meantime, the therapist may opt to apply additional visual bilateral stimulation (BLS).

As a technique in Phase 4, members of the audience may hold hands in a sign of mutual support, or remain silent by themselves during stronger emotional releases. After the Subjective Units of Disturbances (SUDs) of the protagonist has subsided or lowered to a zero, the therapist may proceed to Phase 5 or focus on a second client, depending on the time frame.

When Phase 4 is over, group members may also be recruited to suggest Positive Cognitions (PCs) at the beginning of Phase 5 and repeat the PC in unison during installation. Degrees of participation in the reprocessing of a protagonist's target varies in accordance with the level of group intimacy. Santiago Jacome presented a group intervention where group members formed a circle during Phase 5. They tapped each others' shoulders, while repeating PC aloud (Second Iberoamerican EMDR Conference in Brasília, 2011). Participants were at the same time very satisfied and surprised by the power derived from the exercise.

The EMDR session may be complete or incomplete at the end of the group session. An incomplete session means the protagonist still reports that there is a disturbance when attempting to access the memory being reprocessed, or does not feel the PC as completely true while attempting to access the target memory.

*Sharing and Closure*

Before the official termination of the session, the protagonist returns to the larger circle of the group members. The group facilitator initiates a moment of sharing. During this phase, each group member talks about his or her own experience: what it was like to witness, to support, and to cheer, or negative reactions to having witnessed the reprocessing of the protagonist. The sharing phase may include what the repercussions of the session were, which personal recollections were activated, and what was gained from this session.

Participants are discouraged from intellectually analyzing what just happened. No one is allowed to put a value or judgment on what came up during the session, nor to advise what the protagonist should or should not do about a problem. These are the choices of the client. Interestingly, some group members say that these restrictions bring relief, as group members don't have to take care of other "symbolic siblings" of the group. Rather, their reflections and comments are to be self-focused.

The sharing that takes place after the individual intervention functions as an integrative phase, a synthesis of the witnessed experiences of the group. The status of the protagonist is quickly restored to being once again "one of the group" when similar stories fill the void and there are no feelings of any potential separation from the group, after the individual exposure. The witnessing is vital for reinstating a sense of humanness and empowerment in former trauma victims through the activation of empathy. Listening to the reflections from group members helps the protagonist gain new perspectives in relation to a state of former isolation or social awkwardness; he or she typically learns that other people have also experienced similar things and survived them. The sharing phase also aids group members to feel anchored in the present, and thus is an emotional container: stay with it and stay with us. Individuals who undergo the EMDR reprocessing in this collective context have the choice of gradual disclosure, depending on how much trust is shared with the presence of other group members. Therapists should offer some schedule flexibility, in case a group member requires further individual attention as a follow-up session. When requesting an individual follow-up, clients are encouraged to invite another group member, so as not to interrupt the concept of the group dynamics. If a client prefers an individual session, that is also an alternative.

## Testimonials

What follows are written testimonials from participants who took part in a weekend intensive of GEMDR. The group was composed of 10 participants. The theme of the marathon was related to eating habits and social expectations. These clients were the protagonists of two consecutive EMDR sessions related to food/weight/appearance issues. What follows is a summary of their sharing with the group.

The first client was a woman in her early 30s, with a history of bulimia and self-cutting.

> *Client 1: Being in the center (of the group) was challenging for me. Very hard indeed. It is incredible that the theme chosen by me (former ballet dancer) had a lot of connection with this discomfort of being subjected to the staring of others, of what I was supposed to look like. During a significant part of the session I felt like I was being swallowed by the armchair I was sitting in. The awareness of all the eyes staring at me was crushing. The theme that I chose spoke much more of me, of who I actually was, than I had foreseen. I thought the therapist was very sensitive, and capable to identify a key point in all the events I reported, which was my difficulty to maintain positive memories, something I believe is totally related to my constant depressive state, something that has followed me since childhood, without an apparent motive. I loved to actively participate in this group, to leave that*

> *paralysed attitude. It was extremely significant for me. Another highlight of the session was the installation of a positive memory in relation to a part of my body (I can learn from my body), something I can keep with me, and which I may access at any time. That empowered me in such a pleasant way, that I still cannot fully evaluate it. The "little girl" (inner critic) continues here with me. At times, she tells me how to react in certain situations, waking up the same lightness, the joy to see her being wicked, hanging up-side-down in the tree at her grandpa's farm. It is like she tells me: "take it easy!" and I feel like smiling.*
>
> *To observe the other session after mine was a very intense experience, moving, enveloping. I identified myself with many points with what she said, especially with the difficulty to receive affection, in comparison to taking care of others, those outside her family (of origin). At the end of the session we gave her a collective hug and she was capable to receive it, which was very moving. I feel like I let myself feel hugged too. It was great to receive that, which is something hard for me to do.*

The second client was also a woman, in her late-40s, who had been forced to diet by her parents when she was a child. Her parents had high expectations concerning any talent she had, and she did have a few. Instead of a blessing, her skills became a curse, because she was always expected to be outstanding, better than the rest. She recently had difficulty accepting the idea that she can excel. Excellence has become dangerous, and she sabotages and punishes herself before others have the chance to.

> *Client 2: I experienced recollections which seemed very real about the connection with my mother figure, and that triggered my memories of non-acceptance concerning my body image by my parents (having been an overweight child), the constant dieting; the episodes which I today qualify as imposed starvation. It felt so real to recall those nights, when the noises in my belly would not let me sleep, and I had to sneak out of the room and steal food from the fridge in the kitchen, because they wanted me to always look pretty. So, the inability of my parents to love me for who I was; the identification of the physical and emotional hunger; the external demands for perfection, all of these destroyed my inborn talents, and the recognition of these thoughts that I don't deserve to be successful or be happy, because my success meant an avalanche of parental demands for further perfection. During the session I realized I am not a victim of my life, as that little girl that I used to be, and that I can be the balanced, beautiful, and winning woman, who has always strived to give her best, but did not have enough strength to persevere. I will always be above the desired weight, but my bones are large, and this is who I am. I will never be Giselle Bündchen or the other Victoria's Secret skinny goddesses, but I don't have to be them in order to accomplish what I want. What caught my attention was not how much one theme led to the next, but how it moved most of the group members. I like it that in EMDR there is no right or wrong in relation to what themes come up (into awareness), but how everything is used, and the associative network proves to us the immense possibilities of events which impacted us in the past and present.*

> *Whenever I hear "go with that," it gives me a sense of safety and confirms that we cannot take ourselves for granted, because these memories form our individuality, our uniqueness. Apart from being a miracle therapy, in this group I feel really welcomed and cozy.*

Another participant, who just observed these two sessions, describes on the following day how the stories were important for her, an opportunity to think about herself:

> *Client 3: Yesterday, while observing the sessions, I felt that we were taking care of us all. By being in the group, the identifications are inevitable–largely because we hear from others what fits into our ears. At first, I felt that this personal implication in someone else's story could not be simultaneous with the taking care of the other. With this group I learned a bit better, in affective terms, about how engaging myself can be a way of taking care of myself, to the extent that we may hold and be held in our difficulties.*

Still another participant shared her impressions on the following day. Her comments suggested significant changes and self-evaluations, simply by observing the EMDR therapy of her fellow group members:

> *Client 4: Based on the EMDR sessions that I saw with my group colleagues, I felt very moved; I felt empathy for them. When I got home and went to sleep, I kept thinking about what it would be like when my turn came (EMDR session). I also thought about my personal issues and floated back to earlier experiences in my childhood. Last night I dreamt that one of my group colleagues had been the therapist in my session, and that it had been a really cool session.*
>
> *This morning there was a situation at home, involving my daughter and I, and it made me feel very upset. After examining my memories related to that moment and my body, I felt calmer because I remembered how difficult it had been when she was born, and maybe that is why I am so overprotective of her, and feel very sad when I notice there was a flaw in my relationship with her. I guess that now I know what I have to address in the group.*

Another participant made comments related to the impact of observing the sessions, and connected the observation to the activation of personal issues, as well as those concerning other relevant persons in her family network:

> *Client 5: Observing the sessions has been very enriching for my personal learning. As part of the group, it was challenging to maintain the attention all the time, but a tactic that I used was to observe the expressions of each participant–both the clients and the other group members. It was beautiful to see how the stories unfolded. What mobilized me the most was the possibility of having witnessed the "transformation" of each one. It was emotionally moving having watched up close the processes that were much more complex than they seemed at first. The therapist said something during the session on bulimia*

*that struck me (an interweave), though I do not have eating disorders or issues with my personal image. He said something about the difficulty that some people have to maintain good memories, which made me ponder on how many good things I have been able to maintain in life. As for the first session, I saw a lot of my mother in the client, which moved me and made me make a comment of support at the end of the session.*

## Potential Downsides for Clients Taking Part in a GEMDR

I've found that the reprocessing in a group setting often becomes more emotionally intense. However, instead of inducing fear and reducing safety, this typically tends to fortify bonds and forge a sense of responsibility for the well-being of group peers and for personal boundaries. As sessions progress, these encounters bring about a kind of awareness, of being on the same boat, and there is no need for feelings of shame or helplessness. These reactions may be uncomfortable for those with low affect tolerance.

When an often anticipated reproach from peers in the group does not happen, there is room for emotional relief, coupled with feelings of forgiveness and redemption. However, in the meantime clients who take part in a GEMDR are exposed to more traumatic material than they are used to and there is the possibility that the shared stories will trigger unresolved issues. This vicarious exposure to trauma-based stories from other group members may activate early recollections and unusual feelings.

Another hindrance that may evolve from switching from individual to group EMDR is sharing the therapist, who may be busy attending to the needs of other group members during the session. The participant may feel helpless, envious, inadequate, or abandoned. Whenever possible, the presence of a second therapist is advisable, so that the tasks of maintaining group stability are not centered around a single individual. However, as clients develop a more solid relationship with the therapist, irrational perceptions of being rejected or betrayed diminish as their readiness to offer empathy and support becomes more available to group peers.

I have found that despite these potential downsides inherent to any group dynamics, the advantages of emotional support, collective resignification of traumatic experiences, and enhancement of interpersonal skills far outweigh these possible obstacles. As Siegel (2012) didactically summarizes, "In essence, we come to 'resonate' with the other person, and two 'me's' become a 'we'. This whole set of connections—from mirror neurons to middle prefrontal maps enabling compassion and empathy—is called the 'resonance circuitry'" (p. 308). This process is then amplified, as members engage in the group interaction and become a larger we.

GEMDR provides a plethora of opportunities for the dynamic interactive repair of traumatic experiences and the development of social and emotional skills needed for an adult, oriented here and now. The transition from the "I" to the "We" helps chronically isolated clients experience socialization in a protected environment, as well as the acquisition of new senses of humanness in the group setting.

## SUMMARY

EMDR carried out in a group setting has been depicted by different authors, but not presented as a continuous psychotherapeutic context for engaging individuals who suffer from trauma, cultural bias, or social isolation. The reprocessing of emotionally laden material may trigger traumatic memory networks and destabilize other group members, so previous psychological screening and preparation of participants are essential. The emotional support of the group, and the sharing of experiences, opens up new meanings to traumatic experiences, gives participants the opportunity to practice compassion and self-empathy, and allows them to experience shared gains witnessing each other's EMDR work. The purpose of writing this chapter was to describe the method of adapting EMDR therapy to a group setting on a regular basis, or for weekend intensives to take advantage of the power of group experience for the teams of individual members.

The need for attachment repair in clients may be best addressed at the discretion of the therapist, whether in an individual or a group format, but the capacity to comfort, to empathize, and offer attachment models that mobilize mirror neurons seems to multiply in a group. The therapist is not the sole provider of help and other group members may at times be more in tune with the emotional wavelength of the client, depending on the issue that is reprocessed.

I have noticed a connection between the themes of successive EMDR sessions, as if an invisible thread is established. It is as if the group forms its own associative network, drawn from the interaction of sequentially reprocessed narratives. Thematic association in groups appears to replicate the progression of individual memory associations observable in individual EMDR sessions. More research should be carried out in relation to these and other phenomena pertaining to group dynamics. The complexity of the multiple variables at play seems suited for a qualitative evaluation of these intricacies that are so intrinsic to group interactions.

## REFERENCES

American Psychiatric Association (2013). Diagnostic and statistical manual of mental disorders (5th ed.). Arlington, VA: American Psychiatric Publishing.

Aron, L. (1996). *A meeting of minds: Mutuality in psychoanalysis*. Hillsdale, NJ: Analytic Press.

Bohleber, W. (2013). The concept of intersubjectivity in psychoanalysis: Taking critical stock. *International Journal of Psychoanalysis, 94*, 799–823.

Cozolino, L. J. (2014). *The neuroscience of human relationships: Attachment and the developing social brain* (2nd ed.). New York, NY: W. W. Norton.

Dworkin, M. (2005). *EMDR and the relational imperative: The therapeutic relationship in EMDR treatment*. New York, NY: Routledge

Ginot, E. (2015). *The neuropsychology of the unconscious: Integrating brain and mind in psychotherapy*. New York, NY: W. W. Norton.

Jarero, I., Artigas, L., Uribe, S., & Miranda, A. (2014). EMDR therapy humanitarian trauma recovery interventions in Latin America and the Caribbean. *Journal of EMDR Practice and Research, 8*(4), 260–268.

Kellerman, P. F., & Hudgins, M. K. (Eds.). (1988). *Psychodrama with trauma survivors: Acting out your pain*. London, UK: Jessica Kingsley Publishers.

Korn, D. L., & Leeds, A. M. (2002). Preliminary evidence of efficacy for EMDR resource development and installation in the stabilization phase of treatment of complex post-traumatic stress disorder. *Journal of Clinical Psychology, 58*(12), 1465–1487.

Luber, M. (2009). *Eye movement desensitization and reprocessing (EMDR) scripted protocols: Basics and special situations*. New York, NY: Springer Publishing Company.

Mitchell, S. A. (2000). *Relationality: From attachment to intersubjectivity*. Hillsdale, NJ: Analytic Press.

Monteiro, A. M. (2014). Group and individual EMDR therapy in the humanitarian assistance project in southern Brazil. *Revista Iberoamericana de Psicotraumatología y Disociación, 6*(3), 1–19.

Schore, A. N. (2012). *The science of the art of psychotherapy*. New York, NY: W. W. Norton.

Siegel, D. J. (2012). *The developing mind: How relationships and the brain interact to shape who we are* (2nd ed.). New York, NY: Guilford Press.

# SECTION IV

# Addressing Sexual/Affectional Orientation and Gender Diversity

CHAPTER 11

# EMDR Therapy as Affirmative Care for Transgender and Gender Nonconforming Clients

Sand C. Chang

Transgender and gender nonconforming (TGNC) people have a gender identity that does not fully align with the sex they were assigned at birth. They are a vastly misunderstood group of people who experience far higher rates of trauma, discrimination, and suicide risk than people who are cisgender (i.e., people who feel that their assigned sex at birth matches their own internal sense of who they are; Clements-Nolle, Marx, & Katz, 2006; Grant et al., 2011). Despite rapidly changing policies in the law and increased access to health care coverage in some parts of the world, as well as increasing visibility in the media, TGNC people continue to be underrepresented and underserved in medical and mental health settings.

In this chapter, I introduce the basic concepts and terms related to the experiences and lives of TGNC people. Common misconceptions are addressed in order to build a basic awareness of the needs of TGNC people. For therapists who have little to no experience working with TGNC individuals, this foundational knowledge will be crucial for developing clinical rapport and providing affirming and effective treatment. However, rather than use this chapter alone as a sole source of information about TGNC people, clinicians without prior experience with this population are advised to seek additional training and consultation.

Next, the author discusses the ways in which TGNC people are affected by transphobia or anti-trans bias, ranging from microaggressions to overt acts of violence. While every TGNC person has a unique experience, varying widely based on other intersecting cultural identities, there are themes that many TGNC people frequently encounter. This chapter focuses on those themes.

The third section of this chapter discusses the various ways that eye movement desensitization and reprocessing (EMDR) therapy may be used to help provide affirmative care when working with TGNC people. This includes recommendations for how to utilize the standard three-pronged protocol and eight-phase approach (Shapiro, 2001) to best meet the needs of TGNC clients, illustrating the healing potential of EMDR therapy in creating a cohesive sense of stability, safety, and self for this client population. Finally, a case vignette is used to illustrate the application of EMDR therapy and the use of a Resource Development and Installation (RDI) protocol to assist TGNC people in healing experiences of trauma.

The material in this chapter is a culmination of over 15 years of clinical experience providing trauma-informed care to TGNC clients. In addition, I have a personal cultural identity as a Chinese American person with a TGNC identity, and I find it essential to examine my own subjectivity in approaching work with TGNC clients (as with all clients). Therefore, therapist self-reflection (regardless of gender identity) is an emphasis of any therapeutic work with TGNC people.

## TGNC PEOPLE: TERMINOLOGY AND FOUNDATIONAL CONCEPTS

Gender variance and nonconformity have existed throughout time and in many cultures (Feinberg, 1996; Miller & Nichols, 2012; Schmidt, 2003; Stryker, 2008). When describing gender diversity and TGNC identity, language varies based on contexts such as geographic region and cultural background. Before learning how to use EMDR therapy when working with TGNC communities, it is necessary to understand key foundational constructs and terminology as they are used in this chapter. These key term definitions were developed based on the usage within the TGNC communities; professional literature put forth by health care, legal, advocacy, and professional organizations serving the TGNC community; and my experience of working within TGNC communities for over 15 years.

*Sex assigned at birth* or *assigned sex* refers to the gender marker, typically "M" for male or "F" for female, on one's birth certificate and based on external genitalia.

The *gender binary* is a system of classifying sex and gender into two fixed, mutually exclusive categories of male/man/masculine and female/woman/feminine (Cashore & Tuason, 2009). The gender binary is deeply embedded into Western culture and some non-Western cultures.

*Gender role* is a pattern of appearance, personality, and behavior that, in a given culture, is associated with being a boy/man/male or being a girl/woman/female. Gender role may or may not conform to what is expected based on a person's sex assigned at birth. *Gender expression* is the way that one expresses one's gender role outwardly through appearance, clothing, accessories, and behavior.

*Gender identity* is one's internal sense of being a man, woman, or an alternate gender that exists outside of the gender binary. Because gender identity cannot always be determined by looking at a person and may or may not correspond with sex assigned at birth, it is important to rely on each individual's self-identification.

*Cisgender* describes a person whose sex assigned at birth and gender identity are more or less congruent. In most societies, it is assumed that all people are or should be cisgender. Being cisgender comes with certain privileges, ranging from a complete unawareness that one is cisgender to being able to access public restrooms without the threat of harassment or violence.

*Transgender* (sometimes abbreviated as *trans*) describes a person for whom sex assigned at birth and gender identity are not fully aligned. *Gender nonconforming* (*GNC*) refers to people whose gender identities and/or expressions do not fit with the norms associated with sex assigned at birth. The acronym *TGNC* is used throughout this chapter to refer broadly to TGNC people.

*Nonbinary* is used to describe a range of identities that fall outside of the gender binary. An example of nonbinary identitiy is *genderqueer*, which describes a person who may identify as both man and woman, neither man nor woman, fluidly moving between genders, or embodying a third or unique gender.

*Self-identification* or *self-determination* is based on the idea that not all aspects of a person's cultural identity can be determined objectively or perceived accurately by others. Therefore, it is necessary to rely on each individual's inherent sense of their own identity and the language (e.g., name, pronouns) the individual designates to describe their gender.

*Transition* is a process that some TGNC people undergo when shifting toward a gender role that differs from the one associated with the sex assigned at birth. Aspects of transition may include *social transition* (e.g., changes in gender expression, gender role, name, pronoun, and gender marker) and *medical transition* (e.g., hormone therapy, surgeries). Not all TGNC people desire medical transition, and many who do cannot afford to do so.

*Gender dysphoria* describes an experience of distress that some, but not all, TGNC people report in relation to the incongruence between their sex assigned at birth and gender identity (Knudson, De Cuypere, & Bockting, 2010). Gender dysphoria may be general or more specific to one body part (e.g., breasts, genitals) and is often a motivation to seek out gender-affirming medical care and/or mental health treatment. *Gender dysphoria* also appears in the *Diagnostic and Statistical Manual of Mental Disorders*, Fifth Edition (*DSM-5*; American Psychiatric Association, 2013) as a mental health diagnosis characterized by a "marked incongruence between" a person's sex assigned at birth and gender identity (American Psychiatric Association, 2013, p. 453). This diagnosis remains controversial, as it does not allow for a pathology-free TGNC experience (MacCulloch, 2010).

*Anti-trans bias* (sometimes referred to as *transphobia*) describes the set of prejudicial attitudes and discriminatory behaviors directed toward TGNC people. TGNC people face anti-trans bias in education, workplaces, medical and mental health care settings, in their own homes, and when attempting to access public spaces such as restrooms or simply walking down the street. Anti-trans bias may lead to blatant violence. It can also result in a lifetime of negative internalized core beliefs about oneself and other TGNC people, otherwise known as *internalized transphobia*.

*Sexual orientation* refers to a person's sexual and emotional attraction to another person and the behavior and/or social affiliation that may result from this attraction (APA, 2015). Some people use specific labels to describe their sexual orientation, such as gay, lesbian, bisexual, queer, heterosexual, or asexual. Sexual orientation and gender identity are often inappropriately conflated, as they are separate constructs that may or may not be related for each individual.

*Intersectionality* is a framework for understanding identity that considers the additive and intersectional nature of cultural identities, systems of oppression, and the power, privilege, and marginalization that may result (Cole, 2009; Crenshaw, 1991). An intersectional approach to working with TGNC clients includes acknowledging other cultural identities, including race/ethnicity, socioeconomic status, age, disability status, immigration status, religion, and sexual orientation.

*Affirmative care or practice* with TGNC people is a client-centered approach that supports self-determination. It is based on the evidence that TGNC people who are affirmed in their gender identities have more positive outcomes (Brill & Pepper, 2008; Byne et al., 2012; Davis & Meier, 2014; Kuhn et al., 2009), including reduced rates of mental health symptoms and HIV risk (Bockting, Miner, Swinburne Romine, Hamilton, & Coleman, 2013; Ryan, 2009). Affirmative care with nonbinary people involves supporting the right to not have to identify as a man or a woman. This approach can also be applied more broadly to respect all aspects of personal and cultural identity.

## Common Misconceptions About TGNC People

TGNC people are frequently misunderstood, sometimes due to a lack of exposure or misinformation that is perpetuated in the media (Namaste, 2000). As a result, TGNC people seeking services may be met with skepticism or even hostility. This section addresses common misconceptions about TGNC people.

Some people assume that TGNC people are gay or lesbian people attempting to transition so that they may access heterosexual privilege. This assumption is erroneous, as there are people of all sexual orientations who are TGNC (e.g., gay trans men, lesbian trans women, bisexual GNC individuals, and heterosexual trans women). This assumption also inappropriately conflates sexual orientation and gender identity.

Another assumption is that TGNC people are mentally ill. Prior to the current *DSM-5* (American Psychiatric Association, 2013), all TGNC people were assumed to have gender identity disorder (American Psychiatric Association, 1980). Some experts in TGNC mental health argue that it is not one's internal identity that is disordered, but rather the social reaction that cannot accept human diversity (APA, 2015; Lev, 2004). Even the current diagnosis of gender dysphoria is not applicable to all TGNC people (Coleman et al., 2011), yet this diagnosis is frequently required to justify medical necessity for gender-affirming medical interventions (Drescher, 2010).

Yet another mistaken belief is that all TGNC people want to have a "sex change" in order to live as the "opposite" sex. First, there is no single surgery that denotes a "sex change." The concept of a "sex change" oversimplifies transition by characterizing an event rather than a complex process that may involve a number of gender-affirming procedures. Second, the term *opposite* is a misnomer, as male is not the opposite of female, men are not the opposite of women, and masculine is not the opposite of feminine. These constructs are not mutually exclusive categories, but rather variations in human diversity. It is more useful and accurate to employ such terms as "a different sex/gender" or "another sex/gender," to both acknowledge sex and gender as existing on a spectrum and to be more inclusive of people who do not identify with binary concepts of gender.

Clinicians who have not worked with TGNC people are encouraged to seek additional training and consultation in order to build the knowledge, awareness, and skills necessary for providing culturally sensitive and affirming treatment. For more information about gender diversity and TGNC people, please see the American Psychological Association's *Guidelines for Psychological Practice With Transgender and Gender Nonconforming (TGNC) People* (APA, 2015), the American Counseling Association's *Competencies for Counseling With Transgender Clients* (ACA, 2010), and the World Professional Association for Transgender Health's standards of care (WPATH SOC7; Coleman et al., 2011).

## TGNC COMMUNITIES AND TRAUMA

TGNC people report experiences of discrimination and trauma at alarming rates. Compared with the general population, TGNC people are at a high risk of interpersonal violence. In one study, 46% of TGNC people reported being forced to have sex, 60% reported experiencing physical abuse at some point in their lives, and 66% reported experiencing violence in their own homes (Kenagy & Bostwick, 2005). TGNC youth grades K-12 report high incidences of harassment (78%), physical assault (35%), and sexual violence (12%) in educational settings (Grant et al., 2011). Survey research suggests a correlation between sexual violence and suicidality, with 41% of TGNC people who have attempted suicide reporting that they were sexual assault or rape survivors (Clements-Nolle et al., 2006). In addition, TGNC people experience microaggressions, such as others refusing to use their appropriate name and pronoun, and the denial of anti-trans bias (Nadal, Rivera, & Corpus, 2010; Nadal, Skolnik, & Wong, 2012).

Clinicians should be aware of the challenges faced by TGNC people who live at the intersection of multiple marginalized identities (de Vries, 2015; Saketopoulou, 2011). Transgender women of color are often victims of racism, anti-trans bias, and sexism, as well as other, more unique discrimination experiences that arise from the combination of these systems of oppression. These individuals not only have a higher risk of trauma but may also experience minority stress related to not knowing the cause or reason for someone else's mistreatment of them. For example, a transgender woman of color who experiences an attack or even a subtle microaggression may not know if it is due to the color of her skin, being a woman, or being perceived as TGNC. In other instances, it may be nearly impossible to discern homophobia from anti-trans bias as the motive for a hate crime, as they are both based on gender expression (Chakraborti & Hardy, 2015).

It is not uncommon for TGNC people to have negative experiences with health care providers, including therapists (Bradford, Reisner, Honnold, & Xavier, 2013). Within the United States, there is a long history of exploitation of TGNC people, including for the purposes of research (Denny, 2002). Though deemed ineffective and unethical by the WPATH (SOC7; Coleman et al., 2011), some clinicians and religious organizations still practice conversion therapies to attempt to change a TGNC person into being cisgender (Halberstam, 2005). Some TGNC people have histories of psychiatric hospitalization simply because their gender identities did not conform with their sex assigned at birth.

Many TGNC people experience police brutality, and they are less likely to receive help from law enforcement in general (Edelman, 2011; National Coalition of Anti-Violence Programs, 2011; Saffin, 2011). Regardless of whether an individual TGNC person has personally experienced this kind of trauma, simply being aware that systems designed to protect the public may not truly protect them may reinforce a sense that the world is not a safe place or that they do not deserve the same care and protection afforded to others.

Table 11.1 shows examples of sources of trauma or anxiety for TGNC people. This is not an exhaustive list but illustrates some of the more common occurrences. No matter how subtle these experiences are, they can create negative beliefs about oneself and contribute to mental health symptoms such as anxiety disorders,

**TABLE 11.1 Examples of Sources of Trauma for TGNC People**

| |
|---|
| Being asked inappropriate questions about their bodies |
| Being asked, "Are you a boy or a girl?" |
| Being attacked in bathrooms, locker rooms, and other sex-segregated public spaces |
| Bullying |
| Criminalization (e.g., people assuming they are sex workers) |
| Difficulty getting hired due to identity documents not matching |
| Facing racism within LGBT communities |
| Fear of going out in public or being seen by others |
| Feeling judged by other TGNC people for not having an extremely "masculine" or "feminine" presentation |
| Feeling of being born the wrong way or punished by God |
| Hearing transphobic remarks and jokes |
| Medical procedures that are invasive or create vulnerability (e.g., pelvic exams) |
| Nonbinary people feeling invisible or not taken seriously, including by other TGNC people |
| Not being able to wear clothes that feel comfortable, being forced to wear clothes to conform to sex assigned at birth |
| Others finding out about TGNC status if birth name is disclosed (e.g., in a classroom or medical office waiting room) |
| Rejection by family members, partners, or friends due to transgender identity |
| Rejection from previously supportive communities (e.g., LGB communities) |
| Rejection related to coming out as gay, lesbian, bisexual, or queer in the past |
| Religious abuse |
| Sexual assault in jails and prisons |
| Street harassment and assault |
| Surgery[1] or postsurgical complications |
| Trauma inflicted by medical and mental health providers |
| Workplace discrimination |

depression, and addictive or compulsive behaviors that may persist across the life span (Bockting et al., 2013; Fredriksen-Goldsen et al., 2014).

In addition to being educated about the ways that TGNC experience trauma, it is important for clinicians to be aware of individual and community resilience. In the face of adversity, TGNC communities have used certain strengths to build resistance and empowerment (Fruhauf & Orel, 2015; Singh, Hays, & Watson, 2011). It is helpful for EMDR therapists to be attuned to sources of resilience that may be used to support the processing of traumatic events and negative beliefs.

## BUILDING RAPPORT: TIPS FOR EMDR THERAPISTS WORKING WITH TGNC PEOPLE

The following recommendations outline appropriate and respectful ways to interact with TGNC clients. Because experiences can vary greatly, it is best to attend to the

[1] Surgery is not inherently traumatic for all TGNC people. Many people are happy with their choice and outcomes related to surgery. However, surgery can be invasive to the body and may bring up feelings of loss of control related to already vulnerable common surgical sites.

specific needs of each client, follow their[2] lead, and be open to incorporating client feedback.

*Keep an open mind.* Because the real diversity of TGNC people is not necessarily reflected in mainstream media, it is easy to be skeptical when a TGNC person's narrative or experience does not fit common stereotypes. Thus, it is necessary to remember that there are as many ways to be TGNC as there are TGNC people.

*Respect privacy.* It is not appropriate to ask about someone's genitals or surgical history unless that person volunteers this information.

*Maintain a balanced view.* TGNC people are some of the most marginalized in society because the media tends to sensationalize the adversities they face. It is important that therapists maintain a balanced perspective about clients as complex human beings with both strengths and challenges. Clients themselves may not be able to recognize their own assets, charging the therapist with the task of holding positive regard for the client. On the other hand, therapists should refrain from taking the stance of being overly reassuring, as this may be experienced as invalidating of the very real obstacles they face in the social world.

*Respect self-identification.* Healing may occur when a TGNC person is affirmed in their authentic gender identity. This includes using the language and pronouns that a TGNC person asks for in a given moment.

*Ask for consent when addressing somatic sensations and concerns.* Many TGNC people may feel sensitive when others focus on their bodies or may have dysphoria related to certain body parts (Kraemer, Delsignore, Schnyder, & Hepp, 2008). Clinicians should obtain permission at each session rather than assume that if a client is comfortable discussing body sensations at a previous session that this will always be the case. Many clients will appreciate this consideration, as it communicates both respect and understanding.

*Don't guide TGNC clients in imagining themselves as a child unless there has been a thorough conversation about this topic first.* Although many clients benefit from techniques that help them to connect with their younger or child parts, utilizing these techniques without an explicit conversation ahead of time may create an obstacle to progress for TGNC clients. For example, TGNC clients who are asked to picture themselves as small children in the desensitization phase may feel confusion. They may not know if they should envision their younger self as consistent with their actual childhood, being consistent with their assigned sex at birth (which could be triggering), or if they should envision their younger self as consistent with the gender that feels authentic to them today. Time should be taken during the preparation phase of treatment to discuss the possibility of doing inner child work and to follow the client's lead in terms of the language (e.g., name, pronouns, and gender) that the client feels comfortable with.

*Don't expect TGNC clients to educate you about all things related to gender identity.* It is a therapist's job to take responsibility for learning about concepts unfamiliar to them. It is important that clinicians do not expect a client to use their session time (and financial resources) to provide cultural competency training.

---

[2] The singular form of the pronouns "they/them/their" are used in place of the standard "he/him/his" and "she/her/hers" pronouns to demonstrate the use of gender-neutral pronouns when preferred gender pronoun is unknown or unspecified. These pronouns are also self-designated as a third-person pronoun by some people who identify as nonbinary or genderqueer.

## Common Relational or Transference/Countertransference Themes

Because therapists maintain a gatekeeping function for accessing appropriate health care (Lev, 2009; Singh & Burnes, 2010), TGNC people may have a wide range of feelings about seeking mental health services. Some TGNC people may approach working with a new therapist in a tentative way. Rather than being characterized as defensive or even paranoid, TGNC clients need their therapists to be patient in building rapport and be mindful of past histories of trauma with health professionals. In some cases, it may be necessary to use EMDR therapy to directly target those negative experiences before it is possible to create a safe therapeutic container and effectively address other presenting concerns.

Some TGNC people, aware of the client–therapist power differential, may adopt a "people-pleasing" stance that can be a barrier to expressing true emotions or disclosing information that is crucial in a proper case formulation. This may be especially true if the client is relying on the EMDR therapist not only for psychotherapy but also for an assessment (often referred to as a "letter") for the approval of transition-related medical care. Only therapists with specific gender expertise (often called "gender specialists") are appropriate to take on this task. If a dual role appears to be interfering with the client's progress in treatment, it may be necessary to refer the client to another skilled gender therapist to provide an assessment for medical care.

Therapists may have many different types of reactions toward TGNC clients. Some TGNC clients may have a corrective emotional experience when a cisgender therapist demonstrates ally behavior. It is important to note that being supportive of TGNC people, including respecting self-identification and self-determination, does not mean saying what one thinks the client wants to hear or refraining from appropriately challenging the client when necessary (e.g., when a person's substance abuse is putting them in unsafe situations). Therefore, therapists will benefit in examining their own countertransference regarding their role in relation to TGNC clients.

Therapists who have TGNC identities themselves can also benefit from examining biases about the spectrum of TGNC people in order to refrain from making assumptions about TGNC clients based on their own experiences. Also, TGNC therapists who have not healed their own traumatic experiences may find themselves unable to provide effective treatment when the client presents with similar experiences. This highlights the importance of engaging in clinician-centered, personal growth and healing work in order to prevent a regressive client–therapist relationship, which is one in which the client has surpassed the internal growth work of the therapist in some important regard, especially related to cultural identity and awareness (Carter & Helms, 1992). Another common issue that may arise is the difficulty in tolerating the dual role of being both a therapist/gatekeeper and being a member of the TGNC community. These therapists may experience guilt, a sense of betraying their communities, or a fear that they will be rejected or seen as "other" by their clients (Lurie, 2014). It can be very helpful to consult with other TGNC therapists to manage these countertransference reactions.

Conversely, clinicians who have strong biases against TGNC people living in their affirmed gender or undergoing medical transition should consider whether these biases will get in the way of providing affirmative care to TGNC clients. If a therapist has strong negative reactions toward TGNC people, it is likely that these attitudes will be perceived by clients and thereby do harm. Therefore, it may be the most ethical decision to communicate one's lack of expertise in providing affirming care and to refer clients to a gender specialist.

## APPLICATIONS OF EMDR WITH TGNC CLIENTS

The reasons that TGNC clients seek therapy typically fall into one of categories: (a) to address gender-related concerns such as coming out, transitioning, coping with gender dysphoria, or getting an assessment for medical interventions; (b) to address societal reactions to TGNC identity, such as minority stress, anti-trans bias, harassment, violence, or other forms of trauma, including forced feminization or forced masculinization as a young child (D'Augelli, Grossman, & Starks, 2006); and (c) to address coexisting concerns unrelated to gender. For this client, gender identity may not be the presenting concern, yet it is important that the therapist have basic cultural competence regarding TGNC concerns.

It is important to emphasize that any efforts to change gender identity and/or expression are considered unethical and ineffective (Coleman et al., 2012). This includes behavioral techniques that attempt to make a child conform to gender expectations based on sex assigned at birth. Therefore, it cannot be emphasized enough that therapists should refrain from trying to use EMDR therapy to change gender identity and/or expression to meet societal expectations, *even if a client is struggling with TGNC identity and requests this.*

### Applications of the Three-Pronged Protocol and Eight-Phase Treatment Approach of EMDR Therapy With TGNC Clients

A solid foundation in the standard EMDR protocol, as well as some capacity for creativity and flexibility, will be helpful in facilitating healing work with TGNC people. The eight phases of EMDR therapy provide a clear guideline for application of the three-pronged protocol (Shapiro, 2001). In this section, these phases will be discussed with special consideration for working with TGNC clients, and, where applicable, suggestions for useful questions are presented. Additionally, I suggest the use of one additional phase, termed *therapist humility*, to precede the standard eight phases.

#### Phase 0: Therapist Humility

For any clinician with a strong interest in developing expertise in working with TGNC people, it is necessary to engage in one's own process of increasing cultural competence and humility and acquiring knowledge, awareness, and skills specific to TGNC populations (Cross, Bazron, Dennis, & Isaacs, 1989). Therapist humility may also be regarded as a position, lens, or ongoing dynamic process through which any and all healing may occur rather than a simple or discrete skill that can be attained.

Increasing *knowledge* includes learning about the diversity of TGNC communities and the power structures that create differential experiences between cisgender and TGNC people. Building *awareness* includes investigating and reflecting on one's own gender identity and being aware of how this may shape one's perceptions of people who are both similar and different. For example, cisgender therapists are encouraged to examine unacknowledged cisgender privilege, anti-trans bias, and internalized stereotypes about TGNC people. TGNC therapists are encouraged to examine ways in which they may or may not hold power relative to the client, whether it is due to a different experience of being TGNC or other cultural identity markers such as race, class, or educational background. Finally, cultivating specific *skills* in working with TGNC people will aid in building rapport and allowing for a successful treatment. This includes appreciating self-identification and using respectful language.

## Phase 1: History Taking

A thorough inquiry into each client's background and trauma history, with a special emphasis on attachment, is essential in planning the course of treatment. Trauma experiences may or may not be related to gender identity or TGNC experience. At times when gender identity does not appear to be relevant to the specific target (e.g., phobia, car accident) and later emerges as somehow connected to the target, therapists should allow this discovery to occur naturally and refrain from inappropriately probing or suggesting these connections as this may injure rapport and derail the treatment. No TGNC client wants to be seen solely as a TGNC person to the exclusion of other relevant identities and experiences.

If the client's experience of being TGNC is relevant to the target, it is important to determine where the distress is located. Some TGNC feel conflict internally, whereas others do not feel conflicted about gender identity but feel tension and conflict from the external world. Examples of useful clarification questions include:

1. "Do you have a problem with being transgender (gender nonconforming, genderqueer, whatever language the client uses as self-identification), or is it others who have a problem with it?"
2. "If both, can you tell me what percent is your own discomfort and how much is due to the discomfort or unsupportiveness of others?"
3. "Which important people in your life have supported you in expressing your gender authentically? Which important people in your life have not been supportive?"

These questions may help to identify attachment wounds, as well as indicate specific ways in which the client may need to be prepared or resourced in the next phase of treatment from an attached-focused approach (Manfield, 2010; Parnell, 2013). Another task of this phase is to identify specific targets for processing and to group events into similar themes or as having the same Negative Cognitions (NCs). It is not advised, even if the client requests this, to begin with a severe trauma such as surviving an assault, hate crime, or life-threatening event without having a sense of whether the client can tolerate this level of intensity without dissociating. It is beneficial to be cautious and begin with something more akin to a microaggression and then to build competency toward working on more severe traumas, especially if the client is new to EMDR therapy as a modality.

## Phase 2: Preparation

In this phase, it is important to thoroughly assess positive coping resources or sources of resilience, as well as maladaptive coping mechanisms (e.g., numbing or addictive behaviors). For many TGNC clients who have posttraumatic stress disorder (PTSD) or severe trauma histories, some maladaptive coping mechanisms may be seen as means of survival. A harm reduction approach may help some TGNC clients reduce numbing behaviors while concurrently building a set of adaptive coping skills and tools (Clements-Nolle, Marx, Guzman, & Katz, 2001; Hwahng et al., 2012). Grounding exercises such as mindful breathing and gentle stretching may also be helpful, especially for clients who dissociate.

RDI of a calm or peaceful place (Shapiro, 2001) or a resource figure (Schmidt, 1999, 2001) may be helpful during this phase within and between sessions. If the client did not have significant caregivers who provided love, nurturance, or unconditional acceptance, especially with regard to gender identity and/or expression, it will be strategically valuable at this point to aid in the development of ideal caregivers. It is suggested that the therapist refrain from suggesting the gender of the caregiver(s) and allow the client to choose a gender (if any at all). For example, clinicians should be careful to refrain from suggesting the necessity of both mother and father figures, as this may reinforce a heteronormative family structure and gender norms that may not be ideal for every client's worldview. If the client is able to describe this ideal caregiver, it is appropriate to ask, "What pronoun would you like for me to use to refer to this figure?"

Another resource figure that may be particularly helpful and powerful for some TGNC clients is the future empowered transitioned self (hereby referred to as FETS), which is a visualization and activation of the client in their affirmed gender (i.e., the gender that is congruent with his or her internal sense of who he or she is). A sample script for developing the FETS is provided at the end of this chapter. It is important to reiterate that not all TGNC people desire all aspects of transition (e.g., medical, social, and legal) and that for these clients, the concept of transition may be used very broadly to simply suggest a transformation into the person the client would like to be (e.g., assertive, confident).

## Phase 3: Assessment

The assessment phase of EMDR therapy with TGNC clients should be relatively similar to work with non-TGNC or cisgender clients, with identifying a visual image, NC self-referential belief, alternative Positive Cognition (PC), the validity or strength of the positive cognition (Validity of Cognition [VoC]), the related emotion, the Subjective Units of Disturbances (SUDs) rating, and body sensations. As mentioned previously, it is helpful to ask for consent to discuss physical sensations. This may simply be worded as, "Are you comfortable discussing body sensations today?"

## Phases 4 and 5: Desensitization and Installation

The desensitization phase, as applied to working with TGNC people, should be similar to work with non-TGNC or cisgender clients. Elements of the initial target will evolve through different sets of bilateral stimulation (BLS) with intermittent guiding verbalizations (e.g., "Go with that") and cognitive interweaves from the therapist. When employing cognitive interweaves, the therapist should be careful not to invalidate the client's reality related to anti-trans bias. Emphasis can be on choice and an empowered response in the face of a very real system of oppression that can make a TGNC person's life difficult on a day-to-day basis.

### Phase 6: Body Scan

During this phase, special attention should be given to bodily sensations that were specifically identified in the assessment phase. For TGNC people who report having persistent gender-based dysphoria related to one or more aspects of their body, it may not be realistic for EMDR processing to fully eliminate this somatic experience, as medical interventions may be necessary to reduce this kind of dysphoria. Residual or baseline physical or emotional discomfort related to the body should not be construed as a sign of ineffective EMDR processing.

### Phases 7 and 8: Closure and Reevaluation

These last two phases of the standard EMDR protocol are the same for TGNC clients as for other clients.

## FETS AS A POSITIVE RESOURCE

The following script was designed to help TGNC people access and activate a powerful resource figure within them. This script was developed over time and informed by several TGNC clients who spontaneously and independently created a future self that had overcome past and present challenges and could assure them that they would be okay. Coupled with BLS, this script may be used as part of EMDR processing or on its own as a tool for positive coping or resource development.

Because "transition" is not a concept or goal that every TGNC can relate to, it is important to emphasize to clients that transition can be used very broadly and in whichever way feels most fitting to them. Because many TGNC people find power in being able to designate the language that feels the most affirming to them, this script may be tailored to match the needs of each client. As previously mentioned, it is necessary to ask clients if they feel comfortable with the exploration of physical cues or sensations and to cater this script accordingly.

## Script

*Begin by getting into a comfortable position, with your feet on the floor and eyes closed or resting gently on something in front of you. Then take a few deep breaths, noticing how your body feels as you inhale and exhale.*

*Imagine you are in a peaceful, comfortable place, somewhere you've been or somewhere you'd like to go, real or imaginary. Take a few deep breaths and just take in the sense of calm and comfort around you.*

*Start to notice that there is a warm, welcoming energy present in the room with you. Somehow you know that this is a part of you, a part of you that you do not know well yet but will come to know in the future. Somehow you sense that this figure is here to witness you in your healing process and to support you in any moment that you need help. This is your future empowered (transitioned) self. You can give this presence a name if you wish. This future self can be whatever gender feels right. If this presence has a human or visual shape or form, just notice what this looks like.*

*Take a moment to allow yourself to sit with this loving presence and to take in the sense of being nurtured, accepted, and protected. If you'd like, you can ask for this presence to hold you or cradle you. Take in the comfort of knowing that this figure is you and has survived through all the difficulties and pain that it took to reach this state of calm and empowerment. This figure invites you to reach out for help at any time and especially wants you to know how much you are loved and that you are not alone. When you are ready, you can open your eyes.*

After this visualization (often paired with BLS), the client's vision of and relationship with the FETS figure may be further developed or discussed. The use of this figure in EMDR processing work can be immensely powerful in instilling a sense of hope.

## CASE EXAMPLE: A SENSITIVE MAN

Greg, a 31-year-old White trans man (pronouns: he, him, or his), came to therapy early in his transition from female to male. He had already had chest reconstructive surgery at age 25, and at that time it was the only gender-affirming medical intervention he desired. Over time, however, he realized that he wanted to begin hormone therapy in order to develop masculine secondary sex characteristics and be perceived as a man in society. While he felt this was essential in order to achieve a sense of internal and external congruence, starting hormone therapy also brought up conflict for him. Having studied different forms of oppression and worked as an activist for social change, Greg reported feeling conflicted about gaining heterosexual White male privilege. He feared that if he was perceived as a man, which is what he desired, it would create pressure for him to conform to gender role expectations that were not in line with his values. As much as Greg understood from a cognitive standpoint that he could choose to be and embody who he truly wanted to be, at a deeper emotional level he was scared that he would either comply with societal demands or be ridiculed for not complying with them. He was plagued with fear and indecision.

While gathering Greg's history (Phase 1), I asked questions about his gender socialization. We discussed how his father, a working class man, had exhibited a "tough" exterior and endorsed traditional gender roles. Greg was teased as a kid for being a tomboy, and his parents favored his sister, who had a more "feminine" gender expression. Greg identified feelings of self-doubt and avoidance because his family was not one in which feelings were validated. He recalled many times of being frankly told that his feelings were mistaken or wrong. Phase 2, or preparation, with Greg involved identifying ways in which he had been strong, resilient, and used resources to survive difficult times in his life, including his experience of coming out as attracted to women as a teenager and expressing himself creatively as a writer. It was during this phase that Greg identified all the characteristics that he would hope to embody in a FETS. We paired this image with BLS to install a sense of connection with this future self. He reported finding this satisfying and was excited to be asked, "*What kind of man do you want to be?*" This created space for him to define himself differently from the traditional gender ideals modeled for him. He giggled in delight as he relayed to me his vision of his future self: "He's a rugged mountain-man with a beard wearing Carhardt jeans and a tight pink top. He's soft-spoken, yet confident and comfortable in his skin."

During assessment (Phase 3), Greg identified a memory of himself as a young child being given a choice of two toys, choosing the one he wanted instead of the one he thought he "should," and then being ridiculed by his sister. He identified the core negative belief about himself to be, "I have to hide". Through desensitization and installation (Phases 4 and 5), Greg again utilized the concept of the FETS, which led to an intense release of anger and grief before materializing the PCs of "It's okay to feel" and "It's okay to be me". Here is an excerpt from that session:

**Greg:** "I don't understand. I feel so stupid."

**Therapist:** *<BLS>*

**Greg:** "I just can't get it right. And my parents did nothing. I think they even laughed at me and just let her humiliate me."

**Therapist:** *<BLS>*

**Greg:** "I know it's stupid now, but I just needed someone to support me, to explain what was going on. I'm so confused."

**Therapist:** *Who could do that for you?*

**Greg:** "I want to say my parents . . . but they just couldn't . . . I don't know."

**Therapist:** *Could that future self we discussed earlier come in to support you?*

**Greg:** "Umm, I think so."

**Therapist:** *Imagine that he's there with you. You can ask him for support, for guidance, for whatever it is you need in this moment. <BLS>* [Greg begins to alternate between sobbing and shaking angrily. I encourage him to keep allowing whatever comes up to come up.]

**Greg:** "He's explaining to me that all of this isn't for me, that I can feel whatever I feel. It's okay for it to not make sense."

**Therapist:** *<BLS>*

**Greg:** "He's proud of me. He's there, he picks me up. He tells me that there are no expectations and no secrets. I don't have to hide anymore."

**Therapist:** *<BLS>*

**Greg:** "Now we're taking a walk together. He's explaining to me that it's okay to have feelings, even if I am a boy. He says that feelings aren't something that need to be explained. They can just be. I don't need to justify it for it to be valid."

During this session, Greg's SUDs reduced from an initial 7 to 0. During subsequent sessions, Greg became more confident in the beliefs that he could choose to be his authentic self, as a sensitive man with both "masculine" and "feminine" qualities at the same time. In a sense, much of his EMDR therapy work was about releasing him from the binds of the gender binary and an invalidating early environment that taught him to hide or hold back from choosing from what he really wanted.

## SUMMARY

In this chapter, fundamental information about TGNC people's lives, including ways in which they may experience trauma, were introduced. Special considerations for the application of EMDR therapy and the eight-phase standard protocol were reviewed. Finally, I reviewed an example of a positive resource figure that could be utilized during EMDR therapy and used a client case to demonstrate the use of this resource. As there is no research to date specifically linking the application of EMDR therapy to psychotherapeutic and healing work with TGNC people, more developments are necessary to create a comprehensive model of treatment. However, this chapter serves as a basis for the development of further possibilities for people of diverse gender identities and expressions.

## REFERENCES


American Counseling Association. (2010). American Counseling Association competencies for counseling with transgender clients. *Journal of LGBT Issues in Counseling, 4*, 135–159. doi:10.1080/15538605.2010.524839

American Psychiatric Association. (1980). *Diagnostic and statistical manual of mental disorders* (3rd ed.). Washington, DC: Author.

American Psychiatric Association. (2013). *Diagnostic and statistical manual of mental disorders* (5th ed.). Washington, DC: Author.

American Psychological Association. (2015). *Guidelines for psychological practice with transgender and gender nonconforming people*. Retrieved from http://www.apa.org/practice/guidelines/transgender.pdf

Bockting, W. O., Miner, M. H., Swinburne Romine, R. E., Hamilton, A., & Coleman, E. (2013). Stigma, mental health, and resilience in an online sample of the U.S. transgender population. *American Journal of Public Health, 103*, 943–951. doi:10.2105/AJPH.2013.301241

Bradford, J., Reisner, S. L., Honnold, J. A., & Xavier, J. (2013). Experiences of transgender-related discrimination and implications for health: Results from the Virginia Transgender Health Initiative Study. *American Journal of Public Health, 103*, 1820–1829. doi:10.2105/AJPH.2012.300796

Brill, S., & Pepper, R. (2008). *The transgender child: A handbook for families and professionals*. San Francisco, CA: Cleis Press.

Byne, W., Bradley, S. J., Coleman, E., Eyler, A. E., Green, R., Menvielle, E. J., . . . Tompkins, D. A. (2012). Report of the American Psychiatric Association task force on the treatment of gender identity disorder. *Archives of Sexual Behavior, 41*, 759–796. doi:10.1007/s10508-012-9975-x

Carter, R. T., & Helms, J. E. (1992). The counseling process as defined by relationship types: A test of Helms's interactional model. *Journal of Multicultural Counseling and Development, 20*(4), 181–201.

Cashore, C., & Tuason, T. G. (2009). Negotiating the binary: Identity and social justice for bisexual and transgender individuals. *Journal of Gay & Lesbian Social Services, 21*(4), 374–401.

Chakraborti, N., & Hardy, S. J. (2015). *LGB&T hate crime reporting: Identifying barriers and solutions*. Retrieved from http://lancslgbt.org.uk/web/wp-content/uploads/2015/06/EHRC-Final-Report-Lieces-Uni.pdf

Clements-Nolle, K., Marx, R., Guzman, R., & Katz, M. (2001). HIV prevalence, risk behaviors, health care use, and mental health status of transgender persons: Implications for public health intervention. *American Journal of Public Health, 91*(6), 915.

Clements-Nolle, K., Marx, R., & Katz, M. (2006). Attempted suicide among transgender persons: The influence of gender-based discrimination and victimization. *Journal of Homosexuality, 51*, 53–69. doi:10.1300/J082v51n03_04

Cole, E. R. (2009). Intersectionality and research in psychology. *American Psychologist, 64*(3), 170–180. doi:10.1037/a0014564

Coleman, E., Bockting, W., Botzer, M., Cohen-Kettenis, P., DeCuypere, G., Feldman, J., . . . Zucker, K. (2011). Standards of care for the health of transsexual, transgender, and gender nonconforming people, 7th version. *International Journal of Transgenderism, 13*, 165–232. doi:10.1080/15532739.2011.700873

Crenshaw, K. (1991). Mapping the margins: Intersectionality, identity politics, and violence against women of color. *Stanford Law Review, 43*, 1241–1299. doi:10.2307/1229039

Cross, T., Bazron, B., Dennis, K., & Isaacs, M. (1989). *Towards a culturally competent system of care* (Vol. 1). Washington, DC: Georgetown University Child Development Center, CASSP Technical Assistance Center.

D'Augelli, A. R., Grossman, A. H., & Starks, M. T. (2006). Childhood gender atypicality, victimization, and PTSD among lesbian, gay and bisexual youth. *Journal of Interpersonal Violence, 21*, 1462–1482.

Davis, S. A., & Meier, S. C. (2014). Effects of testosterone treatment and chest reconstruction surgery on mental health and sexuality in female-to-male transgender people. *International Journal of Sexual Health, 26*, 113–128. doi:10.1080/19317611.2013.833152

de Vries, K. M. (2015). Transgender people of color at the center: Conceptualizing a new intersectional model. *Ethnicities, 15*(1), 3–27. doi:10.1177/1468796814547058

Denny, D. (2002). The politics of diagnosis and a diagnosis of politics: How the university-affiliated gender clinics failed to meet the needs of transsexual people. *Transgender Tapestry, 98*, 17–27.

Drescher, J. (2010). Queer diagnoses: Parallels and contrast in the history of homosexuality, gender variance, and the diagnostic statistical manual. *Archives of Sexual Behavior, 39*, 427–460.

Edelman, E. A. (2011). "This area has been declared a prostitution free zone": Discursive formations of space, the state, and trans "sex worker" bodies. *Journal of Homosexuality, 58*, 848–864. doi:10.1080/00918369.2011.581928

Feinberg, L. (1996). *Transgender warriors: Making history from Joan of Arc to Dennis Rodman*. Boston, MA: Beacon Press.

Fredriksen-Goldsen, K. I., Cook-Daniels, L., Kim, H. J., Erosheva, E. A., Emlet, C. A., Hoy-Ellis, C. P., . . . Muraco, A. (2014). Physical and mental health of transgender older adults: An at-risk and underserved population. *Gerontologist, 54*(3), 488–500. doi:10.1093/geront/gnt021

Fruhauf, C. A., & Orel, N. A. (2015). Fostering resilience in LGBT aging individuals and families. In N. A. Orel & C. A. Fruhauf (Eds.), *The lives of LGBT older adults: Understanding challenges and resilience* (pp. 217–227). Washington, DC: American Psychological Association.

Grant, J. M., Mottet, L. A., Tanis, J., Harrison, J., Herman, J. L., & Kiesling, M. (2011). *Injustice at every turn: A report of the national transgender discrimination survey*. Washington, DC: National Center for Transgender Equality & National Gay and Lesbian Task Force. Retrieved from http://endtransdiscrimination.org/PDFs/NTDS_Report.pdf

Halberstam, J. (2005). *In a queer time and place: Transgender bodies, subcultural lives*. New York, NY: NYU Press.

Hwahng, S. J., Allen, B., Zadoretzky, C., Barber, H., McKnight, C., & Des Jarlais, D. (2012). *Resiliencies, vulnerabilities, and health disparities among low-income transgender people of color at New York City harm reduction programs*. New York, NY: Baron Edmond de Rothschild Chemical Dependency Institute, Mount Sinai Beth Israel (formerly Beth Israel Medical Center).

Kenagy, G. P., & Bostwick, W. B. (2005). Health and social service needs of transgender people in Chicago. *International Journal of Transgenderism, 8*(2–3), 57–66. doi:10.1300/J485v08n02_06

Knudson, G., De Cuypere, G., & Bockting, W. (2010). Recommendations for revision of the DSM diagnosis of gender identity disorders: Consensus statement of the World Professional Association for Transgendered Health. *International Journal of Transgenderism, 12,* 115–118. doi:10.1080/15532739.2010.509215

Kraemer, B., Delsignore, A., Schnyder, U., & Hepp, U. (2008). Body image and transsexualism. *Psychopathology*, 41, 96–100.

Kuhn, A., Brodmer, C., Stadlmayer, W., Kuhn, P., Mueller, M. D., & Birkhauser, M. (2009). Quality of life 15 years after sex reassignment surgery for transsexualism. *Fertility and Sterility, 92,* 1685–1689. doi:10.1016/j.fertnstert.2008.08.126

Lev, A. I. (2004). *Transgender emergence: Therapeutic guidelines for working with gender-variant people and their families.* New York, NY: Routledge.

Lev, A. I. (2009). The ten tasks of the mental health provider: Recommendations for revision of the World Professional Association for Transgender Health's Standards of Care. *International Journal of Transgenderism, 11,* 74–99. doi:10.1080/15532730903008032

Lurie, S. B. (2014). *Exploring the impacts of disclosure for transgender and gender non-conforming therapists* (MSW thesis).

MacCulloch, T. (2010). Constructions of truth, gate-keeping, and the power of diagnostic labels. *Issues in Mental Health Nursing, 31,* 151–152.

Manfield, P. (2010). *Dyadic resourcing. Creating a foundation for processing trauma.* Charleston, SC: Cornucopia Publishers.

Miller, J., & Nichols, A. (2012). Identity, sexuality and commercial sex among Sri Lankan nachchi. *Sexualities, 15,* 554–569. doi:10.1177/1363460712446120

Nadal, K. L., Rivera, D. P., & Corpus, M. J. H. (2010). Sexual orientation and transgender microaggressions in everyday life: Experiences of lesbians, gays, bisexuals, and transgender individuals. In D. W. Sue (Ed.), *Microaggressions and marginality: Manifestation, dynamics, and impact* (pp. 217–240). New York, NY: Wiley.

Nadal, K. L., Skolnik, A., & Wong, Y. (2012). Interpersonal and systemic microaggressions toward transgender people: Implications for counseling. *Journal of LGBT Issues in Counseling, 6,* 55–82. doi:10.1080/15538605.2012.648583

Namaste, V. K. (2000). *Invisible lives: The erasure of transsexual and transgendered people.* Chicago, IL: University of Chicago.

National Coalition of Anti-Violence Programs. (2011). Hate violence against lesbian, gay, bisexual, transgender, queer, and HIV-affected communities in the United States in 2011: A report from the National Coalition of Anti-Violence Programs. New York, NY: Author. Retrieved from http://avp.org/storage/documents/Reports/2012_NCAVP_2011_HV_Report.pdf

Parnell, L. (2013). *Attachment-focused EMDR: Healing relational trauma.* New York, NY: W. W. Norton.

Ryan, C. (2009). *Supportive families, healthy children: Helping families with lesbian, gay, bisexual & transgender children.* San Francisco, CA: Family Acceptance Project, Marian Wright Edelman Institute, San Francisco State University. Retrieved from http://familyproject.sfsu.edu/publications

Saffin, L. A. (2011). Identities under seige: Violence against transpersons of color. In E. A. Stanley & N. Smith (Eds.), *Captive genders: Trans embodiment and the prison industrial complex* (pp. 141–162). Oakland, CA: AK Press.

Saketopoulou, A. (2011). Minding the gap: Intersections between gender, race, and class in work with gender variant children. *Psychoanalytic Dialogues: The International Journal of Relational Perspectives, 21,* 192–209.

Schmidt, S. J. (1999, March). Resource-focused EMDR: Integration of ego state therapy, alternating bilateral stimulation, and art therapy. *EMDRIA Newsletter, 4,* 10–13, 25–28.

Schmidt, S. J. (2001, December). Meeting needs with a resource sandwich. *EMDRIA Newsletter (Special Edition), 6,* 28–31.

Schmidt, J. (2003). Paradise lost? Social change and Fa'afafine in Samoa. *Current Sociology, 51*, 417–432. doi:10.1177/0011392103051003014

Shapiro, F. (2001). *Eye movement desensitization and reprocessing: Basic principles, protocols, and procedures* (2nd ed.). New York, NY: Guilford Press.

Singh, A. A., & Burnes, T. R. (2010). Shifting the counselor role from gatekeeping to advocacy: Ten strategies for using the competencies for counseling with transgender clients for individual and social change. *Journal of LGBT Issues in Counseling, 4*(3–4), 241–255.

Singh, A. A., Hays, D. G., & Watson, L. S. (2011). Strength in the face of adversity: Resilience strategies of transgender individuals. *Journal of Counseling and Development, 89*, 20–27.

Stryker, S. (2008). *Transgender history*. Berkeley, CA: Seal Press.

CHAPTER 12

# EMDR Therapy With Lesbian/Gay/ Bisexual Clients

John M. O'Brien

Is eye movement desensitization and reprocessing (EMDR) therapy with gays and lesbians different? Although treatment is similar in many ways, there are experiences that sexual minorities face in American culture that will impact the issues that clients bring to treatment and traumas that can be effectively targeted with EMDR. In this chapter, the unique elements of EMDR therapy with gays/lesbians/bisexuals are reviewed. This chapter restricts itself to issues of concern for lesbian, gay, bisexual individuals, but clinicians need to be aware that there are unique concerns for all clients under the LGBTQQI umbrella: lesbian, gay, bisexual, transgender, queer, questioning, and intersex.

Lesbians and gay men are more likely than heterosexuals to present for mental health treatment and are more likely to experience trauma (Cochran, Sullivan, & Mays, 2003; Roberts, Austin, Corliss, Vandermorris, & Koenen, 2010). Despite recent changes in American culture toward sexual minorities (including legalizing gay marriage), gays/lesbians/bisexuals continue to feel marginalized. Stigma/discrimination and deficits in social support likely increase the incidence of psychological disorders (Cochran et al., 2003).

Therapists therefore need to be prepared to provide treatments to lesbians and gay men that are sensitive to the unique needs of this population. The purpose of this chapter is to outline the experiences of oppression of sexual minorities and to review how EMDR therapy might be used to help clients heal. Case vignettes are used to demonstrate EMDR therapy's utility in working with this population.

## EXPERIENCES OF OPPRESSION

The beginning of the modern gay rights movements in the United States occurred in 1969. Police raided the Stonewall, a bar in Greenwich Village in New York City that was frequented by members of the gay community and began to arrest some of the customers. At this point, for the first time, the crowd fought back against the police, leading to several days of rioting and protests. This event resulted in the creation of gay pride events and the formation of many national gay and lesbian advocacy groups (Silverstein, 1991).

The United States has become an increasingly accepting environment for gays and lesbians over the last four decades, including the recent Supreme Court decision upholding gay marriage (Goetting, 2015). In spite of these gains, sexual minorities continue to face significant discrimination and bias in both their work and personal lives. Negative beliefs about gays and lesbians can lead to overt discriminatory behaviors and violence against this population. Experiences of discrimination based on sexual orientation can contribute to poorer mental health outcomes (Bostwick, Boyd, Hughes, West, & McCabe, 2014).

Internalized homophobia occurs when LGB persons internalize negative societal beliefs and begin to believe them about themselves. Often, individuals are unaware of these beliefs but they can exert great power. Internalized homophobia has implications for levels of self-care and can trigger psychiatric symptoms (Williamson, 2000).

Sexual minorities can also experience discrimination in housing, social services, or health care (Hillman & Hinrichsen, 2014). Many lesbians and gay men fear discrimination in retirement communities as well as assisted living facilities and nursing homes (Jackson, Johnson, & Roberts, 2008). They often "go back in the closet" in these places, rather than face shame and humiliation.

*"I am gay." A 65-year-old man, newly admitted to a nursing home on the outskirts of a large Mid-Atlantic city, scribbled this statement on a piece of paper before sliding it across the table to his new psychologist. The resident held his finger up to his lips, looked cautiously out into the hallway, and whispered "shhh" before taking the piece of paper back and ripping it into tiny pieces (Hillman & Hinrichsen, 2014, p. 269).*

## Microaggressions

Microaggressions are "subtle insults that are delivered through dismissive looks, gestures, and tones (verbal, nonverbal and over visual) that are often directed toward people of color" (Sue & Constantine, 2007, p. 137). Whether intentional or unintentional, these behaviors can exert a powerful and negative effect on the psychological well-being of members of minority groups (Ong, Burrow, Fuller-Rowell, Ja, & Sue, 2013). Microaggressions have also been identified in the lives of lesbians and gay men (Platt & Lenzen, 2013). Sexual minorities experience more problems as they become increasingly visible, leading to beliefs that they are abnormal and deserve to be treated in hostile and discriminatory ways (Herek, Gillis, & Cogan, 2015).

*A gay male psychology intern was treating a gay male client and decided that it was important to talk about countertransference issues in supervision. When he came out to his supervisor in the discussion, he thought that it was important to acknowledge his gay identity when discussing the case. His supervisor responded, "I don't think that you need to talk about that. I don't talk about who I sleep with and neither should you."*

One of the major differences between people of color and sexual minorities relates to the choice of disclosure. Racial minority individuals are identifiable by external physical qualities. Gays/lesbians can decide whether or not to "come out" to others (acknowledging identity as gay/lesbian), based on the environment and/or their own level of comfort with who they are. Many gays/lesbians/bisexuals choose not to talk about their sexual minority status to avoid rejection, retaliation, and the potential loss of social support (Platt & Lenzen, 2013). Coming out is not a one-time event but rather a process that is ongoing through many life situations.

### Homosexuality and Psychotherapy

Until the late 1970s, much of the focus in therapy for gay men and lesbians was to change them into heterosexuals (Davison, 2001). Clinicians used various methods to alter sexual orientation. Treatments encouraged patients to engage in traditional gender-role behaviors in order to complete their developmental process. Many gay men and lesbians avoided therapy due to dissatisfaction with their treatment or what they heard from friends (Langdridge, 2007).

In the mid-1970s, homosexuality was removed as an official mental health diagnosis (APA, 1974). Despite this change, some in the mental health field continued to promulgate the idea that homosexuality was a disease that could be cured via "conversion therapy" or "reorientation therapy" (APA, 2009). In fact, there seemed to be an increase in these treatments in the 1990s by people who sought to stigmatize gays/lesbians as morally flawed, spiritually weak, or developmentally defective (APA, 2009). Advocates of conversion therapy reported only a 30% success rate in changing sexual orientation, leaving 70% of clients as "treatment failures." These clients had entered treatment with distress about their lesbian/gay identity and many left with the additional symptoms of exacerbated depression, sexual dysfunction, avoidance of intimacy, and low self-esteem, among others (Haldeman, 2002).

Since the resurgence of treatments to change sexual orientation, many professional associations have submitted public statements arguing for a ban on conversion therapy. Yet, there are still those who argue for the potential efficacy and merits of conversion therapy (Beckstead, 2012). Many gays and lesbians remain wary of seeking therapy or are dissatisfied with their experiences in mental health treatment (Butler, 2009).

## CLINICAL ISSUES AND EMDR THERAPY

Lesbian, gay, and bisexual clients may present to therapy with issues that have no relationship to their sexual orientation. Alternatively, they may come to treatment with issues that are not a consequence of their lack of acceptance of their sexual orientation but rather others' lack of acceptance of it. In addition, there are other issues unique to therapy with sexual minorities that may benefit from treatment with EMDR. The following is an exploration of some of these issues.

### Religious/Spirituality

Some gays/lesbians grow up in religions that are welcoming and affirming faith communities for sexual minorities. These individuals have little to no difficulty in reconciling their spirituality and sexuality. However, others grow up in faith communities that are invalidating or openly hostile to homosexuals. For these people, integrating sexuality and spirituality becomes much more difficult and many sexual minorities abandon their faith (Shallenberger, 1998). An additional challenge can be the negative response of progressives or other members of the gay community to a lesbian or gay man's disclosure that he/she is active in a religion (Hodge, 2005). This leaves the individual in the uncomfortable position of conforming to the religion's teachings, rejecting themselves or accepting themselves, and rejecting the religion (Bowland, Foster, & Vosler, 2013).

Some religious communities have recently made changes in their treatment of sexual minorities. For example, some Christian, Jewish, and nondenominational churches advertise themselves as "open and affirming communities" that welcome gays/lesbians. Advocacy groups, such as Soulforce (www.soulforce.org), have developed nationally to end discriminatory behaviors by religious institutions. There is a great deal of support available to those who wish to integrate religion, spirituality, and sexuality. Clinicians may be critical sources of support to help these individuals (a) challenge harmful religious interpretations, (b) identify gay affirmative religious leaders and religious communities, and (c) connect with supportive peers (Bowland et al., 2013).

*Adam was a 21-year-old gay male college student who presented for outpatient therapy upon referral from his primary care physician. He presented with symptoms of depression and anxiety that were impairing his academic performance and social functioning. He had few friends and remained at home on most weekend days.*

*In the initial assessment, Adam noted that he had recently come out to his parents. He and his family were members of a conservative Christian church that viewed homosexuality as sinful and that taught him that "homosexuals will go straight to hell." Adam knew that he was gay and he felt trapped between his growing self-awareness of who he was and the dictates of his religion.*

*To his parents' credit, they were trying to be supportive of Adam. Although they were initially completely rejecting of him and of his disclosure, they educated themselves enough about gay/lesbian issues to adopt a more tolerant stance of their son's sexual orientation. While they still maintained that being gay was a sin, they sought to support their son as best they could.*

*Adam's therapy was critical to helping him develop a positive identity as a gay man. He was encouraged to become more educated about the lives of gays and lesbians via readings and websites. Over time, he took the risk of exploring campus resources to support sexual minorities and attended a meeting of the lesbian/gay student organization. He slowly developed social connections in the gay community and grew toward greater acceptance of himself.*

*EMDR therapy was an important component of his treatment. Adam used Resource Development (RDI; Korn & Leeds, 2002) and created resources that helped him to tolerate difficult times. He developed a resource of his guardian angel, watching over him and encircling him with love. He was able to utilize this and other resources when he began to feel hopeless about his life or after a difficult interaction with his parents or other family members that reinforced negative beliefs about gays/lesbians.*

## Sexuality

Much of the research on gender and sexuality has been based on heterosexuality, making it difficult to draw conclusions about the experiences of sexual minorities (Missildine, Feldstein, Punzalan, & Parsons, 2005). In addition, there are differences in the experiences of gays and lesbians. For example, at least one study showed that women's sexuality tends to be more fluid than men's over the course of their lifetime, making women more likely than men to identify as bisexual (Diamond, 2008).

Studies of lesbian sexuality have been limited in focus with specific emphasis on the frequency of sexual activity. Lesbian couples have been found to have genital sex less frequently than gay male couples and heterosexual couples (Cohen & Byers, 2014). This has often been used to label lesbians in long-term relationships as low in sexual desire. However, recent research indicates that both genital and nongenital sexual behaviors were present in their relationships and contributed to sexual satisfaction in lesbians (Cohen & Byers, 2014). It would appear that sexual intimacy and sexual satisfaction remain an important part of long-term relationships in lesbian couples.

Gay men tend to express sexuality in different ways than heterosexual men. Some gay men in committed relationships are nonmonogamous, although rates of monogamy in gay male couples have been increasing steadily (Gotta et al., 2011). There are a variety of sexual behaviors within the gay male community and a wider acceptance of anonymous sex and polyamory as compared with the heterosexual community (Hosking, 2013). Couples who allow for extra-dyadic sex do not necessarily experience lower relationship quality as compared with couples that choose monogamy. Rather, it depends on the agreements that the couple have about this behavior and whether or not these rules are broken (Hosking, 2013).

*Thomas was a 32-year-old gay man who worked for an oil company as a service tech. He spent much of his day on the road, providing regular maintenance as well as emergency service to customers. He had worked for 12 years for the same family owned business and he loved his job.*

*When he first presented to treatment, he complained of symptoms of anxiety and depression. Thomas disclosed that he recently learned that he was HIV positive and he struggled with the belief that he was permanently damaged. The clinician utilized cognitive-behavior therapy to stabilize his mood and to enhance his coping. However, after eight sessions, Thomas precipitously dropped out of treatment.*

*Two years later, he reentered treatment with the same clinician. He noted that he was previously not ready to deal with his real issue. Thomas had a secret: He was a sex addict. He was motivated to enter treatment this time as his addiction had been discovered. His partner found evidence of Thomas's sexual exploits on his smartphone and was threatening to leave him. Thomas had been using the flexibility of his job to engage in sexual hookups during the day. Prior to the use of his smartphone, he had frequented cruising areas where he often engaged in anonymous sex.*

*Treatment focused on stabilizing Thomas's current depression and anxiety. He was also referred to a 12-step group, Sex Addicts Anonymous. He and his partner entered couples treatment and were able to slowly rebuild trust in their relationship.*

*EMDR therapy was critical in helping Thomas heal from his sex addiction. After establishing adequate resources, he and his clinician used the Hase protocol (Hase, 2010) to target urges to fall back into old behaviors. Several trauma memories were processed with the Standard Protocol that were underneath his urges to act out sexually. He was able to reduce his psychiatric symptoms and to maintain sobriety by adhering to his bottom line behaviors of sexuality.*

## HIV/AIDS

AIDS was initially known as GRID (gay-related immune deficiency) as it was first diagnosed in the United States among homosexual men. In other parts of the world, it was first seen in heterosexuals (Cadwell, 1994). In searching for the genesis of the "gay plague," scientists examined behaviors of gay men, specifically related to sexuality. The assumption was quickly drawn that HIV/AIDS was rooted in promiscuous sexual behavior, despite evidence of a wide variety of sexual behaviors in persons with HIV/AIDS. People became more afraid of the increasingly visible gay community because a belief developed that gay men were the carriers of this disease and were solely responsible for AIDS (Cadwell, 1994).

An HIV/AIDS diagnosis often put individuals in the position of having to "come out" to others, not only as gay but also as HIV positive. This can still be true. Many people who acknowledge their sexual orientation and/or their HIV status are marginalized. HIV-positive individuals can view themselves as "dirty" or "diseased." Personal ads for dating or online chat will sometimes contain references to whether the person is "clean" (HIV negative) or "dirty" (HIV positive). The use of these terms can lead the HIV-positive individual to feel further stigmatized, often leading to significant self-hatred (Linde, 1994).

*Adam was a 55-year-old gay man who presented for treatment of comorbid depression and substance abuse. Adam was experiencing conflicts with his partner of 10 years. He acknowledged that he was drinking alcohol more than he wanted to and that it was affecting his relationship. Treatment focused on helping Adam to stabilize his depression and to learn effective ways to manage his drinking.*

*After several months in treatment, Adam acknowledged to his therapist that he had experienced emotional, physical, and sexual abuse as a child/adolescent. He went on to tearfully tell his clinician of his HIV-positive status and how this was a barrier to intimacy in his relationship. His clinician told Adam about EMDR therapy and how it might help target the effects of the trauma that were likely contributing to his depression.*

*Adam created a memory list that focused around the belief that, "I am defective and unlovable." One of the most pivotal memories that he targeted was the day that he went for a routine HIV test and learned of his HIV-positive status. Once he had processed the sadness and shame that he held around this memory, he was able to feel better about himself and to initiate conversations with his partner about their physical relationship much more easily.*

## Trauma

The experiences of sexual minorities have been largely absent from the study of trauma (Brown & Pantalone, 2011). Researchers are now finding that lesbians and gay men experience higher levels of childhood abuse, interpersonal violence, sexual assault, and domestic violence as compared with heterosexuals (Balsam, Rothblum, & Beauchaine, 2005). Sometimes, the experience of "coming out" to family (telling family about being gay/lesbian/bisexual) can be traumatic and even lead to violence (Swindell & Pryce, 2007). Racial and ethnic minority gays and lesbians have even higher rates of abuse compared with Caucasians (Balsam, Lehavot, Beadnell, & Circo, 2010).

Lesbians, gay men, bisexuals, and even heterosexuals who have ever had a same-sex sexual experience have higher rates of risk of developing posttraumatic stress disorder (PTSD) as compared with heterosexuals without these experiences when faced with a current trauma (Roberts et al., 2010). The type of trauma (childhood abuse and interpersonal violence) as well as the age when the trauma was experienced were identified as two key variables contributing to these higher rates. In addition, the stress of heterosexist oppression and consequent emotional vulnerability places gays and lesbians at greater risk for more complicated trauma responses, leading to a greater likelihood of developing PTSD in those who experience potentially traumatic events (Bandermann & Szymanski, 2014).

As a result of these increased risk factors, clinicians need to carefully assess the trauma histories of their lesbian/gay clients. Many variables that are common in the lives of sexual minorities can contribute to the increased risk for experiencing potentially traumatic events. Gender atypical behavior, the experience of hate crimes, substance abuse, social isolation, and the consequent risk-taking behavior can contribute to a great likelihood of exposure to traumatic events and a greater risk of PTSD (Roberts et al., 2010). This was true for the following client.

*Betty, a 33-year-old White lesbian, presented to treatment due to increasing distress associated with the breakup of a 10-year relationship. After 3 years in couples therapy, she and her partner decided to end their relationship and Betty was devastated. She was crying uncontrollably and had great difficulty managing her emotions, especially when she was at her nursing job at a local hospital.*

*This was Betty's first experience in therapy. She initially denied the experience of trauma in her background. However, as she grew to trust her clinician more deeply, she began to talk about her history. Betty's parents divorced when she was 6. She and her five older siblings were left with their mother who was suddenly a single parent. Her mother became emotionally overwhelmed and left the children to "fend for themselves." At age 9, one of Betty's older brothers sexually abused her for a period of several months. She told no one. Another brother began to use substances and to act erratically. At one point, he came home high on methamphetamine and began to threaten family members with physical harm. The police were not called and her mother never discussed the incident with Betty. She left home as soon as she got into college and never went back.*

*Betty also examined her relationship with her ex-partner. She realized that she had been emotionally abused in this relationship but she had never identified these behaviors in this way. She became increasingly concerned about her judgment of potential future partners and made statements that she would never be in a relationship again.*

*EMDR therapy was introduced to Betty. Although she was initially hesitant to use these techniques, Betty agreed to try EMDR. After a successful experience with Resource Development (Korn & Leeds, 2002), Betty created a list of some of her most intense trauma memories that made her feel powerless and overwhelmed. As she began to work through these memories with the Standard Protocol, she grew to trust herself and her instincts. She felt less stress in her life in general and she began to be open to a new relationship.*

## Family of Origin Issues

Families exert a powerful influence on an individual's perception of self. "Coming out" as gay or lesbian to one's family members often serves as a major event in an individual's life as he/she integrates sexual orientation into his/her overall identity. The reactions of family members, whether of acceptance or rejection, can lead the individual toward greater self-acceptance or increasing levels of internalized homophobia (i.e., negative self-talk, shame, depression, and anxiety) that complicate his/her ability to come out to others. The outcome of the coming out process can also have implications for present and future relationships between family members (Diamond & Shpigel, 2014).

Some parents and family members will be supportive. However, even among those individuals who are supportive, there can still be a struggle to accept their loved one. Over half of parents react initially with some amount of negativity to their child's coming out (Diamond & Shpigel, 2014). Many of these parents will ultimately grow to accept their child but a good number remain firmly rejecting of their child's coming out. This can have direct consequences for the child. A parent's ongoing invalidation, rejection, or even abuse can exert a powerful negative effect on that individual. The effects of these negative responses can include internalized homophobia, increased depression with suicidal ideation, increased use of substances, and expectations that others will be rejecting (Diamond & Shpigel, 2014).

Lack of support from family of origin can also be an ongoing issue for lesbian/gay adults. Many will cope with this stressor by either denying their lesbian/gay identity or by limiting contact with family. They will often create "families of choice" as sources of support. These families of choice may include some family members or coworkers but they are often composed primarily of friends who serve as a protective circle for the individual and/or their relationship (Blumer & Murphy, 2011).

*Matthew entered therapy in crisis. He was a 26-year-old graduate student in music from a religiously conservative family. He had struggled with same-sex attraction for years as it was labeled as sinful in his religious tradition. He became highly suicidal and presented to the emergency room at a local hospital. He was referred to outpatient therapy.*

*Initial treatment focused on helping Matthew grow in self-acceptance. He needed significant psychoeducation, including information about how others in his own religious tradition viewed sexual orientation in much more supportive ways. He developed a much stronger sense of self and took risks in coming out to friends in his graduate program and in the local community. He discussed whether or not to come out to family members with his clinician and remained reticent to do so.*

*During a family visit back home, his mother asked him directly if he were gay. He had grown up with the belief that it was never okay to lie to one's parents so he came out to her. This set off a firestorm of negativity, culminating in Matthew being taken to their minister for an "exorcism." When Matthew returned to sessions after this visit, he was experiencing a resurgence of suicidal thinking. Trauma processing was an essential component of his healing from this episode. Fortunately, he had created a "family of choice" in his life and he relied heavily on this protective circle. It would be years before his family could begin to accept him as a gay man and he could begin to share more of his life with them.*

## Marriage

In comparison with gay male couples, lesbian couples are more likely to get married and/or seek legal recognition of their relationships as compared with gay male couples (Badgett & Herman, 2011). Herek (2002) found that gay men faced higher levels of homophobia as compared with lesbians. This may be a primary reason why gay men hesitate to make their relationships more visible. Ocobock (2013) studied 32 legally married gay men and found that half of the sample experienced some negative responses from family members, including a reexperiencing of rejection from some family members and new experiences of rejection from family that had been supportive.

Many people assume that if sexual minorities can marry, then all couples *should* get married. Family and friends may assume that their lesbian/gay loved one wants to marry and pressure them to do so. This may sometimes be a source of stress for the individual or for a couple, if one partner is against marriage or is hesitating, as the following case demonstrates.

*Ella was a 28-year-old lesbian who presented for outpatient treatment upon a referral from her primary care doctor. Ella had been experiencing increasing amounts of stress in her job in the insurance industry and she had developed few resources to cope. Ella had 4 years of sobriety from alcohol addiction and she wanted to maintain her recovery. EMDR therapy strategies, such as Resource Development (Korn & Leeds, 2002) and urge management (CravEx: Hase, 2010), were utilized and played a critical role in helping Ella maintain sobriety.*

*Fairly early in treatment, Ella began to talk about her relationship with Mary, a woman who was 10 years older. She and Mary had been together 5 years and had lived together in Mary's house for the last four. Ella was contributing to mortgage payments and household expenses. Ella had been pushing Mary to get married since the federal government now officially recognized gay marriage. Mary was still reticent to commit. A standoff developed in their relationship and the topic of marriage was a hot button issue for conflict.*

*Ella was encouraged to process her reasons for pushing for marriage. She articulated that she wanted some security in her life and wanted her financial contributions to be recognized. Her therapist suggested that she and Mary meet with an attorney to discuss nonmarital options that might accomplish what Ella needed.*

*The meeting with the attorney clarified their options. Mary talked about the reasons for her reticence to marry and that she wanted some financial protections for her acquired possessions. They were able to talk this through and Mary proposed to a very happy Ella.*

## Socialization/Isolation

Social isolation is a risk factor that can contribute to unhealthy risk-taking behavior, resulting in the greater likelihood of experiencing potentially traumatic events (Roberts et al., 2010). Lesbian/gay youth who withdraw socially may do so as a result of peer/family rejection as well as harassment at the hands of their heterosexual peers (Johnson & Amella, 2014). As sexual minorities begin to experience the benefits of greater social acceptance (especially among younger generations), gay/lesbian-specific social outlets are disappearing in favor of "mixed" venues. One consequence of this social change is that adults who were comfortable seeking connection and support in the "gay only" venues find themselves at a loss for finding social support as readily available. These individuals rely more heavily now on social media and Internet chatrooms for social support, placing them at greater health risks (Poon, Ho, Wong, Wong, & Lee, 2005).

Evaluating the client's degree of social support is a critical component of preparation for EMDR therapy as clients need to possess both internal and external resources. As noted earlier, sexual minorities are at greater risk of being socially isolated at any age as compared with heterosexual individuals. This may be due to psychiatric symptoms, substance abuse, or an ongoing struggle with issues related to sexual orientation and socialization.

*Edward was a 31-year-old gay White male graduate student studying English when he came to treatment. He had first experienced episodes of panic when he was in college. At that time, he was given medication to manage these symptoms. He relied heavily on the medication and became anxious if he thought that he would run out. However, after a brief experience in therapy when he first experienced symptoms in college, he had not been in treatment since then.*

*Edward presented with symptoms of panic. The panic attacks initially resurfaced when he took his first exam in graduate school. He was now experiencing them at unpredictable times.*

*Edward noted a history of emotional, physical, and sexual abuse perpetrated by his parents, other relatives, and peers. He disclosed a history of being raped at the age of 12 by a boy 1-year older. He reported significant shame about these experiences and was not currently sexually active. Edward had few friends and spent most of his weekends playing video games.*

*Treatment focused initially on teaching Edward mindfulness-based self-regulation skills. He received education about panic disorder and trauma. Once he developed better coping skills, Edward was informed about EMDR therapy and he expressed a willingness to try it. Several memories were targeted with the Standard Protocol that focused on feelings of powerlessness. Perhaps most critical was the processing of the rape that he experienced at age 12.*

*Edward reported that he felt less anxious and better able to manage social situations. He began to take more risks and went to the local gay bar for the first time with friends. Edward understood the connection between his current symptoms and past experiences. He started to date.*

## Substance Abuse

Sexual minorities have long been identified as a group at greater risk for substance abuse. Most early studies of gay and lesbian alcohol use recruited participants at gay bars and found very high rates of alcohol problems in the gay community. More recent research has established that rates of alcohol problems in sexual minorities are not as high as once believed but they still remain somewhat higher than the general population (Hughes, 2005).

Club drugs are substances that are used to heighten sexual/sensual experience at local clubs, all night raves, or at "circuit parties" that are weekend long events. Drugs in this class include Ecstasy, crystal methamphetamine, ketamine, GHB, and cocaine, among others. Use of these drugs may lead to overdose, unprotected sex, and exposure to HIV or other sexually transmitted diseases (Nanín & Parsons, 2006). Although the use of these drugs seems to be decreasing overall, HIV-positive gay men use these drugs at higher rates than HIV-negative gay men (Pantalone, Bimbi, Holder, Golub, & Parsons, 2010).

Cochran et al. (2003) studied nonmedical drug use and dependence in lesbians and gay men in the United States. They compared sexual minorities with a comparable heterosexual population. Both gay men and lesbians reported consistently higher rates of lifetime and recent drug use as compared with heterosexuals. For both lesbians and gay men in this study, marijuana was the drug most likely to be associated with drug addiction. This was true in the following case.

*Barry was a 27-year-old hair stylist who came to treatment due to escalating depression and anxiety. He had a long history of episodes of persistent depressive disorder, dating back to adolescence. He also reported a long history of substance use including alcohol, marijuana, prescription drugs, and crystal methamphetamine that started about the same time. Barry had been in substance abuse treatment several times. He had succeeded in eliminating crystal meth and prescription drug abuse from his life. However, he continued to drink with friends on occasion and smoked marijuana daily.*

*Barry disclosed a history of emotional and physical abuse by parents when he was young. He also reported a history of anti-gay bullying that started in middle school. Barry noted that he began to use substances as a way to fit in and to "numb out."*

*Barry stated that he wanted to feel better and he said that he was open to discussing his alcohol and marijuana use. However, as therapy began to focus more directly on his substance use, he became less motivated to change. He had been living with a boyfriend of 1 year and as his marijuana use escalated, his partner expressed greater frustration with Barry's behavior. His therapist pointed out that Barry was choosing his relationship with drugs over his partner. Barry resisted. His boyfriend broke off the relationship and moved out. Barry smoked more and then became increasingly more depressed. He then began to question his choice.*

*His clinician utilized a combination of motivational interviewing techniques and some EMDR Resource Development (Korn & Leeds, 2002) during times when Barry was not smoking. After several months of living alone and being socially isolated, he realized that he no longer wanted a "committed relationship with marijuana." EMDR therapy then progressed to the use of the CravEx protocol (Hase, 2010) to deal with his addiction-related issues. The Standard Protocol helped Barry to process some of his past traumas from his early life. He began to see things more clearly.*

*Barry sought out his ex-partner and expressed his regret about their relationship. Although hesitant, his ex-lover agreed to remain in contact with Barry as he continued his healing. Barry began to attend a 12-step group and seek out sober supports. Slowly, he and his ex-partner began to move toward the possibility of reconciliation and they entered couples therapy after a support meeting with Barry's clinician.*

## SUMMARY

Lesbian/gay/bisexual clients are at increased risk of experiencing potentially traumatic events and developing PTSD. Many continue to experience significant distress as a result of encountering oppression in American culture, despite recent positive changes in societal acceptance. Clinicians must be mindful of these issues in conceptualizing a gay/lesbian client's presenting concerns or his/her reticence to open up in treatment. Sexual minority clients may be more hesitant to provide clinicians with the "whole story" of their lives until they are sure that the clinician is a "safe" person.

EMDR therapy can be different with gays, lesbians, and bisexuals. Some targets for EMDR processing may include life experiences related to religion/spirituality, sexuality, family of origin issues, marriage, social isolation, and substance abuse. Sexual minorities are not the only ones to deal with these concerns but they may present with a unique configuration of the issues. Therapists should be aware of the needs of LGB clients and take care to not replicate the experiences of invalidation that are so much a part of the everyday lives of these individuals. EMDR therapy can be an important component of providing services to this population.

## REFERENCES


American Psychiatric Association (APA). (1974). Position statement on homosexuality and civil rights. *American Journal of Psychiatry, 131*, 497.

American Psychological Association (APA). (2009). *Report of the American Psychological Association Task Force on appropriate therapeutic responses to sexual orientation*. Washington, DC: Author.

Badgett, M. V. L., & Herman, J. L. (2011). *Patterns of relationship recognition by same-sex couples in the United States*. Los Angeles, CA: The Williams Institute.

Balsam, K. F., Lehavot, K., Beadnell, B., & Circo, E. (2010). Childhood abuse and mental health indicators among ethnically diverse lesbian, gay, and bisexual adults. *Journal of Consulting and Clinical Psychology, 78*(4), 459–468.

Balsam, K. F., Rothblum, E. D., & Beauchaine, T. P. (2005). Victimization over the life span: A comparison of lesbian, gay, bisexual, and heterosexual siblings. *Journal of Consulting and Clinical Psychology, 73*, 477–487.

Bandermann, K. M., & Szymanski, D. M. (2014). Exploring coping mediators between heterosexist oppression and posttraumatic stress symptoms among lesbian, gay, and bisexual persons. *Psychology of Sexual Orientation and Gender Diversity, 1*(3), 213–224.

Beckstead, A. (2012). Can we change sexual orientation? *Archives of Sexual Behavior, 41*(1), 121–134.

Blumer, M. C., & Murphy, M. J. (2011). Alaskan gay males' couple experiences of societal non-support: Coping through families of choice and therapeutic means. *Contemporary Family Therapy: An International Journal, 33*(3), 273–290.

Bostwick, W. B., Boyd, C. J., Hughes, T. L., West, B. T., & McCabe, S. E. (2014). Discrimination and mental health among lesbian, gay, and bisexual adults in the United States. *The American Journal of Orthopsychiatry, 84*(1), 35–45.

Bowland, S. E., Foster, K., & Vosler, A. R. (2013). Culturally competent and spiritually sensitive therapy with lesbian and gay Christians. *Social Work, 58*(4), 321–332.

Brown, L. S., & Pantalone, D. (2011). Lesbian, gay, bisexual, and transgender issues in trauma psychology: A topic comes out of the closet. *Traumatology, 17*(2), 1–3.

Butler, C. (2009). Sexual and gender minority therapy and systemic practice. *Journal of Family Therapy, 31*, 339–358.

Cadwell, S. (1994). Twice removed: The stigma suffered by gay men with AIDS. In S. Cadwell, R. Burnham, & M. Forstein (Eds.), *Therapists on the front line: Psychotherapy with gay men in the age of AIDS* (pp. 3–24). Washington, DC: American Psychiatric Press.

Cochran, S. D., Sullivan, J. G., & Mays, V. M. (2003). Prevalence of mental disorders, psychological distress, and mental health services use among lesbian, gay, and bisexual adults in the United States. *Journal of Consulting and Clinical Psychology, 71*, 53–61.

Cohen, J. N., & Byers, E. S. (2014). Beyond lesbian bed death: Enhancing our understanding of the sexuality of sexual-minority women in relationships. *Journal of Sex Research, 51*(8), 893–903.

Davison, G. C. (2001). Conceptual and ethical issues in therapy for the psychological problems of gay men, lesbians, and bisexuals. *Journal of Clinical Psychology, 57*(5), 695–704.

Diamond, G. M., & Shpigel, M. S. (2014). Attachment-based family therapy for lesbian and gay young adults and their persistently non-accepting parents. *Professional Psychology: Research and Practice, 45*(4), 258–268.

Diamond, L. M. (2008). Female bisexuality from adolescence to adulthood: Results from a 10-year longitudinal study. *Developmental Psychology, 44*, 5–14.

Goetting, N. (2015). More than just the last gay marriage case. *National Lawyers Guild Review, 72*(1), 55–61.

Gotta, G., Green, R., Rothblum, E., Solomon, S., Balsam, K., & Schwartz, P. (2011). Heterosexual, lesbian, and gay male relationships: A comparison of couples in 1975 and 2000. *Family Process, 50*(3), 353–376.

Haldeman, D. C. (2002). Therapeutic antidotes: Helping gay and bisexual men recover from conversion therapies. *Journal of Gay & Lesbian Psychotherapy, 5*(3–4), 117–130.

Hase, M. (2010). CravEx: An EMDR approach to treat substance abuse and addiction. In M. Luber (Ed.), *EMDR scripted protocols* (pp. 467–488). New York, NY: W. W. Norton.

Herek, G. M. (2002). Gender gaps in public opinion about gay men and lesbians. *Public Opinion Quarterly, 66*, 40–66.

Herek, G. M., Gillis, J. R., & Cogan, J. C. (2015). Internalized stigma among sexual minority adults: Insights from a social psychological perspective. *Stigma and Health, 1*(S), 18–34.

Hillman, J., & Hinrichsen, G. A. (2014). Promoting an affirming, competent practice with older lesbian and gay adults. *Professional Psychology: Research and Practice, 45*(4), 269–277.

Hodge, D. R. (2005). Epistemological frameworks, homosexuality, and religion: How people of faith understand the intersection between homosexuality and religion. *Social Work, 50*(3), 207–218.

Hosking, W. (2013). Agreements about extradyadic sex in gay men's relationships: Exploring differences in relationship quality by agreement type and rule-breaking behavior. *Journal of Homosexuality, 60*(5), 711–733.

Hughes, T. (2005). Alcohol use and alcohol-related problems among lesbians and gay men. *Annual Review of Nursing Research, 23*, 283–325.

Jackson, N. C., Johnson, M. J., & Roberts, R. (2008). The potential impact of discrimination fears of older gays, lesbians, bisexuals and transgender individuals living in small- to moderate-sized cities on long-term health care. *Journal of Homosexuality, 54*(3), 325–339.

Johnson, M. J., & Amella, E. J. (2014). Isolation of lesbian, gay, bisexual and transgender youth: A dimensional concept analysis. *Journal of Advanced Nursing, 70*(3), 523–532.

Korn, D. L., & Leeds, A. M. (2002). Preliminary evidence of efficacy for EMDR resource development and installation in the stabilization phase of treatment and complex posttraumatic stress disorder. *Journal of Clinical Psychology, 58*(12), 1465–1487.

Langdridge, D. (2007). Gay affirmative therapy: A theoretical framework and defence. *Journal of Gay & Lesbian Psychotherapy, 11*(1–2), 27–43.

Linde, R. (1994). Impact of AIDS on adult gay male development: Implications for psychotherapy. In S. Cadwell, R. Burnham, & M. Forstein (Eds.), *Therapists on the front line: Psychotherapy with gay men in the age of AIDS* (pp. 25–51). Washington, DC: American Psychiatric Press.

Missildine, W., Feldstein, G., Punzalan, J. C., & Parsons, J. T. (2005). S/he loves me, s/he loves me not: Questioning heterosexist assumptions of gender differences for romantic and sexually motivated behaviors. *Sexual Addiction & Compulsivity, 12*(1), 65–74.

Nanín, J. E., & Parsons, J. T. (2006). Club drug use and risky sex among gay and bisexual men in New York City. *Journal of Gay & Lesbian Psychotherapy, 10*(3–4), 111–122.

Ocobock, A. (2013). The power and limits of marriage: Married gay men's family relationships. *Journal of Marriage & Family, 75*(1), 191–205.

Ong, A. D., Burrow, A. L., Fuller-Rowell, T. E., Ja, N. M., & Sue, D. W. (2013). Racial microaggressions and daily well-being among Asian Americans. *Journal of Counseling Psychology, 60*(2), 188–199.

Pantalone, D., Bimbi, D., Holder, C., Golub, S., & Parsons, J. (2010). Consistency and change in club drug use by sexual minority men in New York City, 2002 to 2007. *American Journal of Public Health, 100*(10), 1892–1895.

Platt, L. F., & Lenzen, A. L. (2013). Sexual orientation microaggressions and the experience of sexual minorities. *Journal of Homosexuality, 60*(7), 1011–1034.

Poon, M., Ho, P., Wong, J., Wong, G., & Lee, R. (2005). Psychosocial experiences of east and southeast Asian men who use gay Internet chatrooms in Toronto: An implication for HIV/AIDS prevention. *Ethnicity & Health, 10*(2), 145–167.

Roberts, A. L., Austin, S. B., Corliss, H. L., Vandermorris, A. K., & Koenen, K. C. (2010). Pervasive trauma exposure among US sexual orientation minority adults and risk of posttraumatic stress disorder. *American Journal of Public Health, 100*(12), 2433–2441.

Shallenberger, D. (1998). *Reclaiming the spirit: Gay men and lesbians come to terms with religion*. New Brunswick, NJ: Rutgers University Press.

Silverstein, C. (1991). Psychotherapy and psychotherapists: A history. In C. Silverstein (Ed.), *Gays, lesbians, and their therapists* (pp. 1–14). New York, NY: W. W. Norton.

Sue, D. W., & Constantine, M. G. (2007). Racial microaggressions as instigators of difficult dialogues on race: Implications for student affairs educators and students. *College Student Affairs Journal, 26*(2), 136–143.

Swindell, M., & Pryce, J. (2007). Self-disclosure stress. In W. Meezman & J. Martin (Eds.), *Handbook of research with gay, lesbian, bisexual & transgender populations* (pp. 159–171). New York, NY: Routledge.

Williamson, I. (2000). Internalized homophobia and health issues affecting lesbians and gay men. *Health Education Research, 15*(1), 97–107.

CHAPTER 13

# Sex Assignment, Gender Assignment, and Affectional Orientation: Applying Continua of Congruence to Dismantle Dichotomies

Earl Grey

Understanding the variance across the sex/gender/affectional continua is a foundational part of clinical practice with gender-influenced client issues. All clients have biological developments that lead to sex/gender/affectional differentiation and variance. As a specialist in this topic area, I have discovered that most of my clients have experienced indirect clinical barriers that required focused treatment on sex/gender/affectional issues. In this chapter, I share how I have improved positive treatment outcomes by integrating a sex/gender/affectional continua and Eriksonian psychosocial development across all phases of eye movement desensitization and reprocessing (EMDR) therapy. This chapter offers an explanation of sex/gender/affectional continua and Erik Erikson's psychosocial stage of adolescence, ego identity versus role confusion.

## OPERATIONAL DEFINITIONS

*Sex assignment:* the sex organs that one has physically developed

*Gender assignment:* the imprinted neurological gender identity

*Gender orientation:* biologically imprinted behavioral instincts related to gender identity

*Affectional orientation:* the physical and emotional attraction and arousal stimulated through attachment (*Affectional orientation* replaces sexual orientation because the word *sexual* limits the concept to physical arousal only.)

*Congruent:* the consistencies of sex, gender, and affectional orientations

*Incongruence:* the graduated variance between sex, gender, and affectional orientations

Four case examples bring life to the integration of targeting sex/gender/affectional issues:

1. Wilhelm, a fully *congruent* male, who had a strong blocking belief that "men do not cry."
2. Ash, a client living with intersex conditions of Klinefelter syndrome and a micropenis condition who had a multitude of developmental experiences resulting in their decision that they are permanently unlovable (*they* is the client's preferred pronoun).
3. Sean, a transgender male (female-to-male) adolescent, who faced issues of powerlessness.
4. Finally, Clay, a self-identified incongruent male who questioned his "sexual orientation."

These cases provide examples of how to integrate the sex/gender/affectional continua and the Eriksonian adolescent psychosocial stage through the eight phases of EMDR therapy. However, before we apply the concepts, we must discuss the biological imprinting of human sex assignment, gender assignment, and affectional orientation.

## BIOLOGICAL DEVELOPMENT

All zygotes begin their in utero development as female. The mutation to the male sex organs and neurological release of gender related hormones occur congruently. Although they occur congruently, the actual development of sex and gender are separate processes occurring independent of each other. There is a relationship to the two phases of development (i.e., hormones, brain structures), but sex development and gender development are not mutually exclusive in the in utero development literature (Swaab, 2004). To operationalize sex and gender, we refer to sex as related to the sexual organs that physically develop externally (i.e., what is between one's legs) and gender as the neurological imprinting of femaleness and maleness in the brain (i.e., what is between one's ears).

## SEX ASSIGNMENT

Sex assignment has two primary developmental components in utero, hormonal and chromosomal. Testosterone is the hormone required to initiate the mutation from a female zygote to a male zygote. This sex differentiating mutation occurs around the eighth week of development. The neurological differentiation of gender does not occur until the second trimester around weeks 18 to 24. Although related, these two differentiation processes (physical and neurological) are independent of one another. The physical change is due to the presence of a Y chromosome unless there are intersex conditions resulting from variance in the chromosomal differentiation. The presence of the Y chromosome initiates the release of testosterone to stimulate the physical development of testes and a penis (Pardue & Wizemann, 2001). The conditions necessary for sex differentiation are extremely sensitive and vulnerable. Since the sex differentiation occurs around the eighth week of development, the likelihood of "imperfect" conditions resulting in sex assignment variations is common (up to 1 in 66 humans) (Balen, Creighton, Davies, MacDougall, & Stanhope, 2004). If any variances in chromosomal or hormonal conditions occur in utero, the zygote's differentiation can result in an incongruent mutation.

The results of an incongruent mutation can range from unnoticeable sex variations to developing an intersexed condition. An intersex condition occurs when an individual has some internal or external physical qualities of more than one sex assignment. The example of the greatest incongruent mutation is an individual born with both male and female sex organs. Scholars on intersex conditions identify roughly 14 known intersex conditions. To gain more knowledge on intersex conditions, please refer to the Recommended Website section of this chapter.

The aforementioned explanation of variances in differentiating sex assignments in utero supports that sex assignment is a continuum ranging from female to male. Hence, the following continuum is a more accurate tool to gather sex assignment information:

**Sex Assignment**
**(Sex Organs)**
**Female to Male**

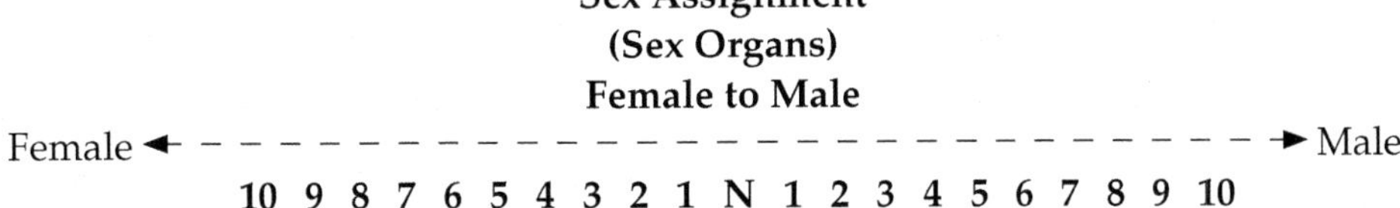


*The aforementioned continuum and those to follow are scales, which I developed and represent a synthesis of my interpretations of sex/gender/affection spectra. These scales have been a clinically useful tool. I have included additional resources at the end of this chapter for further reading.*

## GENDER ASSIGNMENT AND ORIENTATION

Similar to sex differentiation, gender differentiation is exceptionally sensitive to the exposure of hormones. For congruent gender mutation, the zygotic brain must receive the accurate hormone levels at a precise time to develop congruent gender-to-sex assignments. Only specific conditions result in congruent sex/gender assignment. The flooding of testosterone in combination with androgen, in part, is responsible for neurological gender mutations (Pardue & Wizemann, 2001; Swaab, 2004; Swaab & Garcia-Falgueras, 2009). During the exposure to hormones, the differentiation imprints the gender assignment in the brain (i.e., the variation of maleness to femaleness). Gender orientation also imprints during gender differentiation.

Gender orientation is the imprinted behavioral instincts that inform one's general manner (i.e., variations of feminine to masculine). The client's culture and context define the qualitative meanings of "masculine" and "feminine," even though gender orientation is imprinted. These concepts support the use of the following two continua to assess the variations on a person's gender assignment and orientation:

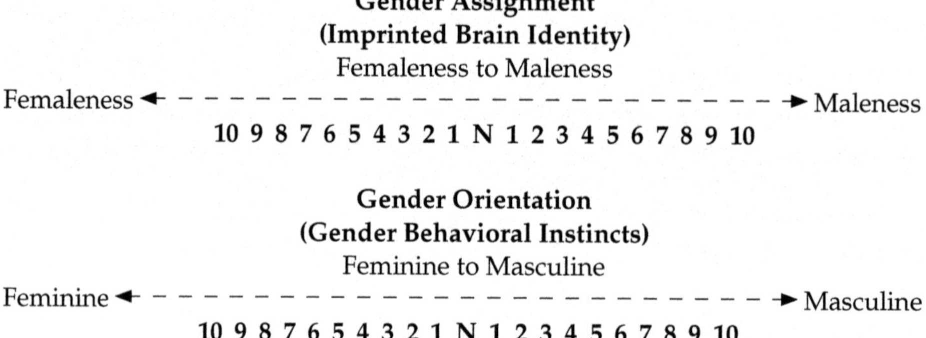


The previous continua summarize key elements necessary to accurately educate our clients. A script for educating clients is included later in this chapter.

## AFFECTIONAL ORIENTATION

Affectional orientation is a conceptual framework developed because of the variances in sex and gender assignment. I find that affectional orientation more accurately describes what the general public calls sexual orientation. *Sexual orientation* suggests that only physical attractions and arousals, based on sex assignment, factor into intimate relationships. An attachment-oriented clinician recognizes that intimate relationships depend on significantly more factors than physical attractions and arousals. Affectional orientation inclusively incorporates factors of physical attraction and arousal with characteristics of emotional attraction and arousal. Emotional attractions and arousals are fundamental in building attachments. *Sexual orientation* diminishes the emotional elements of attachment and often results in an inaccurate dichotomy of heterosexual or homosexual. Some progressive individuals are able to include bisexuality as an additional label. However, the variance of affectional orientation is greater than only three descriptors. Affectional orientation offers an inclusive continuum to inform understanding on how one is attracted to building intimate relationships. *Affectional orientation* includes physical characteristics that promote arousal and attraction, behavioral characteristics that affect both physical and emotional arousal and attraction, and personality traits that speak to emotional arousal and attraction. *Affectional orientation* honors the complexity of intimate attachments, without reducing relationships to simply sex assignment.

In the interest of translating the complexity of intimate attachment to simplified and usable tools, affectional orientation is distilled into two categories: physical attraction/arousal and emotional attraction/arousal, although the potential combinations of physical and emotional orientations are infinitely abstract. The following is an overly simplified scale of the physical affectional orientation ranging between masculine to feminine physical attraction/arousal. These descriptors are based on the clients' cultural definition of masculinity and femininity. Any discussion is dependent on the personal/cultural vernacular of the individual to define what physical characteristics most attract/arouse them.

The emotional affectional orientation continuum ranges from dominance (leader) to submissiveness (follower). These descriptors distill many emotional factors to an oversimplified but usable range. The rationale for using dominance to submissiveness is grounded in our human instinct to respond to threat. All humans have the fight, flight, and freeze survival instincts. Under stress, some people have a stronger drive to *flight* or desire to be protected, while others have a stronger drive to *fight* or protect others. The concept of protection is important in building secure attachment (Ainsworth & Bowlby, 1991; Bowlby, 1988). This information leads to using the following continua for affectional orientation:

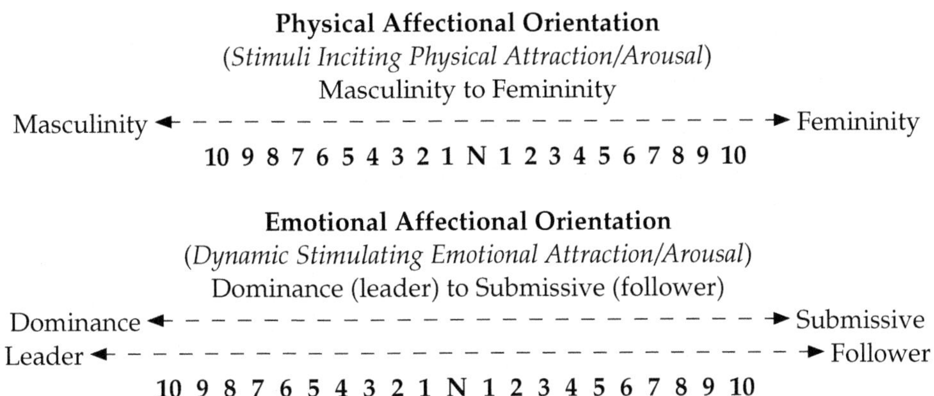


## APPLYING THE CONCEPTS

To give life to the concepts of these sex/gender/affectional continua, let us consider generic American social expectations regarding sex/gender/affectional orientation. Conventional expectation is that a sex assignment falling toward the side of male continuum (M1) will also have a strong gender identity of maleness, an imprinted propensity to behave in masculine manners toward stimuli, be physically aroused by stimuli that possesses femininity, and emotionally attracted to more submissive/follower individuals in an intimate relationship (Table 13.1).

**TABLE 13.1 Sex/Gender/Affectional Continua Example: M1**

| Sex Assignment | | | | | | | | | | |
|---|---|---|---|---|---|---|---|---|---|---|
| Female ← - - - - - - - - - - - - - - - - - - - - - - → Male | | | | | | | | | | |
| 10 9 | 8 7 | 6 5 | 4 3 | 2 1 | N | 1 2 | 3 4 | 5 6 | 7 <u>**8**</u> | 9 10 |
| Gender Assignment | | | | | | | | | | |
| Femaleness ← - - - - - - - - - - - - - - - - - - - - → Maleness | | | | | | | | | | |
| 10 9 | 8 7 | 6 5 | 4 3 | 2 1 | N | 1 2 | 3 4 | 5 6 | 7 8 | <u>9</u> 10 |
| Gender Orientation | | | | | | | | | | |
| Feminine ← - - - - - - - - - - - - - - - - - - - - → Masculine | | | | | | | | | | |
| 10 9 | 8 7 | 6 5 | 4 3 | 2 1 | N | 1 2 | 3 4 | 5 6 | <u>7</u> 8 | 9 10 |
| Physical Affectional Orientation | | | | | | | | | | |
| Masculinity ← - - - - - - - - - - - - - - - - - - - - → Femininity | | | | | | | | | | |
| 10 9 | 8 7 | 6 5 | 4 3 | 2 1 | N | 1 2 | 3 4 | 5 6 | 7 8 | <u>9</u> 10 |
| Emotional Affectional Orientation | | | | | | | | | | |
| Leader ← - - - - - - - - - - - - - - - - - - - - → Follower | | | | | | | | | | |
| 10 9 | 8 7 | 6 5 | 4 3 | 2 1 | N | 1 2 | 3 4 | 5 6 | 7 8 | 9 <u>***10***</u> |

Thus, American social expectation is that a sex-assigned female (F1) will have greater femaleness, will be oriented with feminine gender behaviors, will be physically aroused by masculinity, and will be emotionally attracted to more dominant individuals (Table 13.2).

When we compare the results of the two people that are congruent across the sex/gender/affectional continua, we see that the more vertical the line the greater the congruence across the continua items.

Since affectional orientation is a result of the imprinted gender assignment variances, clinicians can make errors when relying on the traditional dichotomy of sex and gender. Most people make assumptions using the generalized descriptors of M1 and F1 as a baseline. What happens if we rely on this baseline but there is not congruence? This was the case with my client "Clay." Clay self-identified as a "heterosexual male." He sought assistance because he was struggling with an internal conflict between his physical and emotional orientations. His presenting problem was confusion about his sexual orientation. On our first session, I offered him education on the biology of sex/gender differentiation. We then used the continua of sex assignment, gender assignment, gender orientation, and affectional orientations so that Clay could self-rate his authentic identity. He identified himself as a male at an 8. He also shared that he rated himself an 8 on sex assignment due to his physical characteristics that made him look "male." He self-rated on the gender assignment continuum as a 4 in maleness. He explained that "men should not be as sensitive" as him and that he had historically found himself building

**TABLE 13.2 Sex/Gender/Affectional Continua Example: F1**

| Sex Assignment | | | | | | | | | | |
|---|---|---|---|---|---|---|---|---|---|---|
| Female ← – – – – – – – – – – – – – – – – – – – – → Male | | | | | | | | | | |
| 10 9 | 8 7 | 6 5 | 4 3 | 2 1 | N | 1 2 | 3 4 | 5 6 | 7 8 | 9 10 |
| Gender Assignment | | | | | | | | | | |
| Femaleness ← – – – – – – – – – – – – – – – – – – – – → Maleness | | | | | | | | | | |
| 10 9 | 8 7 | 6 5 | 4 3 | 2 1 | N | 1 2 | 3 4 | 5 6 | 7 8 | 9 10 |
| Gender Orientation | | | | | | | | | | |
| Feminine ← – – – – – – – – – – – – – – – – – – – – → Masculine | | | | | | | | | | |
| 10 9 | 8 7 | 6 5 | 4 3 | 2 1 | N | 1 2 | 3 4 | 5 6 | 7 8 | 9 10 |
| Physical Affectional Orientation | | | | | | | | | | |
| Masculinity ← – – – – – – – – – – – – – – – – – – – – → Femininity | | | | | | | | | | |
| 10 9 | 8 7 | 6 5 | 4 3 | 2 1 | N | 1 2 | 3 4 | 5 6 | 7 8 | 9 10 |
| Emotional Affectional Orientation | | | | | | | | | | |
| Leader ← – – – – – – – – – – – – – – – – – – – – → Follower | | | | | | | | | | |
| 10 9 | 8 7 | 6 5 | 4 3 | 2 1 | N | 1 2 | 3 4 | 5 6 | 7 8 | 9 10 |

closer connections to women. He rated his gender orientation as a 9 on masculine, as he assessed himself as being perceived as a strong man. On the physical affectional orientation continuum, he identified himself as being attracted and aroused at the *N*. The *N* rating stands for *neutral*, including characteristics of both sides of the respective continuum. He further rated himself an 8 on the dominance/leader side of emotional attractiveness and arousal. The results of his continua are given in Table 13.3.

His continua indicate a diagonal line. The greater the angles of the diagonal lines, the greater the incongruence across the sex/gender/affectional identity. His perception of his variance across the continua provided him a framework to understand *why* he was struggling, and, more specifically, with *what* he was struggling. He explained that he was generally attracted to individuals with a female sex assignment, possessing femaleness in gender assignments and a moderate feminine gender orientation. He explained that he appreciated a woman who can do "man activities" with him. His affectional orientations were perplexing to him. He recognized that he was very attracted and aroused by a more androgynous looking female and greatly desired her to be a dominant leader in the relationship. Because of his confusion about his affectional orientations, he confided that he had explored activities with feminine gay men. In permitting himself to explore both physical attractions/arousals and emotional attractions/arousals with men, he was overwhelmed with confusion that guided him to question his identity. In this first session, we were able to open his perspective to the array of possibilities in his identity.

**TABLE 13.3 Sex/Gender/Affectional Continua: Clay**

| Sex Assignment | | | | | | | | | | |
|---|---|---|---|---|---|---|---|---|---|---|
| Female ← | | | | | | | | | | → Male |
| 10 9 | 8 7 | 6 5 | 4 3 | 2 1 | N | 1 2 | 3 4 | 5 6 | 7 **8** | 9 10 |
| Gender Assignment | | | | | | | | | | |
| Femaleness ← | | | | | | | | | | → Maleness |
| 10 9 | 8 7 | 6 5 | 4 3 | 2 1 | N | 1 2 | 3 **4** | 5 6 | 7 8 | 9 10 |
| Gender Orientation | | | | | | | | | | |
| Feminine ← | | | | | | | | | | → Masculine |
| 10 9 | 8 7 | 6 5 | 4 3 | 2 1 | N | 1 2 | 3 4 | 5 6 | 7 8 | **9** 10 |
| Physical Affectional Orientation | | | | | | | | | | |
| Masculinity ← | | | | | | | | | | → Femininity |
| 10 9 | 8 7 | 6 5 | 4 3 | 2 1 | **N** | 1 2 | 3 4 | 5 6 | 7 8 | 9 10 |
| Emotional Affectional Orientation | | | | | | | | | | |
| Leader ← | | | | | | | | | | → Follower |
| 10 9 | **8** 7 | 6 5 | 4 3 | 2 1 | N | 1 2 | 3 4 | 5 6 | 7 8 | 9 10 |

Until that session, he was "afraid" that he was gay since he only thought there were two options, "straight or gay." He did not believe in bisexuality.

The example of Clay's first session is an initial illustration of the sex/gender/affectional concepts intersected with Shapiro's (2001) adaptive information processing (AIP) model. A goal of EMDR therapy is to promote choices in how one can more accurately perceive past, present, and future experiences (Shapiro, 2001). The AIP tenets justified offering this education to Clay during Phase 1 so that he could reevaluate how he conceptualized his issues.

## APPLICATION TO EMDR CASE CONCEPTUALIZATION

### Case Examples

Incorporating the sex/gender/affectional continua into initial intake/first session allows for a more comprehensive conceptualization of the issues. The following four cases are used for the remainder of this chapter to illustrate how to synthesize and apply the sex/gender/affectional developmental continua, developmental theory, and AIP model throughout each phase of EMDR therapy of the concepts.

Wilhelm was a congruent male in his mid-40s. He grew up in a two-parent family with a younger brother and younger sister. His parents conducted the household under the assumption that the male was the breadwinner and the woman managed the children and home. His description of his family aligned with what he referred to as "traditional family values" with sex/gender assignment behaviors. Wilhelm also served his country in combat. He sought treatment for complex posttraumatic stress disorder (PTSD) he identified as related to his combat experiences. His overall treatment goals were to (a) eliminate the symptoms of PTSD, (b) increase self-acceptance, and (c) improve his interactions with his wife. The target sequencing plans largely focused on his experiences during his time in combat. The primary decisions Wilhelm reported about himself were "I am evil, I am damaged, and I am weak." His treatment consisted of weekly EMDR therapy sessions over a period of 21 months. At the end of his treatment, he achieved a significant decrease in the symptoms of PTSD, significantly increased his self-acceptance and self-confidence, and improved his ability to manage his interactions with his wife. Wilhelm rated himself as a congruent male (Table 13.4) who benefited from synthesizing the sex/gender/affectional concepts, developmental theory, and the AIP model.

Ash is a client living with the intersex condition Klinefelter syndrome and a micropenis condition. I refer to Ash using plural pronouns (e.g., they, theirs). These pronouns are how they felt most authentically acknowledged. I completed extensive assessment on dissociative issues and none were evident. Ash had a multitude of developmental experiences resulting in their decision that they are *permanently unlovable.* Ash's appearance reflected a sex assignment of male. Ash also had subtly noticeable breast development. Ash identified sex assignment as male, but both male and female in their gender assignment and orientation. In some areas of life,

**TABLE 13.4** Sex/Gender/Affectional Continua for Example: Wilhelm

| Sex Assignment | | | | | | | | | | |
|---|---|---|---|---|---|---|---|---|---|---|
| Female ← | | | | | | | | | | → Male |
| 10 9 | 8 7 | 6 5 | 4 3 | 2 1 | N | 1 2 | 3 4 | 5 6 | 7 8 | 9 **10** |
| **Gender Assignment** | | | | | | | | | | |
| Femaleness ← | | | | | | | | | | → Maleness |
| 10 9 | 8 7 | 6 5 | 4 3 | 2 1 | N | 1 2 | 3 4 | 5 6 | 7 8 | 9 **10** |
| **Gender Orientation** | | | | | | | | | | |
| Feminine ← | | | | | | | | | | → Masculine |
| 10 9 | 8 7 | 6 5 | 4 3 | 2 1 | N | 1 2 | 3 4 | 5 6 | 7 8 | **9** 10 |
| **Physical Affectional Orientation** | | | | | | | | | | |
| Masculinity ← | | | | | | | | | | → Femininity |
| 10 9 | 8 7 | 6 5 | 4 3 | 2 1 | N | 1 2 | 3 4 | 5 6 | 7 8 | **9** 10 |
| **Emotional Affectional Orientation** | | | | | | | | | | |
| Leader ← | | | | | | | | | | → Follower |
| 10 9 | 8 7 | 6 5 | 4 3 | 2 1 | N | 1 2 | 3 4 | 5 6 | 7 8 | 9 **10** |

they were oriented toward a more feminine approach to the world. In other areas, they were oriented toward a more masculine approach to the world. Ash sought treatment specifically to (a) increase self-esteem and self-confidence, (b) improve skills to interact socially, (c) identify safe environments, and (d) increase self-pride toward being able to advocate for their needs. Ash had no reported history of life-threatening traumas. All target sequencing plans directly related to interactions with parents, peers, teachers, and coworkers. Ash chose to be isolated socially to avoid additional ridiculing and bullying. Ash's treatment consisted of weekly to biweekly sessions over a 5-year and 7-month period. EMDR therapy was the primary treatment for Ash's goals. Periodically, Ash needed specific therapeutic life management skills. At the end of treatment Ash's self-esteem and self-confidence had improved, they identified a focus of improving their interactions at their place of employment, and they began to advocate for their needs at their job. Ash's continua ratings proved very incongruent (Table 13.5).

Sean is an incongruent male (female sex assignment and male gender assignment). Sean was a 13-year-old female-to-male, preoperative, transgendered male. "Preoperative" refers to an individual who is actively working toward sex reassignment surgery. His parents referred him for treatment. He was living in an intact family with a younger brother. He had identified himself as male since he was 4 years old. His mother was supportive of Sean's identity. His father had concerns and questioned the validity of Sean's gender identity. The overall treatment goals were to (a) improve self-esteem, (b) build a family dynamic that supports Sean's goals to transition, and (c) expand Sean's sphere of comfortable social situations.

**TABLE 13.5 Sex/Gender/Affectional Continua for Example: Ash**

| Sex Assignment | | | | | | | | | | |
|---|---|---|---|---|---|---|---|---|---|---|
| Female ← | | | | | | | | | | → Male |
| 10 9 | 8 7 | 6 5 | 4 3 | 2 1 | N | **1** 2 | 3 4 | 5 6 | 7 8 | 9 10 |
| Gender Assignment | | | | | | | | | | |
| Femaleness ← | | | | | | | | | | → Maleness |
| 10 9 | 8 7 | 6 5 | 4 3 | 2 1 | N | 1 2 | **3** 4 | 5 6 | 7 8 | 9 10 |
| Gender Orientation | | | | | | | | | | |
| Feminine ← | | | | | | | | | | → Masculine |
| 10 9 | **8** 7 | 6 5 | 4 3 | 2 1 | N | 1 2 | 3 4 | 5 6 | 7 8 | 9 10 |
| Physical Affectional Orientation | | | | | | | | | | |
| Masculinity ← | | | | | | | | | | → Femininity |
| 10 9 | 8 7 | 6 5 | 4 3 | **2** 1 | N | 1 2 | 3 4 | 5 6 | 7 8 | 9 10 |
| Emotional Affectional Orientation | | | | | | | | | | |
| Leader ← | | | | | | | | | | → Follower |
| 10 9 | 8 7 | 6 5 | 4 3 | 2 1 | *N* | 1 2 | 3 4 | 5 6 | 7 8 | 9 10 |

Sean's target sequencing focused on experiences in school with teachers and peers. Sean's treatment consisted of weekly EMDR sessions over a period of 13 months. At the end of treatment, Sean reported to be fully supported by his family, was able to participate in selective social situations that he deemed as safe, and had significantly improved his self-esteem and self-confidence. The result of treatment led his parents to move forward with sex reassignment surgery. Sean is an example for an incongruent sex gender assignment (Table 13.6).

Clay presented as a congruent male with incongruent affectional orientations in his late 30s. He self-referred because he was questioning his "sexual orientation." He grew up in a blended family where his mother and stepfather treated each other as equals. He had no blood siblings and three stepbrothers. He had been in a committed relationship with what he described as a "very feminine female" for 7 years. He had participated in sexual activities with males. His sexual experiences drove him to question his orientation. His overall treatment goals were to (a) increase understanding of the motivation behind his sexual activities, (b) determine how he can authentically identify himself, and (c) resolve his conflicts between his emotional and physical attractions. Clay's target sequencing plan addressed experiences in school with teachers, his brothers, his current partner, and his recent sexual activities. Clay's treatment consisted of weekly EMDR sessions over a period of 9 months. At the end of treatment, Clay reported to have gained clarity in his motivation and desires, was able to accept his authentic identity as having unexpectedly incongruent affectional orientations, and was able to articulate to his partner what emotional traits and physical stimuli best attracted and aroused him. The result of treatment

**TABLE 13.6 Sex/Gender/Affectional Continua for Example: Sean**

| Sex Assignment | | | | | | | | | | |
|---|---|---|---|---|---|---|---|---|---|---|
| Female ◄ – – – – – – – – – – – – – – – – – – – – – – – – – ► Male | | | | | | | | | | |
| 10 9 | 8 <u>7</u> | 6 5 | 4 3 | 2 1 | N | 1 2 | 3 4 | 5 6 | 7 8 | 9 10 |
| Gender Assignment | | | | | | | | | | |
| Femaleness ◄ – – – – – – – – – – – – – – – – – – – – – – – – – ► Maleness | | | | | | | | | | |
| 10 9 | 8 7 | 6 5 | 4 3 | 2 1 | N | 1 2 | 3 4 | 5 6 | 7 8 | 9 **<u>10</u>** |
| Gender Orientation | | | | | | | | | | |
| Feminine ◄ – – – – – – – – – – – – – – – – – – – – – – – – – ► Masculine | | | | | | | | | | |
| 10 9 | 8 7 | 6 5 | 4 3 | 2 1 | N | 1 2 | 3 4 | 5 6 | 7 **<u>8</u>** | 9 10 |
| Physical Affectional Orientation | | | | | | | | | | |
| Masculinity ◄ – – – – – – – – – – – – – – – – – – – – – – – – – ► Femininity | | | | | | | | | | |
| 10 9 | 8 7 | 6 5 | 4 3 | 2 1 | N | 1 2 | 3 4 | 5 6 | 7 **<u>8</u>** | 9 10 |
| Emotional Affectional Orientation | | | | | | | | | | |
| Leader ◄ – – – – – – – – – – – – – – – – – – – – – – – – – ► Follower | | | | | | | | | | |
| 10 9 | 8 7 | 6 5 | 4 3 | 2 1 | N | 1 2 | 3 4 | 5 6 | <u>7</u> 8 | 9 10 |

led him to build a stronger relationship with his "very feminine female" partner. Clay is an example of incongruent affectional orientations (Table 13.7)

## AIP Model Expanded

Effective EMDR therapy treatment planning and case conceptualization requires the application of AIP model tenets (Shapiro, 2001). Attempting to use individual EMDR interventions without applying the AIP model tenets often results in poor treatment outcomes. The AIP model helps conceptualize cases and posits that past disturbing experiences feed current symptoms, issues, challenges, or problems (Shapiro, 2001). Adding the sex/gender/affectional continua and Eriksonian psychosexual developmental stage expands the case conceptualization.

Conceptualizing these issues includes assessing the experiential effects that sex/gender/affectional congruence/incongruence have had on the person's identity. Once the sex/gender/affectional continua are used, we can integrate Erik Erikson's psychosocial stage related to successful completion of the adolescent psychosocial stage: ego identity versus role confusion.

The adolescent Eriksonian stage, by definition, governs how one will interact with his or her authentic or dictated identity including body image and sex roles (Erikson, 1997). Bee (1992) explained that successful completion of this stage leads to an identity or "self" that is integrated with one's goals, aspiration, body image, and applicable sex roles. These factors support a correlation between the adolescent psychosocial stage and issues of sex/gender/affectional incongruence. If an

**TABLE 13.7** Sex/Gender/Affectional Continua for Example: Clay

| Sex Assignment | | | | | | | | | | |
|---|---|---|---|---|---|---|---|---|---|---|
| Female ← - - - - - - - - - - - - - - - - - - - → Male | | | | | | | | | | |
| 10 9 | 8 7 | 6 5 | 4 3 | 2 1 | N | 1 2 | 3 4 | 5 6 | 7 **8** | 9 10 |
| Gender Assignment | | | | | | | | | | |
| Femaleness ← - - - - - - - - - - - - - - - - - - - → Maleness | | | | | | | | | | |
| 10 9 | 8 7 | 6 5 | 4 3 | 2 1 | N | 1 2 | 3 **4** | 5 6 | 7 8 | 9 10 |
| Gender Orientation | | | | | | | | | | |
| Feminine ←————————————————→ Masculine | | | | | | | | | | |
| 10 9 | 8 7 | 6 5 | 4 3 | 2 1 | N | 1 2 | 3 4 | 5 6 | 7 8 | **9** 10 |
| Physical Affectional Orientation | | | | | | | | | | |
| Masculinity ← - - - - - - - - - - - - - - - - - - - → Femininity | | | | | | | | | | |
| 10 9 | 8 7 | 6 5 | 4 3 | 2 1 | **N** | 1 2 | 3 4 | 5 6 | 7 8 | 9 10 |
| Emotional Affectional Orientation | | | | | | | | | | |
| Leader ← - - - - - - - - - - - - - - - - - - - → Follower | | | | | | | | | | |
| 10 9 | **8** 7 | 6 5 | 4 3 | 2 1 | N | 1 2 | 3 4 | 5 6 | 7 8 | 9 10 |

individual achieves an authentic identity (ego identity) then he or she gains the virtue of fidelity to his or her "self's" goals, aspiration, body image, and applicable sex roles. If a person remains stuck in role confusion, then an identity crisis emerges compromising the success of all future psychosocial stages. Erikson's theory suggests that if a stage is not successfully completed, a person can "rework" that stage to success (Erikson, 1997).

During history taking, I explore the adolescent stage in relation to the client's goals, aspirations, body image, and applicable sex role experiences. The client can self-rate the elements as disturbing, neutral, and/or satisfying. Probing open-ended questions can help the client divide the experiences into two categories: "exploring who I am" (ego identity) or "complying with whom I am told to be" (role confusion). As we assess the client's experiences, we are able to better assess the level of success the client has achieved. A clinician who does not specialize in sex/gender/affectional issues can apply the aforementioned steps to apply these concepts to his or her clients. In doing so, the clinician will begin to expand the conceptualization of his or her clients and increase the inclusivity of the whole person's identity.

All four cases shared self-rated levels of disturbance during adolescence. They all also confirmed that they had a "felt sense" of role confusion. As a result, Wilhelm, Ash, Sean, and Clay did not gain the virtue of identity fidelity. Without fidelity to self, role confusion, in part, stimulated the symptoms for which they sought treatment. In Wilhelm's case of congruent sex/gender assignment, there were qualities that he identified as "feminine" and "inappropriate" for men. Sean's treatment occurred during his adolescent developmental stage, which helped prevent an unsuccessful resolution in this ego identity versus role confusion. Sean's supportive parents played a significantly positive role in moving toward successful completion of his adolescent psychosocial stage. Sean faced challenges because of the bullying he endured, inciting generalized fear around his identity. He began to develop internalized sexism, which interfered with his success in this psychosocial stage. The challenge with Ash was more significant due to the complexity of their sex/gender assignments. In their case, the lack of fidelity and role confusion directly related to their goals, aspirations, body image, and applicable sex role. Building a target-sequencing plan around disturbing experiences that interfered with ego identity versus role confusion, for Ash, was the primary focus of treatment. When we were able to identify Ash's role confusion as a challenge, treatment outcomes improved and progressed more efficiently. Initially, I mistakenly did not integrate Eriksonian psychosocial stages as part of Ash's original case conceptualization. In Clay's case, he had a relatively successful adolescent stage with regard to his goals, aspirations, and body image. In assessing his adolescent psychosocial stage, we discovered that he had "always" struggled with what was acceptable and appropriate with applicable sex roles.

## SEX/GENDER/AFFECTIONAL CONSIDERATIONS AND THE EIGHT PHASES OF EMDR

The following offers some suggestions for how to integrate sex/gender/affectional incongruence and psychosocial development appropriately into each of the eight phases of the EMDR therapy.

It is important to be prepared to incorporate attention to sex/gender/affectional identity concepts including cultural and contextual sensitivity beginning in Phase 1, History Taking This often requires some client education related to the continua of sex/gender/affectional congruence. I offer the following script to clients as an educational overview:

> Sex, gender, and affectional differentiation occur in utero. Sex assignment develops by the eighth week of the pregnancy. This phase identifies the specific genitalia that will develop. Then, from weeks 8 to 17, development is generally not concentrated on sex or gender assignment. Around weeks 18 through 24, the brain begins to develop its gender assignment. All babies begin as female and mutate if their sex and/or gender assignment is to move towards being male. During weeks 18 through 24, the timing and conditions of development must be perfect for a fully congruent sex/gender/affectional differentiation. Because pregnancy and development at these stages are so sensitive, it is very common for this complex mutation to result in some level of incongruence. Because of the complexity, I'm going to ask specific questions about how you experience your gender assignment in relationship to the issues to which you're seeking assistance.

Many clients have follow-up questions and need to discuss the concept more. In most cases, clients accept the information and move forward. During history taking, I pose questions like:

1. What did you learn about how others with your sex assignment should behave?
2. What did you learn about how others with your gender assignment should behave?
3. What expectations do others have of how you should behave that have been challenging?
4. What expectations do you have of how you should live your life that have been challenging?
5. How did you decide to manage and present being the gender that you identify?

These questions are designed to stimulate consideration of how the sex/gender/affectional concepts might intertwine with clients' life experiences. You may find that other questions are more effective for your practice. Individuals with congruent sex/gender/affectional identities typically have not considered these questions and therefore may have diminished the effect of their congruence. For those who do not have fully congruent sex/gender affectional identities, these questions provide an opportunity and validation to honor their full array of experience.

The Eriksonian psychosocial state concepts can be used to gather as much detail as possible about the identity development during clients' adolescence. Specifically, ask about the goals they had in their teen years, the content of their daydreams, promises they made to themselves during this time, sexual fantasies, sexual behaviors, and ideas about their body image. Depending on the client, you may need to expand your education and/or questions on any item within these topics. Part of the intention of combining sex/gender/affectional congruence and an assessment of the psychosocial adolescent stage into history taking is to avoid unintentionally perpetuating sexism oppression. These steps are an additional way for the non-specialist clinician to incorporate sex/gender/affectional concepts into his or her practice. This small act can effect positive social change.

During the Preparation phase, I have found that those who have sex/gender/affectional incongruence benefit greatly from resources that validate their complete authentic identity. When developing a calm/safe place with a client with incongruence, follow the standard protocol for a calm/safe place. Then, as part of expanding the details, you can ask the client to describe his or her complete authentic self in that place and add features that allow him or her to feel calmer and more authentic.

In most cases, these additions have resulted in clients feeling greater acceptance, value, and calmness when employing a calm/safe place for affect regulation. In the case of Wilhelm, there was no requirement to include sex/gender/affectional identity concepts into his calm/safe place. His calm/safe place was in the mountains with a waterfall, a cool temperature, and quiet. For Sean, he had better access to his calm/safe place when he added male physical characteristics and descriptors of himself. I offered Clay the sex/gender/affectional enhancements to his snowcapped mountains. He shared that the enhancements were not relevant to the calm/safe place. I learned here that it is better to be conservative when offering these enhancements. With Ash, I intentionally avoided incorporating sex/gender/affectional identity enhancements to their calm/safe place at first. My rationale was driven by the standard protocol, since a high level of disturbance existed around their identity; these enhancements could contaminate the resource. Ash identified a beach scene with blue water, white sand, clear blue sky with white puffy clouds, and a warm temperature. We heightened the experience with smells of coconut, sounds of the wave and seagulls, drinking ice-cold lemonade, and feeling the sun on their face. Ash struggled with establishing this calm place. We attempted three other places (i.e., being in the clouds, near a lake, and an imaginary place in a pool of warm chocolate pudding). None of these calm places would take hold. At that point, I decided to incorporate sex/gender/affectional enhancements. We included the enhancement that allowed Ash to return to the beach scene and was able to describe seeing themselves with long dark hair, wearing square shorts that were multicolored camouflage, seeing their sun-kissed skin, having medium length nails, and feeling a soothing sensation that was moving from their stomach to their throat. Once we had these elements, the calm/safe place was quickly established and the enhancements supported the development. Ash labeled this location as "freedom." This calm/safe place remained effective for Ash's affect regulation for the entire 5 plus years of treatment.

Generally speaking, EMDR Phases 3 to 6 need no alterations. The standard Phase 3 protocol is vital in assuring that the target ignites the reprocessing. Guide clients to find the smallest piece of the image that causes the greatest disturbance because issues of sex/gender/affectional incongruence can remain too broad without a very small specific detail in the image or input item of the target.

During Phase 4, I have incorporated specific interweaves that are helpful with sex/gender/affectional incongruence. For example, in Wilhelm's case, he was struggling with the image of an "act" that prevented him from accessing his sadness. During reprocessing, his system was looping on a specific image. I used what I call the little/big perspectives (e.g., what would it be like if you saw/heard/felt that through big/little eyes/ears/feelings). I interweaved the little versus the big concept. After the fourth return to this image, I asked him if he saw the image through little eyes or big eyes. He shared that he saw the image through big eyes. I responded with "What would it be like if you saw the image through little eyes?" From there I moved him back into reprocessing, adding rapid bilateral stimulation (BLS). The big/little interweave broke the loop, accessed the emotion, and moved Wilhelm back into natural reprocessing. When I conceptualize the big versus little interweave, I do not prescribe what big versus little means or represents. I simply use big/little to shift the perspective. Therefore, in Wilhelm's case, if he had said he sees the image through little eyes, I would have asked, "What would it be like if you saw the image through big eyes?" Big/little is relative to the individual's experience. I find it to be an error if I assume that little means a younger person and big means an older person. I have found that sometimes "big eyes" means eyes wide open.

I have found great value in the use of a temporary Positive Cognition (PC). At the end of each session, I find it helpful to identify a PC that can be believed and has a Validity of Cognition (VoC) of 6 or 7. When a client has truly reprocessed target issues and the Subjective Units of Disturbances (SUDs) is zero, the initial (or revised) PC can often be installed when paired with a reprocessed target to a VoC of 7. In my experience, fully reprocessed targets are not achieved in every session. Often the SUD decreases, but additional reprocessing is necessary. In cases where the SUD is not 0, I ask the client to reevaluate the PC. If the VoC is not a 7, we collectively work to titrate the PC toward a belief that the client could rate at 7.

For example, in Sean's treatment, there was a particular target regarding his brother that required multiple sessions to achieve 0/7/clear. The PC related to the original target was "I am okay as I am." At the end of the first reprocessing session, "I am okay as I am" was still the accurate PC, but Sean rated the VoC at a 2. I offered a titrated form of the PC: "I **can** be okay as I am." Sean was able to rate the VoC for this PC at a 5. I titrated the PC further to "I can learn to be okay as I am." Sean rated this PC at a 7. Therefore, we installed "I can learn to be okay as I am" with the target. The second and third session the PC remained "I can learn to be okay as I am" at a 7. On the fourth session Sean was able to articulate that "I can be okay as I am" was a more accurate PC at a 7. Another six sessions installing "I can be okay as I am" at a 7 led us to our final session on this target to achieving a VoC of 7 with the PC: "I am okay as I am." By incorporating a titrated PC during the Installation phase and assuring the PC is a VoC of 7, I have found better treatment outcomes consistently. This is an alteration to the standard protocol, but due to the generalized nature of sex/gender/affectional incongruence, adjusting the PC to reach a VoC of 7 for the specific session seems to support positive treatment outcomes while improving affect regulation between sessions. The "temporary Positive Cognition" also can be used as an additional tool as part of Phase 7, Closure.

To assist in Phase 8, Reevaluation, with clients who have challenges with sex/gender/affectional incongruence, I request a log specifically about experiences or stimuli that relate to their perceived incongruence experiences. By tracking these "triggers," clients have become more aware of effect and level of incongruence. The logged data informs both an evolving case conceptualization and opportunities for resources to empower the client. Items identified in these logs are not always directly related to the target. Reprocessing sex/gender/affectional incongruence seems to resolve more efficiently by integrating logs to the EMDR treatment.

## COMMON PATTERNS WITH SEX/GENDER/AFFECTIONAL INCONGRUENCE

There is a multitude of biases, discriminations, and threats when one is living with incongruence. American society typically neglects to differentiate sex assignments, gender identity, and affectional orientation. These socially ignorant patterns create adverse conditions for those with incongruent identities. For example, Clay (incongruent affectional orientation) made an effort to find support within his close friendships. He spoke to two of his friends separately to gain support through his confusion. Unfortunately, in both attempts he was met with strong ridicule and humiliation. Over time, these threats evolved into internalized threats and self-deprecating beliefs. This ongoing adversity manifested as general fear of interacting with his family and friends, even though his experience was with only two people.

Conversely, Wilhelm grew up in a family that placed great value on traditional male behaviors; he then participated in a military activity that also valued traditional male behaviors. The work on his combat trauma emphasized the intrusive nature of his blocking beliefs regarding what it means to be a "man." Wilhelm and I could not effectively reprocess any of his life-threatening combat trauma without reprocessing the traumatic memories that were limiting his ability to accept his "humanness" in addition to his "maleness." The use of the concepts in this chapter supported Wilhelm's effective reprocessing of his sadness. He shared that the work we did in targeting his perspective on his own gender was "important" for him to "change." Identity incongruence informs clients' perspectives on their memories. Clinicians have a profound opportunity to build every client's awareness of the influences to his or her identity. Both congruent and incongruent sex/gender/affectional identities produce, at a minimum, barriers that appear to be blocking beliefs. It can be harmful to avoid these identity barriers more comprehensively as they influence the reprocessing. These blocking beliefs are embedded in character and personality traits and should be part of the target-sequencing plan.

Another common issue for identity challenges interfering with reprocessing is internalized sexism. In Ash's case, their experiences around their sex/gender assignment resulted in crippling internalized sexism that cultivated generalized self-hatred. In the 5+ years of treatment, the first 4 years focused on decreasing and ultimately eliminating the generalized self-hatred by targeting the experiences that supported their internalized sexism. One of the targets that reached significant resolution surrounded a high school experience. We targeted a pattern of a relational dynamic in physical education class. Ash's sex assignment of being an incongruent male required an assignment to a "male" physical education class. Ash craved the opportunity to participate with the female physical education teachers.

The target: The image was seeing a specific female teacher smiling at them during a physical education class. The Negative Cognition was "I am unlovable"; the PC was "I am lovable." The VoC was 1, the emotions related to the target were scared and sad. In that moment in the session, Ash was experiencing an SUDs score of 8. We followed the standard protocol for Phase 4 (Desensitization). The blocking belief that arose sporadically during that reprocessing session surrounded Ash's decision that because they were incongruently assigned in sex and gender, they did not deserve and did not possess the human quality to be loved because of their intersex condition. I employed interweaves related to the purpose of the belief, shifted attention to body sensation, and used perspective changes to try to address the blocking belief. Ash's personal traits were very organized around Ash's belief of being undeserving. The blocking belief was so impactful that we had to target disturbing physical experiences separate from the events. We were able to identify the body sensation that directly connected to the Negative Cognition of "I am unlovable." There was a "tight rock" in Ash's groin area. By using the float back/affect bridge jointly, we found a very early memory, around the age of 1 year old, where Ash remembered their father changing their diaper for the first time, then gasping, and then screaming for Ash's mother. Ash determined that because of their intersex condition, they must not possess the necessary traits to be loved.

We developed a target-sequencing plan around the body sensation and the decision that Ash did not possess the necessary traits to be loved. Ash identified the first (touchstone) memory as the memory of their father at 1 year old. We used the standard 3 to 8 phases of EMDR therapy to target that 1-year-old experience. We focused on that target issue for 23 sessions before we were able to come to a resolution with an SUDs of 1 and a VoC of 7 for the belief "I can deserve love." Although not an ideal resolution, we agreed that this was ecologically sound for Ash. This is an extreme case, but it illustrates the depth in which internalized sexism influences identity development.

## SUMMARY

Clients who struggle with sex/gender/affectional incongruence typically have some awareness of the experiences that produce disturbing patterns. When a person recognizes the pervasiveness of his or her identity incongruences, that person is better prepared to find resolution in therapy. As clinicians, we must understand the development and influence that sex/gender/affectional incongruences have on the human experience. It is easy for clinicians to default to a historical perspective of a dichotomous sex (male or female), gender (male or female), and sexual orientation (hetero or homo). Unfortunately, focusing on sex/gender/affectional identities from a dichotomous perspective can misunderstand and marginalize a client's experiences, perpetuate sexism, and overlook injustices. I have found in over a decade of work in this area that sex/gender/affectional dimensions are a powerful component of human experience. One cannot accurately say that every client has issues with his or her sex/gender/affectional congruence. However, sex/gender/affectional incongruence, at any level, can influence the client's presenting problems. Culturally sensitive clinicians value the idea that every individual perceives experiences differently, and can conceptualize sex/gender/affectional congruence is similar to a fingerprint that it is biologically imprinted. Through families of origin, education, relationships, and social perceptions, incongruence is pathologized and exacerbated. The sex/gender/affectional continua and Eriksonian adolescent psychosocial stage complements the AIP model and the eight phases of EMDR therapy to be more culturally sensitive. These alterations and enhancements have promoted efficient and positive treatment outcomes for many of my clients, including Wilhelm, Sean, Ash, and Clay.

## Recommended Website Resources

*Intersex conditions:* To read more about intersex conditions, a great starting point is the Intersex Society of North America (ISNA). http://www.isna.org/. This website provides scholarship and knowledge to increase understanding of intersex conditions. The historic case of John/Joan provides a foundational case example of the biological variance in sex and gender differentiation in identical twins.

*Transgendered/transsexual resources:* For more information about transgendered issues, please go to the World Professional Association for Transgender Health www.wpath.org.

*Affectional orientations (i.e., sexual orientation):* For more information about affectional orientation knowledge, research, and support, there are many resources on the Kinsey Institute's website: www.kinseyinstitute.org.

*Erik Erikson resources:* Finally, if you would like more information on the fundamentals of the Eriksonian psychosocial stage and his contributions, please start with the Institute: www.erikson.edu.

*Other spectra/continuum examples:* http://americantransman.com/, http://itspronouncedmetrosexual.com, http://profriend.webs.com/continuum.htm

## REFERENCES


Ainsworth, M. D. S., & Bowlby, J. (1991). An ethological approach to personality development. *American Psychologist, 46*, 331–341.

Balen, A. H., Creighton, S. M., Davies, M. C., MacDougall, J., & Stanhope, R. (Eds.). (2004). *Pediatric and adolescent gynecology: A multidisciplinary approach.* Cambridge, UK: Cambridge University Press.

Bee, H. L. (1992). *The developing child.* London, UK: Harper Collins.

Bowlby, J. (1988). *A secure base: Parent–child attachment and healthy human development.* New York, NY: Basic Books.

Erikson, E. H. (1997). *The life cycle completed.* New York, NY: W. W. Norton.

Pardue, M. L., & Wizemann, T. M. (Eds.). (2001). *Exploring the biological contributions to human health: Does sex matter?* Washington, DC: National Academies Press.

Shapiro, F. (2001). *Eye movement desensitization and reprocessing, basic principles, protocols and procedures* (2nd ed.). New York: Guilford Press.

Swaab, D. F. (2004). Sexual differentiation of the human brain: Relevance for gender identity, transsexualism and sexual orientation. *Journal of Gynecological Endocrinology, 19*, 301–312.

Swaab, D. F., & Garcia-Falgueras, A. (2009). Sexual hormones and the brain: An essential alliance for sexual identity and sexual orientation. *Journal of Endocrine Development, 17*, 22–35.

## Blank Continua for Clinical Use

| Sex/Gender/Affectional Continua | | | | | | | | | | |
|---|---|---|---|---|---|---|---|---|---|---|
| Sex Assignment | | | | | | | | | | |
| Female ← – – – – – – – – – – – – – – – – → Male | | | | | | | | | | |
| 10 9 | 8 7 | 6 5 | 4 3 | 2 1 | N | 1 2 | 3 4 | 5 6 | 7 *8* | 9 10 |
| Gender Assignment | | | | | | | | | | |
| Femaleness ← – – – – – – – – – – – – – – – – → Maleness | | | | | | | | | | |
| 10 9 | 8 7 | 6 5 | 4 3 | 2 1 | N | 1 2 | 3 4 | 5 6 | 7 8 | *9* 10 |
| Gender Orientation | | | | | | | | | | |
| Feminine ← – – – – – – – – – – – – – – – – → Masculine | | | | | | | | | | |
| 10 9 | 8 7 | 6 5 | 4 3 | 2 1 | N | 1 2 | 3 4 | 5 6 | *7* 8 | 9 10 |
| Physical Affectional Orientation | | | | | | | | | | |
| Masculinity ← – – – – – – – – – – – – – – – – → Femininity | | | | | | | | | | |
| 10 9 | 8 7 | 6 5 | 4 3 | 2 1 | N | 1 2 | 3 4 | 5 6 | 7 8 | *9* 10 |
| Emotional Affectional Orientation | | | | | | | | | | |
| Leader ← – – – – – – – – – – – – – – – – → Follower | | | | | | | | | | |
| 10 9 | 8 7 | 6 5 | 4 3 | 2 1 | N | 1 2 | 3 4 | 5 6 | 7 8 | 9 *10* |

# SECTION V

# Specific Cultures and Social Stigma

CHAPTER 14

# The Transgenerational Impact of Anti-Semitism

Ruth Heber and Karen Alter-Reid

## IDENTIFY EMDR TARGETS TO HEAL INTERNALIZED STIGMA AND EXPAND IDENTITY

Individuals traumatized by catastrophic events exhibit a myriad of symptoms, including affective, somatic, and ideational impairments associated with posttraumatic stress disorder (PTSD). Historically, the diagnosis of PTSD did not appear in the *Diagnostic and Statistical Manual of Mental Disorders* (*DSM*) until 1980. Since then, several trauma-specific treatment approaches have been developed (e.g., eye movement desensitization and reprocessing [EMDR], relational psychoanalysis, and cognitive processing therapy). The complexity of trauma-related symptoms and disabilities need to be understood in the reciprocal social context within which they unfold. The family can mitigate, exacerbate, or perpetuate the individual's symptoms. Families who have experienced catastrophic events may have few resources to support it's members and may in fact further traumatize them.

In spite of advances in the field of trauma therapy, there is still no *DSM-5* (American Psychiatric Association, 2013) diagnosis for generational trauma. Support for such a diagnosis comes from the findings of scientists and clinicians who examine the transmission of trauma from biological, epigenetic, and psychological perspectives (Danieli, 1998; Diorio & Meaney, 2007; Kestenberg, 1982; Yehuda et al., 2000, 2005). That is, they are focusing upon symptoms exhibited by children of traumatized people that may be directly related to their parents' or grandparents' experiences. Such transmission has been observed in generations of survivors of wars, genocide, chronic discrimination, and slavery (Jasienska, 2009; Lev-Wiesel, 2007; Nagata, 1990; Salberg, 2015). Wars and genocide frequently lead to displacements and mass migrations of survivors, who, having lost their way of life and community, must then cope with a myriad of new challenges and develop new skills in order to survive and reestablish themselves in foreign environs.

The expression of trauma-related symptoms appears to be influenced both by nature and nurture within a particular cultural setting. For example, stigma internalized by target populations, within a specific cultural context, has been shown to be transmitted to survivors' children in the form of distorted or damaged self-identity, fragile social agency, and a foreshortened sense of future (Coyle, 2014; Laub, 1998; Shabad, 1993). Intriguingly, second generation symptoms sometimes include flashbacks of events they have never experienced themselves, but have only heard about from direct or indirect sources. Similarly, repetitive dreams, nightmares, hypervigilance, fears of danger, hypoarousal, powerlessness, and avoidance behaviors have been reported (Brothers, 2014; Salberg, 2015).

Particular challenges were faced by people who emigrated from their homelands as children. Those children had not been included in their parents' decision to resettle, didn't fully grasp the necessity to leave everything they had known behind, and were ill prepared for the challenges posed by integration in countries whose culture, customs, and language were foreign to them. Such circumstances frequently led to confusion as to one's place in the world. Their belongingness was challenged by lack of meaningful communication with people of the host country with whom they had no shared history and whose lifestyles, experiences, and points of reference sharply diverge from their own.

Frequently, self-esteem was further bruised by the family's diminished social and economic status consequent upon displacement; a decline that the children could not understand. The families' capacities to help their children tended to be further compromised by the imperatives of survival; by their struggles to reclaim their lives in a strange land, put food on the table, and educate their offspring in whom they saw their future. Those were the parents who spoke in a funny accent, dressed in odd ways, had strange table manners, didn't understand the American sense of humor, and could not swoon over popular stage idols. It was not uncommon for the children to become ashamed of their parents, and distance from them, thus further perpetuating their sense of nonbelongingness and defectiveness.

Lack of continuity and fracture in cultural, personal, and family narratives is of major importance in maladaptation. The children were not cushioned by a shared family history; there were secrets, and fragmented, or inappropriately related stories; there were friends and relatives who were never mentioned; and there were moments of silence and discomfort that everyone ignored. Further discontinuity was one of time—there was the time before the disaster, the time during the disaster, and the time after. The children belonged to the disjointed "after."

In this chapter, we emphasize the need for the clinician to acquaint herself with the patient's culture, mores, lore, and metaphors so as to understand the patient within a meaningful context. We underscore the utility of taking a thorough longitudinal history that can help in understanding current symptoms not otherwise accounted for, and help us identify potential EMDR targets. We also argue that successful treatment includes both reprocessing of trauma and the reconstruction of a coherent, meaningful life narrative.

Our deliberations are limited to Jewish populations with experiences of anti-Semitism and illustrated by a case study. They can, however, apply to many different populations with cultural variants. We write from the perspective of EMDR therapists who believe that trauma is contextualized both in individual and collective narratives, and will show how the individual's narrative is shaped by parental overdisclosure, underdisclosure, gaps, and secrets.

## EMDR THERAPY: THE "INTAKE": HISTORY TAKING, PREPARATION, CASE CONCEPTUALIZATION, AND TREATMENT PLANNING

Damaged self-esteem, identity, and alienation in second generation offspring of survivors of anti-Semitic atrocities, such as European pogroms and the Holocaust, can be addressed with EMDR treatment. As a first step, the intake process is critical to gathering the relevant information necessary to create linkages between presenting symptoms and targets related to generational trauma, internalized stigma, and identity. For work with second generation survivors, it is requisite that the intake be expanded to include generational history. It is only with a widened historical lens that the therapist can stay attuned to the way each second generation survivor internalized the traumatic generational experiences, metabolized them, and processed them—incompletely or to adaptive resolution.

### History Taking: Understanding the Cultural Context

The EMDR trauma therapist working with one or multiple generations of genocides needs to be familiar with the broader impact of mass genocide on the psyche, the impact of internalized oppression (Nickerson, 2010), and the unique factors that continue to impact upon offspring's identity formation. Thus, knowledge about the contextual culture in which the traumatic experiences occurred helps the therapist to identify transgenerational wounds and to select appropriate EMDR targets.

#### The Cultural Context of Anti-Semitism and Jewish Narrative

Anti-Semitism dates back across generations, often resulting in mass genocides and other cruelties of war and accompanied losses. To this day, the word *Jew* holds a pejorative meaning in some countries. "Jew" as a derogatory label classifies and defines a population, and Jews often identify with this pejorative (e.g., Jew the moneylender; the big nose; the gold hoarder; the dirty, lazy child; the Christ killer). As societies often in exile, Jews tried to maintain their positive core identity via community-anchored rituals, written narratives (e.g., the Torah, the Talmud), and oral lore.

This passing down of accounts from one generation to the next includes giving voice to the history of persecution and overcoming of traumatic experiences. These narratives, often replete with the trials, tribulations, and ultimately the joys and triumphs, become embedded in traditions. One of the best known of these traditions is the Passover Seder in which parents recount the story of the Jewish people's enslavement in Egypt, their escape, wandering episodes in the desert, and ultimate freedom.

In keeping with the tradition of Jewish narrative, "never forget" became the dictum of many Jewish groups in the aftermath of the Holocaust. This refers to the notion that only by teaching and educating the next generation about the Holocaust can Jews learn to be on alert to anti-Semitism facing future generations.

However, the recounting of traumatic experiences, when left unmetabolized, tends to be "given voice" in anxious and/or dissociated way. For many survivors of the Holocaust and of the communist regime's anti-Semitic assaults, such unprocessed memories interfere with the capacity to give a coherent narrative; they are not able to recapture and tell their memories in the form of a story that is sequential and is told with appropriate affect and logical conclusions.

Histories of trauma within this population continue to leave narratives disrupted to a point where they can no longer contain the individual or collective trauma. When experiencing posttraumatic stress symptoms, the past is present and there is still no ending to the narrative, no capacity to integrate victim experiences with survival experiences. "Never forget" becomes a haunting experience rather than an empowering and reflective experience. It stands in contrast to other Jewish narratives where there is a lesson learned to impart, a proud resiliency and survivorship, a beginning, middle, and conclusion to a story.

Survivors may anxiously tell their children too much of their experiences, relate sensory details of lived or witnessed horrors, or speak too often about their recalled traumatic events. Conversely, they may tell next to nothing of their personal traumatic lives to their children and families.

Together with the injunction never to forget, in this traumatized population, there is a counter-injunction, the conspiracy of silence; silence because it is too painful to recall, because there are no words to describe the horror, because no one who was not there would understand, because words themselves diminish the magnitude of the disaster, and silence because parents don't want to inflict pain of their suffering upon their offspring. This forced silence oftentimes results in unprocessed fragments and dissociations, rendering the narrative incoherent. We recognize such fragments in bits of the stories, allusions, jokes, and gestures that appear out of context; and we see dissociation in memories with gaps in continuity, stripped of details, or in diffusions of time, and in expressions of affects that are split from contents.

Children of these survivors sense their parents' pain without a contextual understanding of a verbal narrative. In some cases, the traumatic events are learned by reading or hearing others' stories outside of the family, leaving the second generation to fill in gaps and reconstruct their parents' narratives by themselves.

When considering the cultural context of second generation patients, it is important for the therapist to take note of two types of potential losses. The first is the loss of a regulated, coherent narrative in which to develop a continual sense of self; a narrative that defines the self and one's place within a stable familiar context with known norms and expectations. The second is a deep cultural loss of storytelling and passing wisdom to the next generation as is the case with emigrants who only tangentially identified with Judaism and considered themselves the assimilated citizens of a given host country until that host country singled them out as Jews and turned upon them. Here, there is a disruption not only of the individual's narrative, but also the lack of an anchor of the survivor's story within a larger communal narrative of Jewish history and identity marked by oppression, trauma, resilience, and survivorship.

## Taking a Transgenerational History: The Centrality of Thorough Pretrauma, Trauma, and Posttrauma History Taking

For effective treatment of transgenerational trauma in survivor offspring, the history taking must be expanded from the patient's own life history to include a strong generational/ancestral history. It is only from here that generational themes and resources, as well as targets associated with the genesis of the patient's symptoms, will become clear. Expanded, longitudinal generational history gathering should include (a) "Before the trauma" experiences of the survivor's family including resources within the family and religious/cultural identifications before anti-Semitic genocide, (b) the specific genocide trauma experiences, (c) the "trauma(s) after the genocide trauma" including insults associated with a series of displacements into a host culture where one is made to feel "other," and (d) the experiences of resiliency after the trauma.

In the case of the Holocaust and other genocides, it is important to assist the patient in developing a coherent family "before" and "after" narrative so that adaptive memory networks regarding prewar status and norms and postwar resiliency and survival adaptations can be acknowledged. This will help the patient toward integration of both positive and negative memories across time and result in a more fluid, integrated, self, and family narrative.

## Gathering Prewar Trauma History of Parents and/or Grandparents' Lives

Patients often know something of their parents' or grandparents' traumatic experiences but do not have access to much of a prewar narrative. In these cases, the patient can be encouraged to do some investigative work with family members, other survivors, written accounts, and other historical documents, so that a workable genogram/sociogram can be established and the narrative can begin to be constructed.

Areas for investigative inquiry can include: What was going on in the place before the war? For example, what is the history of the region? What were their parents' and grandparents' professions and places in that society? What about previous generations? What were the religious and cultural affiliations? What were their parents' and grandparents' dreams? Were there family secrets? What was the family lore? What was the environmental norm pretrauma? Even before Hitler, persecution was an expected norm in much of Western Europe. How did the family adapt to this? What were their strengths? How did they get through?

## Gathering Family Genocide Trauma Experiences

At the beginning of treatment, patients may know only pieces or fragments of their parents' experiences during the genocide or war. Sometimes, the trauma history is so huge and diffuse, for example, "the Holocaust," "the Ukrainian pogroms," that it overwhelms the individuals' conceptual and affective schemas to a point where they cannot identify the unique family threads to cull out singular events out of the chaotic, undifferentiated black totality of a collective tragedy filled with numbing humiliation, demoralization, and countless losses: loss of country, community, family, education, identity. It is the therapist's task to help each patient develop specific neural networks associated with his or her unique family history during the catastrophe. As the patient talks, the therapist questions and helps the patient make distinctions between the cognitive and affective threads, assess how much detail of the parental story the patient actually knows, and how much the patient intuits, confabulates, or imagines. At times, exploring the context and intent of parental disclosure, as well as their nonverbal cues, emotional discrepancies, and behavioral patterns, can contribute to the understanding of the patients' perceptions and difficulties.

Attunement to the affective patterns is essential—is there a diminished capacity to express certain affects and/or is there a pattern of unfiltered affect that hinders the patient's self-regulating capacities? Oftentimes, feelings don't get expressed for years or for generations because of numbing during traumatic events. Some individuals don't let themselves feel anything until experiencing the safety of the therapist's office; after all, survival at one time depended on the individuals' capacity to quash pain and fear, as well as self-control to the point of suppression reflexes, such as coughing, sneezing, and even startling. For example, historically the patient's parents may have learned that if someone walked behind them, they had to pretend not to hear and not to show any hesitation lest they be noticed and identified as Jews. The patient may similarly show inhibition of behaviors and feelings, although no current danger calls for such control. The task entails exploring behaviors, affects, and other hyperaroused states, and determining what historical precipitants occurred in the patient's own experiences. Thus, for example, when the uncalled feeling of shame surfaces, the therapist needs to question whether the shame belongs to the present, to personal experiences, or to the family's past.

It is from this type of listening that we can begin to understand the patient's symptoms and identify the residues of the family trauma that are central to the treatment planning. For survivor offspring, the dissociative or incoherent narrative—the story that has no beginning, a muddled present, and a stifled possible future—is told in disordered snippets and fragments, and with feelings that are not always appropriate to the content of the story. In attending not just to what is told, but also to the way narratives are related, the therapist starts to understand attachment raptures that may have occurred both with the survivor parent(s) and with the parent's larger culture and history. Often, one of the goals in treatment is the repair of filial bonds and reacquaintance with oneself within one's own culture. This gives the individuals the context for understanding their experiences and, at times, promotes capacity for continuing the tradition of integrated cultural storytelling.

## Gathering Postwar Trauma History

The therapist needs to inquire what happened before and during the traumatic times, as well as what happened after—how the survivors were able to deal with their losses and challenges, build new lives and adapt to new realities. Just like the patients may be lacking in information of the parents "before the war," they may also have failed to develop the narrative of the family "after the war." The patient may need to gather information about that period as well. Often, as discussed previously, postwar migration is filled with further humiliations and difficult transitions into new cultures, which the parents lived but seldom talked about; whatever they were doing was simply necessary for survival. The information about the "after" may also be triumphant. The very fact of survival in the face of new challenges bears testimony to the family's strength.

## History Taking: Noting Emergent Themes

Throughout the course of the prewar, war, and postwar history taking, the therapist begins to identify themes that are threaded through the patient's narratives. Frequently, for second generation survivors, the themes tend to be repetitive and are suggestive of a sense of alienation and not belonging, feelings of defectiveness and inadequacy, a felt sense of danger, vulnerability, and lack of control. Often-heard Negative Cognitions (NCs) associated with these themes include "I don't belong," "I don't deserve," "I'm not good enough," "I'm shameful," "I'm in danger," "I have no control." Affects that accompany these NCs range from shame and fear to rage and surrender. It is not unusual for these themes to become more focused during the reprocessing stage when personal and ancestral memories begin to connect to the identified themes.

## Developing a Treatment Plan

*The search for targets:* Once themes are identified, the therapist and patient pull the lens back and collaboratively construct an appropriate treatment plan. In the context of transgenerational treatment, appropriate targets include (a) traumatic experiences from the patient's own life, (b) trauma of past generations' experiences told to or imagined by the patient, be they fragments or cohesive memories, and (c) symptoms not accounted for in any way. The determining factor for target selection is current symptoms whose genesis may be unprocessed trauma.

## Clinical Case Illustration

Regina is a 50-year-old, bright, creative, and articulate woman born in the former Soviet Union. Her grandparents survived the Russian pogroms, and her parents were raised in Stalinist Russia and survived World War II. Regina and her younger sister were raised in an anti-Semitic, communist regime, and emigrated to the United States with their parents when Regina was 14 years old. Regina and her Russian-born husband have two children, a 25-year-old daughter and a 22-year-old son. They live in the suburbs.

### History Taking Expanded to Include Transgenerational History

Regina's presenting issues in treatment were depression and anxiety. She immediately reported that she was clinically depressed, noting long periods of staying in bed, irritability, and angry outbursts. She stated that for the past 15 years, ever since work-related emotional and financial stress befell her family, she felt as if she were living in a war zone, fluctuating between feelings of surrender and anger. Her descriptions of self included, "Anger envelops me," "I don't speak up . . . like sheep going to the slaughter," "When I surrender, I don't have to feel fear." She also described a pattern of absorption in fantasy and periods of dissociation. She berated herself for not having been a safety net for her two children while they were growing up, noting that her children were sometimes ashamed of her.

During the first session and without prompting, Regina began to intermittently relate pieces of her history. Listening to these pieces of history, it felt as though there was little differentiation between traumatic events of her own life and of the generations before her. It was as though her sense of identity was engulfed by both helpless and enraged reactivity to one long, unending trauma. During the first session, she related her sense of self as "other" who didn't belong in the American culture and whose life was marked by endurance of hardships with no end in sight. These included remarks about the following incidents (eventual EMDR targets):

- Growing up with a mother who was constantly anxious about safety: ". . . getting me to a doctor in the Ukraine when I was sick was frightening . . . if the doctor was anti-Semitic, I might not get proper care . . . my mother still sees everything as a crisis, a life-threatening event, no matter how insignificant in the eyes of others."
- Being molested at age 13 in Italy (en route to the United States) by a shopkeeper, already familiar with nonverbal parental communications of internalized stigma and powerlessness, "These things happen to us, this is our fate and we can't talk about it."
- Her 1 month stay at a welfare hotel when first immigrating to the United States: "I will always be that person, an immigrant fighting her way from the welfare hotel."
- Witnessing the 9/11 attacks on the World Trade Center: "We Russians all ordered Israeli gas masks, water . . . we all knew the horror of war, stories of our parents and grandparents' wars."

During the first stage of treatment, Regina's therapy focused on developing stabilization and affect regulation strategies while continuing with history taking. Particular attention was paid to present grounding since Regina reported that she lived mostly in the past or in future fantasy. Differentiating between past danger and the present safety in the therapist's office became a staple. Regina felt a sense of safety during sessions but never let the therapist forget that bad things could and do happen outside of the office. She spoke of anti-Semitic events in the United States and abroad, insisting that there was little safety for Jews anywhere. She and other Jews could be lulled into disclosing their Jewish identities and beliefs, but it would come back to bite them. She felt unsafe expressing her outrage on social media about international anti-Semitic incidents, stating that she could not rule out that future "regimes" would round her up to an amphitheater and oppress her as a result of her comments.

Positive affect tolerance was also addressed in this stage of treatment because Regina reported that as a Russian, she did not know pleasure; suffering, she said, was a Russian imperative, "sacrificing for Mother Russia" was an obligation, a way of life, and it was transgenerational. Growing up in Russia, she identified with the "suck it up, life is hard" imperative. Joy was for the Americans, people who could live their lives without the "burdens of their histories." Slowly over time, Regina was able to sit in sessions for longer periods of time with small moments of joy, and allow for resourcing in memories/experiences of being in nature, intellectual curiosity from her youth, and blissful times when her children were little.

Since Regina brought in parts of family narrative from the outset of treatment, history taking and finding targets included both (a) float backs to her own life experiences, and (b) recognition of family themes and exploration of possible generational targets. The therapist noted both the narrative content and the way the narrative was conveyed. When asked, Regina said that family stories were told to her either with high levels of detail and distress or there was silence about the history. The patient related instances of listening to unprocessed trauma narratives from her grandmother. One example was the grandmother's flat and casual affect while talking about her experiences of witnessing anti-Semitic raids in which the men in her family were slaughtered. In these narratives, her grandmother's effects of horror and fear were not integrated into her descriptions. At other times, Regina's grandmother's stories about poverty, violence, and fleeing the Ukraine to escape concentration camps were told in a hyperaroused state, marked by unfiltered angst and horrifying details of the dead.

Filling in the patient's autobiographic historical gaps, along with the therapist filling in her own educational gaps about Russian history, helped provide further context. The therapist asked questions to become more fully acquainted with life in Stalinist and postrevolution communist Russia, community and family norms pre-pogroms and war, and postimmigration experiences with her family and the host culture. Inquiry about individual and family strengths and resources was central to the beginning stages of developing a more cohesive narrative from generational victim of anti-Semitism to survivorship and the reclaiming of that which had been lost along the way.

Growing up in the Ukraine in the 1960s and 1970s, and identifying with Judaism was simply not an option. Jews had been oppressed, killed, ridiculed, and deprived of their identity over decades. Regina herself had not overtly known that being Jewish was "bad" until she entered kindergarten. There, she was labeled "dirty kike" because of her curly hair. In telling her parents about incidents of anti-Semitism at school, Regina remembered a sense of helplessness in their faces, as if there was nothing they could say or do to comfort or empower her. She became confused about her identity as a Jew. The cultural and familial climates were ripe for internalized oppression and shameful identity.

Later on in life, Regina's mother filled her in on particular incidents that resulted in deidentification with their religion; for example, being given a ratty blanket for her baby when Regina was born (the nicer blankets were allocated to non-Jewish Russian newborns in the maternity wards); and Jewish friends and relatives being denied admittance to universities and jobs. Regina's father, an intellectual, decided to leave the country when he realized that his daughters would not be able to go to college in the Soviet Union because their "race" was Jewish. Emigrating meant leaving family and roots behind, and not knowing if further contact would be allowed, but it was the only hope for a better future for his children. Regina stated that the younger generation wanted to flee toward freedom but they still held on to a sense of abandoning their history of suffering.

From emigration to present day, Regina's identification with both Russian and Jewish suffering continued. She viewed herself as a shameful immigrant who had to climb her way up in a world that could never belong to her. Despite freedom to celebrate Jewish holidays openly in the United States and a growing yet tentatively held open identification with her Judaism, she remained fearful of prejudice. She was adamant that adopting a sense of rightful belonging would be like learning a new language and that self-compassion was unfathomable. Regina's postimmigration history did not yet have a hopeful narrative and held few threads of acknowledged adaptive resolution. Glimpses of a future orientation came only with Regina's guarded hope that her children might feel the right to enjoy their American citizenship and thrive in this culture.

### Listening to the Affective Narrative

Regina's storytelling in treatment was marked by states of hyper- and hypoarousal, alternating between flattened affect, self-denigrating remarks, and irritable, fearful affect concerning her own and her children's safety. Tenderness emerged over time when the therapist encouraged her toward nurturing of the traumatized child and adolescent self.

Psychoeducation was a central part of history taking and preparation. Eventually, Regina began the process of threading together her affective narrative in a more coherent and regulated manner. The therapist assisted in this process by normalizing the patients reactions by informing her that people whose parents suffered trauma often transmitted their pain or distress to their children. The therapist further conveyed that therapy could aid in disentangling her parents' traumatic history from her own, and that identification and processing of transgenerational themes could give way to the expansion of her identity. This information gave Regina a sense of the possibility of healing.

As therapy progressed, Regina was able to recognize and identify her parents' anxious affect, triggers, and behaviors. In so doing, she also recognized that she had been mirroring their affect and behavior, and took stock of her own triggers.

### Emerging Themes, Negative Beliefs, and Adaptations to Transgenerational Trauma

The following themes emerged over the transgenerational history taking and intake process. These themes are common for second generation survivors of anti-Semitic atrocities and manifested in Regina's life in the following ways:

- *Ruptures, discontinuities, and disconnects:* Regina's parents and grandparents had to uproot, flee from pogroms and threats of concentration camps, and ultimately rupture ties to their homeland. During her Russian childhood, Regina's life was marked by discontinuity from generational Jewish traditions and narratives, and later, disconnections between her background and American culture.
- *Lack of differentiation of traumas:* Regina's early narratives were marked by jumpiness between her great grandparent's pogrom history, grandparent's war trauma history, her own molestation, and other immigration-related traumas, the witnessing of 9/11, and subsequent traumatic experiences.
- *Lack of magnitude differential between events, adverse experiences, and massive trauma:* Regina described that if someone in her family fell and sprained an ankle, the "crisis" was responded to with the same intensity of anxious and fearful affect as if someone had been violently attacked.

- *Lack of perceived sense of safety in the world:* For Regina, being a Jew meant that she and her fellow Jewish citizens were always in danger of being hated, shamed, discriminated against, and even killed.
- *Inability to be soothed or to provide soothing:* Suffering, rather than soothing, was a Russian cultural norm. Soothing was also withheld by others as represented by the dirty blanket given to Regina's mother to wrap her baby in at the hospital at birth. Regina's identification with the nondeserving, unsoothed, shameful Jewish baby contributed to her sense that she lacked the capacity to provide adequate soothing to her own children.
- *Sense of helplessness and powerlessness:* This was transmitted from prior generations' experiences with anti-Semitism, expressed in Regina's parents' helpless nonverbal responses to being wounded in school by anti-Semitic incidents, her molestation at age 13, and later, in Regina's lack of felt sense of agency at work and with her children.
- *Defectiveness pervading lifelong identity:* Shame was the manifestation of internalized stigma related to generational shaming about one's identification as Jewish, expressing itself later in Regina's generalized sense of being different and inferior to Americans' bold, deserving, and competent stances.
- *Diminished expectation of pleasure and joy:* For Regina, opportunities to experience joy were scarce. Pleasure and joy were not affects particularly valued by or modeled within Russian culture. Regina was also unable to access or recall felt or expressed acts of triumph in her own family of origin.

These themes can be conceptualized as belonging to one of three categories: defectiveness, danger, or helplessness. For Regina, these themes expressed themselves in the following NCs: "I am not good enough, I don't deserve joy, I don't belong, I am in danger, and I am helpless." Dominant (and generational) defensive/adaptive structures and symptoms related to these themes were conceptualized as follows: Defectiveness schemas were associated with Regina's adaptations of avoidance, numbed affect, identity as sufferer, and diminished ability to experience joy; danger schemas were associated with adaptations of hypervigilance, anticipation of danger and catastrophic experiences, narrative fragmentations, and repetitions; helplessness schemas were linked to symptoms of surrender (self-annihilation) alternating with rage (alienating others), dissociation, and a foreshortened sense of future.

## Treatment Planning, Finding Targets and Reprocessing

At this stage of treatment, safety and self-regulation in the office had been established, and the uncovering of family/generational patterns had helped Regina to begin to differentiate between past and present. She and the therapist were then able to collaborate upon a treatment plan to address the original presenting symptoms (major depression and anxiety) within the context of a broader recognition of the generational origins of some of these learned adaptations. Targets for reprocessing experiences of joylessness, anxiety, and helplessness had been identified during history taking while others emerged as new hidden or unprocessed generational "nodes" during reprocessing sessions.

The following descriptions and synopses are from three reprocessing sessions that took place while the treatment plan focused upon Regina's symptoms of depression. The sessions illustrate how the processing of theme-based, relevant targets by second generation trauma survivors can proceed toward adaptive resolution marked by the reclaiming of what was lost and expansion of identity. The authors note, through use of italics in parentheses, the times during sessions when transgenerational themes were being processed.

## Synopsis of EMDR Treatment Plan

The symptom focus for the part of treatment described was depression/joylessness. The recent experience/picture identified was sitting in a dark room in her house on a beautiful day while it was bright outside. The NC was Joy is dangerous (*transgenerational*). "I am incapable of joy," and the Positive Cognition (PC) was "I can learn to generate joy in my life and the life of my family."

Float backs led to identification of several target memories, ranging from 7 years old through adulthood, which were linked by the negative core belief. Regina's future goal was to be capable of rising above the trauma and suffering to experiencing joyous moments. It took some time for Regina to come up with a future goal; initially, a life without suffering was not an option as her suffering identity shielded her from vulnerability and further possibilities of being shamed or endangered. This tie to the adaptation, also conceived of as a blocking belief, was verbally processed before continuing with the treatment plan.

The touchstone memory was being timid and afraid in school ". . . I have to be careful not to get picked on. I was Jewish, different, I couldn't be free and playful like the other kids." The representative image for this touchstone target was watching the other children playing; the associated NC, "The joy that's out there is not meant for me. I am stifled and joyless"; and the PC, "I am free to feel joy today." The Validity of Cognition was 3, the emotion sadness, the Subjective Units of Disturbances (SUDs) an 8, and her body sensations were "in my chest, like my breath is taken away."

Between sets, Regina's feedback to the therapist, prompted by "What are you with now?" included the following: "You have to be very careful, quiet, and not show joy because you're Jewish (*generational*). If I'm joyful, they'll kick the shit out of me. No one was joyful in my family; no stories of joy" (*generational*). During the next sets, Regina began to reflect on the "sadness and awfulness" of these types of experiences and tearfully related a more recent memory of her mother's friend saying (about non-Jews): "They don't know what we know; at any moment, things can go bad" (*generational*). She then linked to a potential adaptive network: "My friend's father took him for boxing lessons. He was able to express the injustice. If I could've boxed, I'd feel more powerful and in charge of my own safety. I needed to develop something—physical strength—to be in a position to beat someone up. The feeling of not being able to stand up to anyone was institutionalized. My father couldn't get his PhD because he was Jewish. My grandpa was beaten up in a food line because someone called him 'Jew' (*generational*)." Regina's associations included memories of her parents' helplessness in the face of injustice and her own experiences watching Russian and Holocaust films depicting anti-Semitic atrocities. A few sets later,

Regina linked into a positive network: "You know, I've been thinking about boxing for a long time and imagine it would feel quite good . . . better than being helpless."

Regina came in the following week and stated, "I'd like to go to a Mikvah (Jewish ritual bath). It's about being Jewish . . . an attempt at repair, healing, reclaiming self and self-identity, returning to my roots in a Jewish community . . . these tears are about getting older, my life passing by. I have great kids; where was I? I never knew. I was in my own self-centered mode of misery."

Regina's processing and reflection had clearly continued between sessions. Her expressed wish to go to a mikvah seemed to indicate that she had accessed pretrauma intergenerational memories of Jewish ritual and identity, enabling a reclaiming of her own partially lost Jewish identity. Regina's guilt about not having had more access to these healing and joyful feelings while raising her children may have been generational guilt—Regina's parents and grandparents had to hide their Jewish identity for long periods of time, unwittingly depriving their children of the possibilities of joy in their heritage.

Regina continued by relating a fantasy that connected her to a previously disavowed community: "I would have made a great Rabbi's wife . . . I have the skills to be in this role, to build a community. In my life, I never got to be the nurturer. Being the Rabbi's wife, the 'mother' of the community . . . it's all over me, it's what I'm capable of. I was a really nice girl, then shit happened. . . . You know, I may take tango lessons . . . I made some phone calls to find dance studios." A sense of playfulness and anticipated joy had come to consciousness.

When the therapist returned her to the incompletely reprocessed target, Regina's SUDs had gone down to 6 and the sadness she felt was related to what her childhood should have been, stating "It's like the after-taste of war and struggle. I was never part of the war but it's still in the air (*generational*)." During reprocessing, Regina tapped into positive neural networks. She recalled a fourth grade Jewish teacher who was joyful and whom she admired; reported that the words, "It's going to be okay," began to superimpose and then infuse many of her own traumatic memories and calm her body; stated "I was a beautiful woman who could've done a million things. I got in my own way . . . others knew I could rise to the top but I acted like I couldn't." Between sets she described how she had felt like a wanderer (*generational*) who had stopped looking for a herd, and how she hoped that her daughter would pay attention to models of resilient women like Cheryl Sandberg. She imagined herself serving as one of those resilient women, feeling strong and confident enough to look in the mirror and say (quoting a *Saturday Night Live* character skit), "I am good enough, I am smart enough, I am worth it."

During this reprocessing session, Regina described a new perspective on the impact anti-Semitism had on her sense of worth, differentiated between her own and her parents' trauma, linked to memories and thoughts of joyful and resilient Jewish role models with whom she could identify, and began to imagine and playfully step into an image of herself as a more confident woman in her current life. It continued to be of central importance to Regina that she be able to impart this sense of herself to her children.

During the third session, Regina reported that her daughter had begun to openly express anger at her; she recognized this open expression of anger as an important departure from her family's history of numbing and detachment from rage. Regina also reported binge watching movies about the Holocaust, looking for answers ". . . Could it have been different? The anxiety, the fear, the angst, could my parents have done it differently? Will my kids get something different?" Regina particularly reflected on the film *Life Is Beautiful*, where a father shields his son from the pain and anguish of the Holocaust. "My parents couldn't do it, they were incapable but I needed and deserved nurturing."

When the target memory was reaccessed, the SUDs had dropped to a 4. Between sets, Regina linked to childhood memories of sitting on her grandmother's lap, feeling helpless as she was told stories of hiding while Jewish men were slaughtered, and of a younger brother's death related to poverty. Regina recounted the story of her great grandmother crying for well beyond the 30 days, which marks the end of the initial period of Jewish mourning. Regina's reaction to these stories was, "How can I have joy when there's so much anger and grief in my past, so much death and torture?" ". . . Your parents couldn't help you, the government is abusing you, the neighbors are anti-Semitic." She began to express anger about her own legacy of helplessness. The session ended with Regina deliberating over her right to express anger at her parents, recognizing they were traumatized children and were themselves linked to generations of "helpless children walking through the desert and war zones." She then shifted to an empathic stance with them and ultimately with herself, relating through bittersweet tears, "They deserved joy. Maybe **I** deserve joy?"

At the close of the session, Regina stated that watching Holocaust-themed films was an empowering experience for her, noting an emerging sense of identification and belongingness. Through tears, she said, "I hear other people's stories, it doesn't end with them. Someone's hearing their stories. There's something very important about this. I'm looking for solutions. How did they survive?" The therapist was humbled by the injunction she probably would have given Regina not to put herself at risk for retraumatization by watching the films. In this moment, Regina brought the therapist in as a cowitness to the trauma so that they could jointly acknowledge that these horrors happened and validate the unfathomable pain.

Regina continued to immerse herself in her ancestral history of anti-Semitism and began to differentiate herself from those who suffered before her. She consciously directed herself to joyful and peaceful experiences, seeking alternative solutions to her own generational alienation and joylessness. Regina gradually reentered the work world with a different stance, even surprising herself to find she was acting at times like a "nonalarmist American" both in her professional and family life.

Through continued processing of targets, Regina's adaptations have been shifting from a passive defensive structure of helplessness, for example, "It's useless to fight back" to a more active stance of speaking the truth of her history, and shaping future dreams with a sense of healthy entitlement. Regina has begun to ask herself, "What will bring me joy?" She recently stated, ". . . Maybe I have a little sense of excitement, maybe it's not the end of the world, maybe I can thrive . . . . maybe I can do it. . . ." She then proudly recounted a recent incident in which she delivered a sense of hopefulness and future orientation to a despairing family member of a previous generation. This shift away from comingling with depression to being a messenger of hope delighted Regina.

## SUMMARY

For patients with intergenerational trauma histories that include oppression, war, genocide, and immigration to a new culture, it is important to develop a treatment plan that includes attention to the patient's affective and cognitive narratives of this history. It is recommended that the EMDR therapist widen the lens during history taking, preparation, and case conceptualization beyond the patient's individual trauma experiences to identify possible transmission of transgenerational wounding and related themes for EMDR processing targets. Suggestions are made for how the therapist can assist the second generation patient toward the development of a coherent and regulated narrative that includes preoppression generational experiences, parental trauma experiences, and posttrauma adaptations and resources. If there are gaps in historical knowledge, it is recommended that the therapist and patient educate themselves regarding the cultural context in which the generational trauma occurred. The clinical case illustrated in this chapter described the treatment of a second generation patient whose family survived Ukranian pogroms, World War II, rampant anti-Semitic atrocities, and immigration-related trauma. The themes and treatment issues identified are generalizable to other stigmatized populations with cultural variants.

## REFERENCES


American Psychiatric Association. (2013). *Diagnostic and statistical manual of mental disorders* (5th ed.). Arlington, VA: American Psychiatric Publishing.

Brothers, D. (2014). Traumatic attachments: Intergenerational trauma, dissociation, and the analytic relationship. *International Journal of Psychoanalytic Self Psychology*, 9, 3–15.

Coyle, S. (2014). Intergenerational trauma—Legacies of loss. *Social Work Today*, 14(3), 18.

Danieli, Y. (Ed.). (1998). *International handbook of multigenerational legacies of trauma*. New York, NY: Plenum Press.

Diorio, J., & Meaney, M. J. (2007). Maternal programming of defensive responses through sustained effects on gene expression. *Journal of Psychiatry and Neuroscience, 32*(4), 275–284.

Jasienska, G. (2009). Low birth weight of contemporary African Americans: An intergenerational effect of slavery? *American Journal of Human Biology, 21*, 16–24.

Kestenberg, J. (1982). A metapsychological assessment based on an analysis of a survivor's child. In M. S. Bergman & M. E. Jucovy (Eds.), *Generations of the Holocaust*. New York, NY: Basic Books.

Laub, D. (1998). The empty circle: Children of survivors and the limits of reconstruction. *Journal of the American Psychoanalytic Association, 46*, 507–529.

Lev-Wiesel, R. (2007). Intergenerational transmission of trauma across three generations. *Qualitative Social Work, 6*(1), 75–94.

Nagata, D. K. (1990). The Japanese American internment: Exploring the transgenerational consequences of traumatic stress. *Journal of Traumatic Stress, 3*, 47–69.

Nickerson, M. (2010). *Undoing stigma: EMDR applications in the dismantling of socially based internalized oppression and prejudice: Theory, examples and practicum*. Presented at the EMDR International Association conference.

Salberg, J. (2015). The texture of traumatic attachment: Presence and ghostly absence in transgenerational transmission. *Psychoanalytic Quarterly, 84*(1), 21–46.

Shabad, P. (1993). Repetition and incomplete mourning: The intergenerational transmission of traumatic themes. *Psychoanalytic Quarterly, 10(1)*, 61–75.

Yehuda, R., Bierer, L. M., Schmeidler, J., Aferiat, D. H., Breslau, I., & Dolan, S. (2000). Low cortisol and risk for PTSD in adult offspring of Holocaust survivors. *American Journal of Psychiatry, 157*(8), 1252–1259.

Yehuda, R., Engel, S. M., Brand, S. R., Secki, J., Marcus, S. M., & Berkowitz, G. S. (2005). Transgenerational effects of posttraumatic stress disorder in babies of mothers exposed to the World Trade Center attacks during pregnancy. *Journal of Clinical Endocrinology & Metabolism, 90*, 4115–4118. doi:10. 1210/jc.2005-0550

CHAPTER 15

# Left Out and Left Behind: EMDR and the Cultural Construction of Intellectual Disability

Joseph C. Yaskin and Andrew J. Seubert

People with intellectual disability (ID) are excluded from life experiences that people perceived as nondisabled take for granted. Their social and economic exclusions are the results of commonly held attitudes and beliefs about the population so embedded in social structure, public policy, and family behavior that they persist despite decades of reform and advocacy efforts. The tenacity of negative bias toward people with ID is rooted in their construction as a surplus population and a community burden (Farber, 1967). Historically, people with ID were identified as disabled "because they failed to adapt socially to their environment" (Schalock et al., 2007). People with ID, then, are left out and left behind (Cummins & Lau, 2003).

The authors intend this chapter to complement an emerging body of research that points to eye movement desensitization and reprocessing (EMDR) as an effective treatment for trauma in the ID population. Excerpts of clinical process are presented, not only to illustrate, but also to encourage the reader to replace culturally grounded negative stereotypes (usually unrealized or, at least, unnoticed) with a compassionate and humane understanding of people with ID as *individuals*. In their own work facilitating trauma repair with individuals identified as intellectually disabled, the authors observed that the label itself had a deterministic effect, creating a chain of common adverse life experiences that kindled into trauma. Herein lies the challenge—and the opportunity—for clinicians practicing EMDR therapy. We invite our colleagues to take part in repairing psychic harm, deeply embedded, from a dysfunctional and disabling cultural script, one person at a time.

## CONCEPTS AND PREMISES

The authors' common clinical experience has led them to the conviction, validated in the research literature, that people with ID have rich internal lives, yet suffer from mental illnesses in general (Bouras & Szymanski, 1997; Emerson, 2003), including trauma (Doyle & Mitchell, 2003). A significant body of research in peer-reviewed literature supports the authors' convictions implicit in this chapter, namely that (a) people with ID suffer mental illness co-occurring with ID, (b) adverse life experiences of people with ID kindle symptoms of trauma (Martorell & Tsakanikos, 2008), and (c) psychotherapeutic treatment is effective in this underserved population (Thompson Prout & Browning, 2011; Willner, 2005).

The therapist treating a person with ID for trauma will notice that the cultural construction of his or her disability, and consequent stigma, is *lived* and remembered, persistent and ever present in every domain of treatment. It is part of the trauma history itself and complicates the establishment of internal resources, relationships with caregivers, and the quest to satisfy hopes and aspirations. It can also be present in the therapeutic dyad, requiring the therapist to explore transference and countertransference due to the internalization of the cultural construction. The authors found that, throughout the eight phases of EMDR psychotherapy, and particularly during trauma processing, many clients with ID challenged their cultural construction as they built an improved sense of self, never established in early development. Reprocessing trauma required clients (particularly those in the mild range of disability) to confront their shame story, the false belief that they *are* their disability and that the disability *defines* their potential. This case of mistaken identity between self and disability (Seubert, in Shapiro, 2005) typically colors the self-perception of the client and often the therapist's perception of the client as well.

The fields of disability studies and medical anthropology present disability as an *idea*, a cultural construction, where functional limitation and impairment are not biological constants, but environmental variables, mediated by context, including culture (Anastasiou & Kauffman, 2013). The authors acknowledge that social construction of people with ID varies by culture, as does the cultural construction of mental illness in people with disability (Littlewood, 2006). Negative beliefs prevailing in Western culture about people with IDs include ideas that they are a burden, that they are dangerous, that they are strange, and that they don't have emotions (Scior, 2011).

## THE PRESENTING ISSUE: CONTRIBUTION OF CULTURAL CONSTRUCTS TO THE TRAUMA BURDEN

While processing experiences of exclusion from childhood milestones and rites of passage, our clients recalled the hurt—experienced like it was yesterday—of life events, like a younger brother who got his driving permit, while the clients were always "escorted." They were often placed in "special" classes and segregated elsewhere. These clients knew, and mourned for, what they missed (e.g., "That cute girl/handsome boy in the house across the street? Not for me!"). These clients knew there was something not right with them. They talked about being excluded, and they knew they were missing important life experiences that brought identity and meaning. Greenwald wrote that risk for trauma is mediated by temperament, attachment status, and proximity to the event. It must also include grief, loss, and life changes as a result of the trauma (Greenwald, 2007). In this context, we understand that childhood losses resulting from the cultural construction of the disability are risk factors for adult trauma.

Clients with ID treated by the authors suffered repeated and varied negative life experiences that kindled into a cluster of symptoms now widely understood as complex trauma (Herman, 1992). This term, not specific to people with

ID, "describes both children's exposure to multiple traumatic events, often of an invasive, interpersonal nature, and the wide-ranging, long-term impact of this exposure" (Complex Trauma | National Child Traumatic Stress Network—Child Trauma Home, 2015). Consistent with this and other descriptions of that long-term impact, primary trauma features presenting among our clients were deficits in self-regulation, including problems with anger and anxiety management, disordered attachment patterns, and aggressive behaviors. With these impairments, trauma becomes another developmental disorder (Cloitre et al., 2009), adding to the challenges of ID.

Part of the burden of trauma, particularly complex trauma, is the internal narrative—the stories people tell themselves, about themselves—to make sense of a traumatic experience (Newman, Riggs, & Roth, 1997). The story builds over time, and through development: "I'm broken," "I am invisible," "I am worthless," "I'm a loser, hopeless, helpless." These negative beliefs are interwoven with reexperiencing of both traumatic events and the accompanying feeling-states to create a story that slips in and out of awareness, originally a strategy for coping, later a counterproductive dysfunction.

The authors suggest that lived, day-to-day experience internalizes the prevailing, negative cultural construction of people with ID. It follows, then, that these harmful cultural constructions increase the vulnerability of people with ID to complex trauma. Some research suggests that people with ID may be at a greater risk of developing posttraumatic stress disorder (PTSD) consequent to traumatic life events (Wigwam, Taylor, & Halton, 2014). Lived experience (dictated, in large part, by stigma encoded into social structures) reinforces the internalized belief that the person with ID is "other" and "useless" (Jahoda, Wilson, Stalker, & Cairney, 2010). The child with ID experiences that cultural introject (onto both self and family) as unspoken shame, which leads to the internalization of the stigma (Crocker & Major, 1989).

## CASE ILLUSTRATION: THE FACE OF COMPLEX TRAUMA IN AN ADOLESCENT WITH INTELLECTUAL DISABILITY

We present a case review of a young man we will call Mitchell, illustrating the burden of shame associated with negative cultural construction kindling into trauma. The case also demonstrates adaptations of EMDR therapy to cognitive impairment. Mitchell, 19, was born with Down syndrome. He struggled to finish high school in a rural, small town in northern Pennsylvania. With an emerging sense of loss, Mitchell watched as his older brother mastered school subjects, succeeded as captain of his football team, and attracted the most popular girls in school. His younger sister, also quite intelligent and socially comfortable, left Mitchell behind developmentally. Mitchell noticed all of this and internalized a shame-based stigma (Ali, Hassiotis, Strydom, & King, 2012).

> "She's only 16!" he exclaimed. "I'm two years older. She can drive our car, and I still can't! When's my turn?!"

His parents had nothing left to say. No excuses, no promises. "I know it's not fair," his mother would sometimes reply. "But life isn't always fair." She had nothing else to say.

And then there was the "girlfriend," or Mitchell's fantasized girlfriend. She was perky, confident, and sexy. She danced with Mitchell one time at a high school dance. He fell for her. Misunderstanding a brief dance with a classmate, Mitchell attributed meaning to the encounter that reflected his loneliness and need, not reality. Mitchell was convinced that the sophomore was "his girl." Until he saw her holding hands with a nondisabled friend.

Mitchell turned to the black-and-white thinking that people with complex trauma employ to manage emotional overwhelm. "She hates me! I know it. Why does it always happen this way?" he half questioned his therapist, who felt as helpless as his parents often did.

Mitchell's story, the one he told himself, got darker, more discouraging. "Mainstreamed" into his local schools (i.e., not segregated from able classmates), Mitchell never quite fit in. Family, friends, caregivers, and teachers treated him kindly, sparing him the teasing and bullying that children with ID often endure (Horner-Johnson & Drum, 2006). But Mitchell saw his peers pass through the milestones culturally identified with the transition from adolescence to adulthood. As their lives moved on, Mitchell's did not. High school was a series of disappointments and painful experiences.

## Preparation Phase

Various aspects of EMDR treatment were translated from established protocols into concrete terms for Mitchell. For example, he learned to describe his subjective distress by spreading his hands apart. The greater the distance, the greater the pain. Hands brought together in a prayer-like posture meant the disturbance was gone. For the most part, Mitchell was not able to use the scales for Subjective Units of Disturbance (SUD) and Validity of Cognition (VoC). They were too confusing for him, so they were combined into one scale: 0 to 10. Zero, in his terms, stood for "sucky." Ten indicated "peachy."

At times Mitchell and his therapist used eye movements, but mostly they employed an electronic device that provided bilateral stimulation through sound and vibration. Images representing feelings were drawn on paper and laid out on the floor (most of the sessions were floor based, with Mitchell and his therapist sitting across from each other). Mitchell had the most trouble tolerating the "something's wrong with me" feeling (aka shame). Photos, newspaper clips, and other resources were also spread out on the floor. Anytime Mitchell wanted to indicate a feeling or to access a positive resource to balance and tolerate strong affect, but didn't feel like verbalizing, he only needed to point.

## Treatment Phase

The stage was set after a few months of preparation. Mitchell felt badly because his best friend, Justin, and his family went on a trip to Disney World without him. Justin, also born with Down syndrome, was 1 year Mitchell's senior. Justin and Mitchell—and their families—were previously inseparable. Mitchell, his shame activated, interpreted his exclusion from the Disney trip as a painful rejection.

In treatment, Mitchell was asked to imagine Justin's family in Florida, enjoying Disney World, without him. Because it was difficult for Mitchell to focus on anything for too long, much less something uncomfortable, the therapist spoke to Mitchell during the processing. The therapist also returned to the original target image frequently, to sustain Mitchell's attention. These adjustments were adaptations of standard EMDR protocols to accommodate the client's disability. Further adaptations included the spreading of hands to communicate intensity of distress. Additionally, the therapist didn't insist on establishing negative/positive cognitions since Mitchell was reluctant to process this event and the therapist wanted to keep Mitchell in touch with the "something's wrong with me" feeling. Cognitions would arise and be recognized spontaneously during the processing.

Seubert utilized eye movements, and, within 10 to 12 sets of bilateral eye movement, Mitchell declared that he felt really good ("peachy") even when he thought of Justin at Disney World. Then, as Mitchell was about to leave, Mom entered.

> "I think Mitchell is doing much better," the therapist told her.
> "But what's going to happen when Justin's family gets back and shows all those photos with Mitchell missing in all of them?" she replied.
> There were no options here. The therapist elected to support processing with EMDR on the spot, leaving aside the standard protocol.

**Therapist:** "Your mom's got a point, Mitchell. How about you just stand there, imagine a photo of Justin's family in Disney World and you're not in the picture. And then just follow my hand back and forth."

**Mitchell:** "Sure!"

Standing there in the doorway, Mom looking on, they did four sets of eye movements. After each, Mitchell felt better. He pushed his therapist's outspread hands closer together to indicate his relief, incremental with each set. After four sets, Mitchell looked at his therapist, smiled, and pushed his hands completely together. "I just love Justin!" By facing this future feared event, Mitchell's love for his disabled friend was able to trump the shame of perceived rejection.

## CLINICAL CONSIDERATION: THE CULTURAL CONSTRUCTION AND DIAGNOSTIC OVERSHADOWING

The majority culture tags an individual who has an ID with *stigma* that discredits the true complexity of his or her identity and reduces the bearer "from a whole and usual person to a tainted, discounted one" (Goffman, 2009). Consequent to stigma, population-level neglect by exclusion from all kinds of social goods continues (Nibert, 1995). Particularly harmful is exclusion from equal access to health care. The price people with ID pay for unequal access to health care is represented in studies that identified diverse negative health outcomes, from higher prevalence of obesity (Bhaumik, Watson, Thorp, Tyrer, & McGrother, 2008) to higher incidence of premature death (Heslop et al., 2014). The research literature also shows that the generalization of ID into an all-inclusive diagnosis is a significant cause of inequalities in mental health care (Chaplin, 2011).

The phenomenon of dismissed psychiatric symptoms is described in the literature with the term *diagnostic overshadowing* (Jopp & Keys, 2001). People with ID must deal with a milieu of caregivers who see depression, anxiety, adjustment disorders, and PTSD as attributes of the ID diagnosis. In this reductionist framework, a person's suffering and psychiatric symptoms are reduced to blunt behavior management strategies that employ operant conditioning, psychiatric medication, or both. Behavior management with psychiatric medication, but with no diagnosis supporting the psychiatrist's medication choice, remains common. Over and over, attending psychiatrists, who were gatekeepers of admission to inpatient care, denied access to clients of the first author, rationalizing the exclusion from needed care with statements along the lines of, "We have observed the patient for more than 24 hours, and we don't see any evidence of psychiatric illness. We only observed Axis II conditions. *It's just behavior.*"

## DIAGNOSTIC OVERSHADOWING: SYMPTOM PRESENTATION

People with ID and psychiatric disorders are often undiagnosed because the symptoms look different from standard symptom presentation. Psychiatric symptoms are often expressed as behavior (Bobińska, Florkowski, Smigielski, & Gałecki, 2009). Given impaired awareness of—and limited ability to express—internal experience, clients with ID often act out with behavior destructive to themselves, or to others, or to property. Concern among clinicians about widespread deficits in accurate differential diagnoses—specifically, failure to identify disordered behavior as a symptom of psychiatric illness—led to the creation of a new psychiatric classification system devised specifically for use with adults with IDs, the DC-LD (Cooper, Melville, & Einfeld, 2003).

## THE LEGACY OF ABUSE

The consequences of challenging behavior misattributed to the ID diagnosis, harmful to today, were often catastrophic in the era of institutional care. Memories of coercive, inhumane interventions haunt those of us who witnessed the harm. The second author remembers Tammy, a client living in an institution where the author consulted many years ago. Tammy was diagnosed with ID and labeled with "anger management problems," attributed to the ID diagnosis. Her anger was part of the temperament of a woman with strong feelings and a lively spirit. However, her anger was uncontrollable at times and perceived as an untreatable danger to caretakers. The recommended treatment was a lobotomy. Tammy was never again the same, no longer angry and no longer functioning as she had before. Another client, Jane, was a resident of the same institution. Presenting with outbursts of anger and sadness, her behavior plan to manage outbursts was restraint and dousing with spray bottles. This continued until the behavior, viewed as part of Jane's ID profile rather than as an emotional communication, ceased.

People with ID suffered population level, institutionalized abuse that persisted from the late 19th century into the 1970s. That abuse included medical experimentation and forced sterilization. While these and other extreme practices of abuse are now viewed culturally as unacceptable, stigma, grounded in negative generalizations about this population, persists today, as does maltreatment (Horner-Johnson & Drum, 2006).

## CLINICAL CONSIDERATION: CULTURAL CONSTRUCTION AND DISSOCIATION

The authors hypothesize that dissociation, pathological type, is a common adaptive mechanism in the population of people with ID and co-occurring trauma. While this is certainly the case in our own practice histories, we present this hypothesis with some caution, given the absence of support in the research literature. Nevertheless, we suggest that the EMDR therapist treating people with ID and co-occurring trauma without assessing for dissociative disorders risks overlooking a critical factor, while opening the doors to potential, emotional, and even physical harm. Failure to identify dissociation can derail the treatment process, even when dissociation presents in its more mild and common forms.

### Case Illustration: Jamie

Jamie was a 35-year-old female client of our first author. The author's failure to pick up on Jamie's severe dissociation almost led to physical harm, potentially even death. By installing a *safe place* resource, the author thought he would be on solid ground as he guided Jamie through what was planned as two brief sets of reinforcing eye movements—her first experience of bilateral stimulation. At the start of the second set, Jamie's affect changed from open and smiling (she was remembering comfort from her grandmother) to terror, eyes downcast, facial muscles clenched. She suddenly appeared much younger than her chronological age. This presentation lasted just a moment—then Jamie was gone from the treatment room, and out the front door of the human services agency. A moment later, there was the sound of a vehicle honking and an extraordinarily loud screech of brakes coming from the street. The author found himself outside the front door, watching Jamie as she stood in front of a pickup truck, clinging to the driver, sobbing and screaming.

Later, the therapist learned that Jamie's memory of affection from her grandmother associated to her a subsequent return home where her mother took jealous revenge on her by scalding her with boiling water. Jamie later said that she felt herself "leaving my body" as the second set of eye movement began, and then reexperienced mom's abuse as an event occurring here and now—some 30 years after the abuse occurred. She had no memory of running out of the office and throwing herself in front of traffic. In Jamie's internal experience, she was not a grown woman, 35, fleeing a therapy session to throw herself in front of a pickup truck. Jamie's action was driven by the intrusion of an ego state that maintained separate awareness, stuck at 5 years old, suffering intolerable terror, containing it so that Jamie, as she experienced herself day to day, could survive. Jamie's symptoms, at the most severe end of the dissociative spectrum, fit the definition for dissociative identity disorder (DID). It was once thought that DID and ID were mutually exclusive because of the intelligence presumed necessary to maintain ego states that exclude each other from awareness. The authors' clinical experience seems to indicate the opposite.

This case reinforces the point that complex trauma impairs not just an individual's emotional development, but also—with a dissociative system established to tolerate terror—the structure of self, creating a compounded vulnerability for people with ID. Recent conceptualizations of dissociation have refined what was once thought a spectrum into "a dichotomy between two qualitatively different phenomena: detachment (an altered state of consciousness with a felt sense of alienation) and compartmentalization (an inability to bring normally accessible information to consciousness)" (Holmes et al., 2005). Van der Kolk represented dissociation as a phenomenon that is, at once, a memory disorder and also a functional adaptation for surviving intolerable terror, on a spectrum with other adaptations, such as PTSD and somatization (van der Kolk & Fisler, 1995). Given our expanded understanding of "trauma," clients with ID experience innumerable moments of emotional pain and discouragement. It then stands to reason that these clients would employ various forms and degrees of dissociation, usually undetected due to the reality of diagnostic overshadowing. Where there is trauma, there is, most often, dissociation.

## Case Study: Vanessa

A severe level of dissociation also appeared in Vanessa, a 25-year-old female who was referred to the second author because of what had been described as "lying and game playing in order to get attention." Also mildly disabled, Vanessa, like James, had little awareness of her emotions, and little tolerance for states of anxiety and panic.

When triggered, Vanessa, out of desperation, "cried for help" in the only way she knew, threatening self-harm and/or suicide. In those moments, as the second author discovered, she stared like the proverbial deer in the headlight, her posture froze, and she perseverated continuously, "I don't want to go back! I hate it there! I have to be punished!"

When Vanessa quieted down, she sometimes remembered the flashback she had just experienced (dissociation presenting as depersonalization) and sometimes did not (dissociation with a shift in ego state and amnesia, similar to Jamie, the client who reexperienced childhood abuse during a safe-place installation). Her parents informed the second author that she had talked about her victimization in high school, where she was lured into having sex with an older boy, whom Vanessa had regarded as the love of her life. The following day he called the relationship off and slept with her best friend.

Vanessa's dissociated reexperiencing was not a feature of ID presenting as behavior. It was unfinished business, "talked about" with other therapists, but with attendance neither to the dissociative symptoms of PTSD, nor to the underlying emotional harm. At present, the author continues to explore ways of helping Vanessa stay present, which requires: (a) being conscious of entering different states, (b) an awareness of early warning signals of dissociation, and (c) the ability to manage and to experience emotions (Chu, Dell, van der Hart, & Cardeña, 2011).

The first author, treating people with dissociative presentations of PTSD and ID in community settings, saw dissociative reexperiencing set off allegations of abuse against paid caregivers in a half-dozen incidents, involving three clients in a period of 5 years. The scenario, in all six cases: Overnight, the client had a nightmare where past abuse was reexperienced, and the reexperiencing continued in a dissociated, semiwakeful state, with absorption. Still in a state of dissociative absorption, the client reported that abuse (usually, sexual assault) had just happened when the morning caregiver came in to relieve overnight staff. In each of the six incidents, the allegations against the night staff were found to be without merit, but only after the caregiver was suspended while the incident was investigated. The abuse had actually taken place, just not at the time the client reported it. The client's dissociated sense of time and present reality confused past with present, dream state with daylight. Abuse had occurred, but earlier in life, in other settings. The point being that the clients weren't lying, nor did abuse take place at the hands of the staff. A necessary adaptation of trauma therapy with these clients to create a sense of actual safety was an arrangement in which treatment sessions were conducted with a third party present and instructed to keep the therapist and the client in constant line of sight.

## CLINICAL CONSIDERATION: THE CAREGIVING WORLD AND ATTACHMENT

For clinicians new to providing psychotherapy to people with ID, the authors strongly recommend a person-in-environment approach, where the intervening clinician learns about the people who care for the individual and perhaps engage them as (potential) supporters in the trauma recovery process. Competence treating attachment disorders is also helpful because they are often the root cause of the "challenging" behavior cited as the reason for referral to treatment. People with ID depend on other people in a way that the majority population does not. Most depend on family or professional caregivers for significant help with activities of daily living (ADLs). A consequence of the need for care is that people with ID rarely have significant control over their environment. They live with their families of origin through adulthood, or they are placed in community homes with agencies that often give lip service to choice, while giving a person placed in their care only a limited opportunity to choose where or with whom they live. The intervening clinician may find that attitudes and beliefs of family and professional caregivers create an emotionally unsafe environment for the client, complicating and extending the stabilization stage of treatment. The therapist may or may not have an opportunity to intervene in the environment.

The authors encourage a perspective drawn from family systems theory and suggest that the intervening clinician take a carefully considered, yet expansive, view of boundaries. One consequence of the cultural construction of people with ID as less deserving than the general population is that caregivers, including doctors and psychotherapists, often disregard boundaries demanded by ethics and the law. The intervening clinician should be wary of these violations and take care not to collude in them, particularly when colleagues violate the right to privacy in general and HIPAA specifically. The first author, working in the publicly funded community system of care, found these violations commonplace among case managers and providers of residential care. The reader is encouraged to note the client's attachment patterns with caregivers, first, as an indicator of trauma, and, second, as a cause of retraumatization and compromised stability (Cottis, 2008).

Disabled clients with disordered attachment styles (Bowlby, 1980) are vulnerable to attachment rupture when siblings leave home or when parents take a break for a day or two, leaving someone else in charge. When, as often happens, these clients are moved into some form of residence or group home, they may experience the break with family as traumatic. Professional caregivers may become figures in a disordered attachment schema (De Schipper & Schuengel, 2010), where the relationship is doomed to an outcome of disappointment and perceived betrayal. Pathology aside, relationships between a person with ID and paid caregivers are often nurturing and intimate. When paid caregivers leave, the loss can be profound and unacknowledged. Where there is a need for repair of disordered attachment patterns, the circle of support surrounding the disabled person must function as a family like, nurturing structure that provides the secure attachment of Winnicott's "good enough" environment (Winnicott, 1960).

When a caregiver leaves, the caregiving circle must support the individual in processing the loss. The circle of caregivers must grow into something like a family where members understand the language and the needs of its vulnerable brother or sister, the kind of family in which members communicate and support each other and do their own emotional work. The line between healthy interdependence and pathologic reenactment of negative attachment experience can blur when the person with ID has cascaded through his or her life course with repeated attachment ruptures, experienced as trauma, because the need for repair of early attachment experience was never quite met. Both authors saw, over and over again, clients with ID exhausting the caregivers (family members and professionals) they relied on, as attachment distress was acted out through self-injurious and other challenging behaviors.

The person with ID and co-occurring trauma, then, may have disordered patterns of relationships that create tough demands across the entire caregiving network. As mentioned earlier, caregivers must work in close collaboration so that trauma symptoms are understood and addressed with compassion. Therapists providing more than the usual skill building and problem solving for ID clients must consult with and educate parents about trauma symptoms that may look like manipulation to the person providing day-to-day care. Additional teaching is needed to make direct caregivers aware of some of the possible ripple effects of treatment in between sessions (spontaneous processing/flashbacks, irritability, and hypervigilance). With more understanding of an ID client's process, caregivers are more likely to respond to challenging behaviors and reactions with patience and compassion.

Adolescents and adults who continue living with their parents face their own challenges. Attitudes and beliefs in the family may have a negative impact on the individual. For example, complications arise when parents deny the severity of a child's impairment due to their own pain in seeing their child miss out on one developmental milestone after another. Imagine your own child stepping into his or her life with hands and feet chained to heavy weights, as you stand by, watching helplessly as he or she struggles. It is this grief, realizing the life their child will never be able to live, and the powerlessness of it all, that parents of children with ID must face if they are to be emotionally present for their offspring. Other parents may have trouble letting a child with a disability leave the nest, fall, and fly, because a sense of shared vulnerability creates black-and-white thinking about the disability. Parents also experience stress in connection with challenging behavior

(Hassall, Rose, & McDonald, 2005). Clinicians providing interventions may need to support parents and families in letting go of rigid attitudes and beliefs, in embracing their grief and seeing the child with disability as he or she is, with vulnerabilities and resources that change over time. Everyone has the need and potential for self-determination that deserves recognition and validation. But that process can be challenging for caring families where the struggle to adjust is unresolved as the child with disability grows up. It is a very precarious tightrope these parents must walk.

Parents must nurture themselves and their marriage, as well as attend to stress that may present among siblings (Hassall et al., 2005). Agencies must support residential staff, with the need for self-care acknowledged in policy and practice, at all levels of the organization (Bloom, 2013). The intervening clinician may need to facilitate such nurturing and self-care by providing training in related skills and by collaborating with the treatment team to make social support and other appropriate resources available (Devereux, Hastings, Noone, Firth, & Totsika, 2009).

## SUMMARY

This chapter is intended to provide a primer for the EMDR therapist interested in treating posttraumatic stress in people with ID. We have discussed the cultural construction of ID to support clinicians in recognizing environmental challenges to trauma treatment consequent to culturally mediated attitudes and beliefs. The role of these factors in the etiology of trauma is also essential knowledge. The authors intend that their overview of the cultural construction of ID provide the reader with a unifying framework for the clinical considerations of diagnostic overshadowing, dissociation, and disordered attachment/caregiver concerns.

The underlying concept is simple: stigma is toxic. It contributes to health inequalities that leave many people with ID suffering psychiatric symptoms that are misunderstood, incorrectly treated, or not treated at all. Additionally, stigma itself contributes to the burden of psychiatric illness among people with ID, because it feeds the persistent exclusion and neglect that translates to adverse life experience, irreconcilable with a stable sense of self. It is hoped that this chapter prompts renewed attention to the mental health needs of this vulnerable population in general and, in particular, to the need for improved access to care, inclusive of informed, differential diagnostics.

It is also hoped that this chapter suggests directions for future research specific to people with ID. This research must address gaps in knowledge regarding the impact of trauma in the lives of clients with ID, as well as the limited access to trauma treatment for these clients. Research must also support and encourage best practices in the clinical treatment of trauma, including effectiveness and validation studies of adjusted protocols, such as those presented in these pages.

In conclusion, we ask our colleagues: What makes trauma work worthwhile? There is the reward of seeing clients improve. There is the joy of bearing witness to a person's transcendence from suffering and confusion to connection and identity. There is the sacred opportunity to support people in moving from powerlessness and reactivity to some measure of self-efficacy. These are the rich rewards the authors experienced treating people with ID for posttraumatic stress. We invite the reader to let go of any limiting beliefs about individuals with ID, and, instead, to regard people who carry that label as individuals, each with his or her own story, each with his or her own capacity for transcendence. They are worth our time.

## REFERENCES


Ali, A., Hassiotis, A., Strydom, A., & King, M. (2012). Self stigma in people with intellectual disabilities and courtesy stigma in family carers: A systematic review. *Research in Developmental Disabilities, 33*(6), 2122–2140. doi:10.1016/j.ridd.2012.06.013

Anastasiou, D., & Kauffman, J. M. (2013). The social model of disability: Dichotomy between impairment and disability. *Journal of Medicine and Philosophy, 38*(4), 441–459. doi:10.1093/jmp/jht026

Bhaumik, S., Watson, J. M., Thorp, C. F., Tyrer, F., & McGrother, C. W. (2008). Body mass index in adults with intellectual disability: Distribution, associations and service implications: A population-based prevalence study. *Journal of Intellectual Disability Research, 52*(Pt. 4), 287–298. doi:10.1111/j.1365-2788.2007.01018.x

Bloom, S. L. (2013). *Creating sanctuary: Toward the evolution of sane societies* (revised ed.). London, UK: Routledge. Retrieved from https://books.google.com/books?hl=en&lr=&id=m6w9Vb_qXrcC&pgis=1

Bobińska, K., Florkowski, A., Smigielski, J., & Gałecki, P. (2009). [Psychiatric diagnostic problems of mentally retarded patients]. *Polski Merkuriusz Lekarski: Organ Polskiego Towarzystwa Lekarskiego, 27*(160), 318–325. Retrieved from http://www.ncbi.nlm.nih.gov/pubmed/19928662

Bouras, N., & Szymanski, L. (1997). Review article: Services for people with mental retardation and psychiatric disorders: U.S.-UK comparative overview. *International Journal of Social Psychiatry, 43*(1), 64–71. doi:10.1177/002076409704300106

Bowlby, J. (1980). *Attachment and loss* (Vol. 3). New York, NY: Basic Books. Retrieved from https://books.google.com/books?hl=en&lr=&id=pNS5wfCMh0cC&pgis=1

Chaplin, R. (2011). Mental health services for people with intellectual disabilities. *Current Opinion in Psychiatry, 24*(5), 372–376. doi:10.1097/YCO.0b013e3283472524

Chu, J., Dell, P., van der Hart, O., & Cardeña, E. (2011). Guidelines for treating dissociative identity disorder in adults, third revision. *Journal of Trauma & Dissociation: The Official Journal of the International Society for the Study of Dissociation, 12*(2), 115–187. doi:10.1080/15299732.2011.537247

Cloitre, M., Stolbach, B. C., Herman, J. L., van der Kolk, B., Pynoos, R., Wang, J., & Petkova, E. (2009). A developmental approach to complex PTSD: Childhood and adult cumulative trauma as predictors of symptom complexity. *Journal of Traumatic Stress, 22*(5), 399–408. doi:10.1002/jts.20444

Complex Trauma | National Child Traumatic Stress Network—Child Trauma Home. (2015). Retrieved from http://www.nctsn.org/trauma-types/complex-trauma

Cooper, S.-A., Melville, C. A., & Einfeld, S. L. (2003). Psychiatric diagnosis, intellectual disabilities and diagnostic criteria for psychiatric disorders for use with adults with learning disabilities/mental retardation (DC-LD). *Journal of Intellectual Disability Research, 47*(s1), 3–15. doi:10.1046/j.1365-2788.47.s1.2.x

Cottis, T. E. (2008). *Intellectual disability, trauma and psychotherapy* (Vol. 3). London: Routledge. Retrieved from https://books.google.com/books?hl=en&lr=&id=pVt9AgAAQBAJ&pgis=1

Crocker, J., & Major, B. (1989). Social stigma and self-esteem: The self-protective properties of stigma. *Psychological Review, 96*, 608–630.

Cummins, R. A., & Lau, A. L. D. (2003). Community integration or community exposure? A review and discussion in relation to people with an intellectual disability. *Journal of Applied Research in Intellectual Disabilities, 16*(2), 145–157. doi:10.1046/j.1468-3148.2003.00157.x

De Schipper, J. C., & Schuengel, C. (2010). Attachment behaviour towards support staff in young people with intellectual disabilities: Associations with challenging behaviour. *Journal of Intellectual Disability Research: JIDR, 54*(7), 584–596. doi:10.1111/j.1365-2788.2010.01288.x

Devereux, J. M., Hastings, R. P., Noone, S. J., Firth, A., & Totsika, V. (2009). Social support and coping as mediators or moderators of the impact of work stressors on burnout in intellectual disability support staff. *Research in Developmental Disabilities, 30*(2), 367–377. doi:10.1016/j.ridd.2008.07.002

Doyle, C., & Mitchell, D. (2003). Post-traumatic stress disorder and people with learning disabilities: A literature based discussion. *Journal of Intellectual Disabilities, 7*(1), 23–33. doi:10.1177/1469004703007001603

Emerson, E. (2003). Prevalence of psychiatric disorders in children and adolescents with and without intellectual disability. *Journal of Intellectual Disability Research, 47*(Pt. 1), 51–58. Retrieved from http://www.ncbi.nlm.nih.gov/pubmed/12558695

Farber, B. (1967). *Mental retardation; Its social context and social consequences.* Retrieved from http://eric.ed.gov/?id=ED035133

Goffman, E. (2009). *Stigma: Notes on the management of spoiled identity* (Vol. 24). New York, NY: Simon and Schuster. Retrieved from https://books.google.com/books?hl=en&lr=&id=zuMFXuTMAqAC&pgis=1

Greenwald, R. (2007). *EMDR within a phase model of trauma-informed treatment.* New York, NY: Haworth Press.

Greenwald, R. (2013). Progressive counting within a phase model of trauma-informed treatment. New York, NY: Routledge.

Hassall, R., Rose, J., & McDonald, J. (2005). Parenting stress in mothers of children with an intellectual disability: The effects of parental cognitions in relation to child characteristics and family support. *Journal of Intellectual Disability Research, 49*(Pt. 6), 405–418. doi:10.1111/j.1365-2788.2005.00673.x

Herman, J. L. (1992). Complex PTSD: A syndrome in survivors of prolonged and repeated trauma. *Journal of Traumatic Stress, 5*(3), 377–391. doi:10.1002/jts.2490050305

Heslop, P., Blair, P. S., Fleming, P., Hoghton, M., Marriott, A., & Russ, L. (2014). The confidential inquiry into premature deaths of people with intellectual disabilities in the UK: A population-based study. *Lancet, 383*(9920), 889–895. doi:10.1016/S0140-6736(13)62026-7

Holmes, E. A., Brown, R. J., Mansell, W., Fearon, R. P., Hunter, E. C., Frasquilho, F., & Oakley, D. A. (2005). Are there two qualitatively distinct forms of dissociation? A review and some clinical implications. *Clinical Psychology Review, 25*(1), 1–23. doi:10.1016/j.cpr.2004.08.006

Horner-Johnson, W., & Drum, C. E. (2006). Prevalence of maltreatment of people with intellectual disabilities: A review of recently published research. *Mental Retardation and Developmental Disabilities Research Reviews, 12*(1), 57–69. doi:10.1002/mrdd.20097

Jahoda, A., Wilson, A., Stalker, K., & Cairney, A. (2010). Living with stigma and the self-perceptions of people with mild intellectual disabilities. *Journal of Social Issues, 66*(3), 521–534. doi:10.1111/j.1540-4560.2010.01660.x

Jopp, D. A., & Keys, C. B. (2001). Diagnostic overshadowing reviewed and reconsidered. *American Journal of Mental Retardation, 106*(5), 416–433. doi:10.1352/0895-8017(2001)106<0416:DORAR>2.0.CO;2

Littlewood, R. (2006). Mental health and intellectual disability: Culture and diversity. *Journal of Intellectual Disability Research, 50*(Pt. 8), 555–560. doi:10.1111/j.1365-2788.2006.00834.x

Martorell, A., & Tsakanikos, E. (2008). Traumatic experiences and life events in people with intellectual disability. *Current Opinion in Psychiatry, 21*(5), 445–448.

Retrieved from http://journals.lww.com/co-psychiatry/Abstract/2008/09000/Traumatic_experiences_and_life_events_in_people.4.aspx

Newman, E., Riggs, D. S., & Roth, S. (1997). Thematic resolution, PTSD, and complex PTSD: The relationship between meaning and trauma-related diagnoses. *Journal of Traumatic Stress, 10*(2), 197–213. doi:10.1002/jts.2490100204

Nibert, D. A. (1995). The political economy of developmental disability. *Critical Sociology, 21*(1), 59–80. doi:10.1177/089692059502100103

Schalock, R. L., Luckasson, R. A., Shogren, K. A., Borthwick-Duffy, S., Bradley, V., & Buntinx, W. H. (2007). The renaming of mental retardation: Understanding the change to the term intellectual disability. *Intellectual and Developmental Disabilities, 45*(2), 116–124. doi:10.1352/1934-9556(2007)45[116:TROMRU]2.0.CO;2

Scior, K. (2011). Public awareness, attitudes and beliefs regarding intellectual disability: A systematic review. *Research in Developmental Disabilities, 32*(6), 2164–2182. doi:10.1016/j.ridd.2011.07.005

Shapiro, R. (2005). *EMDR solutions: Pathways to healing*. New York, NY: W. W. Norton. Retrieved from https://books.google.com/books?hl=en&lr=&id=7TtuG6uy26kC&pgis=1

Thompson Prout, H., & Browning, B. K. (2011). Psychotherapy with persons with intellectual disabilities: A review of effectiveness research. *Advances in Mental Health and Intellectual Disabilities, 5*(5), 53–59. doi:10.1108/20441281111180673

van der Kolk, B. A., & Fisler, R. (1995). Dissociation and the fragmentary nature of traumatic memories: Overview and exploratory study. *Journal of Traumatic Stress, 8*(4), 505–525. doi:10.1002/jts.2490080402

Wigham, S., Taylor, J. L., & Hatton, C. (2014). A prospective study of the relationship between adverse life events and trauma in adults with mild to moderate intellectual disabilities. *Journal of Intellectual Disability Research, 58*(12), 1131–1140.

Willner, P. (2005). The effectiveness of psychotherapeutic interventions for people with learning disabilities: A critical overview. *Journal of Intellectual Disability Research, 49* (Pt. 1), 73–85. doi:10.1111/j.1365-2788.2005.00633.x

Winnicott, D. W. (1960). The theory of the parent-infant relationship. *International Journal of Psycho-Analysis, 41*, 585–595. Retrieved from http://www.ncbi.nlm.nih.gov/pubmed/13785877

CHAPTER 16

# "People Like Me Don't Get Mentally Ill": Social Identity Theory, EMDR, and the Uniformed Services

Liz Royle

*I was in the Falklands and Northern Ireland in the Army so I probably don't need to tell you what that was like and what I saw and what I did in those situations. In the police force I've been to you know child murders, horrendous road traffic accidents, stuff like that, I've just about seen it all and I've not had a problem. I hope I never do, I think I've got the strength of character, the mental strength, not to, but if ever I did get to that point where I did lose it, where I couldn't face anything like that, I think I would be so disgusted with myself . . . I'm not quite sure but I wouldn't really think of myself as a person anymore. I would just be completely contemptuous of myself. I hope, and I'm confident that I'll never get there.*

—David, 10 years Army service, 16 years police service

The strength of feeling from people such as David can be shocking and bewildering to eye movement desensitization and reprocessing (EMDR) therapists new to working with clients from the armed forces and police service (hereon referred to as Uniformed Services Personnel [USP]). Although EMDR has been successfully used to address psychological trauma with USP (Keenan & Royle, 2008; Lansing, Amen, Hanks, & Rudy, 2005; Russell, 2006; Silver, Rogers, & Russell, 2008), offering effective trauma psychotherapy is not necessarily enough to engage individuals in a course of treatment. Reluctance to access mental health services is a common phenomenon among USP, with the stigma of mental illness and help-seeking thought to be a major influence (Hoge et al., 2004; Iversen et al., 2011; Kim et al., 2011; Royle, Keenan, & Farrell, 2009).

A social identity approach may offer therapists some insight into how this group can be better served. This chapter begins with a cultural perspective explaining how the social group identity of USP influences their attitudes toward mental illness and psychotherapy. The chapter moves on to consider the perceived differences between USP and mental health professionals, and how this gap can be bridged, before discussing more specifically how therapists can bring this information into their EMDR practice. This is illustrated throughout with case material from three USP who served in the UK Armed Forces before joining the police service and who self-define with a strong USP social identity:

David[1] (quoted earlier) displayed symptoms of psychological trauma but would not access treatment.

Matthew[1] (9 years Royal Navy service, 10 years police service) was diagnosed with posttraumatic stress disorder (PTSD) and received EMDR.

Rob[1] (6 years Army service, 12 years police service) was also diagnosed with PTSD and had nondirective therapy before being offered EMDR.

## THE SOCIAL GROUP IDENTITY OF UNIFORMED SERVICES PERSONNEL

Social identity theory describes social group identity as "that part of an individual's self-concept which derives from his knowledge of his membership of a social group (or groups) together with the value and emotional significance attached to that membership" (Tajfel, 1978, p. 63). It is possible to act as members of a specific group defining ourselves as "us" and "we" rather than "me" and "I" (Turner, 1985), but a group can only be a group when it is compared against others. Social Identity Theory explains this via the concept of the ***in-group*** and ***out-group*** (Tajfel, 1978). For members of the uniformed services, in-group identification is strengthened through shared language, occupational experience, and appearance (including uniform) along with their unique role in society of authority, protection and collective action under threat. They are the people who are relied on to run toward danger as civilians run away from it.

Once an individual has self-identified as belonging to an in-group, that person views himself or herself as somehow different from those who do not share that group identity. This act of ***cognitive separation*** into in-groups and out-groups provides members not only with the group label (e.g., police officer), but also with attitudes and behaviors that are appropriate to that in-group, known as ***group norms*** (Tajfel, 1978). These norms can determine how strongly another individual or out-group is perceived as "like us," depending on how closely their group norms match. Group norms determine attitudes to help-seeking and symptoms of illness, thereby influencing physical and mental health, mortality, and suicide rates (Jetten, Haslam, & Haslam, 2012).

For the uniformed services, four norms are particularly influential when it comes to engaging in treatment for mental health problems (Royle, 2015), but it is important to recognize their adaptive intention and the crucial role they play in the group's success. Table 16.1 shows the traits synonymous with these norms and examples of the types of cognition associated with the in-group identity.

[1] Names and identifying features changed to preserve anonymity.

**TABLE 16.1** Group Norms, Related Traits, and Examples of Cognitions

| NORM | RELATED TRAITS | POSITIVE COGNITIONS |
|---|---|---|
| Mission focus | Empowerment<br>Control<br>Focus<br>Commitment to the job<br>Orientation toward action<br>Decisiveness<br>Pragmatism | I am capable.<br>I am in control.<br>I can trust my judgment. |
| Strength and control | Emotional and physical strengths<br>Logical, clear thinking<br>Self-discipline<br>Self-sufficiency | I am strong.<br>I am in control.<br>I can handle this.<br>I am invulnerable. |
| Cohesion | Loyalty<br>Protection of peers<br>Attachment | I am supported.<br>I belong.<br>I am loved.<br>I am safe. |
| Be the best | Pride<br>Smart appearance<br>Self-esteem | I am worthy. |

## Norm Number 1: Mission Focus

In a collective culture such as the armed forces, an individual must defer to the group mission and let his or her own needs come second. Similarly, on the operational police frontline, the job is paramount; ultimately, lives may depend on getting it done properly. In-group members must quickly become focused, pragmatic, and able to act quickly and decisively.

Remaining focused on the objective during an operation provides psychological protection whereby structure and action detract from the emotional nature of the situation.

> We sort of protect ourselves with the cloak of doing the job. You're not concentrating and thinking about what's actually going on. You're not just standing there thinking, "oh my God I'm going to die." You've got a job to do. (Matthew)

In adherence to mission focus, the ethos when first experiencing mental health problems is often to "crack on." This focus on the job can initially be an adaptive coping strategy. Work can be a welcome distraction from personal problems, preventing rumination and offering an opportunity for the person to feel empowered and in control of at least one part of his or her life. Issues may arise when the individual relies on keeping active to avoid dealing with problems. Without opportunity for reflection, distressing events may not be assimilated. Continual strain will inevitably cause issues of exhaustion and burnout. And what begins as an adaptive coping strategy quickly becomes maladaptive.

## Norm Number 2: Strength and Control

Being mentally strong and controlling emotions is necessary in operational situations and allows high-stress situations to be managed with maximum effectiveness. Emotional urges (especially the natural urge to flee from danger) must be contained and suppressed. Psychological distancing, for example, through the use of gallows humor and compartmentalization allows unpleasant things to be dealt with, at least temporarily. It is therefore a highly adaptive response when dealing with operational demands. In order to maintain control, individuals must be self-sufficient and able to endure adversity. In military basic training, physical and mental strengths are forged through hardship and individuals are expected to maintain a stoical attitude to any distress. This ability to suppress the inner experience of pain is seen as developing strength of character, mental fitness, and tolerance to pain.

> It's a mental thing for me to shut my locker door and whatever I've dealt with that day, I turn the key and that's me finished. It's all locked in there, good bad or ugly whatever. (David)

The adaptive, short-term skill of showing strength and control may become bound up in the individual's identity. The person can begin to believe that he or she can deal with challenges by "toughing them out." Where this is successful, it bolsters the view that "people like me don't need help." At its extreme, they feel invulnerable and are blind to signs that they need external help. If the internal reaction to distressing events needs to be suppressed during the mission, then sometime after it is over, it must be dealt with.

An individual may need to temporarily withdraw from others (often reflecting on whether the job was done properly) to deal with any arising emotions privately. This does not violate the norm as it is in keeping with self-sufficiency. However, the mental strain of longer term compartmentalization and suppression can lead to distressing symptoms of intrusion. Avoidance may mean that problems are ignored or dismissed, leading to a slow and subtle deterioration over later years.

## Norm Number 3: Cohesion

The military knows that individuals must have a higher purpose for sacrificing their safety. Through building camaraderie they ensure peers will be drawn to support each other and persist in the face of severe hardship. In battle, this united front is essential to survival and successful completion of the mission. Whether it is in theater or on the edge of a public order police incident, without collective action, it is every man for himself.

> Ultimately I need to know that, if the shit hits the fan and you're in a fight, or a situation, that they're going to be there to support you. You fight for the guys who are alongside you . . . and the core task is to get everybody home. Safe and sound. (Matthew)

Accessing peer support and talking through experiences can be both preventative and remedial when it comes to mental health. Peer-delivered interventions can help to reduce stigma and indeed critical incident stress management (Mitchell & Everly, 2001) and the Royal Navy's Trauma Risk Incident Management (Greenberg, Langston, Iversen, & Wessely, 2011) deliberately harness this resource.

> When people show you empathy because they've come through the same factory that you have, the same mould as you have, they've experienced what you've experienced, then they have a right to nod their head and say I know how you're feeling mate, because they've been there. (David)

However, cohesive peer support can also be a negative influence where group norms lead people to damaging forms of coping, such as alcohol abuse, or create a reluctance to engage with external support. Banter and gallows humor can discourage serious conversations about peers' distress. Peers may collude in ignoring or covering up issues, often in a misguided attempt to protect the individual from outside judgment.

Relying solely on peer support can lead to the fear of being rejected by those peers just at the time they are most needed. Self-withdrawal often occurs as peers are avoided for fear of exposure and subsequent rejection.

> The success or failure of a unit depends on its overall strength. If someone is "different" they become a weak link in the chain which could ultimately jeopardise the strength and safety of a unit. (Rob)

According to Social Identity Theory, peer support will only be available provided the individual is a credible group member (Kellezi & Reicher, 2012). Membership does not merely come through a particular uniform but via group norms. Peers may feel uncomfortable around affected individuals or blame them for having problems. Given the norm of cohesion, it can be perplexing to see this "abandonment" when problems surface. However, it is easier to understand the punitive attitudes of peers when their group values (and therefore collective identity) are threatened.

## Norm Number 4: Be the Best

Military mottoes promise membership of an exclusive and elite group—Be the Best (British Army), Rise Above the Rest (Royal Air Force). Pride comes from meeting standards, and succeeding where others have failed. Service cements this through regimental pride and competitive rivalry. Inspections, smart uniforms, and parades all build self-discipline and pride in the individual and that reflects on the whole group. Appearance matters.

> I mean look at me—totally bulled shoes and the rest—but that's the way we are. That's how you're built up in the forces to think you are the best from being very, very young. You're told you are the best at

> what you do. You're not just the best in the British forces. You're the best in the world. (Rob)

Pride also comes from mission focus—the satisfaction of a job well done. There is good reason for instilling this norm. In the military, a lack of pride in the job could lead to sloppy standards. This could compromise safety if an individual loses pride in taking care of his or her kit or weapons, or in adhering to drill and procedures. The police service carries much of this same pride in appearance and carrying out a vital role. Being a police officer was traditionally a social role that brought status and expectations of high standards of behavior, morality, and professionalism. Mental health problems can feel like a failure in maintaining standards. In Matthew's case, this manifested as obsessive-compulsive disorder.

> I'll put it in military terms, the fear was that I'd appear to be a minger, meaning that I didn't care about anything and everything was dirty. Yeah, I'd be judged on cleanliness. I'd be judged professionally. If I was summonsed to court or asked to go to court to give evidence, that, to me, would be a question of my professionalism. I took it horrendously personally. (Matthew)

If membership of the in-group brings pride, then breaching group norms will mean the individual is now part of the out-group and this often brings shame.

## Shattering Beliefs and Group Norms

These four group norms are important to the group's success but also dictate how members cope with problems. What happens, though, when the strategies of focusing on the job and being strong and controlled are not enough? When peers cannot offer support that properly alleviates distress? Or when the individual's impaired functioning means his or her own high standards drop? Not all mental health problems carry stigma. It is acceptable to be temporarily affected and earn a break after an arduous mission or "earned" trauma but, because the group generally enjoys the challenge of high adrenalin operational action, a subjective judgment is applied to mental illness that is events based. Events need to be "significant" or concerns will be raised about affected individuals being "fit for purpose."

> I do think that not being able to cope with some of the things we have to see and do is a reflection of perhaps not being as mentally strong or not having the mental aptitude to do this job. (David)

Accepting a mental health problem may necessitate "comparing oneself with an internal notion of other people who have problems" (Brown, Creel, Engel, Herrell, & Hoge, 2011, p. 800). In other words, it compels one to compare himself or herself with someone who is not "fit for purpose." To preserve their identity, individuals may deny a problem, ignore or dismiss symptoms, or believe they just "need a break." This denial or nonawareness of a greater problem stems from the dissonance between the strongly valued USP identity (in-group) and the identity of someone with a problem who needs external support (out-group). Resulting thoughts of *this can't be happening to me*, and *people like me don't get mentally ill*, typify the internal resistance to this.

> Most of the time I couldn't see it. I thought I must have been really tired. All I need is to be signed off for a few days so I can sort myself out. Until you admit it to yourself then you don't put yourself forward to get the right treatment. But again it's back to the stigma. If I don't tell people that I'm mentally ill then it doesn't matter because I won't be. (Rob)

Help-seeking implicitly requires the personal acceptance of a problem that cannot be handled alone. Self-reliance and suppression are barriers to treatment in both police and military populations. Individuals feel they can handle the issues themselves, preferring to minimize effects. Often, professional support is only accessed when impairment is severe or there is concern that behavior resulting from mental distress will have severely negative consequences.

At that point, not only is there psychological trauma from the causal event(s) but also from the shattered sense of self. Table 16.2 shows how the previously positive and adaptive norms create negative beliefs when mental health problems arise.

**TABLE 16.2** Breached Norms and Examples of Negative Cognitions

| GROUP NORM | EVIDENCE OF BREACHING THE NORM | NEGATIVE COGNITIONS |
|---|---|---|
| Mission focus | Inability to perform at work<br>Anticipated fear of no longer being able to do the job and of being removed from the unit<br>Recognition of risky behavior that may impact on the job | I am useless.<br>I am out of control. |
| Strength and control | Inability to contain intrusive traumatic material<br>Inability to control emotions<br>Fear of approaching this level of inability—recognition of the growing strain | I am weak.<br>I am out of control.<br>I cannot handle this.<br>I am in danger.<br>I am "mad." |
| Cohesion | Withdrawal<br>Isolation<br>Fear of being rejected by peers | I am alone.<br>I no longer belong.<br>I am unloved.<br>I am in danger. |
| Be the best | Letting standards slide<br>Fear of exposure<br>Feelings of failure and shame<br>Self-stigma through comparing self with other people who have mental health problems | I am worthless. |

> For a serviceman who prizes self-control it was very scary . . . it felt like a massive, massive sign of weakness in myself. I've served in wars and in the police—people like me don't get mentally ill. I think you see yourself as indestructible, totally. How can this be happening to me? (Rob)

If admitting a problem to oneself is hard enough, having external "evidence" of this can be devastating. Rob unwittingly found himself referred to a psychiatrist.

> I flipped and trashed his office—kicked his table over, kicked the drinks over. Why am I here? What am I doing with this man? I'm not mad! I've seen One Flew Over the Cuckoo's Nest! I was embarrassed. I was angry. I became totally irrational in one second, totally irrational. (Rob)

This identity conflict can lead to an intolerable existential crisis for some USP, in which they question the very foundations of their life. Unresolved, this may lead to suicide ideation, the blocking out of reality through alcohol, raging against the crisis with violence, or self-expulsion from the group and even from society due to overwhelming shame. The stronger the person identifies with the social group identity, the harder this identity crisis may be. Being action oriented, once a problem is disclosed, fast movement is required in order to seize the window of opportunity before defenses are bolstered. An awareness of these challenges may offer the opportunity for mental health providers to ease the route to help-seeking.

## CULTURE CLASH: "ROUGHTY TOUGHTY" MEETS "PINK AND FLUFFY"

The USP social group identity and norms influence the therapist–client relationship before therapy even begins. Social Identity Theory emphasizes the importance of in-group support as being most credible and acceptable. When USP contemplate accessing out-group support (i.e., a mental health professional), their perception of the extent of difference will generally reflect the potential for engagement. If mental health services are not perceived to share norms, then the gap between the two groups will be wider. The related traits (see Table 16.1) provide a starting point for considering shared norms.

Stereotypes of "pink and fluffy" are common when USP think about therapists. People associated with this stereotype are polar opposite to the "roughty toughty" world of mission focus and strength and control and very much out-group.

> There's two sides within the police, the frontline operational side and there's the pink and fluffy side—"is there anything you'd like to share with me?"—all this sort of stuff that training put in place 15 years ago, which just goes against the grain for most frontline police officers, male and female. They view people in that sort of environment almost as the enemy. I was dreading the, right, ok pull up a beanbag and tell me all about it, at which point if it had been that I would have stood up and walked out in disgust. (Matthew)

Therapists from different theoretical backgrounds will bring their own norms. It is important that practitioners consider these before working with this group so as to avoid damaging clashes such as the one Rob experienced.

> I didn't relate to her at all—very patronising. You sit there, and I'm talking to her and they're looking away and they go (adopts soft tone) "just read this passage from this book." What? "Just read this" It's like a poem or whatever they give you, and I'm like what you giving me this for? (soft voice) "tell me what you're feeling about that." It's a poem about a door or about grass or, are you going to talk to me about my problem? And they go "no, read this, read this." (Rob)

A useful way for therapists to consider their own norms before working with this group is to honestly reflect on the following questions. This exercise may also reveal any underlying or subtle stereotypes (positive and negative) that the therapist holds in relation to USP:

- What do you associate with this group? Think about how you would describe the stereotypical group member to someone who knew absolutely nothing about the uniformed services.
- What emotions/sensations do they invoke in you? Consider this from the perspective of meeting an individual member of the uniformed services as well as from the perspective of you meeting the group as an outsider.
- How closely do you identify with the associated traits (see Table 16.1)?
- How acceptable is it to you to see strategies of emotional suppression and a focus on being active as adaptive?
- What are your views on helping people to recover so that they can return to a job where they may again face psychological trauma and danger?

No matter how much a therapist considers himself or herself to be nonjudgmental, when a police client first attends the session in full uniform and body armor, it is important to be aware of any countertransference that is raised. Some clients may, consciously or otherwise, use this appearance to mask their vulnerability and redress perceived issues of power. Furthermore, if the individual feels coerced into attending mental health services, that person may retain what little control he or she has through nonengagement and minimization of issues. A range of common initial defenses—firing questions at the therapist, subtly derisive comments about therapy, "pinning the therapist to the chair" with overly direct eye contact—can be unsettling ways of testing mettle!

USP often fear being judged, particularly for their use of gallows humor or for being "politically incorrect." Previously held notions of someone with mental illness as insincere, not fit for purpose, or a malingerer can lead to anticipation that the therapist will judge him or her similarly. There may also be fear that the individual will be blamed for not being able to cope with what he or she "signed up for." This can result in a negative belief such as *It's my fault. I knew what I was letting myself in for.* Clients may underreport symptoms and therapists need to be wary of collusion in this minimization. Despite the arduous process behind the decision to disclose, Matthew found his concerns were repeatedly dismissed by health professionals.

> We had an in-force counsellor, it's very fluffy but her view was just, well, you know it's just one of those things, nobody likes to see a dead baby, and it was kind of just, you know, if any more issues come back but I think you'll be alright to just let nature take its course. (Matthew)

Professionals need to consider that individuals have a high tolerance to distress and may downplay their real situation to promote personal identity continuity. Screening questionnaires may not provide a true picture.

Opening up, revealing what they perceive as weakness and shame, relies on there being enough trust between the individual and the potential therapist. USP are trained to make fast judgments. Their lives may depend on quickly assessing who is trustworthy and, as said earlier, appearance is an important factor in these assessments. A therapist who prefers working in casual clothes, offers a weak handshake, and presents in a gentle manner can all lead to negative first impressions. Anything that is perceived to be "woolly," ambiguous, or lacking structure is contrary to the traits associated with USP norms. Being direct, straight-talking, confident, and focused on the task in hand can feel more familiar and therefore less threatening.

Appearance includes how services are marketed. Words such as *support* and *help* denote weakness and an inability to be self-sufficient by their very definition. Using them may unintentionally create resistance. It is possible to reframe help-seeking so that it adheres to group norms, for example, a practical solution to a problem, rebuilding strength and control, and developing skills to stay fit and well in the job.

The primary objective of help-seeking must be that the presenting problem will be effectively dealt with. There is often little confidence in the efficacy of mental health services; for many police officers, their notion of mental health services is based on their observations of people in crisis, "revolving door" statutory mental health services, and poor outcomes.

> When I was in custody trying to get people who clearly had lots of serious issues, and had experienced great trauma in their lives . . . the system seemed to fall down. A lot of people were caught between the devil and the deep blue sea and then I've seen people kill themselves. Afterwards. (David)

The individual may question what mental health services could possibly offer. After all, they could not change what had happened. The individual simply had to find coping strategies—and that was something the individual could do for himself or herself.

In-house services, or therapists from a USP background, offer the benefit of being perceived as understanding the language and culture of the uniformed services. Conversely, self-stigma can be reduced when the "shame" of mental health problems is taken as far away from the social group as possible. In that instance, safety comes through the concept of speaking to a complete stranger who will probably never be encountered again. This allows the individual to compartmentalize the problem and reduce the risk of contamination. It also reduces the perceived risk of short- and long-term consequences that organizational in-house services carry.

> If you go within the job, somebody, somewhere will write it down and as soon as that's marked down in any sort of documentation that's a disclosable document to the people that require it and I think that, anyone who's seeking any decent work will never get another decent job again. And that's the God's honest truth, that's the way it is. (David)

Despite these barriers, it is possible for therapists to build bridges in any background or setting. Being recommended by another in-group member is helpful in building trust, as is having links, no matter how small; for example, my father was in the Navy or I have worked with many police officers (provided this is true). It is well worth becoming familiar with the terminology and operational world through seminars, further reading, or discussions with colleagues who are more familiar. It is better to admit to limited knowledge than fake it, as this will likely be quickly discovered.

## CULTURAL CONSIDERATIONS WITHIN THE EIGHT-PHASE PROTOCOL

### History Taking and Preparation

The need for a practical direct approach does not equate to underestimating the relational aspect once rapport and an adequate level of trust have been established. To USP, revealing private thoughts and emotions to another person may not initially be viewed as important. Matthew preferred the metaphor of taking his car to the garage but found disclosure very beneficial.

> If I could've gone down to kwikfit and had an oil change I'd have been fine. But then, I didn't realise what a skilled, clever job they do because they get you to open out without you actually realising it. (Matthew)

A collaborative approach in therapy is helpful, saying for example, "I'm an expert on psychological trauma. You're the expert on you. Together we can crack this." However, cohesion may be tested. USP may stretch boundaries and expect the therapist to be *their* emergency service when in crisis. Act fast and, within reason, be there when needed. This is rarely a client group who becomes overly dependent.

When considering targets for reprocessing in EMDR, therapists need to be mindful of shattered beliefs relating to the social group identity as well as the traumatic events that precede this. Targets for reprocessing fall into two categories (a) the traumatic event(s), and (b) the loss of social group identity.

#### The Traumatic Event(s)

Most USP could provide a long list of potentially traumatic incidents they have been involved in. However, events that the general public may find traumatic can be perceived as exciting, or routine, depending on the individual's belief about his or her ability and willingness to handle such situations. This does not mean that a single traumatic incident is not at the root of issues, but it is helpful to be sensitive to breached norms (see Table 16.2). Norms may be violated where there are elements of an ineffective mission, the perception of betrayal by colleagues, or the organization or the lack of strength, potency, and control in self. These violated norms may then lead to psychological trauma arising from "shattered assumptions" (Janoff-Bulman, 1985) about how things *should* be. Additionally, the diverse tasks required in the police role (some needing the psychological protection and others not) may mean that an officer can arrive at a scene without his or her "protective cloak" fully in place.

When discussing traumatic events, there may be fears of revealing information that could jeopardize security or result in criminal proceedings. Confidentiality boundaries may need to be reemphasized; however, consideration also needs to be given to the safety of the individual at work, particularly if he or she remains in high-risk situations and/or carries lethal weapons. Taking a general trauma history may be seen as intrusive, particularly where a recent traumatic incident appears to be the "obvious" reason for problems. A useful way of framing the need for comprehensive history taking is for the therapist to use this metaphor: "If you were planning on entering into an unfamiliar and potentially charged situation, you would want to do a thorough reconnaissance or surveillance exercise so that you could take the most safe and effective action, wouldn't you? Well this is *my* reconnaissance so that I can work in the best way to help you achieve your goals."

## The Loss of Social Group Identity

> All the roughty toughty stuff . . . that's just the kind of thing that pushes my button, I think that's just who I am. (David)

Therapists should be sensitive to seemingly casual remarks such as "this isn't me," "I don't do this." Rob's assertion that "people like me don't get mentally ill" begs the questions:

- Who are people like you? This is potentially the lost identity.
- Who does get it? The target for reprocessing could be the person he or she now fears he or she has become, for example, "weak," "a waste of a uniform."

An identity conflict is often revealed by how a client fears others will view him or her. This internalized stigma reveals what the individual fears or believes to be true about himself or herself. When exploring such identity issues, it helps to give permission to speak openly without fear of being judged for expressing negative stereotypes.

The loss of social group identity may be more keenly felt when the benefits it provided (e.g., strength, control, pride) compensated for childhood feelings of vulnerability, disempowerment, or shame. USP are sometimes attracted into the uniformed services by a need for attachment or safety or to feel strong and empowered. The organization can become something of a surrogate family and if there are later issues of, for example, betrayal by managers or the system, this may resonate with past, early betrayals. In more complex cases, an individual may have built a new persona and left distressed child emotional parts behind. A therapist should consider ego strength and the need for extended preparation to strengthen this.

If it is necessary to target earlier trauma, there may be strong defenses in place. Nurturing and self-soothing parts are often suppressed by the "crack on" and "toughen up" parts and may need enhancing or installing.

The preparation phase in the EMDR protocol is a good opportunity to rectify misconceptions that therapy is ineffective. Demonstrating expertise may need to precede history taking. For this group, expertise does not come from academic qualifications but utility. Psychoeducation and normalization is particularly important as it gives logic to what may feel irrational and out of control.

> The first thing he did was a physiology lesson. "This is the brain, these are the parts, this is what it does," and I'm thinking this all makes sense. And he laid it all out quite logically and it was easy for me to take onboard. (Rob)

By remembering the purpose and adaptive nature of the group's coping strategies, acceptable alternatives can be reframed. For example:

- In place of suppression—teach containment, affect tolerance, and management.
- In place of keeping busy to avoid and distract—direct the urge to "do" into behavioral activation (e.g., exercise).
- Where peer support networks have been lost, or are being avoided through shame, consider mobilizing alternatives. Online forums can help to normalize reactions, but look for constructive, informed attitudes toward recovery before making recommendations.

By teaching skills to manage symptoms, the individual's sense of mastery begins to be restored. This is crucial. However, providing good psychoeducation and coping strategies may create a dilemma. If crisis has led the client to enter into therapy, once he or she regains some control there may be a premature ending of therapy (Royle et al., 2009). Mental health professionals should be pragmatic and respectful of this and prepare for this potential outcome. Giving a valued experience of therapy (however brief), and being explicit at the outset with the client that this "flight to health" may happen, means an increased ability to contract with them regarding what steps can be taken should it arise (e.g., a follow-up in x months). Without credibility through building skills, the individual is less likely to be engaged and he or she will leave with an impression that therapy was a waste of time and without any benefits at all.

## STARTING REPROCESSING SESSIONS

The emotional tolerance skills and psychoeducation that are taught in the preparation phase will be important when accessing affect during reprocessing sessions. With the norm that emotions and negative thoughts and feelings must be concealed or contained, USP become skilled in portraying a persona and masking "weakness." From their perspective, feeling is a less useful skill than doing. Emotions are illogical, unseen, and ambiguous, hard for the logical, practical, and pragmatic person to grasp. "Reactions" are more palatable than "feelings." There may be fear that the norm for maintaining control will be violated by the "requirement" to expose vulnerability. It is crucial to contain overwhelming emotions and create trust. Accessing emotions too early will result in a fear of losing control, leading clients to lose trust and disengage. A natural urge to suppress feelings may arise during reprocessing and it can help to focus instead on body sensations, or build tolerance to emotions through titrating exposure. The ability to dip in and out of strong feelings affirms the norm of strength and control. Facilitation of this by the therapist is a sign of shared norms and so builds rapport. The stop signal can be used at any point in a session that the client feels his or her self-control slipping, not just during desensitization, thus building trust that power is shared.

Eliciting the negative cognition (NC) in Phase 3 can be problematic as it may be too challenging to verbalize something that negates identity. David's words at the start of the chapter describe the strength of self-loathing he would experience. Asking him to verbalize this as a negative cognition may be too shaming or overwhelming. This needs sensitive handling and therapists may need to initially work with a "lesser" NC, or without one at all, and keep the client grounded in affect rather than cognitions.

Among the emotions that can become overwhelming in this group is anger. Fight, rather than flight, is drummed in as the most appropriate reaction to life-threatening situations.

> In the forces, you're encouraged and developed to become self-reliant and resilient, that traditional British fighting spirit, when the chips are down you come out with guns blazing. (Rob)

Aggression affirms the norm of strength and allows venting and the release of pent up adrenaline. Clients and therapists may be fearful of this coming out, particularly during reprocessing sessions. Clients will often be very aware of their physical strength and the potential for violence if control slips.

The strength of this anger needs to be acknowledged, triggers identified, and psychoeducation and management strategies provided. Explicit risk assessments with plans for maintaining safety offer a sense of control.

Avoiding emotions may be easier outside the therapy room and can manifest as "forgotten" or avoided between session logs. Being trained to remain focused externally on the task rather than on an inner experience discourages the self-reflection that may be helpful; this could be an underdeveloped skill. A reminder that the session makes up a small portion of the client's week, and that he or she holds responsibility for continuing the work for the remaining days, and may engage his or her mission focus provided the therapist offers some structure and strategies for undertaking reflective activities.

## REGAINING CULTURAL IDENTITY

Once reprocessing is underway, awareness of the importance of group norms means culturally sensitive cognitive interweaves can be offered if blocks are encountered.

Examples include the following: When a client is looping on perceived weakness at breaching strength and control, the therapist can ask: "How would you judge a close peer?" This may link to a more compassionate view fueled by the norm of cohesion or, alternatively, reveal the stigmatizing belief that has been internalized (in which case a simple—"Is that always the case?"—may help).

In the heat of a life-threatening situation, a fast appraisal and immediate action is needed; indeed, this is in line with the norm of mission focus. With the clarity and hindsight of a postincident evaluation (by the individual, the organization, or the media), it may appear that this action was unhelpful. Such clinical evaluations may lead to guilt or regret about the outcome. Where this blocks processing, a useful interweave is: "What could have happened if you'd delayed acting?"

Other operational situations may lead to looping shame, guilt, or helplessness. An example is where the client followed a higher level command and then became aware of a disturbing outcome such as severe civilian casualties following a military offensive. An interweave that facilitates recognition of the need to follow orders (mission focus), trust others, and act collectively (cohesion) can be useful. The therapist may ask: "Who took that decision?" "What would happen if people didn't follow orders?" "Could you/they have had all the information in the heat of that moment?"

Where there is shame for breaching the norm of strength and control through admitting mental health problems and accessing therapy, interweaves could include: "If a close peer was feeling this, what would you say to him or her?" "I would imagine coming here is one of the hardest things you've done and took immense courage."

Clients will generally have a sense of the part of themselves that they view as strong, resilient, and courageous, and it may help to use this in an interweave. This part may be closely associated with completing grueling training or handling challenging situations or combat. PTSD is often reified by the client as an enemy; in this instance, those empowered inner resources can be mobilized by the therapist, suggesting that: "Sometimes our hardest battles are the very things that ultimately make us stronger. The strong and determined part of you that got through (basic training/theater/operational situations) will be useful in this battle to beat PTSD."

Feelings of anxiety may be causing shame as the client sees them as evidence of weakness, breaching the norm of strength and control. The therapist can reframe the existence of anxiety and fear as a helpful resource: "I'd imagine in your role an absence of fear can be dangerous and cause people to be reckless. So fear is useful"

This reprocessing and reframing of perceived breaches in group norms (whether they arose through the nature of the traumatic event or through experiencing mental health problems) may enhance the recovery of their group identity. As the client recovers, he or she needs to reassess his or her identity and make sense of the experience. Therapy is not complete until the social identity is reclaimed or acceptably reframed. Rob and Matthew both made this transition successfully, returning to the uniformed services with transformed and strengthened group norms. Mission focus was transformed into a new mission of being better able to guard against the hidden "enemy" and learn more about it, through reading around the subject or getting involved in peer support programs.

Strength and control were renewed through having won the battle.

> I don't like failure, personal failure. It was very, very dark, but I've turned it on its head. And I've never ever, at this moment in time, felt quite this strong for a lot of years. (Rob)

Cohesion was remobilized as a desire to help other group members through inspiring hope and becoming a positive role model.

> I hope it gives them hope. Again it's, probably—fucking hell I wouldn't have thought it would have happened to you because yeah you're one of these sort of ex forces, big TAG,[2] firearms and yet you've still ended up going a little bit wibble, but also, right, you've been there . . . you're back to the old Matthew that we know, so it must be right., I'm happy, I'll go for it. Yeah I'm not sort of sat in an admin job trying to knit fog. (Matthew)

Pride was taken in their new skills. The development of compassion, understanding, and empathy was felt to enrich both personal and professional lives.

These reframed norms, and the positive affect they invoke, can all be enhanced with bilateral stimulation. Such reframing changes the individual's misperception that he or she had become an out-group member by breaching norms. By recognizing the norms from a new perspective, the individual's cultural identity, and place within the in-group, is regained.

## SUMMARY

Society will always require individuals to act collectively in the face of danger to preserve our safety and freedom. The uniformed services create strong group norms deliberately, in order to facilitate this. Focus is often placed on changing the culture of the uniformed services, but change must also come from mental health professionals adapting their work to be culturally more acceptable.

For USP, much of the stigma of seeking mental health is about loss of valued identity. Being aware of cultural identity and understanding how the group norms influence attitudes toward help-seeking may contribute toward reducing this stigma and increasing timely referrals. Therapists can be sensitive to group values and use them to help build rapport. By recognizing their impact throughout the course of therapy, therapists can work with them rather than against them. Most importantly the recovery of a strong cultural identity can be facilitated.

When challenges arise, it is good to remind ourselves of the importance of this work. In honor of that intention, this chapter concludes with a quote from Rob who, despite experiencing a huge identity crisis, finally emerged with his sense of identity renewed. He was asked, if he had the chance to turn back the clock and erase the experience from his life, would he?

> No I don't think I would. The bizarre thing with it is that it's almost a part of my life . . . it's me and I understand who I am and it's made me the person I am today with the different experiences I've had. And it keeps me alive, emotionally, it makes me grateful for who I am, what I have and where I am. There are times when

[2] Tactical Aid Group—comparable to U.S. SWAT team.

suddenly I'll get a reflection on something and I'll look around and I'll think, some of you people don't know how lucky you are. For every action there is a positive reaction and yeah, I actually do view it quite positively because I've been to the dark side and I've come out. (Rob)

## REFERENCES

Brown, M. C., Creel, A. H., Engel, C. C., Herrell, R. K., & Hoge, C. W. (2011). Factors associated with interest in receiving help for mental health problems in combat veterans returning from deployment to Iraq. *Journal of Nervous and Mental Disease, 199*(10), 797–801.

Greenberg, N., Langston, V., Iversen, A., & Wessely, S. (2011). The acceptability of "Trauma Risk Management" within the UK armed forces. *Occupational Medicine, 61*(3), 184–189.

Hoge, C. W., Castro, C. A., Messer, S. C., McGurk, D., Cotting, D. I., & Koffman, R. I. (2004). Combat duty in Iraq and Afghanistan, mental health problems, and barriers to care. *New England Journal of Medicine, 351*, 13–22.

Iversen, A. C., Van Staden, L., Hacker Hughes, J. G., Greenberg, N., Hotopf, M., Rona, R. J., . . . Fear, N. T. (2011). The stigma of mental health problems and other barriers to care in the UK armed forces. *BMC Health Services Research, 11*, Article 31.

Janoff-Bulman, R. (1985). *Shattered assumptions: Towards a new psychology of trauma*. New York, NY: Free Press.

Jetten, J., Haslam, C., & Haslam, S. A. (Eds.). (2012). *The social cure: Identity, health and well-being*. Hove, East Sussex: Psychology Press.

Keenan, P., & Royle, L. (2008). Vicarious trauma and first responders: A case study utilizing eye movement desensitization and reprocessing (EMDR) as the primary treatment modality. *International Journal of Emergency Mental Health, 9*(4), 291–298.

Kellezi, B., & Reicher, S. D. (2012). Social cure or social curse? The psychological impact of extreme events during the Kosovo conflict. In J. Jetten, C. Haslam, & S. A. Haslam (Eds.), *The social cure: Identity, health and well-being* (pp. 217–233). Hove, East Sussex: Psychology Press.

Kim, P. Y., Britt, T. W., Klocko, R. P., Riviere, L. A., & Adler, A. B. (2011). Stigma, negative attitudes about treatment, and utilization of mental health care among soldiers. *Military Psychology, 23*(1), 65–81.

Lansing, K., Amen, D. G., Hanks, C., & Rudy, L. (2005). High resolution brain SPECT imaging and eye movement desensitization and reprocessing in police officers with PTSD. *Journal of Neuropsychiatry and Clinical Neurosciences, 17*(4), 526–532.

Mitchell, J. T., & Everly, G. S. (2001). *CISD: Critical incident stress debriefing: An operations manual* (3rd ed.). Ellicott City, MD: Chevron.

Royle, L. (2015, June). *Mental health help-seeking amongst police officers with a military background: A theoretical model based on social identity*. Paper presented at the XIV ESTSS Conference Trauma in Changing Societies: Social contexts and clinical practise. Vilnius, Lithuania.

Royle, L., Keenan, P., & Farrell, D. (2009). Issues of stigma for first responders accessing support for posttraumatic stress. *International Journal of Emergency Mental Health, 11*(2), 80–86.

Russell, M. C. (2006). Treating combat-related stress disorders: A multiple case study utilizing eye movement desensitization and reprocessing (EMDR) with battlefield casualties from the Iraqi War. *Military Psychology, 18*(1), 1–18.

Silver, S. M., Rogers, S., & Russell, M. (2008). Eye movement desensitization and reprocessing (EMDR) in the treatment of war veterans. *International Journal of Clinical Psychology, 64*(8), 947–957.

Tajfel, H. (1978). Social categorisation, social identity and social comparison. In H. Tajfel (Ed.), *Differentiation between social groups: Studies in the social psychology of intergroup relations* (pp. 61–76). London, UK: Academic Press.

Turner, J. C. (1985). Social categorisation and the self-concept: A social cognitive theory of group behaviour. In E. J. Lawler (Ed.), *Advances in group processes* (Vol. 2, pp. 77–122). Greenwich, CT: JAI Press.

CHAPTER 17

# EMDR Therapy and the Recovery Community: Relational Imperatives in Treating Addiction

Jamie Marich

Addicts and alcoholics are some of the most misunderstood people in global society. People in active addiction can inflict great harm on others and the wounds caused by addicts can fuel many of the hateful condemnations made by the public. The stigma of being an addict can cast a tremendous barrier—built with the bricks of shame and disgust—that can prevent people from seeking help in the first place. The more that the helping professions learn about the impact of unhealed trauma on addiction progression, the more what we've grown used to simply labeling "addict behavior" can be understood through a more informed, compassionate lens. Creating quality treatment informed by this new understanding does not just require an understanding of trauma and eye movement desensitization and reprocessing (EMDR) therapy. Rather, a comprehensive understanding of what individuals seeking recovery (a term preferred in many circles to the traditional labels of *addict* or *alcoholic*) experience as part of their journey is also required.

In her first article on EMDR in the treatment of chemical dependency, Francine Shapiro (Shapiro, Vogelmann-Sine, & Sine, 1994) recommended the use of EMDR after the initial phase of treatment. Achieving stabilization from the immediate effects of addiction is the primary goal of this initial phase. Shapiro advised that EMDR should never be used in a vacuum but rather as part of a system designed to make the client feel safe and supported. In her landmark book *EMDR: The Breakthrough "Eye Movement" Therapy for Overcoming Stress, Anxiety, and Trauma*, Shapiro proposes that "[EMDR] works best when it is used in conjunction with counseling groups that provide a nurturing atmosphere, such as group therapy, Alcoholics Anonymous (AA), and Narcotics Anonymous (NA)" (Shapiro & Forrest, 1997, p. 178). Shapiro now regards EMDR therapy as a distinct approach to psychotherapy, signifying EMDR's growth and evolution. However, her early writing about integrating EMDR into the treatment of addictive disorders offers sound guidance for introducing EMDR therapy to someone seeking recovery from chemical dependency or other compulsive behaviors often described under the umbrella of addiction (e.g., sex, food, overspending, and gambling).

I guide you through this chapter as a woman in long-term recovery from drug addiction, alcoholism, and codependency, a journey that began in 2002. Being public about my recovery as a professional exposes me to constant criticism from many of my peers. Hearing comments like "talking about being an addict so much undermines your credibility" is evidence to me that stigma and misunderstanding about individuals in recovery is alive and well. Much of this criticism has come from other EMDR therapists. I celebrate the inclusion of the recovering community in this collected volume, especially because EMDR therapy has so much to offer us. I credit EMDR therapy, which I experienced in my early recovery, as the healing modality that invigorated my overall sense of wellness. Inspired by my own journey with EMDR therapy, I decided to get trained so that I could carry this healing art to others in recovery. This decade-long journey led me to where I serve today as an EMDRIA Certified Therapist, Approved Consultant, and training provider.

Shapiro's early wisdom about pairing EMDR with other means of support remains the most culturally appropriate course of action when working with individuals on a path of recovery. Using this larger context of her guidance, I use this chapter to offer practical suggestions from my perspective as an openly identified addict in long-term recovery. The chapter examines EMDR therapy as a powerful healing mechanism in the treatment of addiction and provides insights on future directions. Research citations and case studies are integrated throughout the chapter, and I use pseudonyms in discussing case studies.

## MODELS OF RECOVERY IN THE MODERN ERA

Disparate opinions exist about the utility of 12-step programs and the disease model on which they are based. Some people are adamant that the 12-step path saved their life. Clinical professionals strongly identifying with the 12 steps may insist that embracing this path completely is the only way to get sober and stay sober. Others condemn the 12 steps as being ineffective, unscientific, and even harmful (Glasser, 2015; Peele, 2015). A neutral middle also exists—people who acknowledge the benefit of 12-step programming, yet also recognize that the program does not have to be followed so rigidly in order to be useful. This third group, with which I identify both clinically and personally, largely embraces the idea that 12-step principles are most successful when used in tandem with other therapeutic supports throughout the healing process.

My clinical assumption is that 12-step programming is one of many paths available to help individuals in the pursuit of lifestyle change required for recovery (Marich, 2009a). In the many models of recovery I've studied throughout my career (e.g., 12 step, faith-based recovery, SMART® Recovery, Rational Recovery, Moderation Management, and Refuge Recovery), the single greatest common denominator in success appears to be the success of that model in teaching and promoting lifestyle change. The culturally sensitive EMDR therapist will not impose their biases about the utility of any one model of recovery on their clients; rather, the therapist will facilitate an experience where the client can discover which path will best serve him or her. Part of this openness is allowing clients to choose how they identify (e.g., addict/alcoholic, person in recovery) and how they conceptualize their struggle (e.g., treatable disease, behavioral compulsivity, a biological manifestation of unhealed trauma, or a combination of explanations).

In Shapiro's 1997 book referenced at the beginning of this chapter, an excellent framework for where EMDR therapy fits into the comprehensive picture of lifestyle change required for recovery appears. She details:

1. EMDR should never be used in a vacuum but rather as part of a system designed to make the client feel safe and supported. It works best when it is used in conjunction with counseling groups that provide a nurturing atmosphere, such as group therapy, Alcoholics Anonymous (AA), and Narcotics Anonymous (NA) (p. 178).
2. The goal in doing EMDR with a substance abuser is to touch into and process the negative emotions that are perpetuating their addiction (p. 192).
3. Many addicts who repeatedly relapse have had some kind of life-threatening experience in their history or an experience that they had perceived as life-threatening. These experiences set off a tidal wave of intense anxiety and unbearable feelings of powerlessness. To avoid these feelings (and, therefore, in the logic of automatic connections, to avoid dying), the recovering addict would do whatever it took, even go back to drugs after years of sobriety (p. 197).
4. *Working it through* is not only done on an intellectual level. The goal of EMDR is to work things through on all levels so that the person's *knee-jerk responses* are naturally healthy ones—intellectually, emotionally, and physically (p. 200).

These four major points provide invaluable guidelines for integrating EMDR therapy in working with clients on a path of recovery. The guidelines are explored further with the specific purpose of helping EMDR practitioners with clinical decision making.

## EMDR SHOULD NEVER BE USED IN A VACUUM

As a person in recovery, I get concerned when I hear EMDR therapists say, "Once we clear up the trauma, your desire to drink (or use drugs, or engage in a problematic behavior) will go away." Research such as the ACE Study (Centers for Disease Control and Prevention, 2013) establishes correlations between early childhood trauma and substance use disorders. However, clearing out antecedent traumas with EMDR or any other modality is not necessarily a magic bullet to healing. Although dealing with core traumas is a critical part of the recovery process, targeting that clearance as a primary goal without stabilization, healthy motivation, and adequate sober support is not wise.

EMDR purists may argue that Phase 2 of the eight-phase protocol covers the stabilization component. Within this assumption, it is important to note that one Calm/Safe Place exercise is not sufficient preparation for most on a path of addiction recovery. In addition to guided visualizations like the Calm Safe Place, other skills like progressive muscle relaxation, breath work, grounding techniques, and use of other senses (e.g., sound, taste, touch, and smell) to regulate affect should be in the EMDR therapist's toolkit of skills. Within EMDR literature, Greenwald (2010), Knipe (2014), and Parnell (2008) offer outstanding suggestions for building this skill set. You are also welcome to visit my trauma resources website at www.traumamadesimple.com for guided videos.

More time will need to be spent in EMDR preparation (Phase 2) with those whose main coping mechanisms in life can be described as addictive or focused on numbing intense emotion. Accessing healthy sober support can serve as an important part of the preparation; for many individuals in recovery, 12-step meetings or other groups are the most available source of such support in their communities. I have engaged in the trauma reprocessing phases with people claiming as little as 1 month of sobriety if they are actively working to build and to implement affect tolerance skills associated with EMDR preparation. Others require longer; it is truly a case of the quality of stabilization over the quantity. In a qualitative research project that I conducted with recovering women who received EMDR therapy as part of their own continuing care, the time frame in which the reprocessing phases (3–6) commenced varied from 1 month to 2 years of abstinence (Marich, 2010).

When making decisions about whether or not to move into reprocessing with a client, Dr. Shapiro does not offer specific time guidelines regarding how much sobriety a person should have before engaging in the reprocessing phases of EMDR therapy. My position remains that quality of recovery versus quantity must guide our clinical judgments. As EMDR evolves, more practitioners contend that one can begin EMDR reprocessing even if the client is still using drugs or actively engaged in problematic behaviors. The three main specialty addiction protocols published since the inception of EMDR (e.g., the DeTUR protocol, the CravEx protocol, and the Feeling State Addiction protocol) do not require abstinence (Hase, Schallmayer, & Sack, 2008; Miller, 2012; Popky, 2005). Still, appropriateness must be assessed on a case-by-case basis; in some cases, it would be unwise to use these protocols in the absence of sufficient stabilization and a modicum of abstinence from the drinking/drug use or the problematic behavior. Many EMDR colleagues see this position as too conservative. It is a position that is informed by my own personal experiences with addiction and recovery and my clinical experience in using EMDR with many different types of people in recovery over the last decade.

Many professionals from the addiction field have moved past the rather antiquated notion that an individual must have 2 years of sobriety to successfully target trauma. However, it is always crucial to practice caution when delving into reprocessing. A critical question that should be asked before targeting trauma is whether or not the person in question can handle what might surface during the trauma work, a concept often referred to as assessing for the affective window of tolerance.

Another critical evaluation point in clinical decision making relates to a person's motivation for targeting past traumas. Like many others working with recovering alcoholics and addicts, I've seen clients and fellow 12-steppers get lost on the quest to find out "why I drink/use . . . " at the expense of overall commitment to a new lifestyle. Addiction psychiatrist David Ohlms, MD, disclosed that when he first entered the profession, he dedicated himself to finding the "root cause" of addiction. As Ohlms (1991) recounted in one of his training videos, he treated one alcoholic with serious trauma for about 5 years using psychoanalysis with the goal of helping him resolve the root causes. After much success in psychotherapy, the man ended up dying after relapsing and subsequently being attacked in a bar. As a result of this experience, Ohlms realized that in rigorously exploring possible root causes, he had furnished the man with more excuses for self-pity and, ultimately, more reasons to relapse. He concluded that the therapeutic time could have been better spent helping the man in taking responsibility for his disease, accepting it, and moving forward from there.

Although EMDR therapy can do more than just identify the root causes of addiction, EMDR therapists would be wise to heed Ohlms' caution. In my own EMDR practice, I've seen clients who are not ready to process adverse life experiences get stuck in looping patterns. For a person in recovery who is not committed to a recovery lifestyle, such rumination on the past can be dangerous. Debates between traditional 12-step-oriented addiction counselors and mental health professionals have raged for years about whether the addiction or the mental health symptoms ought to be treated first. In dealing with addiction colleagues I often find myself justifying the need for trauma services. Some of these colleagues are so filled with fear about trauma work potentially leading to destabilization, excuse making, and ultimately relapse. Diving into causality without looking at overall lifestyle change, commitment, support, and motivation is not optimal.

The stages of change—a model developed by Prochaska and DiClemente (1994, with Norcross) and used widely in the mainstream addiction treatment field—provides a useful tool for EMDR therapists in evaluating when to move forward with the reprocessing stages. Intense affect can surface in the use of the specialty addiction protocols (e.g., DeTUR, CravEX, and FSAP) as well. Thus, assessing a client's stage of change is useful in accounting for the larger context no matter how you are using EMDR. The stages of change are *precontemplation* (no desire for change), *contemplation* (beginning to think about change), *preparation* (beginning to take steps toward change), action (proactively working toward goals), and *maintenance* (continuing to engage in wellness to sustain the gains of action). A sixth stage, *termination,* is generally not used by traditional 12-steppers who see their recovery as a state of constant maintenance. From the perspective of sensitivity to the 12-step path, using the stages of change to guide your EMDR case conceptualization is a clinically intelligent way to avoid using EMDR in a vacuum (Marich, 2011; for useful applications also refer to Abel & O'Brien, 2014).

As I discuss in *EMDR Made Simple* (Marich, 2011), EMDR reprocessing work—which includes the specialty protocols—is best pursued when an individual is in the action stage of change. However, in some cases it may be appropriate to pursue in the preparation stage of change. If an individual best fits the description of *precontemplative* or *contemplative,* it is ideal to remain in EMDR Phase 2 preparation strategies and other recovery skill building. Some EMDR targeting may be appropriate in these stages. In such cases I primarily target the motivation issue, using a negative cognition that's blocking the client from accepting wellness (e.g., "I can't handle it," "My addiction is my identity"). Such an approach is safer than immediately targeting their earliest or worst memories.

### Phases 3 and 4 Targeting Sequence Example: Using a Negative Cognition Connected to a Motivational Block

- Image: What image represents the worst part of the incident/issue? ***Seeing my dad come to my rescue after getting arrested for a possession when I was 19—he called me a black sheep.***
- Negative cognition: When you bring up that image, what is the negative belief that goes along with it? ***My addiction is my identity.***

- Positive cognition: What would you like to believe about yourself now, even when that negative memory/issue comes up? ***I am recovering and restored.***
- Validity of Cognition (VoC): What is your gut-level reading of how true that positive statement is right now (1 = completely false through 7 = completely true)? **2**
- Emotion: What emotions or feelings are coming up for you when you link the negative image/worst part with the negative cognition of *my addiction is my identity*? ***embarrassed, sad, disgusted***
- Subjective Units of Disturbances (SUDs): What is your level of distress as we're bringing up these memories/images, negative beliefs, and emotions (0 = no disturbance/neutral through 10 = worst disturbance imaginable)? **7**
- Location of body sensation: What are you noticing in your body in this moment as we're bringing up these memories/images, negative beliefs, and emotions? ***stomach, throat***
- Desensitize (Phase 4): Hold those body sensations together with the negative belief of *my addiction is my identity* and the image of *seeing your dad come to your rescue after getting arrested for a possession when you were 19. Remember that he called you a black sheep.*
- Begin stimulation.

## THE ROLE OF EMDR THERAPY IN WORKING IT THROUGH

After you've accounted for the contextual and other safety factors, the possibilities for using EMDR to target recovery roadblocks are limitless. A major challenge that many in recovery experience is working on the fourth and fifth step. These are often viewed as the steps that cause many people to abandon a 12-step program.

Nancy, one of the first 12-step clients that I guided through the EMDR therapy standard protocol, struggled with Steps 4 and 5 for a long time (Marich, 2009b). These steps require individuals to take a deep look at themselves—the positive and negative traits—and then share what they've found with another person. As a trauma-informed practitioner, it's been evident to me that unhealed trauma can be a significant factor keeping a person from working Steps 4 and 5.

Nancy was a Caucasian female in her mid-40s who was referred to treatment after her third driving under the influence (DUI) charge. She met criteria for alcohol, marijuana, and sedative dependence. Although externally mandated for services, she presented with a high degree of internal motivation, ready to work in an action stage of change. Nancy divulged, "You don't have to convince me I'm an alcoholic. I know what I am. I've just never been able to get past a fourth step . . . and then I always relapse."

History taking revealed that Nancy met the substance dependence criteria since her late teens. As a survivor of multiple childhood sexual traumas, she also met criteria for posttraumatic stress disorder. In the previous decade, she went through five and six treatment episodes (all in a 12-step model) and was not able to achieve any more than 4 months of sobriety. I worked with Nancy during my service at an outpatient rehabilitation center, so I was able to stay with her case from assessment through continuing care. During treatment planning, we decided to directly confront the trauma issues . . . *after* Nancy established enough of a foundation in her recovery. The first component of her treatment plan required her to complete an 8-week outpatient 12-step facilitation (Nowinski & Baker, 2003) treatment group, attend three to four AA meetings a week, and begin working the first three steps with a sponsor.

Nancy completed the 12-step facilitation treatment group successfully, during which time she developed relationships with a sponsor and a support group. We worked on coping and relaxation skills during our individual sessions as she completed the group. Nancy responded very well to breath work and guided visualization exercises. Once her support, coping skills, and sobriety skills were in place, I offered her two possible options: cognitive behavioral therapy (CBT) or EMDR therapy. Because she heard good things about EMDR at a previous treatment center, Nancy opted to use EMDR. We revisited some of her developed coping skills in the context of EMDR Phase 2 preparation, commencing with the reprocessing phases (3–6) when Nancy reported about 3 months of sobriety.

In these sessions, we primarily targeted the negative cognition of "I am shameful," floating back to sexual abuse she experienced at the hands of neighborhood kids. Ultimately, this work led to what she identified as the worst of her sexual traumas—being raped by a close family member at the age of 12. She made multiple connections to sexual assaults she experienced within her toxic marriage to another alcoholic. Nancy cleared all of these targets and she was able to successfully install more positive belief states like "I am worthy." After approximately 10 individual EMDR reprocessing sessions, during which time Nancy continued active AA involvement and worked with her sponsor on the first three steps, Nancy began to write a fourth step. Nancy decided that she wanted me to hear her fifth step. For her, it was important to do a fifth step in an arena where she felt optimally safe. Nowhere does it say that the fifth step needs to be heard by a sponsor or a minister, just *another human being* (Alcoholics Anonymous World Services, 2001). Having a fifth step plan that honored her safety gave her some assurance during her fourth-step process, and after resolving a great deal of toxic shame during her EMDR sessions, Nancy was finally able to work a fourth and fifth step.

Nancy continued to work closely with her sponsor, and she continued sessions every other week with me while she worked through the rest of the steps. In total, Nancy engaged in the treatment process for an entire year, staying sober the entire time. Nancy publicly shared her story at an AA speaker meeting upon celebrating 18 months of sobriety, a remarkable feat considering that she had not previously been able to stay sober any longer than 4 months. Shortly after this first lead, I interviewed Nancy as part of a follow-up research project, and she offered some perspective about her recovery (Marich, 2009b). Nancy credited the combination of EMDR, 12-step work, opening up to a sponsor, seeing addiction as a life-or-death matter, her willingness to change, and deepening her spirituality as factors that worked *together* to help her get sober and well. She also acknowledged that her trauma history made it difficult for her to work the 12 steps of AA during her prior attempts at recovery:

> You can't put anything in the proper perspective. And you can't really get a heads up on what really happened because you were so traumatized and you had such bad experiences and, like in my case, I had the trauma then I had the—I call it the after-effect of my

> ex-husband—pounding over and over and over and over it for like fourteen years after that. I took so much responsibility for it. It was almost like I victimized myself all over again in my mind. (p. 103)

Nancy shared that all of these factors in combination helped her achieve a perspective shift that helped her achieve her goals for recovery. EMDR helped her to put responsibility in its proper perspective—she was able to admit the wrong she did in her addiction without beating herself up for all that was done to her. The last time that Nancy contacted me, she reported 5 years of sobriety.

Standard protocol EMDR can be used any time a person encounters a roadblock on their recovery journey. The key is to understand the basic concept of setting up a target sequence with EMDR therapy. Simply asking the question "What's keeping you stuck?" is powerful. Helping a client come up with an answer to that question and identify a corresponding negative cognition can provide a good opportunity to engage in the floatback process, which can lead to an immensely powerful therapeutic experience.

The extensive qualitative research study I conducted with an ethnically diverse group of women in continuing care (Marich, 2010) took the investigation with Nancy a step further. These women were not my clients, so I had the opportunity to be an objective investigator of EMDR therapy implementation within a 12-step friendly facility. The women's (five African American, four Euro American, and one Iranian) lived experiences suggested that EMDR can be safely and effectively integrated into addiction continuing care as long as proper safety precautions were taken. Just 1 of the 10 women studied credited only EMDR therapy with her sobriety—the majority suggested that other factors like support and lifestyle skills learned while they were in treatment served as critical components in what they were able to achieve.

In the context of this safety and support, the collective sample reported that EMDR therapy allowed them to address the core issues that kept them in an addiction cycle. Ultimately, this standard protocol targeting led to perspective shifts serving the larger recovery process (Marich, 2010). Although many amazing stories of transformation are apparent in the phenomenological data, one woman's interview offered formidable insight on how EMDR can bolster the 12-step recovery process.

Sasha, an African American woman, entered treatment in her mid-40s for cocaine addiction. Acting out and violent behaviors were also issues that needed attention, according to her report. During many previous attempts at addiction recovery, her anger was an obstacle. Sasha was sexually molested as a small child and indicated a long-standing history of discord with her mother. "I am bad" was the core negative cognition defining her identity. I interviewed Sasha when she had 3½ years of continuous sobriety, and at that time, she reflected on the role that anger played for her (Marich, 2009a):

> I was a cesspool of badness . . . of dysfunction. I was very promiscuous . . . I was a liar, a thief, and a cheat. And I was very aggressive, real angry, and I had been molested at the age of 5, and me coming here [to treatment] had really helped me identify all those behaviors I had going on and

> connect the dots on why I did what I did. And in my addiction, I was just angry and I was covering up a lot of feelings, trying to suppress them. So when I came in here, the only feeling I could really identify with was anger. Anger and rage. And by me staying in that addiction as long as I did, I wasn't me, I wasn't my authentic self anymore. I just did what I had to do to survive and did what I did and had to do to get the drugs and alcohol. I was a chronic relapser. And I think that was because, now that I have some awareness of a lot of that, I think it was because I didn't get to none of my core issues. I really didn't. And it was just surfacy stuff: the things you know to say that you say when you do the treatment thing, the treatment jargon. But for me today, it's just totally different, because I've gotten to my core issues. EMDR helped me get in touch with the things, with the resentments I had towards my mom and me wanting to know why my mom didn't love me or care anything about me. During the EMDR, I saw that it's none of my business of why she didn't love me or any of that. I did a lot of crying, I did a lot of that work.

What impressed me about Sasha's interview, and many others in the research, was their ability to use an emotional vocabulary to describe situations that they once found unspeakable. The implications of this dynamic for helping people really dig deep with their recovery journeys are tremendous. In pursuing recovery with this enhanced understanding of trauma's impact on their lives, people may stand a better chance of thriving in recovery as opposed to "white-knuckling it" or just staying abstinent from alcohol, drugs, or other addictive behaviors without true transformation.

Throughout my almost decade-long journey of offering EMDR therapy to people in addiction recovery, I continue to be amazed by how EMDR therapy can play a powerful role for both those in early sobriety (like Nancy and Sasha) and in long-term recovery. Existential questions, often triggered or elicited by adverse life experiences in sobriety, may also arise. "How do I really know what God's will is for my life?" "What is the line between carrying the message of recovery and helping others and possibly becoming consumed by helping others?" "What if life changes and I'm not sure if I believe in a Higher Power . . . or the 12 steps anymore?" EMDR therapy can help people in long-term recovery address these and other questions.

Such was the case for David, who approached me for services after reading about my work with trauma and 12-step recovery. David had 9 years of sobriety from alcohol when he contacted me. A successful businessman, even during his active alcoholism, David changed professions in recovery and pursued an advanced degree to work as a treatment clinician. At the time he came to me for EMDR therapy, he held a prominent leadership position in a treatment setting. Although David was an active member of a 12-step fellowship for many years, he found himself struggling with the rigidity on certain issues as interpreted by many groups. The "God" language was very difficult for him, and as an agnostic he found it even more challenging as he grew in recovery.

David was actively exploring ways to expand his recovery wellness at the time he met me. In the history taking, David revealed that his biological mother relinquished him at the time of his birth. After spending 7 days in a home for unwed mothers, a couple, unable to conceive, adopted him. Five years later they were able to naturally conceive David's younger sister, and then years later they adopted another son from an unwed mother. David explained that, overall, he was well cared for by his adoptive parents and he described his childhood as relatively carefree, yet there were still some unsettling issues that had begun to manifest now that he was in his 50s.

Even though he was sober and successful in his work, he was struggling in many other life domains, namely in connecting with others. He also identified problems with compulsive overeating, even following his sobriety from alcohol. When David presented for EMDR he was unsure if he could describe the relinquishment and experiences connected to being adopted as *trauma*. In our initial history taking session, I explained to David that trauma does not have to meet PTSD criteria for us to name it as trauma, explaining the concept of adverse life experiences as they are described in the adaptive information processing model.

In our initial history taking session I assessed him to be sufficiently stable and capable of handling an extended history. Because David traveled a long distance to see me for services, I asked him to write out as much of a narrative as he was comfortable writing to optimize our time spent in session. Upon reading his presentation, certain statements stood out as trauma-fueled cognitions influencing his presenting maladaptive symptoms. These statements became candidates for EMDR targeting sequences in Phases 3 to 6:

- "I have vague memories of feeling like I was under the microscope whenever I was with people."
- When his friends found out he was adopted (around age 6), they acted in total disbelief and shifted their attitude toward him: "I am guessing I may have felt at the time that something was wrong with that [being adopted]."
- "I felt hugely ashamed and humiliated. I guess more importantly is that it added to my feelings that something was wrong with me. I no longer felt safe around other people or myself."
- "I seemed to become distant or withdrawn. I remember beginning to feel at all times like I didn't belong wherever I went."
- "Some of my fondest childhood memories come from spending time at the lake."
- "I got sober in August 2005, still wondering, as I had my whole life, who I was, where I had come from, and if I had blood family still living."
- At the prospect of meeting his biological half-sister, with whom he was just able to establish contact: "I fear that I'll disappoint them somehow."
- On his general reason for seeking services: "I still feel like a chronic malcontent who is often dissatisfied and rebellious."

In our initial history taking session, I began gathering information about David's existing coping skills, most of which he gained from 12-step exposure. We began discussing a plan for how he could build more body-based coping skills like breathing into his daily regimen. I sent him to some of my online videos that teach breathing and mindfulness skills, and he was willing to try these in between our initial history taking session and our second session. When David presented for his second session, we reviewed which breathing strategies worked the best for him, and discussed other visualizations that might work for distress tolerance. I picked up on his statement in the history that some of his fondest childhood memories came from spending time at a lake where his family vacationed, and we transitioned that into a Calm Safe Place exercise with tactile bilateral stimulation. He chose to alter the safe place for the purpose of the exercise and use the serenity of a Caribbean beach. We also "tapped in" a positive experience that he had at a new 12-step meeting the night before our session.

David responded well to these preparation exercises, and by the third session he expressed readiness to begin reprocessing. I read back the negative self-beliefs that I noted in his narrative, and I asked him to notice which one(s) seemed to most resonate in his body as distressing. For him it was clear: something is wrong with me. He floated that negative cognition back to a memory of two of his childhood friends making a big deal about him being adopted. After attending to other components of the targeting sequence, we begin "going with that."

Within the first two to three sets of bilateral stimulation, David was able to very deeply connect with what was occurring in his body. For David, a self-confessed intellectual with the tendency to overanalyze, being able to sit with body level experience and simply be mindful was vital. At the end of the session when I checked in with him about the initial issue/belief we took through the targeting sequence, he reported a clear body scan and a near zero SUDs. More significantly, his initial goal statement/positive cognition of "I can work through it" was not only completely true, he was able to name two other positive cognitions to claim as completely true: "I am a human being," and "I can trust myself." We ended our session by installing both of those completely true positive cognitions together with the clear body scan.

In the second reprocessing session we revisited the initial memory that we took through the targeting sequence previously to see if anything else may have come up. David reported: "I now have the power to observe it—I was just a kid. I should forgive myself for putting myself through all of that crap." In the spirit of the three-pronged protocol, we commenced this second reprocessing session by having him simply notice how he *presently* views the memory. David spontaneously began articulating new positive beliefs about himself that he was able to integrate and believe were completely true: "I have the power," "I've got this," "I am safe," and "I don't have to protect myself anymore." Additionally, the two positive beliefs that he reported in the previous session held as completely true statements. In our final check-in during that second reprocessing session, David articulated two new positive beliefs of "I am whole" and "I don't feel judged anymore," together with a clear body scan. Said David: "I'm anchored; attached to the present."

In the next session, after checking in with the positive beliefs to make sure that they held their truth, we transitioned into future template work. For his future template, David wanted to work on issues of intimacy and problems connecting with others. David believed that he was *somewhat* confident that he could connect with others. I asked him what kept him from *complete* confidence, and he immediately identified the message that he received in 12-step meetings that *ego is bad*. So I had him consider that notion along with any body experiences that came up as he held it in mind. After applying a few sets of bilateral stimulation, David recognized that he seemed kinder and gentler—and that he could extend that to himself and others. He then made a connection to a famous story in 12-step recovery about the founder Bill Wilson's "bright light experience," and he realized that he finally had something to "give away" to others. Previously, his self-identified "imposter complex" of feeling like a fraud, both personally and professionally, stood in the way. In the next few sets of bilateral stimulation (BLS), he made connections to his family and work life. He ended the session by expressing: "I am more than a victim, a survivor, or a 'rescue,' . . . I am whole." We installed that profound realization as a completely true positive belief.

The final two in-person sessions that I conducted with David focused on reevaluation. The positive beliefs achieved in previous sessions held as completely true statements with a clear body scan. Our natural conversation progressed into discussing what potential pitfalls David might see in moving forward. He stated, "I can find fault like there's a reward for it, at least that's been my pattern." He identified that this tendency began around the time of the target memory we began with at age six, and I had him hold the present experience of that memory together with his insight about finding fault. After a couple of sets of stimulation, he expressed: "That's my head talking, not my heart and my soul." In the next set: "That's a useless energy drain." I also made the decision, in testing out the potency of the generalization effect, to inquire about one of his other negative beliefs identified at the time of history taking: "I am disconnected." I asked him how valid that belief seemed in the moment, and he responded, "It was a delusion—I'm finding the connection within." I had him "go with that" for a few sets, and he ultimately expressed, "I am home." I asked him what, to him, the opposite of "I am disconnected" would be (i.e., his positive cognition) and he said, "I have the capacity to be connected." He reported that was a completely true statement, as it was installed with a clear body scan. David then held that positive belief as he pictured future life scenarios and no distress or concern registered.

David and I followed up via phone call 3 weeks after that last session (part of the reevaluation process) and he noted overall positive progress and maintenance of goals in the weeks since the final in-person session. He said that he was no longer "obsessing" over how he feels, and that he was "over" his feelings of being a fraud. He reported 20 pounds of weight loss in the weeks after his EMDR work, and an increase in faith that everything in his life was going to turn out okay. A final phone call a month later confirmed the maintenance of those achievements. He checked in with me at 3- and 6-month intervals continuing to report maintenance of his EMDR gains. He also indicated further progress in his desire to speak out on adoption issues in the addiction treatment field, working with another collaborator to bring a curriculum to life. In 2015, the book *Do Tell: Stories by Atheists and Agnostics in AA* published David's recovery story; he shared openly and honestly about the adoption component of his story in this venue (see "References" section).

David's case offers an example of EMDR therapy's value as a recovery enhancement measure. Although clinically not meeting the criteria for PTSD upon presentation, it is clear how trauma, especially attachment-related or developmental trauma, continued to cause symptoms of depression and overall disconnection with his life. David's story is a strong example of how EMDR can work very quickly. In many ways, his case allowed for that because he presented for treatment already reasonably stabilized. David had a job, 9 years of sobriety, strong family support, and a willingness to work on himself. Moreover, he came to me already in an action stage of change. For clients at earlier points on the recovery path, EMDR may not progress as smoothly. It may be necessary to practice more patience and utilize more advanced EMDR skills like interweaves. Entering the treatment engagement with this realistic view is critical. Combine this view with the precautions offered on how to work with preparation and the larger context, knowing that you can still make a difference with EMDR therapy.

## SUMMARY: EMDR THERAPY AS "THE MISSING PIECE"

EMDR and addiction specialist Susan Brown (2003) called EMDR the "missing piece" in addiction treatment care. She demonstrated a great respect for traditional addiction approaches in the article that invoked this phrase, yet recognized that there are gaps that need filling. Well-known addiction researchers Zweben and Yeary (2006) made a similar assertion in their landmark article, and I've carried this message of *EMDR as the missing piece* in the various arenas of my work. When fellow 12-steppers or traditional addiction counselors ask me "*Why EMDR?*," I typically answer: Traditional 12-step work gives us a spiritual and lifestyle path for recovery. Treatment centers have customarily added the cognitive-behavioral component to the mix, helping us work with the mind. Yet, little has been done until recent years to work with the body in addiction recovery, especially the legacy of somatic distress left by trauma. This distress is what leads many people to abuse substances in the first place, or it can exacerbate an existing predisposition for addiction.

EMDR therapy, by design, can address all of these issues: the spiritual, the lifestyle, the cognitive, the somatic, and the historical facets of addiction. Targeting adverse life experiences with this approach can help people move beyond simply surviving in life as a person in recovery. Addressing the wounds of these adverse life experiences can help recovering individuals thrive in all areas of their life, just as the adaptive information processing model inspires. The idea of engaging in this full healing process can come with some fear. I often field concerns like, "What if I get so upset that I end up using again?" or "What will it mean for my life if I actually deal with all of this old stuff?" My general response is to first validate the concern. I then explain how the EMDR therapy approach contains an extensive preparation phase that allows us to build the skills one may need to handle addressing these potentially emotional targets. Emphasizing that the client is in control the entire time and always has the power to stop the processing and come back to a stabilizing resource is critical.

We as EMDR therapists tend to get excited about the radical results that EMDR is known to produce regarding trauma resolution. However, I remain most impressed by the safeguards in the EMDR approach (e.g., therapeutic relationship building, the preparation phases, and highlighting client control) that allow clients who identify as being in recovery to feel safe in enhancing their recovery with EMDR. This emphasis on relationship and safety may seem obvious. However, as a member of the community that I covered in this chapter, I attest to the primacy of safety and building the relationship. As individuals in recovery we've been told things like we're lazy, selfish, a waste of a life, and don't want to live in the real world. We've been labeled as the sickest of the sick and told that we can never really change. We've been made to feel weak by those in our families and in the public who proclaim that all we need is a little willpower. Perhaps worst of all, we've been told that we've chosen this life for ourselves. Society and even clinical professionals have referred to us pejoratively as *those people*. Any person in recovery presenting for EMDR will be assessing you, as their treatment provider, to determine if you believe all of these harmful ideas of division and occlusion.

Fadalia is a young woman in recovery from long-term opiate addiction who, with 26 treatment episodes prior to receiving EMDR, was labeled a chronic relapser. When she presented for treatment services at some of the same facilities, it was common for clinicians and medical professionals to roll their eyes at her and chide, "You again?" Fadalia shared that being treated with dignity at the treatment center was a key factor is making her receptive to EMDR therapy (Marich, 2009a, 2010). She noted that everyone at the facility being researched—the clinicians, the medical team, the support staff, the cooks, even the janitors—treated her with respect and made her believe she could get sober. There is a lesson in this simple sharing of lived experience for all of us practicing EMDR therapy. EMDR therapy is more than just a technique or a protocol that can "fix" people, and I am saddened when people view it this way. EMDR therapy is truly an approach that allows for transformation, and getting to know the people we serve before simply reprocessing traumatic memories is paramount.

## REFERENCES

Abel, N., & O'Brien, J. (2014). *Treating addiction with EMDR therapy and the stages of change*. New York, NY: Springer Publishing Company.

Alcoholics Anonymous World Services. (2001). *Alcoholics anonymous* (4th ed.). New York, NY: Author.

Brown, S. (2003). *The missing piece: The case for EMDR-based treatment for posttraumatic stress disorder and co-occurring substance use disorder. LifeForce Trauma Solutions*. Retrieved from http://www.lifeforceservices.com/article_detail.php?recordid=5

Centers for Disease Control and Prevention. (2013). *Major findings, in adverse childhood experiences (ACEs) study*. Retrieved from http://www.cdc.gov/ace/findings.htm

Glasser, G. (2015). The irrationality of Alcoholics Anonymous. *The Atlantic*, April 2015. Retrieved from http://www.theatlantic.com/features/archive/2015/03/the-irrationality-of-alcoholics-anonymous/386255

Greenwald, R. (2010). *EMDR within a phase model of trauma-informed treatment*. Binghampton, NY: Haworth Press.

Hase, M., Schallmayer, S., & Sack, M. (2008). EMDR reprocessing of the addiction memory: Pretreatment, posttreatment, and 1-month follow-up. *Journal of EMDR Practice and Research*, *2*(3), 170–179.

Knipe, J. (2014). *EMDR toolbox: Theory and treatment of complex PTSD and dissociation*. New York, NY: Springer Publishing Company.

Marich, J. (2009a). *EMDR in addiction continuing care: A phenomenological study of women treated in early recovery*. ProQuest Dissertations & Theses: Full Text. (UMI No. 3355347).

Marich, J. (2009b). EMDR in addiction continuing care: Case study of a cross-addicted female's treatment and recovery. *Journal of EMDR Practice and Research, 3*(2), 98–106.

Marich, J. (2010). EMDR in addiction continuing care: A phenomenological study of women in recovery. *Psychology of Addictive Behaviors, 24*(3), 498–507.

Marich, J. (2011). *EMDR made simple: 4 approaches to using EMDR with every client*. Eau Claire, WI: Premier Education & Media.

Miller, R. (2012). Treatment of behavioral addictions using the feeling-state addiction protocol: A multiple baseline study. *Journal of EMDR Practice and Research, 6*(4), 159–169.

Nowinski, J., & Baker, S. (2003). *The twelve-step facilitation handbook* (2nd ed.). Center City, MN: Hazelden.

Ohlms, D. (1991). *The disease of alcoholism: Update* [Video]. Georgetown, TX: FMS Productions/GWC.

Parnell, L. (2008). *Tapping in: A step-by-step guide to activating your healing resources through bilateral stimulation*. Boulder, CO: Sounds True Books.

Peele, S. (2015). *The meaning of addiction: Compulsive experience and its interpretation*. Watertown, MA: Broadrow Publications.

Popky, A. J. (2005). DeTUR, an urge reduction protocol for addictions and dysfunctional behaviors. In R. Shapiro (Ed.), *EMDR solutions: Pathways to healing* (pp. 167–188). New York, NY: W. W. Norton.

Prochaska, J., Norcross, J., & DiClemente, C. (1994). *Changing for good: The revolutionary program that explains the six stages of change and teaches you how to free yourself from bad habits*. New York, NY: William Morrow.

Shapiro, F., & Forrest, M. (1997). *EMDR: The breakthrough "eye movement" therapy for overcoming stress, anxiety, and trauma*. New York, NY: Basic Books.

Shapiro, F., Vogelmann-Sine, S., & Sine, L. (1994). Eye movement desensitization and reprocessing: Treating trauma and substance abuse. *Journal of Psychoactive Drugs, 26*(4), 379–391.

Zweben, J., & Yeary, J. (2006). EMDR in the treatment of addiction. *Journal of Chemical Dependency Treatment, 8*(2), 115–127.

CHAPTER 18

# EMDR With Issues of Appearance, Aging, and Class

Robin Shapiro

## APPEARANCE MATTERS

Culturally defined "attractive" people are more likely to get the job (Gilmore, Beehr, & Love, 1986), the raise (Heilman & Stopeck, 1985), the mate (Jonason, Garcia, Webster, Li, & Fisher, 2015), higher status friends, and better grades (Begley, 2009) than less attractive people. Attractive children receive more attention, especially from strangers. Grade school children become more aware, each year, about the norms of appearance in their schools: what race, body shape, grooming, clothing, and facial structures are acceptable and what is shunned. Regional, social class, family, and gender mores dictate appearance parameters. And ubiquitous media images create often impossible-to-meet expectations of female and male beauty.

Some of our clients have been bullied for the way they look. Many are insecure about their appearance. Some have anxious bodies that overrespond to the threat of social rejection and go round and round with obsessive thoughts about their appearance. And some compulsively work out, starve, and/or have surgery after surgery in an attempt to have an acceptable shape.

As a therapist, your assessments will include your clients' cultural contexts, attachment histories, trauma histories, temperaments, and actual appearances. As an EMDR therapist, you are going to look carefully at clients' cognitions, emotions, and body sensations as you move through their distress. First, clear out the earliest traumas tied to appearance issues. Then, go after what's left. The work naturally goes toward anger, then grief, and then acceptance for the reality of clients' bodies or appearance.

You may want to use the Two-Hand Interweave (Shapiro, 2005a, 2005b) to help pinpoint the distress: "In one hand, hold the way you think you ought to look. In the other hand, hold the way you actually look. <Eye Movements (EMs)> What do you notice now?" Next, ask for the origin of the distress: "When and where did you learn that you were supposed to look like that?" Then target, with the standard protocol, the moment of the realization that there was a standard the client did not match.

## GARDEN VARIETY FAT SHAME

Here is an example of a way-too-typical body-hating woman: "Jodi," a 29-year-old, came to therapy to deal with a bad breakup. After clearing out the trauma-driven distortions and settling into the grieving process, we went after her hatred of her short, round, but not obese, body.

**Therapist:** *Could you put the body you think you should have in one hand, and the body you actually have in the other? Stay with both of those for a moment.* <EMs> *What do you notice now?*

**Jodi:** "The fat body hand feels disgusting!"

**Therapist:** *When's the first time it felt that way?*

**Jodi:** "I was in sixth grade and watching the cool girls laughing together. They all were skinny and had great clothes, and I was a mess."

**Therapist:** *What would that girl say about herself?*

**Jodi:** "I'm fat and ugly and no one should like me."

**Therapist:** *Looking back, what would your adult self say about that girl?*

**Jodi:** "She's okay. She was a working-class kid in a ritzy school and didn't know the rules, but she's a good kid.

**Therapist:** *When you think about watching those girls laughing together, how true does it feel in your gut, one to seven, that you are good enough?*

**Jodi:** "A one."

**Therapist:** *What feeling goes with that scene?*

**Jodi:** "Self-disgust. I guess that's shame."

**Therapist:** *How big is that, one to ten?*

**Jodi:** "Nine."

**Therapist:** *And where in your body does that shame live?*

**Jodi:** "In my curled up neck and shoulders."

**Therapist:** *Go with that.* <EMs>

**Jodi:** "Now I'm remembering every time I saw a skinny girl. And I feel hopeless. I'll never be like that."

**Therapist:** [utilizing Jim Knipe's "Loving Eyes" protocol (2015), which brings the adult sensibility to younger, shamed ego states:] *Can you get in touch with the adult part, the one that thinks you're good enough? Great, go back and get that sixth grader. Bring her up here. Show her around. I want you to imagine you and she are watching a movie of the skinny, rich girls laughing together with your kid looking on and feeling shame.* <EMs> *What does the kid see?*

**Jodi:** "She sees a stupid, fat, yucky kid, who no one should pay attention to."

**Therapist:** *What does your adult see?*

**Jodi:** "She sees that girl being ignored because she's different in a lot of ways. And that kid isn't horribly fat, just not skinny. I think she's cute."

**Therapist:** *Can that adult look over at the kid with loving eyes and explain that to her? Let her know that not fitting in isn't about her appearance, or her goodness."* <EMs>

**Jodi:** "Okay. I'm telling her. It's taking a while for her to believe me….

Now she's settling down, like a big sigh. She feels better."

**Therapist:** *How true does it feel now, that you're good enough?*

**Jodi:** "More now."

**Therapist:** *What's keeping it from being true?*

**Jodi:** "I'm still fat."

**Therapist:** *What's the feeling now?*

**Jodi:** "Angry!"

**Therapist:** *Go with that!* <EMs>

**Jodi:** [while processing] "I hate this body! I'll never get another man … I hate looking in the mirror."

**Therapist:** *How old is that?*

**Jodi:** "Teenager, of course."

**Therapist:** *What was her input about her body?*

**Jodi:** "Every movie, magazine, TV show, everything. And then all the weird social stuff."

**Therapist:** *I wonder what part of that equation deserves your anger.*

**Jodi:** "Well, yeah. Fuck that media trying to sell me that stuff."

**Therapist:** *Go with THAT!* <EMs>

**Jodi:** "I'm feeling better, but I still don't like my fat."

**Therapist:** *Hold the body you think you should have in one hand again, and the one you have in the other. What do you notice this time?*

**Jodi:** "The one I should have is not as skinny as it was earlier today! And I don't feel disgusted anymore at the other one… more like sad."

**Therapist:** *Go with that.* <EMs>

**Jodi:** "You know, it's not so bad. I've got a healthy body. I'm in pretty good shape. I still do get hit on… I'm never going to look like a model, but I'm okay. I mean it. I'm really okay. It's a seven, now.

**Therapist:** *Where do you feel that okayness in your body?*

**Jodi:** "My heart, and believe it or not, my stomach."

**Therapist:** *Go with that!* <EMs>

## FUNNY LOOKING KID

Ned had a round face, a large brow, and very large ears. He came from an upper-class family that prized "fitting in" above all else. As a baby, he was likely diagnosed as an "FLK," a "funny looking kid," the physician's chart note for babies who may have Down syndrome, fetal alcohol syndrome, or an odd-shaped head. As an adult, he looked a little odd, but not unpleasant, and strategically grew his hair and whiskers to hide his face. He came to therapy for depression, and we quickly discovered the shame that kept him "hunkered down."

In his therapy, we started early, using Maureen Kitchur's (2005) strategic developmental model. Kitchur targets trauma in developmental order, positing that the client is developmentally older at each session, and will not be overwhelmed with early material in subsequent work. We started targeting attachment injuries in his early childhood (raised by the staff, not the favored child, etc.), moving on to bullying in grade school and middle school, and to his drug-and-booze-laden high school and college years. Targets tied to appearance included:

1. His father saying, "I never thought a kid of mine would look like you."
2. Name calling and physical bullying from age 10 to 16.
3. His fear of rejection that kept him from asking girls out, which he never did in high school.
4. His reaction to other people's reaction to meeting him for the first time—the "stare."
5. Current beliefs that he will not be liked or connected to (despite having friends and a nice, connectable wife).
6. Fears of saying no because, "someone like me doesn't deserve to."

We used many future templates, including:

1. Running into the "double-take" people have at his appearance. *How would you like to respond to that?*
2. Saying "no" or "I want" and dealing with people's responses.
3. Encountering his image in the mirror.

I pulled out a portrait-sized mirror and had him look at himself. *What's your response to seeing that guy? What would you like to say about him? What feeling arises? How big? Where is it?* In the processing, he went through the anger, grief, and acceptance phases, ending with, "I've got a funny face and people are going to react, and I'm okay." When we imagined the future instances of that, we came up with some funny things to say to new people, changing his dread to a possibility of playful connection.

In about a year of therapy, Ned's depression abated as the trauma dissolved. He no longer saw himself as flawed, just "different." And he had developed humor about his situation, a grand way of bringing perspective to his "funny-looking" face.

## AGING

If we are lucky, aging brings wisdom and growing acceptance of ourselves and our place in the world. Aging inevitably brings bodily change: fat, wrinkles, and declining abilities. We go gray or lose our hair. It takes more effort to maintain strength. New illnesses crop up. Our sexual responses change or disappear. And as we watch our age-mates decline and die, and our own bodies fall apart, we face mortality.

Some people navigate the aging process with grace; grieving, then accepting the alterations of time. Others face their changes with fear and shame. Youthful images pervade media and advertising. For women, forever, and increasingly for men, smooth skin and firm bodies are social currency. For some men, losing bodily strength or the ability to get and maintain an erection is a loss of identity. EMDR therapy will not halt the aging process, but can assist people to mourn their former bodies and accept their current ones.

### The Invisible Woman

"Betty," a composite based on several clients and several conversations I have overheard, was 76, a retired manager, and depressed. She described her younger self as "quite attractive." She said, "If I walked into a store or a party, people would stop what they were doing and say something. Now, I'm invisible. I can't get help at the store. People don't look up when I walk in a room. And it's not just men, it's everyone."

We discussed the social aspects of aging and being seen, and the particular loss she had as a former "hottie" (her word). We had already processed some losses and earlier traumas, when we turned our attention to her appearance. When we processed the body she had versus the body she has, she moved through stages of grief: anger, sadness, hopelessness, and acceptance. The attention-from-others target went differently. We started with the present,

**Therapist:** *Imagine walking into a store, and the clerk looks right through you and helps a younger woman. What do you say to yourself about that?*

**Betty:** "I don't exist. I'm not important."

**Therapist:** *What would you like to know about yourself?*

**Betty:** "I'm here and I matter, dammit!" (VoC 2)

**Therapist:** *When you think about that scene and not existing, what feelings are you having?*

**Betty:** "Anger and helplessness." (UD 8)

**Therapist:** *Where do you feel that?*

**Betty:** "Face, throat, and chest."

**Therapist:** *When's the first time you ever felt that way?*

**Betty:** "... A long time ago. When I was a kid, my mother was depressed, and sometimes couldn't really react to me. I had no idea this was related."

**Therapist:** *Think about your mom not responding, feel that helplessness, and go with that.*

We cleared early targets with her mother and some grade school incidents and Betty began to realize that she had received most of her good attention outside the family, from people responding to the cute little girl and the attractive older girl. She saw that she had leveraged her attractiveness for attention her whole life.

**Therapist:** *So, Betty, were you a worthwhile person, besides your good looks?*

**Betty:** "Sure. I was a good mother . . . I still am. And I did my work well. And I'm nice to people."

**Therapist:** *Where do you feel that goodness in your body? Go with that!* [After we installed her sense of goodness, we came back to the future.]

*Imagine that store clerk again. What do you notice?*

**Betty:** "I'm just mad."

**Therapist:** *Go with that.*

**Betty:** "I still feel stuck."

**Therapist:** *What do you want to do about it?*

**Betty:** "Get her attention."

**Therapist:** *Do it! And go with that.*

**Betty:** "I said, 'Hey Miss, I was here first.' and she waited on me."

**Therapist:** *How does that feel?*

**Betty:** "Good!"

**Therapist:** *Go with that!*

We did another future template with social gatherings. With her new sense of okayness and assertiveness, Betty saw that she could directly ask for attention by approaching people she wanted to be with. In future sessions, she told me that it was working. "I no longer get the immediate attention that I'm used to, but I know how to make my presence known, and get what I need. And you know what? People like me anyway."

## SUMMARY

Appearance issues run through every race, class, gender, and culture and many of our clients. EMDR therapists are trained to work with the "real" trauma of war, sexual abuse, violence, cataclysmic events, and car accidents. The shame that underlies issues of appearance, aging, and socially constructed differences are necessary, appropriate, and helpful targets for many clients. The higher the social class, the more appearance-shaming (Fussell, 1992). People who had no overt abuse may have crippling social shame for minor variations in appearance. Ask your clients if they have any issues with the way they look. You may be surprised at the number of okay-looking men and women who report deep shame at the bodies they inhabit.

## REFERENCES


Begley, S. (2009, July 14). The link between beauty and grades. *Newsweek*.

French, M., Robins, P., Homer, J., & Tapsell, L. (2009, August). Effects of physical attractiveness, personality, and grooming on academic performance in high school. *Labour Economics, 16*(4), 373–382.

Fussell, P. (1992). *Class: A guide through the American status system.* New York, NY: Touchstone.

Gilmore, D. C., Beehr, T. A., & Love, K. G. (1986). Effects of applicant sex, applicant physical attractiveness, type of rater, and type of job on interview decisions. *Journal of Occupational Psychology, 59*, 103–109.

Heilman, M. E., & Stopeck, M. H. (1985). Being attractive, advantage or disadvantage? Performance based evaluations and recommended personnel actions as a function of appearance, sex, and job type. *Organizational Behavior and Human Decision Processes, 35*, 202–215.

Jonason, P. K., Garcia, J. R., Webster, G. D., Li, N. P., & Fisher, H. E. (2015). Relationship deal-breakers: Traits people avoid in potential mates. *Personality and Social Psychology Bulletin, 41*, 1697–1711.

Kitchur, M. (2005). The strategic developmental model for EMDR. In R. Shapiro (Ed.), *EMDR solutions: Pathways to healing.* New York, NY: W. W. Norton.

Knipe, J. (2015). *EMDR toolbox: Theory and treatment of complex PTSD and dissociation.* New York, NY: Springer Publishing Company.

Shapiro, R. (2005a). Cultural and generational introjects. *EMDR solutions: Pathways to healing.* New York, NY: W. W. Norton.

Shapiro, R. (2005b). The two-hand interweave. *EMDR solutions: Pathways to healing.* New York, NY: W. W. Norton.

# SECTION VI

# Global Frontiers of EMDR Intervention

CHAPTER 19

# Learning EMDR in Uganda: An Experiment in Cross-Cultural Collaboration

Rosemary Masters, Elizabeth McConnell, and Josie Juhasz

*Look, I have a file drawer filled with manuals and handbooks from specialized workshops taught by kind, intelligent Americans who came through and left before I could really figure out what their ideas were all about. I would try to use the techniques they taught us for a while but then give up when they just didn't work.*

—Ugandan Mental Health Counselor

"England and America are two countries separated by a common language." Variously attributed to Oscar Wilde, George Bernard Shaw, and Winston Churchill, the quip amuses not least because of its whiff of British condescension—"If only you colonials could speak correctly, how much better we would get along!"[1] Amusing as it may be, the aphorism embodies a powerful truth: Peoples who speak the same language may significantly misunderstand one another because of differences in accent, pronunciation, vocabulary, idioms, common metaphors, culture, and history. Such potential misunderstandings can be compounded when the mother tongue of one or both speakers is not English, and most especially if the subject of communication is a technical subject of which one has extensive knowledge and the other relatively little.

We suggest that more than mutual incomprehension is at stake when the technical elites of one class, region, or country attempt to transmit their skills to individuals of a class, region, or country other than their own. We join the philosopher Freire (1996) who asserts that efforts of educators from privileged elites to communicate their "superior" knowledge to those dealing with the burdens of weak economies, corrupt government, and limited opportunities result in negative consequences. In his radical indictment of the seemingly well-meaning projects of the economically and politically privileged to "educate" those who lack access to

[1] For a discussion as to the origin of the ". . . separated by a common language" quotation, see *English Language and Usage Stack Exchange* (English.stackexchange.com).

the same privileges, he argues that *the process of education itself can become an act of oppression*:

> Pedagogy which begins with the egoistic interests of the oppressors (an egoism cloaked in the false generosity of paternalism) and makes of the oppressed the object of its humanitarianism itself maintains and embodies oppression. (p. 36)

In essence, Freire tells us that when knowledge is delivered from "above" without respect for the culture, values, and perspective of those who receive it, that knowledge cannot be adequately understood, integrated, and employed in a way that is useful to those being "taught" or to the society in which they live. At best the "educatees" waste time and money trying to learn a technique they do not comprehend and cannot use. At worst they are disheartened and ashamed about their own inadequate abilities and the "inferior" culture in which they live.

Freire characterizes the efforts of elites to bestow half-baked and ineffectual education upon the oppressed as a deft means by which elites absolve themselves of the guilt they may experience on encountering the vast inequalities between themselves and the oppressed. If the oppressed fail to benefit from the generosity of the privileged, it can only be due to the inherent inferiority of the oppressed.

While involved in efforts to bring about greater understanding of psychological trauma in Uganda, the authors witnessed more than one instance of what Freire would regard as self-aggrandizement masquerading as altruism. On one occasion we spoke with a group of American teenagers shortly after they had visited a Ugandan orphanage. The smartly clad youngsters had ceremoniously donated soccer balls to the orphanage and, over the course of 2 hours, demonstrated their considerable athletic prowess to the Ugandan youngsters. The Americans appeared delighted by their generosity and seemed oblivious to the fact that the institution they were visiting could barely afford food and clothing for their charges. Replacement soccer balls, even a pump for deflated ones, were unaffordable. We were struck by the boys' lack of curiosity about how their "gifts" may have been experienced. They did not seem to wonder about their impact on the objects of their charity. Were the orphans inspired or discouraged? Did their efforts accomplish temporary or lasting changes? If changes occurred, were they positive or negative? Given their age, it is understandable that these enthusiastic youths were naïve when it came to assessing the utility of their efforts. Ugandan friends have taught us, however, that far more sophisticated educational efforts also fail for similar reasons: too much self-congratulation and too little curiosity.

This chapter considers some of the obstacles to integrated learning that arise when experts in the theory and treatment of psychological trauma attempt to share their skills with colleagues practicing in another country. Such obstacles loom especially large in countries and regions burdened with poverty, histories of civil unrest, corruption, and inadequate infrastructure. Our focus will be on a specific project, one of collaboration between the Uganda Counselling Association and the Trauma Studies Center of the Institute for Contemporary Psychotherapy (which is based in New York City). The project's primary goal was to introduce a model of eye movement desensitization and reprocessing (EMDR) training that would support enduring commitment to and use of EMDR treatment by clinicians who are culturally sensitive to the ethnic groups they serve, and especially by clinicians who are themselves members of the ethnic group they serve.

We begin by describing the specific context in which the project was initiated. We describe, using Freire's perspective, the pitfalls and barriers to authentic learning inherent whenever those with first world technical skills attempt to teach those skills to counterparts in a developing country like Uganda. We recount how we worked with our Ugandan colleagues to avoid those pitfalls and overcome those barriers. We enumerate in detail what we and our Ugandan colleagues learned from each other about adapting the eight phases of EMDR treatment to the Ugandan context. We summarize the pedagogical implications of what we have learned and conclude with thoughts on what it takes to bring effective EMDR training to a country like Uganda.

One final introductory point: We originally titled this chapter, "Teaching EMDR in Uganda." As we reflected on our experiences in Kampala, we had to acknowledge how profoundly reciprocal this project was and how we learned as much as, if not more than, those taking the training; hence, we revised our title to "Learning EMDR in Uganda." We think this title expresses more accurately the mutuality of the experience. For similar reasons, we have avoided using the terms *students* and *trainees* when referring to those who took part in the training because such terms are more hierarchical than is appropriate to what actually took place. Instead we use the terms *colleagues* and *participants* to suggest the degree to which we attempted to make the learning experience, in Freire's terms, truly "dialogic."

## THE CONTEXT OF THE PROJECT

Our observations and recommendations arise out of a specific context. In 2008, two of the authors (Masters and McConnell) were invited to Uganda by Pilgrim Africa, an indigenous nongovernmental organization serving Soroti, a town in the Teso region of north-central Uganda. On the occasion of this visit, they were asked to present a one-day seminar that reviewed the causes of and helpful responses to posttraumatic stress disorder (PTSD). Subsequently, Lois Ochieng, then president of the Uganda Counselling Association, asked us to assist the Association in obtaining training in EMDR for Ugandan mental health practitioners.

Ms. Ochieng explained that because of the extremely high incidence of psychological trauma in Uganda, members of the Association had traveled to other counties eager to learn EMDR. The experience had proved unsatisfactory for a variety of reasons including cost, cultural differences, and difficulties understanding the accents of the trainer and facilitators. More generally, she commented, "We just didn't get it." Her concerns echoed Freire's critique of failed efforts by elites to teach concepts that require not just memorization but an active integration of ideas that can be used as guides for constructive and effective action.

> The more students work at storing the deposits [of information] entrusted to them, the less they develop the critical consciousness which would result from their intervention in the world as transformers of that world. (p. 54)

With considerable acerbity Freire notes that while rote educational efforts are touted as generous, they are in fact designed to "preserve a profitable situation by failing to foster the kind of critical consciousness which might lead the oppressed to challenge a status quo which favors those who hold the economic and political reins of power" (p. 54).

On returning to New York, we proposed that the Trauma Studies Center, a division of the Institute for Contemporary Psychotherapy, would develop a pilot project in concert with the Uganda Counselling Association. The goal of the project would be to develop an approach to EMDR training that would lead to the eventual embedding of this method of trauma treatment in the Ugandan mental health system. We would come to describe this approach as one of *cross-cultural collaboration.*

As we envisioned it, we would arrange for basic EMDR training to be taught in Uganda. During the training, we would be in continual discussion with the participants as to the difficulties they encountered in understanding the model and in employing it in their clinical practice. We would encourage them to figure out how to make the concepts intelligible to their clients and how they might best adapt EMDR to the specific challenges of their own economic, social, and political context. We were, in effect, adopting Freire's injunction that effective education, especially adult education, requires active cognition, not just mere rote learning on the part of *both* student and teacher:

> The teacher is no longer merely the-one-who-teaches, but one who is himself taught in dialogue with the students, who in turn, while being taught, also teach. They become jointly responsible for a process in which all grow. (p. 61)

Our immediate objective was to foster the development of a core of Ugandan therapists who were not just personally skilled in the practice of EMDR, but committed to expanding the pool of Ugandan therapists equipped to treat their own psychologically traumatized people. Our colleague, Dr. William Zangwill, an experienced EMDR trainer, agreed to train and supervise one of the authors (Masters) as the EMDR trainer for the project. Dr. Zangwill also prepared a simplified manual that would be user-friendly in the Ugandan context while remaining within EMDRIA guidelines for such a manual. This experimental model of EMDR training was approved by EMDRIA.

Meanwhile, the Uganda Counselling Association launched a vigorous outreach effort to its members. The Association committed a considerable percentage of its annual funds and membership energies to this project and secured meeting spaces, meals, and training materials for four EMDR trainings. At the end of the four trainings (offered over the course of 5 years) some 60 counselors, all with the equivalent of a U.S. master's degree in mental health counseling or social work, completed EMDR basic training.

To achieve our long-term goal, we aimed to build a sustainable cohort of EMDR therapists who would be committed to training others and to increasing the availability of EMDR to their country's citizens. We cannot claim to have been consistently skilled in eliciting feedback from the participants nor sufficiently sensitive to cultural differences that interfered with learning. What we attempted, however, was commitment to Freire's concept of learning as a process of dialogue. We invited our Ugandan colleagues to tell us when we were violating the norms and rules of their society. We wanted them to show us what worked for them, as well as what didn't. We tried to notice what was comprehensible and what was not. In short, we looked to *them* to educate *us* about them.

## OBSTACLES TO MUTUAL CROSS-CULTURAL LEARNING

During each EMDR training, we made it a point to create opportunities for feedback. As a rule, the training team did not eat lunch together as a group. Rather, we broke up and sat as individuals with our Ugandan colleagues. We solicited discussion and disagreement in the small practice groups where participants felt free to express opinions openly. Each night the team reviewed the day's progress, noting what had gone well and what had not. This willingness to hear and respond to participants' concerns required us to be flexible about the learning plan. Sometimes we needed to review material previously taught. Over time we began to see certain repetitive patterns of difficulty and became more skilled at addressing them.

### Deference to Authority

Uganda, prior to the British protectorate established in the early 20th century, was governed by tribal systems grounded in respect for elders.[2] The chief of a given tribe or clan was presumed to have the wisdom and knowledge necessary for the group. This patriarchal system of deference to the elders was reinforced with the introduction of the 19th century British model of education. For the most part it was based on lecture and rote learning, a method of pedagogy that was, in many respects, the very embodiment of the "bank deposit teaching" that Freire deplores.

This emphasis on deference to authority can be a significant barrier to integrated learning for our Ugandan colleagues. To challenge a trainer's or facilitator's communication as unclear or invalid is to commit a serious breach of good manners, one that risks shaming the trainer or the participants.

Our practice of soliciting input from individuals in their practice groups and during lunch times made it easier for our colleagues to point out problems they had with learning. We characterized the training as collaborative. We celebrated moments when a participant questioned something we said or offered his or her own ideas.

### Formality of Conduct

Intertwined with the Ugandan tradition of deference to authority is an emphasis on formal conduct. The unity of the group as a whole is framed by interactions between those to whom respect is owed and those offering respect. This dynamic reinforces the status of each. In this society, mutual concern for one another is prized. Group

[2] An excellent concise history of Uganda is offered by the University of Pennsylvania's Center for African Studies at the web-address www.africa.upenn.edu/NEH/uhistory.htm

unity is reflected in the custom of beginning official meetings with a Christian prayer. Respect for officials and other leaders is acknowledged by formally identifying and thanking them for their participation. The order of who speaks first and last at a meeting further reinforces the mutual roles and obligations of host and guest. Meetings typically close with another prayer asking God's grace and a safe journey home to the participants.

Americans, with our informality of interpersonal behavior and our goal-oriented tendency to "cut to the chase" and get things done, can unwittingly violate the Ugandan cultural norms. We were tempted, for example, to rush through the opening protocol of offering prayer, being welcomed by and acknowledging the welcome of the leaders of the meeting, and expressing gratitude to the presence of other important officials. We are more likely to interrupt than our Ugandan colleagues and, on occasion, we committed breaches of propriety without having the slightest idea that we were doing so.

## Emphasis on Relationship

Ugandan society is extremely relational. Friends, acquaintances, even strangers are quick to ask about one another's well-being and quick to offer comfort when they notice another person has any kind of distress. A typical exchange between our Ugandan colleagues and us could go like this:

> "How did you sleep last night?"
>
> "Not too well. I am still dealing with jet lag."
>
> "Sorry, sorry! Can I get you some tea? That might make you feel better."

Such expression of concern for the person with whom one is interacting has importance beyond formal manners. Hierarchy implies responsibility. Formality requires attention to the physical and emotional needs of the other. To be alone is to be profoundly bereft in a country that lacks many basic services. Expressions of genuine concern from people we barely knew often surprised us. We suspect that our colleagues may at times have experienced us as a bit cool and brusque. In any case, we tried to remember to be more relational ourselves by frequently inquiring about the health and well-being of our colleagues and their families and by congratulating them when we learned of a marriage or birth of an important family member.

## Other Cultural Issues

A wide range of cultural beliefs, practices, and nuances could have potentially impeded assimilation of EMDR concepts and methods by participants. For example, eye movements in American practice are often stimulated by asking the client to follow two raised fingers. That particular hand gesture, we learned, is a sign of support for a political party. As such, use of two fingers as the point of visual focus could be quite disconcerting Ugandans are keenly aware of the underlying fragility of political order in their society.

In rural areas, EMDR could be interpreted as a form of witchcraft and thereby subject to local fear and suspicion. We learned this information solely by soliciting feedback rather than from spontaneous expressions of concern from participants. Equally important was our asking participants to offer suggestions as to how these problems could be avoided; for example, the search for language to explain EMDR to rural farmers and their families was the subject of much discussion between the training team and participants.

## Separated by a Common Language

English and Kiswahili are Uganda's national languages; however, these are not the mother tongues of most citizens. The country is made up of 56 tribal groups who speak some 40 different languages and dialects. Numerous misunderstandings and confusions can result in the course of EMDR training.

### Accents

We often had difficulty understanding our Ugandan colleagues. We did not always appreciate the fact that our accents could make us unintelligible to them. Our colleagues found our accents especially troublesome when we gave words an American rather than a British emphasis. On the other hand, we sometimes became confused because some Ugandan languages lack common English consonants; for example, some participants pronounced the word *search* as "church."

### Vocabulary

Many words have different meanings to Americans as opposed to those speaking British English. Two simple examples: a car's trunk is its *boot* and its hood is its *bonnet*.

### Idioms

American idioms can carry very different meanings for our Ugandan listeners. For example, American EMDR therapists may instruct a client who has reported a new association, "Go with that," meaning, "Notice that association and see where your mind goes next." To some Ugandans, the phrase is said with a disdainful emphasis that implies, "That's really dumb; don't expect me to believe it"—the opposite of what an American trainer intends to communicate!

### Metaphors

EMDR training uses a great many metaphors. Some of these metaphors did not resonate for our Ugandan colleagues. For example, American EMDR participants are instructed to tell clients that EMDR processing is "Like going through a tunnel. You can see light at the end. It is important to keep moving." When participants were asked if this metaphor made sense, we were told it does not. Uganda has virtually no tunnels of any length. Roads go around mountains, not through them.

The passenger railway system, which once had tunnels, ceased to operate decades ago (L. Ochieng, personal communication, September, 2015).

### Misunderstandings Resulting From Double Translations

Acholi-speaking participants, upon being told to use the phrase "Notice that" during the desensitization phase of the EMDR protocol, translated it in their own minds into an Acholi phrase that has several meanings. Subsequently, in practice sessions the therapists retranslated the Acholi phrase back into an English phrase that was not suited to the context. The client would be asked, "How do you feel about that?"—one of the possible English meanings of the Acholi phrase. The result was that the "client" stopped processing to describe her feelings.

## Economic Realities

There is a vast difference between the buying power of American and Ugandan citizens, even those with comparable educational and professional backgrounds. Failure to be attuned to these differences caused us at times to be insensitive to the reality of our colleagues' lives. For example, we considered recommending that participants purchase Neurotek's "Theratappers" because they were less expensive than the company's light bars. Our Ugandan colleagues pointed out that *both* devices would be unaffordable to many participants. Similarly, supplies such as paper, crayons, markers, white boards, and stuffed animals are not routinely provided in schools or social service agencies. Our suggestions that clients, especially children, should be encouraged to make drawings about their experiences failed to consider that in many settings even such basic items as pens and paper must be supplied by the clinician and, as such, are no small burden to the clinician.

Supplies for the EMDR training itself—manuals, notebooks, blackboard chalk, tear sheets, and especially copying of target assessment sheets and other materials—significantly stressed the budget of the Uganda Counselling Association. Many of the conveniences Americans take for granted, such as waste paper baskets, tissues, and toilet paper, are not routinely available. Discarding of or inattention to such items was experienced as disrespectful to the host organization. Cumulatively, our expectations versus the reality of the Ugandan economy put us at risk of creating, like those teenage soccer players, the sense of futility decried by Freire. We learned to respect the care with which unused materials were carefully gathered and safeguarded at the end of each day's training, and learned to do the same.

## Insufficient Knowledge With Respect to Psychological Trauma

EMDR training in the United States assumes some reasonable familiarity with trauma theory: What is a psychological trauma? What are the symptoms of trauma? What are the underlying neurobiological causes of PTSD and other trauma disorders? What are the fundamental goals of trauma treatment? In the more than 23 years since Herman's (1997) *Trauma and Recovery* was published, many American clinicians who treat trauma survivors have absorbed directly and indirectly the implicit assumptions of trauma theory. This is not a given for most Ugandan clinicians.

We addressed this difference in fundamental trauma knowledge by devoting the first morning of EMDR training to summarizing the basic elements of trauma theory. As the actual EMDR training progressed, we repeatedly referred back to ideas such as linking of neural networks, the concept of adaptive integration, and the ultimate goal of reduction in trauma symptoms. We found that a solid understanding of trauma theory facilitated what Freire termed, "acts of cognition, not transferrals of information" (p. 60). One participant commented:

> What has happened in this training is that there has been "buy in" on our part. It is really exciting for us! EMDR is not just an abstract concept anymore. When we understand why EMDR works, we want to bring it into our clinical practice.

### Infrastructure Problems

Technology created various problems for us. Despite Uganda's advanced development when compared with many African countries, the city of Kampala nonetheless suffers from frequent electrical blackouts and outdated technology. Telephones, especially landlines, often don't work. At critical moments, lack of power delayed copying of important teaching materials. Reliance on flash drives for slide presentations and teaching materials proved risky. The relentless updating of American software often made our computers and those of our Ugandan colleagues mutually incompatible.

And of course there is the bane of so many rapidly developing countries—traffic jams caused by highways inadequate for the number of cars on the road. Participants who arrived late as a result of Uganda's massive transportation problems needed understanding and special attention from facilitators. Overall, tolerance, flexibility, and good humor on the part of the training team when it came to these problems went far to create the atmosphere of mutual respect and learning.

In sum, we faced challenges with respect to cultural norms, language, economics, infrastructure, and lack of specific understanding of trauma. Such challenges, we believe, are inherent with respect to any cross-cultural learning project.

## CHALLENGES TO LEARNING EMDR AS A SPECIFIC MODEL OF TREATMENT

As we introduced each of the eight phases of EMDR treatment to participants, we learned from our colleagues that modifications of language and protocol are required. Many, if not most, of their clients come from rural backgrounds with limited opportunity for education and deeply held animist traditions and beliefs. These differences of culture and education created significant problems for the implementation of the EMDR protocol.

## Phase 1: History Taking

Differences in language and communication style required modification of standard U.S. history taking methods. American diagnostic terms may be unintelligible to Ugandan clients. For example, some of Uganda's languages and dialects have no words for anxiety or depression. Exploring symptoms for these and similar conditions may require very concrete behavioral questions such as "How often do you cry?" "Do you feel dead inside?" "Do you feel like your body shakes like a rattle all the time?"

In a country where there are eight medical doctors for every 100,000 citizens, most people see a medical doctor infrequently and only if severely ill. Many receive care from village healers and know about or have witnessed exorcism rites performed by Christian pastors or animist healers. Proper medical and mental health history taking, especially among the rural poor, needs to include inquiries about the belief that one is possessed by ancestors, malevolent spirits, or the devil.

## Phase 2: Preparation

Finding the right metaphor for trauma itself proved challenging. Our colleagues came up with three possibilities. First they suggested that:

> Trauma is like a neatly packed suitcase that falls off the bed so that shoes and clothing are scattered everywhere.

They quickly recognized that many rural people travel infrequently; so next they suggested that:

> A trauma is like a glass bottle that breaks and pieces scatter everywhere. If you step on a piece it cuts your foot and hurts.

They decided this metaphor may be experience-distant for impoverished people living in refugee camps or the most remote rural areas where plastic containers rather than glass are familiar items of use. Finally, participants were satisfied with this rendition of a traumatic experience:

> A trauma is like a storm that blows the roof off a hut. Straw, nails, poles are scattered everywhere. Healing happens when those materials are put back together and maybe some new things added so that now the house is stronger than ever.

The standard description of EMDR offered to American clients did not strike our Ugandan colleagues as especially illuminating, because the terminology struck them as too abstract. Together with their facilitator, one group developed the following explanation that emphasized sensory and somatically focused experience:

> Your eyes have seen too much horror; your ears have heard too much pain and sadness; your nose has smelled things that have made you

> sick. It is not just your body that has been hurt in terrible ways. The memories of what has happened continue to pain you like unhealed wounds. EMDR can help heal the memories of what has happened.

Participants were asked to develop a culturally appropriate recasting of the standard EMDR tunnel metaphor: "EMDR is like going through a tunnel as rapidly as possible with the goal of reaching the light at the other end." When one of us asked our Ugandan colleagues for a better metaphor, they suggested the following:

> When you think about the pain of what happened, imagine you are deep in the bush where it is dark and the sticks and thorns grab at you. Together you and I will walk out of the bush into the sunlight to a field of grass where the sky is blue. Once you arrive there, the pain will be much less or even gone.

What stands out here is that participants, in collaboration with the facilitator, created a metaphor appropriate to the context of Ugandan lives, the majority of whom live or grew up in rural villages surrounded by dense thorny brush ("the bush"). A seemingly minor, but important detail is the presence of the therapist in the metaphor—"*Together, you and I will walk out of the bush into the sunlight. . . .*" The metaphor assumes a relational experience. The client and therapist are together. In our highly individualized culture, Americans expect, as the old hymn states, that "You have to walk that lonesome valley . . . by yourself." In the powerfully relational society of our colleagues, walking by yourself is unthinkably lonely and dangerous. Here, in our view, is cross-cultural collaboration at its best. We were open to being challenged about our language. Our colleagues found solutions more culturally apt and poetic than we could have ever imagined ourselves.

## Phases 3 and 4: Target Assessment and Desensitization

Emphasis on the visual aspect of a traumatic experience (the picture) did not always create an emotionally powerful target for our Ugandan colleagues. We are not sure why this was the case. In part it may be that Americans, as a result of our universal exposure to movies and television, and the abundance of books and other visually based learning mediums, may relate more powerfully to visual memories, whereas other sensory memories, smells, textures, and especially sounds may be more accessible to Ugandans for whom learning is more aural than visual.[3] We also speculate that the extraordinary level of communal trauma that Uganda has endured in the past 50 years may mean there is reliance on compartmentalization as an adaptive response to terrifying events. A Ugandan response to an account of distressing experiences might be "It is better not to think (or talk) about such things." Inquiring about all the sensory aspects of an experience—how things smelled, the sounds, the tactile sensations associated with an event—resulted in higher Subjective Units of Disturbances (SUDs) ratings, which in turn resulted in more powerful and effective processing.

---

[3] We are grateful to our native South African colleague, Helen Fossberg, for this observation.

Our Ugandan colleagues informed us that the negative and positive cognitions required in the assessment stage of EMDR treatment would be difficult for their clients. Perhaps, they suggested, Americans, with their cultural emphasis on individual initiative and autonomy, are more accustomed to self-reflection and self-analysis than are Ugandan people, whose sense of self is formed in the context of a highly relational and communal culture. In practice sessions, the American facilitators found they needed to provide numerous specific examples of what it meant to have a negative belief about the self: "I am a bad person." "I am in danger." "I am defiled."

Finding a positive cognition (difficult enough for Americans!) was particularly problematic for participants due to cultural prohibitions against what is considered "boasting." Instead, while focusing on the target the client could be asked to think of an action that demonstrates something positive about himself. In response, the client might, for example, say, "I can honor my family by rebuilding our burned home." The client could then be asked, "What are the positive qualities of a person who does such things?" He might then be able to reply with a positive cognition: "Such a person is honorable and loyal."

Participants told us that both the Validity of Cognition (VoC) and subjective units of disturbance scales (VoC and SUDs) would be problematic for many of their clients to understand and apply to their experiences. Fluency with numbers and percentages is far from universal. They recommended using the distance between two hands to demonstrate "a little," "some," and "a lot." Another suggested approach was to ask clients to choose big, medium, and small rocks to describe the SUDs and VoC.

When it came to naming emotions, participants told us they would not emphasize emotional terminology. As a purely linguistic issue, in some of Uganda's languages, the English statement, "What do you feel?" translates as "What do you think?" Emotions, as distinct categories of mental experience, are not easily identified. They again recommended focus on descriptions of the physical sensations that accompany emotions: "Fist in my stomach," "pain in my heart," "burning in my face." Such slow, careful accessing of physical sensations—"Where do you feel the painful experience in your body?"—proved the most effective target enhancement method.

When the "clients" in a practice session became upset, we needed to encourage the "therapists" to continue with the bilateral stimulation. Given the highly relational nature of the society and the tendency to compartmentalize, a Ugandan therapist's first impulse would be to stop the processing prematurely and comfort the client. The value of continued processing ultimately became clear to many participants when they played the role of client in practice sessions. They were often astonished by the seismic shift in their SUDs levels and by the strength of their positive cognitions. This experience fortified their understanding of the importance of continued processing.

## Phases 5 and 6: Installation and Body Scan

Participants reported that focusing on body sensations during the installation procedure was particularly effective. The experience of reduced body activation (as opposed to changes in negative and positive cognitions) helped participants realize the power of the EMDR model. Asking about body sensations in Phase 6 proved especially helpful because it opened up neural networks not previously accessed.

## Phase 7: Closure

A number of issues can arise in the closure phase of an EMDR session. Many clients are likely to be concerned about the possibility that EMDR is some kind of sorcery or witchcraft. Participants suggested that clients should be fully informed about possible aftereffects of an EMDR session. Disturbing dreams, details of memories, new memories, and powerful feelings should all be normalized. Even a marked decrease in the SUDs score should be addressed. When a participant's disturbing memory dropped from a seven to a zero in a practice session, she asked with astonishment and some apprehension, "Is this witchcraft?" Less educated clients might be so scared by the experience that they would refuse further treatment or even seek an exorcism.

Participants pointed out that availability of the therapist for between-session contact is problematic due to clients' lack of access to telephone and e-mail. They suggested that clients be encouraged to identify supportive people to whom they can turn if they become upset and to use culturally consonant restorative activities such as prayer. The American practice of ending a session with instructions on post session issues could seem abrupt to many clients. Prayer, benediction, or other formal rituals would be consistent with the Ugandan emphasis on formality.

## Phase 8: Reevaluation

Regarding post session experiences, participants thought it would be important to inquire specifically about somatic changes. In their view, somatic changes, including increases or decreases in body sensations (e.g., back pain, headaches), could reflect continued between-session processing. Resuming bilateral stimulation in the next session with a focus on the somatic changes would be appropriate.

## Culturally Sensitive Cognitive Interweaves

The EMDR processing protocol recommends intervening when clients are unable to transform self-referential negative beliefs into cognitions that offer more positive and realistic concepts of the self and one's situation. For example, as we taught the concept of cognitive interweaves, we discovered that most Ugandans derive deep comfort from their spiritual traditions, especially the Christian tradition. Our colleagues recommended inquiries about whether, for example, clients could see themselves "Protected in God's hands" or posing a question like, "What would Jesus say if you told him you had run away when the Lord's Resistance Army came into your village instead of staying to protect your family?" Teaching the concept of cognitive interweaves requires particularly careful collaboration between trainers/facilitators and participants, so that effective interweaves are conceptualized in the context of participants' culture and history.

## THE IMPLICATIONS OF WHAT WE LEARNED

We recognize that the suggestions and insights of the participants in our EMDR trainings may not be ones with which other Ugandan clinicians would agree, nor are they necessarily suitable for other countries. For that matter, they may not even be suitable for Ugandan ethnic groups not represented in the project. What was enlightening for us was how much we learned and how much our Ugandan colleagues learned through our process of collaboration. Looking back over our 5 years of training and follow-up supervision, there are some overarching principles that we think are supported by the experiences we have had and the learning we achieved.

### A Relationship of Trust, Openness, and Frankness Is Essential for True Collaboration

We are highly skeptical as to whether a single training achieves lasting integration of EMDR (or any other clinical model for that matter). Given the hierarchical structure and formality of Ugandan society, open expression of doubt or disagreement needs to be repeatedly welcomed. The tendency of the host professionals to idealize their American counterparts must be challenged and their own deep cultural wisdom acknowledged. The willingness to challenge, disagree, and offer one's own ideas requires that participants trust in the openness on the part of the trainer and facilitators. Such trust can only be built if trainings are repeated over a period of years.

### Lasting Change May Require the Support of Indigenous Organizations and Their Leaders

We speculate that, in the absence of a strong, respected indigenous organization that provides training and supervision over time, EMDR risks becoming a model of treatment that remains on the periphery of a developing country's mental health system. We noticed, for example, when we searched the web for "EMDR South Africa," the photographs of 18 therapists were displayed, none of whom, by name or appearance, would be thought to be Black. Similarly, on searching the web for "EMDR Kenya," the website displayed listed EMDRIA, Austin, Texas, as the source for contact information. By way of contrast, a search for "EMDR Cambodia" brings up a national EMDR organization whose membership list appears entirely made up of Cambodian clinicians.

We lack data as to the extent to which EMDR has found its way into any given country's mental health system. Nor do we have explanations for the disparity of results that our web search produced. These are certainly questions worth pursuing. What we can say is that in the case of our project, the Uganda Counselling Association took the lead in recruiting participants and in providing the meeting space, meals, and teaching materials. Our project benefitted incalculably from the leadership of President Ochieng, who was tireless in her support of the project. Without such backing, we believe that EMDR is likely to be an ephemeral discipline, holding no enduring place in a country's mental health system—yet another "helicopter-training," wasting time and resources for all concerned.

## Genuine Learning Requires Attention to the Subjective Experience of Participants

Trainers and facilitators must focus not only on the content of what is taught but also on whether there is engagement and collaboration with participants. As one Ugandan colleague remarked,

> Teaching EMDR requires attention to what you want us to learn and at the same time to whether we are learning it. It's one foot on one side of the stream and one on the other.

Minor details, such as speaking slowly and asking if a particular metaphor or phrase makes sense, seems obvious; yet it is surprisingly hard to do consistently. Since our participants rarely volunteered questions and almost never disagreed with or openly criticized the content of what we were teaching, we could easily miss that they did not understand or agree with what we were saying.

## Celebrate the Skills and Wisdom of Participants

Identifying participants' skills and highlighting their resourceful solutions are essential for genuine learning. For example, one participant spontaneously reported that her housekeeper had collapsed into a mute, dissociated state upon learning of the death of her mother. "What should I have done?" the participant asked. The team stopped the formal teaching and encouraged the participant to describe her interventions in detail. We pointed out how she had first helped the woman become grounded in her body and recover the ability to speak. Using her knowledge of Ugandan funeral traditions, the participant then assisted the woman to connect to appropriate family and community resources. We reminded the group that social support at the time of a traumatic event can be crucial in the prevention of PTSD. We observed that our colleague had intuitively accomplished exactly what trauma theory recommends. Our attitude of inquiry coupled with respect for the participants' knowledge embodies what Freire means when he exhorts us to privilege learning by dialogue as opposed to rote "bank deposit" learning (p. 53).

## The Long-Term Goal Should Be a Vital Core of Committed Ugandan Therapists

We believe that EMDR from the beginning must encourage development of a core of clinicians who will ultimately take over the roles of trainers and facilitators. To that end, we offer ongoing group consultation by SKYPE and have encouraged our colleagues to form a national EMDR Association—a process they have begun. In our most recent training, we invited the most advanced clinicians to assist the American facilitators. The long-term task must be for Ugandans to take on the responsibility for EDMDR standards and training in Uganda.

## SUMMARY

Our project attempted and, we hope, succeeded in introducing EMDR to Uganda in the spirit of Freire's "liberation education." He envisioned a learning environment in which students are encouraged to question and criticize. He insisted that both teacher and student should be considered experts. The former has authority with respect to a body of knowledge, and the latter intimate acquaintance with his or her culture and circumstances. Together we have attempted to shape our mutual pedagogy so as to make EMDR understandable for participants in EMDR trainings and effective as a treatment model that addresses the realities of the lives of Uganda's people.

Key factors in the ongoing success at this stage in the development of EMDR in Uganda include commitment by the Uganda Counselling Association and the Trauma Studies Center to support the training programs over the course of years and the ongoing support of volunteers on both continents. Special credit is due to a core group of Association members who, in the face of enormous demands on their time and energy—not to mention daunting Kampala traffic—have met monthly for peer and SKYPE supervision with U.S. consultants. These intrepid and dedicated counselors have been particularly astute in explaining aspects of Ugandan society to their American colleagues and thereby enable their American colleagues to clarify and modify the EMDR protocol in ways that make that protocol intelligible and workable in the context of Ugandan society. Again we quote Freire:

> Authentic education is not carried on by "A" *for* "B" or by "A" *about* "B," but rather by "A" *with* "B," mediated by the world—a world which impresses and challenges both parties, giving rise to views and opinions about it. (p. 75)

For Americans to be effective in helping to introduce EMDR to a developing country such as Uganda, four fundamental human capacities are required: humility, curiosity, flexibility, and a sense of humor. We must remind ourselves that "we" do not have the answers for "them." Encountering attitudes and values at odds with our own, we must refrain from arguing and remember to ask why. Rather than resent the limitations of a country's infrastructure, we should respect our colleagues' resourcefulness in dealing with them. When the electrical grid goes down or half the participants are late, we must remind ourselves to be flexible and adjust the teaching schedule accordingly. Lastly, we need to laugh, most especially at ourselves. We need to feel okay about being ignorant or learning that we had made some really dumb faux pas. It is our hope that in our capacity to acknowledge our limitations our colleagues can make EMDR their own.

We close this chapter with testimony sent to us by one of our colleagues, the Reverend Dismas Eddie Bwesigye, a pastor and mental health counselor who works tirelessly with some of Uganda's most despairing and destitute trauma survivors.

> I express my thanks that you and your colleagues have taught us how to use EMDR therapy. This method has greatly improved our ability to deal with the endemic problems of our society. . . .

My clients have often been neglected and have had a life long history of trauma. This is common in Uganda, a country in which polygamy is neither illegal nor frowned upon. The majority of the cases I see have had a history of growing up in the home of a cruel stepmother. The country for 20 years has been steeped in a civil war—the Kony—war in which brutal and inhuman atrocities *were* meted on innocent civilians. The victims, who are numerous, do not have the resources necessary to cope. The few who have found their way to the hospital are finding that there is someone with a method that can help get rid of the nightmares and re-experiencing resulting from the horrible incidents they have endured. I have been fortunate that the hospital usually calls on me to help with the more serious cases of PTSD.

In our peer consultation sessions we have attempted to use EMDR on phobias. My particular fear was the fear of heights. I was skeptical when I brought a childhood experience when I froze while climbing a tree. Lo and behold in only one session I have found I can now look out of a window of a high-rise building without the sensation that something was trying to drag me over the ledge. The doubts I had at the beginning are gone and I can attest to the fact that EMDR works.

I see a lot of potential for growth of EMDR as a widely used therapy that will be beneficial to the country. Please continue your efforts with us. I constantly thank God for you and your colleagues. (D. E. Bwesigye, personal communication, August, 2015)

## REFERENCES

Freire, P. (1996). *The pedagogy of the oppressed* (M. B. Ramos, Trans.). London, UK: Penguin Books. (Original work published 1970)

Herman, J. L. (1997). *Trauma and recovery: The aftermath of violence—from domestic abuse to political terror* (Rev. ed.). New York, NY: Basic Books.

CHAPTER 20

# Teaching and Learning EMDR in Diverse Countries and Cultures: When to Start, What to Do, When to Leave

John Hartung

Clinicians and trainers have travelled over the years and around the world to conduct and teach Eye Movement Desensitization and Reprocessing (EMDR), paralleling the global extension of psychology and psychotherapy generally. Some cultural psychologists hoped that increased cross-cultural contact and interchanges would correct the ethnocentrism typical of Western practices. Those who have followed the effects of crossing cultural boundaries, however, question whether this hope is being achieved. Questions have also been raised about how culturally sensitive EMDR teams have acted. Christopher, Wendt, Marecek, and Goodman (2014), writing about foreign helpers in a postdisaster southeast Asian country, mentioned "eye movement desensitization and reprocessing therapy" as one example of Western-derived interventions that "often flew in the face of local ways of being, local ideas of appropriate social interaction, and local norms regarding privacy, dignity, emotional display, personal comportment, and family solidarity" (p. 646). Some of the errors made by foreign helpers were said to be unwitting, others deliberate.

This chapter is intended to contribute to the growing literature on the values of diversity, cross-cultural respect, and empowerment, with special reference to EMDR. It is based on my experiences, direct observation, and secondhand reports during my work over several decades with colleagues in some 30 countries in Asia, Europe, and the Americas. I made my own share of errors as I was learning enough to make the recommendations in this chapter, so I begin with an apology and a note of gratitude to all those colleagues and clients who patiently corrected and tutored me.

The themes covered are, in the author's view, among those most relevant to EMDR globally: space limits require postponement of other important issues such as team development, vicarious traumatization, compassion fatigue, gender issues, and dissociation across cultures. Persons with considerable international experience outside of the EMDR community are cited frequently.

## THE INVITATION: PREPARATION OF THE TRAINING SITE AND PARTICIPANTS

Invitations to teach EMDR come from various sources: local laypeople who read about EMDR on the Internet, practitioners who have studied EMDR elsewhere, and expatriates seeking to offer more help. A first step in the process of engaging in cross-cultural interventions is to wait for a legitimate invitation. Wessells (2009) writes about "disaster parachuting" or "disaster tourism," as when someone impulsively purchases a one-way ticket to an affected area. Wessells reported cases where outsiders used aggressive tactics, broke social norms, and abandoned victims when they left. Outsiders might feel pressed for time and act without having done an assessment, and without predicting possible consequences of helping. In some situations nongovernmental organizations (NGOs) work without coordinating with one another, possibly because the helpers have little understanding of the international humanitarian system. Given that intention is not synonymous with impact, outsiders might sincerely perceive a real need and feel motivated by humanitarian values and still cause chaos *unintentionally*.

Even a local resident might extend an inappropriate invitation, perhaps prematurely, because of a personal need to "do something" for suffering neighbors, perhaps by not knowing that most victims most of the time recover without professional assistance (Bonanno, 2004).

Because emergencies and other pressures can seem to justify economizing on initial planning and fieldwork, EMDR consultants are encouraged to think in the long term. Experienced international consultants realize that disaster victims first seek to survive and feel safe, and to reestablish a sense of place and belonging (Prewitt Diaz, 2008). Psychological first aid involves providing for coping and comfort, something we relearned immediately after the 9/11 attacks in New York City when neither victims nor first responders requested psychotherapy but rather ear acupuncture and massage (S. Reisner, personal communication, 2013). When EMDR consultants and trainers are invited to provide services internationally, the obvious expectation is that we will initially concentrate on EMDR. Frequently, our hosts request training in other modalities as well. I have been approached by many EMDR teams wanting to learn crisis and first aid interventions, coping strategies, and leadership coaching along with or prior to EMDR training.

Sensitive international trainers will have studied cultural norms and nuances in the host country prior to arranging travel plans. Resources useful for EMDR trainers include books (e.g., Hays, 2013; Lowman, 2013; Morrison & Conaway, 2006) and the Internet (updated more frequently than books and journal articles) regarding norms, mores, and other social expectations from country to country. The relative long-range success of these trainers is the topic of the next section.

## THE SPONSOR AND THE LOCAL EMDR TEAM

Ideally, outside trainers will help train both EMDR clinicians and local leaders. When a project begins, local leaders are appropriately assertive, structured, and decisive. As the team develops, these authoritative leaders will hopefully shift into coaching, mentoring, and eventually delegating roles. With attention to succession planning, the local sponsor leaders help team members to develop skills and assume greater authority and responsibility. The best leaders step aside to be replaced while continuing to support and empower those who replace them.

In my experience, these qualities are best described through the situational leadership (SL) model, developed and taught by Ken Blanchard (see kenblanchard.com website). SL is an extensively tested and broadly useful model elaborated through various media. Materials are available in 27 languages. While practicing SL is not essential to the success of a clinical project, I find it necessary for team development. EMDR visiting trainers can help prevent power struggles by selecting a sponsor who already exhibits SL styles. Alternately, the trainer coaches the sponsor to develop relevant SL skills. I encourage all EMDR trainers involved in team development to look into the SL model. I have used SL for many years as a guide for leadership training, and most of my approximately 1,000 coaching clients have told me that SL provides them with special insight in their evolution as leaders. It is immediately useful when selecting sponsors and local EMDR team leaders and serves as a fix-it resource for sponsors who need help in developing new leadership skills. After observing EMDR development in many countries, I have been impressed by the many first-generation leaders who were ambitious and decisive as the programs began, learned new leadership skills as necessary, continued to empower the next generation of leaders, and eventually enjoyed the success of their former students. These critical characteristics embody the fundamental messages of the SL model.

On the other hand, certain errors appear repeatedly among sponsors and team leaders. Sometimes a certain leadership behavior is initially appropriate and effective but is so overpracticed that it becomes a liability. A prime example is when qualities necessary for a start-up interfere with team evolution, as when a directive sponsor (initially very effective) does not eventually shift to more coaching and collaborative leadership. Conflicts commonly occur between strong team members who ask for additional responsibility and sponsors/leaders who continue to micromanage. In these cases, the SL model is useful in teaching the sponsor to appreciate the changing dimensions of leadership. Outside trainers increase their credibility as teachers and model effective strategies by practicing SL themselves.

These interprofessional rivalries can occur anywhere. Physicians and psychiatrists, sometimes privileged by special civil and legal recognition, might fail to recognize the genuine leadership and therapeutic skills of nonmedical professionals, who may in turn compete unnecessarily among themselves. Power struggles can be diminished by inquiring early about local existing professional hierarchies and consulting with different possible sponsors prior to initiating a project.

Where the first EMDR team for whatever reason has not been accepted by the entire local EMDR community, competing local EMDR teams might appear, each recruiting its own followers, each claiming to be legitimate for one reason or another. Sometimes one of these local groups invites outsiders for assistance. Should the outsider accept the invitation? This is controversial, as some regions favor open borders, others sovereignty. The working policy most widely endorsed presently seems to be that where a local EMDR association exists; this group should be consulted, and permission sought, before the outsider enters to treat, teach, or consult.

## UNINTENDED CONSEQUENCES

Receiving an invitation, preparing beforehand, and enjoying a working relationship with a local sponsor does not guarantee success as each of these factors can shift at any time. In one case, a Western expatriate moved to an Eastern country that had only recently ended years of civil war. In spite of daunting challenges she developed alliances with local counselors and other like-minded psychologist expatriates to set up a psychotherapy clinic along with a national, university-based academic program with a trauma and EMDR focus. For several years I trained them in EMDR and other therapies. Once the team became successful, however, the "taxmen" arrived, first to demand bribes, then to close down the clinic when their demands were refused. It was not the end of EMDR, but it did set things back for several years and left the local psychotherapists discouraged. Not infrequently have I been told about variations of the "crab phenomenon." Just as crabs in a pail will reach up and pull down any crab that tries to escape by climbing, so members of a community might conspire to pull back to a low but egalitarian level anyone who dares to surpass others' aspirations and achievements. While this phenomenon can occur anywhere in the world, it seems more prevalent where people have limited opportunities for advancement, or *perceive* things to be so. In scenarios like this, it can help to remember that it is a *success* that provokes most reactions. In one case, where the end of a civil war was still being negotiated, thuggish law enforcers invaded the hotel where our EMDR team resided "to search for weapons." Even though it was a UNICEF-sponsored training, the local powers wanted us to know who was really in charge. Though some visiting team members did not sleep that night, we were in no danger relative to what our local colleagues faced daily for having presumed to reveal their society's dirty secrets to outsiders. Experiences of that kind taught me of the sacred work that can be done by international agencies (e.g., UNICEF) and the courage of those who live at the trauma sites.

In general, anyone whose country of origin has both a humanitarian and a military presence might ask hosts how they view us. Are we friends? Or do they see our work as a political act? I have been challenged in various countries to explain how the United States could be generous on the one hand with foreign aid, while on the other hand installing dictators. It is rare for someone to demand that I take a stand against U.S. policy, but local people do expect me to be informed about international politics and trade, about the realities they face daily, and about how the power of the United States has been experienced through their country's history.

While seeking to do no harm, we remain alert to the possibility that sometimes confronting prejudices provokes more danger. We increase our credibility and perceive empathy when we investigate, learn about, and appreciate the systemic factors involved where we will work and give even closer attention to the realities of the conditions in which our sponsors and teams will remain. This implies identifying with sponsors who enjoy community credibility along with some degree of power and influence. Often (not always) it involves developing alliances with persons who have extra resources, financial and other, as in many countries the ongoing trainings will not be self-supporting, and a project will continue only if the local teams can work, as some colleagues say, "without lucrative purpose." Fortunately, the world is amply populated with persons abundant in both money and generosity.

When success breeds contempt or provokes any variation of the crab phenomenon—that there is not enough abundance to go around—EMDR local sponsors, team leaders, and clinicians will be particularly grateful if we can support them through such rough times. Sometimes they can use EMDR to strengthen ways of distinguishing between real and perceived dangers. In some cases, a national blocking belief against abundance has been identified as an EMDR target. A frequent positive goal has been for each party to focus on doing their best work and to simply allow the free marketplace to recognize this work.

## CONSTANT FEEDBACK

The main protection against preventing or correcting negative consequences, unintended or deliberate, is ongoing discussion with and feedback from hosts who speak honestly. Because outsiders risk being unaware of, and inattentive to, subtle cultural cues when working in unfamiliar environments, it is essential to compare our perceptions and assumptions with those of our local colleagues frequently. Seeking and acting on their feedback invites them to teach and mentor us while helping us correct our errors and learn more suitable conduct. Outsiders need to initiate such dialogues, as local norms of hospitality may mitigate against saying "no," questioning authority, or risking disrespect. Hence, the outsider may err in assuming that the feedback perceived was the feedback intended. I recall a time I unwittingly had offended a group of professors when I raised questions about a form of therapy that, unknown to me, they had been strongly promoting. I did not notice the professors' discomfort and so could not apologize publicly. Not until later did a trusted local colleague tell me about my *faux pas*.

The failure to seek and utilize appropriate feedback may be a particular liability of psychotherapists, who appear to have a distorted perception of their effectiveness (Tracey, Wampold, Lichtenberg, & Goodyear, 2014; Walfish, McAlister, O'Donnell, & Lambert, 2012). In addition, a tendency toward inflated self-appraisal is likely more pronounced when psychotherapists work outside of their customary zones, with cultural cues and norms further off the radar. Clients in other countries may be particularly reluctant to confront an outside authority. Unless the outsiders actively seek feedback, they may make the same errors repeatedly.

Teams can enhance the power of debriefing with a simple design involving a whiteboard divided into sections, where team members' comments are entered regarding what they would like to be "continued" (and with more or less emphasis), "stopped," and "added" in regard to the training. Feedback is based on concrete behavioral observations and the impact of that behavior on others—rather than on motives or intention. Following basic coaching principles makes it easier for the person receiving personal feedback to listen and hear, and less likely to become defensive.

In this regard, it is essential to construct feedback sessions with attention to local norms regarding individual versus group discussion. As I learned from my own errors, some individuals feel reflexively shamed by public attention, *whether the attention is negative and critical or positive and affirming!* On a cultural level, public and group feedback is absolutely taboo in some communities, and the expected context for giving feedback must be recognized and honored. Sometimes relevant norms are not obvious. Outsiders who exercise special care in this regard might ask local colleagues to *coach the coach,* which means requesting feedback about the impact of the feedback given.

When allowed by local norms, outsiders and locals should attend debriefings together and have equal rights to speak and to be heard. While it is obvious that the outsiders have expertise in some topics, in others it is the locals who will teach. For example, because outsiders can confuse "culture" with "country" or geographic territory, locals can help the outsiders to appreciate how their behavior is viewed and how it affects people in the social group where a particular training happens to be taking place. Groups within one country may differ among themselves more than they do with similar groups in another country.

## LOCAL HEALING PRACTICES

While Western psychology, developed in the United States and western Europe, offers evidence-based practices and supportive research to inform consumers and practitioners, "(t)he true history of mental health care includes contributors from around the world during the last several thousand years" (Peterson & Pope, 2010, p. 842). Western trainers who ignore the second of these two tenets might fail to inquire about indigenous healing practices, and local colleagues, awestruck by the visitors, might denigrate their own homegrown healing practices due to modesty or because they worry that their own ideas, especially relative to those of the outside experts, are backward. Although it is important to maintain a critical attitude about some cultural practices (such as female genital mutilation or other examples of gender bias and paternalism), outsiders are encouraged to ask locals how they understand their situation and what they customarily do about it. Otherwise traditional practices could be overlooked that have perfectly beneficial effects, that could enhance EMDR methodology, and that could open the outsiders to the possibility of engaging nonprofessionals in our teaching or preparing of trainers. One form of neocolonialism is teaching only our own methods, especially if they have no basis in the local culture (Dawes & Cairns, 1998).

I have no doubt that I missed many opportunities to learn from my students when I first began my involvement in international service. I am grateful that my colleagues continued to be patient, and willing to share their wisdom. For example, a man in Maharashtra, India, showed me how to hold my fingers to the third eye and the bladder-1 meridian points, a tool I now include in every basic EMDR course as a stabilization strategy. In another instance, a group of Mayan community counselors began one course by asking their oppressors for forgiveness. I was momentarily taken aback until I noticed the similarity to the ancient Hawaiian tradition of Ho'Oponopono (Vitale & Hew, 2007).

Sometimes a local healing tradition is not just complementary to, but synchronous with, EMDR, as when students asked to include drumming (alternating hand tapping) during both resourcing and trauma processing. Not to include this form of bilateral alternating stimulation—perfectly consistent, as it is, with EMDR theory—would have been unthinkable. And an anthropologist in South America, invited as an observer at an EMDR course, told me about the eye movements that had been used for some 500 years by a Toltec community along the Caribbean coast where he had been living.

Van der Kolk (2014) has written of the importance of incorporating movement, dance, and other physical activities in trauma treatment. While recognizing that we know little about how these physically expressive therapies work, he notes that their ability to circumvent the speechlessness that accompanies terror may be one reason they are used as trauma treatment around the world. I consider it a gift to be in a community where art, music, and dance are commonplace.

## THE TRAINING FORMAT

Two factors are blended in this section: how information is delivered, and the pros and cons of group compared with individual learning contexts.

The most successful and highly rated training formats in one country may be irrelevant in another. Lectures, PowerPoint slides, public demonstrations of EMDR with participants, reading from a manual, group versus individual feedback—all may have culture-specific value. It is important to ask students in each specific context how they learn best so that the teaching format is adjusted accordingly.

In communal and group-oriented societies, the experienced outside trainer asks whether the usual training EMDR format, particularly the one-on-one practicum setup, is appropriate. On the one hand, locals might request individual therapy from outsiders if they do not feel they can tell their story locally. On the other hand, highlighting an individual's troubles in treatment can set the person up for subsequent criticism, even humiliation, by other community members. Outsiders are strongly encouraged to ask about possible consequences prior to offering services, particularly when those services will be publicly displayed or known. Any tensions between group and individual formats are best reduced when the student or client is involved in decisions.

When EMDR trainers were few and exclusively English speaking, errors were frequent because original texts were translated word-for-word with minimal consideration of meaning and context. Where participants followed cultural mores to be modest, obedient, and subservient, feedback to trainers was rare and errors remained.

One step that can be taken to prevent cultural disconnects is to develop a manual with the teaching language and the participants' first language written side-by-side.

Manuals can be first translated from English (if this is the trainer's language) into the participants' original language(s), then back-translated into English to check on the initial translations, and to note special issues such as when one language involves concepts unavailable in another language. Many retranslations might be required before a satisfactory final product results. Sometimes no equivalence is possible: the Moken of Indonesia, for example, have no words for *worry* and *want* and they speak of past and future in the present tense. A trainer accustomed to thinking of memory as a past event would need to consult with local colleagues in order to translate a tsunami experience into a treatment target.

Sharing "best practices" and creative teaching tactics is highly recommended. I observed a trainer-candidate in Cambodia who impressed me in many ways, not least because of her vision to develop an EMDR community of therapists throughout Southeast Asia. In one instance, I watched her train in Thailand where participants had come from various countries, had different mother languages, and spoke English as a second language with varying levels of fluency. The trainer-candidate, teaching in English, would lecture for 15 minutes, and then stop to invite the participants to organize themselves into small groups according to first languages where they then back-translated the lecture with each other, discussed and corrected misinterpretations, and finally returned to the main group for another quarter-hour lecture. It was extremely effective, even though—or perhaps because—there was no PowerPoint or other visual aid or even a training manual on which the trainer might depend. In the practicum experiences at this site, the participants worked in their first language and translated for English-speaking facilitators only as necessary. Despite mastery of a second language, a bilingual client may find that certain feelings can be adequately expressed only in one's native tongue (Comas-Diaz, 1989) given that emotions appear to be anchored to the language learned as a child (Guttfreund, 1990).

EMDR offers an important advantage over language-based therapies because EMDR clients need not talk about their experience either before or during processing. As EMDR clinicians know, after traumatic memories and the associated shame and guilt are processed, clients often choose to talk about themselves, perhaps for the first time in their lives. This advantage needs to be highlighted anytime EMDR is proposed to trainees or their funding hosts.

## THE TRAINING-OF-TRAINERS MODEL

The training-of-trainers (TOT) model, long valued by UNICEF and other international organizations, challenges the assumption that providing direct services is inherently positive. While it is still common for outsiders to treat victims of natural and human-caused disasters, the TOT principle implies that the benefits of treatment are outweighed by the resulting dependency and loss of pride experienced by recipients of aid. In a village in tsunami-affected Sri Lanka, no NGOs had ever been present until after the tsunami when 27 different NGOs set up shop. One villager said that people had previously depended on relatives and neighbors when in need; a year after the tsunami they had learned to depend on the NGOs (IASC, 2007). When the NGOs left, community and government credibility had been eroded and the villagers had become disconnected from local helping resources.

In the subtitle of this chapter, "When to Leave" refers to *succession planning*. Beginning with the first group of trainees, the outside trainer identifies possible candidates to become trainers, lead teams, and promote programs. The trainer eventually shifts to the TOT role, developing and supervising these candidates.

Promoting TOT involves a clear agreement that outsiders will generally not treat clients but will offer training, supervision, and consultation for local therapists who will provide treatment and will someday train others to do so. The outsider provides some direct services when demonstrating EMDR during the training course. Teams I work with are willing and able to conduct EMDR while being observed, if only because videos sometimes do not work well.

Oftentimes, members of the training team will also treat one another for secondary trauma (Alter-Reid, Colelli, & Simons, 2014). In one international situation, a member of the local training team arrived traumatized after having served as a witness for a group of peasant farmers harassed by the national army; she could not facilitate until we provided emergency treatment. Because her stance was not necessarily shared by all her local colleagues, she asked to be treated by one of the outside members.

At times local team members postponed their treatment until the outsiders had returned to provide follow-up treatment, a clear indication that they undervalued their own clinicians. To some degree this is realistic, since the outsider team members are often more experienced and effective in EMDR therapy. Perhaps the best policy is *not* to have a policy but to decide whether to provide direct services on a case-by-case basis without condoning attitudes about locals being inferior. Generally, there are always some locals who learn fairly quickly to use EMDR effectively, and these people then earn a reputation as a go-to local resource when the outsiders are absent. Whatever bias there is against referring to local clinicians is relatively short-lived. Throughout this process, it can be repeated that while the outsider has special skills, these will be taught to local colleagues who should then be looked to for support.

## EMDR METHOD VERSUS MODEL

The EMDR method has been empirically validated (Cukor, Olden, Lee, & Difede, 2010). However, the model, based on the adaptive information processing (AIP) hypothesis, has not. Although EMDR trainers favor the AIP to explain how and why EMDR produces benefit, participants may prefer alternatives. Participants in a given culture might endorse a worldview that posits spiritual intervention, or cosmic energy, or some other external factor as the source of healing. Having the outside trainer insist that each person enjoys inherent healing capacities may seem odd; it might even suggest sacrilege to some locals.

Mechanisms of action are hypothetical for virtually all psychotherapies (Kazdin, 2007), and EMDR is no exception. EMDR trainers who promote the AIP too forcefully may alienate some participants who, in turn, might well ask: "Given that neither of us has scientific evidence for our hypothetical mechanisms of action, why is your theory superior to mine?"

## VARIATIONS OF THE EMDR METHOD

I offer for consideration a nonstandard EMDR methodology that I have taught, along with standard EMDR, to several hundred clinicians in many countries. I expect EMDR clinicians that I employ to be competent in both variations so they have options, depending on what best fits their clients. These clinicians consistently tell me that the nonstandard version has been better received by their clients. One noteworthy situation, reported multiple times, is when clients ask for EMDR after having had a negative experience in EMDR months or years earlier. Invariably, these cases involved initial treatment by a therapist who rigidly applied the standard EMDR method. The client experienced too-intense access or bilateral stimulation along with intolerable emotional abreactions and often ended therapy entirely. When these clients eventually sought assistance from one of my students, they were treated with some procedural variations we have learned consistently reported positive outcomes.

When I became the EMDR Institute coordinator for Latin America in 1996, I began to make modifications to the EMDR procedural steps in ways that would honor the basic principles and model and soon thereafter was asked to teach in Asia and Europe. I realized that many trainees had little previous experience as therapists; in some cases, they had memorized the *Diagnostic and Statistical Manual of Mental Disorders* (*DSM*) but knew little about interviewing clients, less about treatment options, and almost nothing about trauma. Though they might have been licensed mental health professionals, they functioned in many ways on a paraprofessional level of clinical expertise. I recall one psychiatrist initiating an EMDR session at a hospital for severely traumatized EMTs. He opened his EMDR training manual, then looked at me and, very transparently, confessed through our translator that, "I've never done a psychotherapy interview. Mostly I prescribe medication without ever getting to know my patient. How do I start?"

Almost immediately, I and the teams I experimented with developed strategies aimed to limit the risks of unnecessary emotional abreactions, dissociation, dropout, and retraumatization. The central objective was to teach EMDR in such a way that traumatic memories could be processed while clients maintained optimal levels of *access, bilateral stimulation,* and *change* (which we called the ABCs of EMDR). We field-tested various modifications to the eight phases for benefit and safety, with reliability checks to ensure that the nonstandard methodology was faithful to EMDR models and principles (i.e., that it was still "EMDR"). Clinicians' experiences regarding "best practices" were gathered from various countries and documented (Hartung & Galvin, 2003, Chapter 4). As changes were fine-tuned, they too were publicized (Hartung & Forgash, 2014).

I do not claim efficacy with this version as it has never been studied under controlled conditions. Nonetheless, through extensive field testing in many countries, with only positive reports so far—and especially the positive reports from persons who had already experienced EMDR negatively—I suggest the modifications which I outline next might comprise one way to change the eight phases so they are safer and, because clients seem more likely to complete treatment.

## Preparation for an EMDR Training Project

The outsider can ask if it is appropriate at the site to isolate a student/clinician/client from the group and to follow the one-on-one model in the training practicum and for subsequent client treatment. If not, the trainer will shift to a group protocol, possibly with an exclusive resourcing focus. This may be temporary, as with time the local team and its clients may become more open to individual treatments.

## Training and Learning Formats

First, check to ensure that the manuals have been back-translated accurately. It is sometimes very effective to have local cotrainers follow an English speaker and repeat the same information in another language, thereby also practicing as teachers. As exemplified earlier, learning can be enhanced by having the main trainer speak briefly, then inviting students to discuss the material in their own first languages.

## Assess Cultural Limits to Self-Disclosure

Ask if local norms support or discourage revealing one's inner world. Students might prefer to learn and practice in relative silence. The trainer can repeat that EMDR therapy *does not require much vocal expression.*

## Ask About the Meaning of "Trauma"

The notion of trauma may be a taboo topic in some places. The very admission of unresolved traumatic memories may be suggestive of weakness, lack of religious faith, and counter to national values that discourage emotional expression. The outsider can discuss this and similar themes during early contacts. There was no counseling center at one university where I trained a trainer; our hosts said that society norms expected the 20,000 students on campus to work hard and succeed. "And if they fail?" I asked. "Suicide, too often," the hosts sadly replied.

We consulted regarding ways to reframe targets, and ended with a model where a center might be opened with a performance enhancement focus: goal setting, study skills, exam taking, heart coherence, and the like. If unpleasant memories just "happened" to appear that might explain why a student was having trouble staying on task and feeling confident, the counselor trained in EMDR might just use that moment to suggest a way to "put the past in the past" before returning to the positive, the future, the performance goals. None of the "t" words (trauma, treatment, and therapy) would be mentioned.

## Phases 1 and 2

These two phases can be merged as a series of preparatory tasks. Stabilization and resourcing, usually Phase 2, may deserve earlier attention. Consider how to incorporate local healing strategies by asking the following questions: Do they reflect communal norms? Are they best done in groups? Resourcing and stabilization strategies can be related to local healing traditions such as acupuncture (China), the chakras (India), eye movements (South American Toltec tradition), bilateral drumming (in many societies), homeopathy (Germany), and so forth.

When taking history, the therapist is encouraged to draw a horizontal timeline, with positives above and negatives below. This allows clients to view their life from past through present to future. If the information below the line outweighs that on the top, more time is taken to find positive memories and/or to develop additional resources. Identifying a treatment target can involve something as simple as pointing to an event. Gaps can be investigated for dissociation.

Performance enhancement protocols may be more properly considered early in treatment. Therapists in any country can make errors during processing, so postponing trauma work can be especially salient where therapists are unaccustomed to observing clients feeling, remembering, and reliving past events. Two validated EMDR performance enhancement protocols have been published (Gracheck, 2010; Hartung, 2009; Korn & Leeds, 2002) and can be used in these phases.

## Phase 3

EMDR students are generally taught that *access* to the target requires inquiring about visual, cognitive, and somatic (emotion and sensation) variables, which in turn are coded in seven questions (image, Negative Cognition [NC], Positive Cognition [PC], Validity of Cognition [VoC], emotion, Subjective Units of Disturbance [SUD], and sensory location). In some situations some of the seven questions are best left unasked.

The *cognitions* aspect of the ICES may most challenge our worldview. In some societies, self-esteem has no meaning apart from the family or group. Sources of meaning may be extended family, kinship, or society, rather than inner dictates (Ho, 1999). The good life may involve obedience, subordination, filial piety, or transcending the self rather than "being true to oneself." Humanistic strains evident in Western psychology and philosophy might be seen as excessive privilege, if not narcissism. Some values not listed as standard EMDR cognitions may have meaning for our hosts, such as "I forgive," "I am repentant," "I extend myself with love," and "God loves me."

In a culture where public displays of *emotion* are strictly prohibited and emotional suppression is valued, trainers avoid suggesting that, "Crying will make you feel better," and offer alternative ways to identify and process symptoms. When working with people more accustomed to suppressing than confronting traumatic memories, and where there is little modeling to favor emotional expression, it is especially important to dose access. The window of tolerance (see the following) is particularly helpful here. Instead of suggesting that the client move through an emotion, therapists can spend time in between bilateral sets to allow clients to lower a SUD level by breath practice and other stabilization strategies.

Targeting only body *sensations* is especially helpful with people who have difficulty with negative beliefs and emotions. In one Buddhist setting following a natural disaster, clients and therapists-in-training tended to suppress unpleasant emotions and thoughts (which reflected poorly on their faith). Given that they were wracked with aches, pains, joint problems, and symptoms of fibromyalgia since the disaster, they were invited to focus only on their chronic pains and to rate them with the SUD scale. Eventually they recognized how body symptoms could be somaticized memories, and how targeting pain still permitted them to disregard any accompanying cognitions, images, or emotions. The value of identifying a body sensation can also help when a person speaks of a symptom unfamiliar to the clinician, such as a feeling of being possessed, of running *amok*, of experiencing an *ataque de nervios*, or even facing existential *angst*.

In other cases a *trigger* may be a preferred treatment target. In these cases, the therapist can encourage the client to see the trigger as a small link to the past so that resolving a trigger is a form of memory processing. An adaptation in these scenarios is to skip past events and cognitions.

The two-handed *dilemma* procedure is an excellent option where clients seek to be healed, but reluctantly so (Shapiro, 2005). Likewise, the use of the SUD to measure *how much do you not want to remember/feel* is an excellent tool that helps a client to approach an issue indirectly with greater safety and containment than occurs in more orthodox memory processing (Knipe, 2005).

Strategies designed to contain or to allow access but in a limited or dosed manner are generally intended to prevent intolerable abreactions and dissociation. In some societies they also enable the client to stay within a preferred range of emotional expression, which might mean saving face or simply feeling more comfortable. I recall watching a group of Asian trainees as they watched a video in which a male European client wept; the trainees looked away, embarrassed by the man's display. Using the window allowed them to slow processing during their own practice sessions and keep their emotional responses within their personalized and culturally acceptable range. It bears repeating for clients that they can remain silent while processing. Clients who wish to speak can do so in the language they spoke when the trauma occurred.

## Phase 4

Variations in the use of bilateral stimulation also involve *dosing*, in this case adjusting the bilateral stimulation so that the client remains in the window of tolerance. The window is used mostly when the client experiences heightened emotion, where clients *and* therapists tend toward suppression (are affect-phobic), where there is no tradition of emotional expression, anytime dissociation is a possibility—and whenever the client asks to stop!

When local clinicians are just beginning EMDR, it is particularly important to take precautions that lower the risk of intolerable abreactions, dissociation, treatment failure, retraumatization, and attrition. The window helps to ensure that the client remains in charge. Whenever the client reports too much emotion, the clinicians can temporarily suspend processing and invite the client to practice self-regulation to return to an acceptable level of emotional access. Processing is then resumed, with even slower bilateral stimulation than before (of course if the client loses access and feels too little emotion, a target can be revisited, though leaving the window of tolerance in this direction is relatively rare in my experience and is largely prevented when access and simulation are dosed downwards from the onset).

To address these issues, many of my students have reported that they begin with a single bilateral stimulation (BLS; rather than the iconic 24), and then gradually increase speed and number in collaboration with the client. To date, everyone who has reported results to me has said that this nonstandard approach to initiating Phase 4 has been safer and, in the process, more effective because it mostly prevents extreme emotional responses and dissociation. There are now many testimonials from clinicians who have done no more than two or three BLS movements in a single set throughout a session and whose clients resolved their targeted memories, reduced their symptoms, and remained present (not dissociated) throughout the EMDR experience. As mentioned earlier, these testimonials are particularly gratifying when the client had engaged in previous and standard EMDR treatment that had not been successful because of too-intense emotional experiencing.

This modification is not necessarily unique. In the EMDR Institute (2012) training manual, the reader is advised that some clients cannot initially tolerate a set of 24 bilateral movements but can initiate EMDR processing if they begin with fewer, sometimes many fewer, than 24 movements in a set. This slow start sometimes proves to be sufficient throughout processing. In sum, EMDR used or begun in these ways is relatively safer, and in the long run more effective in that more clients can tolerate the relatively less intense emotion that results, and reports of dissociation and attrition are minimized.

### Phase 5

The strengthening of positive cognitions can be enhanced with somatic resourcing where positive self-talk is seen as counter to filial piety and communal values.

### Phase 6

Clients can be reminded that their bodies are sources of wisdom and that EMDR is a somatic therapy. Physical symptoms can serve as traumatic memory targets in Phase 3, and remaining aches, pains, and tensions can open up additional memories deserving attention in Phase 6.

### Phase 7

Closing a session may require consultation with local colleagues to identify realistic and appropriate support systems. Teaching ways to handle strong emotions and generally to care for oneself is particularly important when your students are the first ones to be trained in a given region, which may mean that they are also the most experienced clinicians available for consultation and treatment. Examples of self-care strategies from many cultures are described in Hartung (2016).

### Phase 8

Debriefing in subsequent sessions might be difficult when outside trainers leave the region soon after EMDR courses have ended. When the outsider returns, it is particularly important to make time for the clinicians to talk about their experiences since the previous visit. Given that much of the material is unfamiliar, fidelity drift is common, so repeating a previous training schedule may be preferred to teaching new material. When locals have incorporated coping strategies from their own traditions, it is helpful to discuss these innovations to see if they were used to enhance the processing of traumatic memories or if, as I have often witnessed, they were attempts to avoid access and to postpone healing as if to protect the client (and the clinician) from suffering. In some cases, the trainer may want to ask for detailed information from clinical notes: I have noticed that many new clinicians terminate EMDR treatment even though the client reported a high remaining SUD.

## TEACH BOTH STANDARD AND NONSTANDARD EMDR METHODS

The modifications to standard EMDR just summarized are consistent with the EMDR model and principles, congruent with relevant neurobiological findings, and, according to several hundred students in several countries (who have shared their experiences with me), safe, efficient, effective, and more likely to be used subsequently by both clinician and client. The variations on the standard approach described have only been field-tested and are not offered as the only variations possible; it is only one example of what might be incorporated into a training schedule when a trainer wishes to offer variational options of the standard protocol along with the standard eight phases so that clinicians have a choice when the standard procedure—for whatever reason—is not producing benefit. Likewise, when the modified methodology does not work, the clinician can review the standard protocol to see if some critical step in the validated method was missed.

## TRAINING PERSONS WITHOUT MENTAL HEALTH LICENSES ("PARAPROFESSIONALS")

Relying solely on professionals to provide psychotherapy to suffering populations is impractical. A million residents in a "wealthy" country may have access to about 700 mental health professionals, whereas a million residents of a "poor" country may have access to three such professional workers (Jacobs, 2007). It is estimated that over 1.7 million mental health *professionals* will be needed worldwide to meet mental, neurological, and addiction conditions (WHO, 2011). Paradoxically, while it is mostly in the developing world where professional mental health resources are scarce, it is also the region where the greatest needs exist in the form of violent conflicts, man-made and natural disasters, and other traumatic events. Writing in an EMDR context, UN consultant Rolf Carriere noted that involving paraprofessionals is imperative and one possible solution to policy challenges and ethical dilemmas (Carriere, 2014). And clinician Zimmerman (2014) called for combined top-down (university-educated psychotherapists) and bottom-up selection and training. Referring to paraprofessional training in Africa, she wrote about "EMDR light" and on-the-job training for local candidates.

While there is no consensus as to what paraprofessional candidates need to learn in order to meet basic selection criteria as trainers, some preliminary lists have been drafted. Matthess and Sodeman (2014), for example, suggest that all trainer/clinician-candidates study assessment, traumatology, stabilization tools, and various basic relationship skills.

There is little published that describes how the standard eight phases could be modified to enhance paraprofessionals' ability to learn, conduct, and teach EMDR. An exception is the PROPARA model, proposed for use by paraprofessionals in acute critical incidents as complementary to professionals' first aid interventions (Jarero, Amaya, Givaudan, & Miranda, 2013). Hence, EMDR's international extension has been curtailed and paraprofessional resources underappreciated and underutilized.

## THE RELEVANCE OF GROUP PROTOCOLS

EMDR helpers from the West might err in favoring the individual, as evidenced in one-on-one treatment protocols, in cognitions that promote personal self-esteem, and in concepts about self-actualization. In a community-oriented culture, the idea of isolating a single victim for individual treatment can appear peculiar and can harm or disrupt social support systems on a massive scale. In some situations, a person treated alone can be stigmatized after returning to his or her community. Western values of individualism may conflict with norms of community, filial piety, and group esteem (Christopher et al., 2014). Individual treatment is also inefficient and impractical for large-scale disasters or where distances and expenses limit repeated visits to a training site. Considering the numbers of persons who suffer from life challenges and seek help to enhance their healing and recovery, it becomes obvious that individual treatment will never meet the needs of all who suffer.

It is essential to develop ways to provide EMDR treatment in group formats, for resourcing, for teaching coping tools, and for trauma processing. Along with his plea for more training of paraprofessionals, Carriere (2014) also asks for group innovations.

The group protocol developed by the Mexican EMDR team is an example of how EMDR might be applied in group settings across diverse cultures (Jarero & Artigas, 2009; Jarero, Artigas, & Hartung, 2005). This Mexican EMDR team is also developing protocols for possible use by paraprofessionals. Also, Konuk and Zat (2015) wrote about using Elan Shapiro's traumatic episode protocol in group treatment of Syrian refugees residing in Turkey.

## CONCLUDING COMMENTS

Although the suggestions made in this chapter can serve as useful guidelines, there are no substitutes for continuously checking in with both sponsor and participants, and the people they treat. All of us who teach EMDR where language, custom, demeanor, and cues are unfamiliar are encouraged to be humble about our abilities to detect social and cultural cues, to rely on others to assist us, to ask directly about our impact (rather than assuming on the basis of good intentions), to give thanks for feedback, to apologize when we err, and then to make changes. Virtually everyone accepts that to err is human and will forgive us under such conditions. Each of the themes covered in this chapter could comprise a book-length discussion, plus many topics went untouched, so I end with an invitation to colleagues to continue the dialogue.

## REFERENCES

Alter-Reid, K., Colelli, G., & Simons, N. (2014). When disaster strikes our local communities: U.S. EMDR trauma recovery network coordinators reflect on lessons learned. *Journal of EMDR Practice and Research, 8*(4), 205–214.

Bonanno, G. A. (2004). Loss, trauma, and human resilience: Have we underestimated the human capacity to thrive after extremely aversive events? *American Psychologist, 59*(1), 20–28.

Carriere, R. C. (2014). Scaling up what works: Using EMDR to help confront the world's burden of traumatic stress. *Journal of EMDR Practice and Research, 8*(4), 187–195.

Christopher, J. C., Wendt, D. C., Marecek, J., & Goodman, D. M. (2014). Critical cultural awareness: Contributions to a globalizing psychology. *American Psychologist, 69*(7), 645–655.

Comas-Diaz, L. (1989). Culturally relevant issues and treatment implications for Latinos. In D. R. Koslow & E. Pathy (Eds.), *Crossing cultures in mental health* (pp. 25–42). Rockville, MD: U.S. Public Health Service.

Cukor, J., Olden, M., Lee, F., & Difede, J. (2010). Evidence-based treatments for PTSD, new directions, and special challenges. *Annals of the New York Academy of Sciences, 1208*, 82–89.

Dawes, A., & Cairns, E. (1998). The Machel study: Dilemmas of cultural sensitivity and universal rights of children. *Peace and Conflict: Journal of Peace Psychology, 4*, 335–348.

EMDR Institute. (2012, October). *Basic training manual*. Watsonville, CA: EMDR Institute.

Gracheck, K. A. (2010). *Evaluating the effectiveness of EMDR as an athletic performance enhancement intervention* (p. 57). UMI Dissertation Publishing, UMI#3433356.

Guttfreund, D. G. (1990). Effects of language usage on the emotional experience of Spanish-English and English-Spanish bilinguals. *Journal of Consulting and Clinical Psychology, 58*, 604–607.

Hartung, J. (2009). Enhancing positive emotion and performance with EMDR. In M. Luber (Ed.), *EMDR scripted protocols: Basics and special situations* (pp. 339–376). New York, NY: Springer Publishing Company.

Hartung, J. (2016). *Innovative practices from the East and West for bodymind health* (2nd ed.). Singapore: Bodymind Press.

Hartung, J., & Forgash, C. (2014). *Do stabilization strategies improve on the standard EMDR methodology? It is time to ask*. EMDRIA Annual Conference. Denver, CO.

Hartung, J. G., & Galvin, M. D. (2003). *Energy psychology and EMDR: Combining forces to optimize treatment*. New York, NY: W.W. Norton.

Hays, P. A. (2013). *Connecting across cultures: The helper's toolkit*. Thousand Oaks, CA: Sage.

Ho, D. Y. F. (1999). Relational counseling: An Asian perspective on therapeutic interventions. *Psychologische Beitrage, 41*, 99–112.

IASC. (2007). *Inter-agency standing committee guidelines on mental health and psychosocial support in emergency settings*. Geneva, Switzerland: Author.

Jacobs, G. A. (2007). The development and maturation of humanitarian psychology. *American Psychologist, 62*, 932–941.

Jarero, I., Amaya, C., Givaudan, M., & Miranda, A. (2013). EMDR individual protocol for paraprofessional use: A randomized controlled trial with first responders. *Journal of EMDR Practice and Research, 7*(2), 55–64.

Jarero, I., & Artigas, L. (2009). EMDR integrative group treatment protocol. *Journal of EMDR Practice and Research, 3*(4), 287–288.

Jarero, I., Artigas, L., & Hartung, J. G. (2005). Protocolo grupal e integrativo con EMDR: Intervención post-catástrofe para niños y adultos. *Revista de psicotrauma para Iberoamérica, 4*(1), 22–29. Published in 2006 in English: EMDR integrative group treatment. *Journal of Traumatology, 12*, 121–129. Retrieved from http://tmt.sagepub.com/current.dtl

Kazdin, A. E. (2007). Mediators and mechanisms of change in psychotherapy research. *Annual Review of Clinical Psychology, 3*, 1–27. doi:10.1146/annurev.clinpsy.3.022806.091432

Knipe, J. (2005). Treating positive affect to clear pain of unrequited love, codependence, avoidance, and procrastination. In R. Shapiro (Ed.), *EMDR solutions: Pathways to healing*. New York, NY: W. W. Norton.

Konuk, E., & Zat, Z. (2015). Humanitarian programs and interventions in Turkey. *Journal of EMDR Practice and Research, 9*(2), 106–113.

Korn, D. L., & Leeds, A. M. (2002). Preliminary evidence of efficacy for EMDR resource development and installation in the stabilization phase of the treatment of complex posttraumatic stress disorder. *Journal of Clinical Psychology, 58*(12), 1465–1487.

Lowman, R. L. (Ed.). (2013). *Internationalizing multiculturalism: Expanding professional competencies in a globalized world*. Washington, DC: American Psychological Association.

Matthess, H., & Sodeman, U. (2014). Trauma-aid, humanitarian assistance program Germany. *Journal of EMDR Practice and Research, 8*(4), 225–232.

Morrison, T., & Conaway, W. A. (2006). *Kiss, bow, or shake hands*. Avon, MA: Adams Media.

Peterson, P. B., & Pope, M. (2010). Inclusive cultural empathy for successful global leadership. *American Psychologist, 65*, 841–853.

Prewitt Diaz, J. O. (2008). Integrating psychosocial programs in multisector responses to international disasters. *American Psychologist, 63*, 818–827.

Shapiro, R. (2005). The two-hand interweave. In R. Shapiro (Ed.), *EMDR solutions: Pathways to healing*. New York, NY: W. W. Norton.

Tracey, T. J. G., Wampold, B. E., Lichtenberg, J. W., & Goodyear, R. K. (2014). Expertise in psychotherapy: An elusive goal? *American Psychologist, 69*, 218–229.

van der Kolk, B. (2014). *The body keeps the score*. New York, NY: Viking.

Vitale, J., & Hew, I. (2007). *Zero limits: The secret Hawaiian system for wealth, health, peace, and more*. New York, NY: Wiley.

Walfish, S., McAlister, B., O'Donnell, P., & Lambert, M. J. (2012). An investigation of self-assessment bias in mental health providers. *Psychological Reports, 110*, 639–644.

Wessells, M. G. (2009). Do no harm: Toward contextually appropriate psychosocial support in international emergencies. *American Psychologist, 64*(8), 839–854.

World Health Organization (WHO). (2011). *Mental health atlas*. Geneva, Switzerland: Author.

Zimmerman, E. (2014). EMDR humanitarian work: Providing trainings in EMDR therapy to African clinicians. *Journal of EMDR Practice and Research, 8*(4), 240–247.

# Index